THE DEVIL HAS FORECLOSED:

The Private Journal of George Whitwell Parsons,
Volume II,
The Concluding Arizona Years, 1882-87

Transcribed, Edited, Annotated, Indexed,
and with Foreword
By

Lynn R. Bailey

WESTERNLORE PRESS . . . 1997 . . . TUCSON, ARIZONA

Library of Congress Catalog Number 96-60051
ISBN 0-87026-099-5

PRINTED IN THE UNITED STATES OF AMERICA BY WESTERNLORE PRESS

TABLE OF CONTENTS

FOREWORD

George Parsons began keeping a diary not because of a sense of historical awareness, but as a device to purge his emotions following the death of his mother on June 22, 1869. For the next thirty years he recorded his thoughts and observations through good and bad times, from the East coast to California, in Arizona Territory and Sonora, and back in California. His last entry was on December 31, 1929. Seldom did he miss a day, and if he did, George kept notes so that he might recreate his experiences in the journal. The time span of his diary, and its geographical scope, transformed a cathartic exercise into a historical treasure trove.

George's historical awareness dawned slowly, however. It was not until 1885 that he began to view his daily jottings as a possible foundation for a larger literary work, and then only after some urgings by friends and relatives to record his experiences in the Far West. At that time he did not contemplate publication of his diaries, but envisioned a book of reminiscences. Although George had writing aspirations the book was never written, but he eventually recognized the historical value of his diaries, and stipulated in his will that they be published. By the time legal fees and debts were paid, following George's death in January 1933, there was not enough money in the estate to carry out that wish. Fortunately, his relatives and executor donated the 1879-1929 diaries to the Arizona Pioneers' Historical Society, forerunner of the Arizona State Historical Society. Although the gift did not include journals covering 1869 to 1878 (they apparently had been lost or were in the possession of others, probably the latter), the donation was fortuitous.

The 1879-1882 journal, detailing George's debute on the Arizona scene, was immediately recognized as a unique piece of Americana. Between its covers was a record of everyday happenings at one of the West's wildest boomtowns, Tombstone, Arizona Territory. The journal's merit could not be overlooked and in the mid-1930s the Works

Projects Administration put historians to work transcribing it. Despite what one self-style expert says, the WPA workers did a creditable job. With a few exceptions in punctuation, their rendition is exactly as Parsons wrote it, misspellings, lack of paragraphing and all (if you doubt this, then compare the WPA version with the original). Published in mimeograph form in 1939, this version has been extensively mined by researchers seeking data on the life and times of early Tombstone.

Produced in limited edition, the WPA version went quickly out of print, only to be revived in 1972 by Wayne Winters, editor of the Tombstone *Epitaph*. A publisher and typographer by trade, Winters set the WPA transcription in type and issued a thousand hardback copies—a contribution which many have benefitted from ever since. The book went out of print and today commands a high price on the antiquarian book market. Those two editions established George Parsons' identity, and today his diary is considered "one of the classics in that genre." Because of its research value that diary was republished by Westernlore Press in 1996 under the title *A Tenderfoot in Tombstone*, and it too is fast nearing out-of-print status. This companion volume is the logical conclusion to Parsons Tombstone saga. For benefit of those who do not have *A Tenderfoot in Tombstone*, it is appropriate to repeat some biographical data relative to the diarist, with minor update, of course.

George Whitwell Parsons was a Easterner, trained as a banker, who wanted to carve a niche for himself in hardrock mining. To do so, he picked Tombstone, Arizona Territory, one of America's most isolated silver camps. Although he failed to attain that goal, he left a journal which every serious student of Cochise County history has utilized. Until recently not much was known about George's life before coming to Arizona.

George Whitwell Parsons had distinguished ancestors. A brother of his great-grandmother was a general on George Washington's staff, and great-grandfather Josiah Parsons was a patriot at Bunker Hill. Born in Washington, D.C., on August 26, 1850, George was the eldest son of Samuel Miller Parsons of Wiscasset, Maine, who obtained a degree from Yale Law School in 1843. The elder Parsons, however, moved to Brooklyn, New York, to practice law. His wife was Virginia Whitwell of Richmond, Virginia. She attended Mrs. English's Boarding School at Georgetown and was a classmate of Jessie Benton, who became the wife of Pathfinder John C. Fremont. Virginia Parsons bore five children, two sons: George Whitwell and Samuel (born 1869), and three daughters: Emeline (born 1854 whom George refers to as sister); Alice (born 1855 and nicknamed Strallus), and Mary (born 1858), who died in childhood. Emeline and Alice received much of their education at a Pennsylvania girls' seminary, and Sam attended college but dropped out due to ill-health. George was educated in New York public schools and worked in his father's Wall Street law office.

Hating New York winters and not wanting to be a lawyer, George moved to Key Biscayne, Florida, in 1874. He survived in the South by salvaging lumber from wrecked vessels, which he resold. He stayed less than two years, departing Florida for the Far West after nearly drowning one night in a hurricane off Cape Sable. Taking passage to Panama, he crossed the Isthmus on horseback, and arrived in Los Angeles, where he stayed a short while. His ultimate destination was San Francisco, which he reached in 1876. He took a job as clerk in the National Gold Bank and Trust Company. That job too was shortlived. Decline of Comstock mining began the year Parsons arrived in California, devastating California's banking institutions, and the National Gold Bank failed in 1879.

Out of a job, George Parsons was depressed. "Thirty years of age and nothing ahead. . . . My future is discouraging," he wrote in his journal on December 19, 1879. George was down but he was not out. His residence in San Francisco, the economic hub of the Pacific Coast and the center of Western mining and finance, had opened his eyes to opportunities. Bank employment had put him in touch with men who shaped Western commerce and industry. He was bombarded daily, either in conversation with financiers and promoters or from newspaper accounts, of gold and silver strikes in the Far West. No doubt about it, mining was the way of the future and George wanted to be part of it. Just how, he was not certain. "I think after all, that mines promise more for me and I wouldn't be surprised to find myself in them before many days," he wrote on January 5, 1880. "I'm tough and strong and know how to get along with the working classes." (A rather arrogant comment in light of subsequent events revealed in his journal.)

During the latter months of 1879 San Francisco was alive with news of the Tombstone silver strike. Although most of its mines were being developed with capital raised in Philadelphia and Boston, San Francisco foundries were working around the clock fabricating hoists, mills, and powerplants for the district. Tombstone was the talk of the Bay City and in mid-January George decided to go there "and begin as a common miner. Learn the business and stick to it." On February 4,

1880, George and Milton Clapp, a friend who had also worked for the National Gold Bank, boarded a third class car attached to a Southern Pacific freight train which took them to Casa Grande, the line's terminus in Arizona at the time. From there they traveled by stage to Tucson. On the morning of February 17, 1880, Parsons and Clapp boarded a stage at the Old Pueblo and set out for the silver camp. Nearly twelve hours later they stepped out of the crowded conveyance into an all male society bent on extracting wealth from the earth. Tombstone of 1880 was a primitive world; a world Parsons quickly sized up. It was a "very lively camp" of 2,000 population; a rough place with a "hard crowd," where everyone went heeled. No law other than miner's and that doesn't sit and deliberate but acts at once," Parsons observed. Above all, he sensed "money was there," an endearing quality to an ex-banker. George made his decision, he would stay in Tombstone and make mining his profession.

For seven years George Whitwell Parsons toiled in southeastern Arizona and northern Sonora, most of the time at Tombstone. He witnessed the camp's murder and mayhem period of 1880-81, during which time he nearly lost his life in a fire that swept the town. That period, as George recorded it, is found in *A Tenderfoot in Tombstone*.

The old adage, "what doesn't kill you, strengthens you," was never more true than in Parsons' case. By 1883 George had made the transition from a tenderfoot to a knowledgeable mining man, savvy to the rigors and dangers of frontier living. His transition from San Francisco banker to diehard frontiersman is evident in his journals from 1882 to 1887. Here in published form are George Parsons' struggles in Sonora, first trying to establish a quartz mill, then eking out an existence managing a company store at Nacosari, and finally plunging into gold mining in the nearby mountains which bankrupted him and forced his return to Tombstone.

The town he returned to was no longer the youthful boomtown he first wrote about, where violence and personal vendettas were common place. By 1883 Tombstone was a mature mining community with law abiding citizens whose fortunes were dependent upon success of the district's mines. That too would change when a succession of calamities brought economic chaos to the town. Mines were flooded, there was a bank failure, newly-installed pumping equipment broke, the price of silver pummeted forcing a reduction of wages, miners struck, and the mining companies responded with a lockout. If that was not enough, the headframe and hoist of the Grand Central Mine burned, destroying that company's pumping capacity. George Parsons observed it all, from boom to bust.

Although this portion of George's journal lacks much of the blood-and-guts drama of 1880-81, it is a wonderful social commentary. It portrays the precariousness of mine and mill operation; the difficulties Americans faced in getting their equipment across the "line" and through Mexican customs; and the hardships of prying wealth from the earth. George paints a dismal picture of everyday happenings at Tombstone: how its citizens lived, played, and in some instances died. His journal brings to life many Cochise county stalwarts; the diary is a directory of the real movers and shakers of southeastern Arizona and northern Mexico. Dr. George E. Goodfellow, an expert in the treatment of gunshot wounds figures large in George's account, as does lawyers William Herring and B. L. Peel, land speculators J. S. Clark, and Michael Gray. Parsons partied with military elite at Henry C. Hooker's Sierra Bonita Ranch, and frequently visited the ranch of Theodore White and John V. Vickers, the forerunner of the great Chiricahua Cattle Company. For a time George toyed with the thought of becoming a cattleman, an improbable idea. At any rate, his descriptions of roundups in the Sulphur Spring Valley are among the best ever written. George also rubbed elbows with Sonoran autocrat Ignacio Pesqueira and Samuel Brannan, California's first millionaire, who as an old man was trying, with help of his son Sam Jr., to resurrect a squandered fortune by promoting a colonizing scheme at the headwaters of the Rio Yaqui in Sonora.

Like the 1880-81 portion of the journal, this segment is primarily a mining document, but its scope is much boarder than just the Tombstone District. George takes the reader from Nacosari, Sonora, where former state historian Thomas Farish and his brother William were developing copper mines discovered by California pioneer Cornelius T. Cutler, to mining localities in the Huachuca and Dragoon Mountains. Parsons concludes his journal at Oro Blanco, south of Tucson, where he carried out assessment work for George Cheyney on mining properties that would ultimately develop into the camp of Ruby.

No man writes a daily narrative without revealing his personality traits. That was true in the earlier portion of Parsons' diary and it is evident in this segment. George remains ever religious, prudish, and somewhat masochistic. He drinks, plays billiards, and experiences lust for Daisy Clark, teenage daughter of J. S. Clark, mining engineer and one of the promoters of the Tombstone Townsite Company. Athough

George laments that all eligible women are married, that deficiency did not stop him from seeking their company in gadfly fashion. As mentioned in the introduction to *A Tenderfoot in Tombstone*, the code of Western conduct, "live and let live," was foreign to George. Although he was honest and hardworking, he was not a likeable man. Many of his Sonoran and Tombstone relationships soured, always because of the failings of others. That was also true of his private life. The love of his life, Nathalie, stood him up in New York and married another. While George condemned philanders, in loneliness he turned to Mrs. Stevens, a divorcee. His torrid fling, however, created pangs of guilt, and that relationship ended when Mrs. Stevens left Tombstone with U.S. Marshal William Kidder Meade. All that remained for George were memories which he eased by reading a book on infidelity. To George fantasy was always better than reality.

There is no denying that George was complex. Never a slacker, he worked hard at whatever he did, be it mining gold, running a quartz mill, managing stores, auditing county books, or serving on a grand jury. His diary reveals a desire to enter the journalistic arena. Having seen his acquaintances slaughtered by Apaches, George like most Tombstoners, detested George Crook's Indian policy. When the opportunity arose to let the country know what was going on in Arizona, he sought to correct what he considered military ineptitude. In spring of 1883 he blasted the nation's Apache policy in an interview which appeared in the Chicago *Tribune* (it is included in this volume). And Harry Ellington Brook, Indian War correspondent for the *Epitaph* and several West Coast papers, utilized George's knowledge of what was going on in southeastern Arizona during the later phases of the Geronimo campaign. Parsons' observations appeared in the *Epitaph* and Tucson newspapers, and his scathing commentary relative to George Crook was published by the San Francisco *Chronicle*. Three of these writings/interviews are included in this volume, as is an article George wrote for the Los Angeles *Mining Review* long after he left Tombstone. But I don't want to rehash Parsons' diary. It is up to the reader to use this volume as he sees fit. I do, however, want to say a little about my transcription.

I have transcribed this five-year segment of the Private Journal as George wrote it. Abbreviations, with and without periods, have been retained. Archiac words and mispellings have been left, but always followed with an inserted *sic* or corrected notation. No phrases have been moved around. Except for some deletion of em-dashes, sentence structure has not been changed, and light punctuation (commas or semi-colons) have been added to improve readability. Participles dangle where they may. Redundancies and superfluous comments such as climatic observations and phrases like "nothing doing today" have been omitted. Only two segments have been cut: George's visit to New York City and Washington, D.C., and a mine inspection tour to Northern California; deleted for the sake of brevity. A publisher has to think about costs too. Researchers desiring this information can find it in Parsons' pocket diaries at the Arizona Historical Society, Tucson. Despite what some claim, the diaries are readable, his handwriting with few exceptions, perfectly legible. I have attempted to identify persons cited in the diaries by inserting within brackets, initials or first names, but only where those names first appear. Because of Parsons' numerous abbreviations, insertions at every point where an initial appears would be distracting and add to the length of the book. Where possible, individuals listed in the index have either full names or initials. To give meatiness to George's comments on prominent individuals and moments of historic significance I have added footnotes.

Now for some acknowledgments. I would like to thank the librarians at the Arizona Historical Society for allowing me to xerox George Parsons pocket diaries. A debt of gratitude also goes to Bob Pugh, dealer of Arizoniana, who urged me to complete the project. On numerous occasions Neil Carmony, editor of *Whiskey, Six-guns & Redlight Ladies*, George Hand's saloon diary, and more recently *Apache Days and Tombstone Nights: John Clum's Autobiography*, perked my interest in Cochise County characters and sustained my decision to answer detractors of Parsons' earlier printed editions by making available this historical document. Without his kindness I would not have carried this project to completion. Historian and biographer Don Chaput also provided historical documentation and indirect encouragement. And the Santa Cruz Island Foundation furnished information on the later years of John V. Vickers and graciously allowed publication of a photograph of that entrepreneur. Last but certainly not least, I want to acknowledge Anne, my wife and helpmate, who has assisted my endeavors for twenty-nine years.

Lynn R. Bailey
Tucson, Arizona
January 19, 1997

George W. Parsons "a la Mexicano." In the past this photo has often been mistakenly identified as John P. Clum. See diary entry of May 19, 1886 (page 220), for details relative to this photograph. *(Photo courtesy Arizona Historical Society, Tucson)*

1882

Wednesday, June 28, 1882: Was delayed in getting off this a.m. till nearly 10 o'clock and then had a hard load for my horse. Didn't know he was in such a bad way till I got off. He had a very bad distemper. Sheath was badly swollen, back sore; while I was about sick from bad blood I guess, and had a large boil in a bad spot for riding horseback, but by leaning forward I managed it. Was anxious to get away from Tombstone. Went by way of Lewis Springs and again met soldiers and refreshed. Showery in afternoon and my new rubber coat came in handy. Met the notorious Pete Spence* with a villainous looking gang between Lewis and Crystal Springs, driving four cattle. Long hard ride and I didn't reach the Custom House** till nearly nine o'clock. Ten hours to make 40 miles. Met Capt. Payotte who gave some good points about my horse, saving me some cash, and we then had long talk about the quicksilver. Am afraid it will eventually be confiscated. Slept dressed, fleas troublesome.

Thursday, June 29: A hot day's ride. Horse bad and my boil no better. Had a hard time of it walking and pushing horse to Woodward's, about 30 miles. Met Geo. W[oodward] with two horses about eight miles from the C[ustom] H[ouse], going to Tombstone for Foley. Put up at W's. Horse and self played [out]. Adobe house new, quite nice.

Friday, June 30, 1882: Unable to sleep a wink all night on account of fleas. They were terrible and this a.m. I was one mass of sores. They seem to poison my flesh. A hard night of it, smoking, prowling around, and longing for morning. What a relief it was to see the first streaks of dawn. Young Hohstadt kind and hospitable. They have a Mexican boy; young horse thief whom they caught and who is obliged now to be their slave [peon]. Rather a hard looking youngster. The Indians reported as Apaches in the scare a month since are now thought to be Pimas smuggling gold dust into Arizona. Things quiet now in the Indian line. Made a good start and in a couple of hours arrived at locality. New country to me as I was never over Hohstadt's mine trail before. First person I saw proved to be [J.

*The notorious Pete Spence, or Spencer, figured in several encounters with the Earp brothers, and was implicated in the murder of Morgan Earp.
**The Custom House was located at Palominas, Sonora, in the San Pedro Valley, nine miles south of the international line. It was closed in 1890 in favor of Fronteras, fifty miles south of the border.

L.] Redfern and the place Hohstadt's. A new one he is building when he proposes mining from the Ojo de Agua. Found them building a large corral. R looked extremely well and hearty. Life a grand thing for him. Quarter to a half mile beyond was the mill site and mill going up. All hands well, making good headway. Boiler and engine up and battery doing well. [Charles] Godfrey a fine workman. A man named Bob Matheson, friend of his, assists him while Cap, Frazer and a Mexican hand, "Rocks," do other things. Too expensive to bring water from the river, so a well has been started and a good flow is expected before 20 feet is reached. Very slim camp; no houses built. Cap made himself a shed and the others crame into what was intended for a log cabin, but has only three ties laid and a few boards covering. Very little protection against the rain for anybody.

Saturday, July 1, 1882: Couldn't stand fleas in the enclosure, so I went outside and had to strip. Finally after taking off everything, rolling up in my blanket and lying outside on the grass instead of inside on the dirt, I managed to get some sleep. Two days and nights without it and I needed it badly. The boys have a good thing on me. We walked over to Hohstadt's and staid there late talking last evening, and as stated, I laid down in the enclosure. While fighting the fleas I heard something drop, and raising on my elbow, looked around for a tarantula or centipede, as those things are not at all uncommon. In fact, Bob was bitten by a centipede the other day. All of a sudden I saw something jump on to Godfrey's blankets and poke its head into them at [the] locality of his feet. While it was evidently hard at work nosing around, I cautiously reached for Redfern's riding boots, and when opportunity arrived, I let drive with all of my might at the supprised possum or coon, when to my consternation up rose G, his head where I supposed his feet to be and wanted to know the "row" in a not very amiable frame of mind. I soothed him as much as possible, and as no particular damage was done, it was all right but it was a close shave, for his face was slightly scraped, his arms and a tree receiving the full force of the blow. Supposing his position reversed, I mistook the throwing about of his arms for an animal.

Am very glad I didn't have my pistol under my head, a matter I was regretting, as the consequences would probably have been very serious. Godfrey has a bad habit of throwing his arms about and I was positive of an animal preying on something at the time. After the excitement was over I thought R would kill himself laughing. He kept it up for a full hour. In fact, most all did. It was so supremely ridiculous — my actions, G's surprise and the whole business. Then my peeling off everything and rolling up in an old shawl, not blanket, on the ground, made them laugh. I last remember seeing R's cigarette in the darkness and hearing him tapering off into subdued laughs.

Work going ahead quite well. Grub rather at a discount. A well is being sunk to save ditching from the river. Not very promising for water I think. Too much water. No meat and I went off on a hunt but instead of finding game discovered a ledge and some fine rock. Lost it this afternoon.

Can find it though I am quite sure by going original way. Plenty of rattle-snakes about and one needs to be careful. Cap has a fine skin filled with sand and last night while R, Finch and I were going to camp a big fellow crossed the road just ahead of R and got his quietus. Larger than in Arizona. I sleep with a hair rope stretched around me on the grass or will after tonight. Very little travel now, all travel is opposite us, short distance on other side of the river.

Sunday, July 2, 1882: Plenty of showers and some terrible lightning too. A terrible thing happened near Hohstadt's, the upper place, on Friday evening when the lightning was very bad. H came in and told us last night during the storm, and while a party of Mexicans were traveling this way, the lightning struck a burro on which were a boy and woman, the latter behind. The animal and boy were instantly killed, and the woman [who] was supposed to have [been killed], was laid out for burial but revived after a while. Mrs. H nursed her. Her hair was burned from her head, her right ear and breast badly lacerated, while the burro was literally cut in two, and the boy had a hole in his body. Quiet day. No work to speak of and I was much pleased as my wish was respected. R and John H went off hunting and killed three deer, having an exciting time, so now there is meat in camp once more. One year ago [President] Garfield was killed and I hope we will soon have the news of his assassin's death. I was positive in a discussion with others that the ass[assin] was hung June 30th, the day set by his trial.

Monday, July 3, 1882: R and I took a walk today and I followed my course of the other day very straight and struck my find with no trouble. While there we were caught in a mild thunder storm and was badly exposed on the summit. One flash near us caused us hastily to throw away our arms, ammunition, pick, etc., which we had hardly done when a crash and flash came together and we looked at each other to see if either had been hurt. Something had evidently struck very near. R's head hurt him a few minutes. Hohstadt let himself loose tonight and got off several very good horse yarns before the camp fire while M discussed some of the milk and our pipes. Cap will go with me to survey ledge probably tomorrow.

Tuesday, July 4, 1882: Our National Holiday and on foreign soil. Celebrated it by working harder than heretofore. R and G revived old times by striking drill in blasting, engine and boiler, battery, pan. Up tonight and very little remains to be done. Must have some lumber somehow. How I don't know. I haven't any money and am afraid R's short and can't meet present demands, he looks so little ahead. Frazer sick today and off duty. I brought Cap and R together yesterday and had a plain talk, saying we must not have dissension, that we should work with one another as it was to our best interests. We now had to make money, not trouble.

Wednesday, July 5, 1882: Bad time this morning. Godfrey disclosed his intention to quit and return to town today as the grub was unfit to eat and he couldn't work without eating. He is perfectly right, the only wonder to me is that he did not kick before. He did threaten to leave several times before I came down. Pretty hard to work as he does and then subsist on bread and water. If the flour was only decent, he said, he would not care. Beef spoils. We have no bacon and no Arizona flour; using a very inferior article from Magdalena that grits between one's teeth. It's hard luck. Cap got Godfrey into [a] better frame of mind and tomorrow R and I will corral several of Hohstadt's cows up river and than some milk. We can then have some decent bread from sour milk instead of the poor attempts with sour dough. Tough living all around. Nothing but bread and coffee and G doesn't drink that. We ought to have a store of provisions, at least $100 worth from Charleston and Tombstone. Made my bed on the carpenter bench last night, suspending rubber blanket to the partly made bough roof, and now I will be O.K. and not have to take a nightly struggling on the grass. Stage passed this a.m. and brought news of the hanging of [Charles] Guiteau [President Garfield's assassin]. At last justice done. Good thing on Redfern. He killed a big rattlesnake, six footer, several weeks ago and skinned it, throwing the skinned snake up the gulch. A week or more later, while walking the same gulch, he saw the remains and went for them lively, returning to camp with the story of having killed another huge snake. He retired very early when it was found that he had attacked the poor lifeless carcass of the snake he had killed and skinned. That throws my boot business of the other night altogether in the shade.

Thursday, July 6, 1882: R & I tried some time to catch horses this a.m. and R finally gave it up. I then went for them alone and finally corralled them some distance off. R afraid of rattlesnakes. We then went up the road to "Haniueriche" [sic, Janarerachi] about five miles to hunt some milk cows Hohstadt said we could use. I struck a deer on my trail and after finding R and getting his rifle, hunted the deer again and got a fine bead on him, but the barrel was empty and deer got away. Result of having hammer at half cock with nothing in the breech. R had a good square meal at the adobe house and I got left. While resting there along came Graham of San Francisco on his way to Flinn's gold properties west of Bacuachi about 20 miles. Got S[an] F[rancisco] *Call* of the 30th from him. R and I in the afternoon helped to drive some 50 head [of] cattle down for Hohstadt to his new place. Very hard work indeed, rough on man and horse. Great time in corral after cattle arrived, catching and marking some of the calves. R got his hand in lassoing and I tried it a while, great sport. Cap says very little now-a-days. I don't propose to be left by him after all the trouble he has caused me. Am getting used to my hard board bed. Ground pleasanter and softer but too many chigs and centipedes. Country reminds me strongly of the East with its fine large mountains, greenery, winding stream and fire flies in the evenings.

Friday, July 7, 1882: Very warm weather, yet we will probably be cooled off before long as rain is threatened. Mill about completed as much as possible before requiring lumber. Cap away last night — telling me that Geo

Woodward had sent for him on business — returned today. Had a long talk with him tonight alone. He still retains peculiar ideas of his connection with the mill notwithstanding the different talks I have had with him. It seems very hard for one to get his ideas correct in the matter. Had a plain talk with him tonight with particular reference to R's connection with us and my own interest and hope now we understand matters. After all trouble, bother, worry and annoyance I have had with Cap Hanson, I do not propose to be left by him now, and shall see that I am not. He doesn't like R at all and that is now my chief trouble. I hardly think though that Cap will go back on me.

R and I partly constructed a small corral today for our two cows and calves. Had a circus trying to milk. R held calf, "Rock," [the] Mexican, lassoed cow and milked while I held rope around her horns. Every now and then cows would make a break and we would move around lively. Rather broncoish. Mill about up now, except lumber part of it.

Saturday, July 8, 1882. Cap and I took pick and shovel this a.m. to examine my find. That didn't amount to much, but we traced up the float and found a fine large ledge which we will prospect later on. Ledge looks like a fine one, copper probably. Had a hard time of it prospecting without water, and the sun was terrible. Good properties are well earned by us if we get any. Hohstadt has to go to Bacuachi tomorrow, and I think of going along. Cap in better humor today. He, Godfrey and Bob left tonight for Tombstone. Cap to see about lumber either at Huachuca or Cananeas.

Sunday, July 9, 1882: Got away this a.m. Beautiful ride most of the distance, well shaded and watered. About 25 miles to Bacuachi and we made it about noon. A typical Mexican town a thousand years behind the age. On the edge of town we saw several of their carts drawn by oxen with raw hide straps bound around their horns. The wagons or carts are a sight very like the old pictures. The wheels are solid wood cut bodily out of a log and rounded and these work on a wooden axle, simply a log run under the body of the wagon with places at each end cut out for the wheels. The play of the wheels was remarkable. No tires, spokes or felloes and no close fitting. Bacuachi is a very old place; no one seemed to know how old, but thought to be all of 150 years, and is built on a hill or high mesa as are most if not all of the Mexican towns, to be better protected against Indians.*

We rode into one of the back yards or corrals and tied horses and presently got something to eat. Met several parties I knew — Mitchell of New Zealand and Australia, who stopped in the Huachucas a while, and Manning on his first trip down here, and Ketchum who was chased by the Indians a while ago when Lowry was killed at their mine, 16 miles distant. Water here is brought into town in canvas sacks on burros. Went to see

*This is the antiquated spelling of Bacoachi, in the District of Cananea. The town was older than most people thought at the time, being founded by Captain Simon Lazo de la Vega on September 28, 1649.

the mill this afternoon, all hands, and had a time finding it. It seemed to be washing day for the women as many were at work rubbing their clothes on large flat stones worn smooth by constant use. We got off the road and in several quite secluded spots surprised several parties of girls in our costume, but they didn't scare much. Finally reached the primitive mill, and it is primitive indeed. Water power moving two small stones which grind about 150 pounds a day at a charge of 75 cents for the whole. Money making process. I believe there is money to be made in this country in milling flour and will consider the matter when able. Met old Jesus. He is a great old fellow or in common parlance — "a daisy." They have a great way in this country of naming children after the day they are born on. Didn't get anything to eat till quite late and then I found a straw mat which I slept on in the yard close to the horses. Men, dogs, horses, chickens, and all, often sleep together.

I forgot to speak about the threshing machine consisting of four horses hitched to a post and driven by a mounted Mexican around and around, over and through the grain. Also about the old church with its three bells which are said to have a history and to be old. Tortillas for supper and they went well. For good coffee and a magnifico way of cooking frijoles, or beans, the Mexicans cannot be beaten. Don Juan Hohstadt seemed to be well known. Domingo certainly treated us well. Very hot in Bacuachi. Met Graham close to town returning.

Monday, July 10, 1882: Hohstadt's suit with "Dandy Jim" and Mortimer was compromised this a.m., and M got away between two and three p.m. This morning R had his horse shod by the only apology for a blacksmith in the place. His anvil was an old cannon and his bellows consisted of something resembling a pair of old boot legs which had to be pulled alternately. The only redeeming feature in the outfit was the pretty wife. Met Hayes on the road and got rid of the balance of our mescal with his help. Reached camp after dark a while and found everything all O.K. Graham kindly took our pan, shoe and die to Tombstone.

Tuesday, July 11, 1882: Met Finch on the road last evening who told us that Corrella [Corella] had suddenly died in Tombstone on the street of heart disease.* I was much taken back, having been much with C of late, and he was going to be of great use to us. He was a good man.

Wednesday, July 12, 1882: Am much worried about poor Correla's death. His poor wife is to be pitied. R and I took horses today and went about eight miles from camp on a turkey hunt, staying in the mountains all night. We camped in a very wild and picturesque piece of country — well worth a visit to see the wonderfully shaped rocks on the mountain tops.

Thursday, July 13, 1882: Off early to catch a turkey. Thousands of signs but no birds, though we started up a few deer. Caught in rain going home but my rubber coat, just received, saved me.

*Don Manuel M. Corella, formerly a practicing attorney in Tucson, was appointed Mexican consul at Tombstone in May 1882.

Friday, July 14, 1882: The boys digging for Hohstadt's house exhumed remains of a baby probably in an olla, also skeleton of an old party lying between two layers of rock. I saved some of the teeth. While writing this up this afternoon, a terrific storm burst and threatened wholesale destruction for a while. I covered this [diary] and sought refuge by standing on the bunks with head close to the few boards over me. The wind and rain swept through with great force blowing down our sheltered eating place and a large tree near by to which R's horse was tied. Was very afraid of lightning. Since the late death I am cautious. This is camp life with a vengeance. Wish we had some shelter. Don't like to have to do as the animals, take the wetting and wait for the sun to dry by. Every night we are anxious but thus far have not been much troubled. My rubber coat keeps my face dry and part of my body when it does rain in the night and we can only hope that these tornados will come in the day time. Not as many snakes, tarantulas and centipedes as expected so we cannot complain very much. Such is primitive life in Sonora.

Hayes arrived from Arispe shortly after storm pretty well soaked. R staid with John H. He looks after himself pretty well. I prefer to stay with the camp as much as possible. The owner of an extensive smuggling outfit visited us today for the second time and we are now pretty good friends. He is a traveler. The first authenticated news of Guiteau's hanging we got from him today from an *Illustrated Police Gazette*.

Saturday, July 15, 1882: Hayes and I went hunting this afternoon. Thousands of signs but we got no deer. He found a good mine though I guess when alone, and I struck something to be investigated. Splendid prospecting country and we propose to look at it well. There is money for us here I know it. Hope our privations will now earn something.

Sunday, July 16, 1882: I caught a Gila Monster yesterday afternoon on the way home and this a.m. Frazer skinned it for me. I have now a worthy companion for my alligator and crocodile in San Francisco at Clapp's. It's a beautiful specimen and has just shed its old scales. R went with Hayes this a.m. to see his new find, after which H went on to the Huachucas, taking some rock to be assayed. R brought back some fine looking specimens. [Ledge] seven feet across and a big thing — copper evidently. H will not allow Cap to come in although we both tried, R directly. He is down on Cap for something and would not listen to his having anything to do with it. Indians have probably done us a service in keeping away prospectors. We are in now at the first blush and must hold our ground. Another hard rain today and I was caught while washing at the river. R and I have, we think, a big thing in our find of last Tuesday. In Tombstone it would certainly be a very big thing. We have now one copper and one silver, besides Hayes' new find, and other rich float to trace up. We'll go out tomorrow for that I think. The day of rest but no change except stoppage of work on the mill. What a life it is in this wilderness. I would like some people I know to try this life a while. Cap and Bob arrived tonight and brought no mail but a few papers. Very singular, something is wrong. No friends for Godfrey and the Dickinsons.

Monday, July 17, 1882: Under the circumstances I thought it best for R and me to go to Tombstone today to arrange matters and smooth our existing troubles. So about 1:30 we started, and after a tiresome ride through darkness and rain, reached the Custom House at 9:30. We refreshed horse and man at [José] Elias's and then pushed on, but felt very tired a few miles beyond the C.H. and after picketing horses, slept a little while by the road side and reached Tombstone about two p.m.

We stopped to see Mrs. Clapp a few minutes while on the way to the house in our rough attire, armed, and she was very glad to see us and extended a cordial welcome. [She] was looking better than I expected. Mrs. Richardson was there. Had a good square meal tonight and slept well.

Tuesday, July 18, 1882: Little Harry looking well and growing. Mrs. [Catherine (Kate)] Goodfellow's infant died today from general bleeding, and by request of Doc & Mrs. G, I wrote Mrs. Goodfellow at Oakland the particulars. Didn't know Doc could feel so much.

Wednesday, July 19, 1882: First time R has been in Tombstone in three months. All of our friends very glad to see us. We dined at Milton's tonight by invitation and had a very enjoyable evening. Pacified Godfrey, as R's remittance is delayed. R very poor manager indeed. Am afraid he will injure my credit unless I am very careful. Got some provisions today, or R did, to pack out on old Sam tomorrow. G left him behind for us, he starting this a.m. with wife and outfit in a covered wagon for the camp.

Tuesday, July 20, 1882: Just after turning in last night, the fire alarm sounded, and the blaze being between our horses on one side and grub on the other, we got up there as quickly as possible and found the hook and ladder Co., house and adjoining lodging house in flames. Huachuca Co. and P. W. Smith and Co. stopped what looked at one time as though it might be another terrible conflagration. R got off this a.m. with pack horse but returned in a little while saying he could not manage him, so I had to do up my business in a hurry and leave much undone so as to go tomorrow. Wanted very much to stay over Sunday and see and hear the new Minister [Isaac T.] Bagnall. [Endicott] Peabody left day before my arrival. Had a pleasant surprise at Clapp's the night we dined there. Later Mr. and Mrs. [Frank] Earl, Rev. Bagnell and a lawyer named Strout I think, of Portland, Maine, spent evening. Had a very pleasant talk with Strout who knows Wiscasset and many of the people—Judge [George E.] and Mrs. Berry on hand too.

Friday, July 21, 1882: After many vexatious delays got started about 10 o'clock. R forgot pistol of course a few miles out and had to return. I took pack to Lewis Springs. There met Gilman returning from Sonora. Very heavy rain storm here for a while. Horse began to play out at Hereford. Here we met Capt. [J. C.] Thompson and Company with Indian scouts. Feared Indian trouble but were reassured and proceeded. Crossed river at

Ochoaville but had to camp at trees and Sam's back was sickening when pack was taken off. No pack saddle, only riding, and it cut into his rotten flesh.

Saturday, July 22, 1882: Camped in a very pretty spot last night and slept in our hammocks suspended from the trees. During the night a coyote or wolf came for our grub and I fired at him hardly awakening R. With his deafness and sound sleeping he is like the dead. Had to pack our saddle at times this a.m., drive Sam ahead and foot it to the C.H. five miles. Very hot time of it. Found [Con T.] Cutler there.* A long interview about our quicksilver and a very unsatisfactory one. The gray found still there. No one talks English and we only happened to strike Cutler. At his suggestion I wrote a letter to [Alexander] Willard, Consul at Guaymas, which Cutler will forward with a few words of his own. Thus the matter has been started. Had a hard time of it tonight. Señor Elias provided us very kindly with a burro which we packed and about three p.m. started for home. Walked the 30 miles to Woodward's. That is, walked the animals and made Woodward's about one or two a.m. Black as Egypt going through canyon. Could see only white pack on burro bobbing up and down. Fire flies of tremendous size. Handled pistol once thinking someone was crossing path with a light.

Sunday, July 23, 1882: Santa María outfit on hand at Woodward's. Good meal with them this a.m. 1,000 [peso] fine at C.H.—secured time. Finally reached home this a.m. and got tent up this afternoon and things inside just ahead of rain.

Monday, July 24, 1882: Got things in order this a.m. and straightened up. Got some birds with new shot gun. Found Bob quite sick when we arrived.

Tuesday, July 25, 1882: Ashman and Watts arrived Wednesday and staid night with us. Ash very anxious for me to go with him to Cumpas to see his mine there. Indian news not very cheery from that quarter, but good chance to see the country so guess I'll go.

Wednesday, July 26, 1882: Wrote this up this a.m. and now I will get horse and go. I need a change anyway. This state of things here is not encouraging and is very provoking.

Thursday, July 27, 1882: Made a start this a.m. and reached Bacuachi in afternoon, 25 miles distant. Met Ketchum who wanted to trade me a mule for my horse, but I didn't see it. From all accounts Indians are plentiful be-

---

*Forty-nine year old Cornelius T. Cutler, an early California pioneer, was born in Damrisutta, Maine. In 1861 he went to Sinaloa, Mexico, in company with William Penn Johnson and engaged in cotton growing with success. The French invasion broke up the business and Cutler was sentenced to be shot; but his persuasive arguments saved his life. Cutler was then arrested by Mexican forces, and escaped during a French attack. He made his way back to the United States and participated in the opening of the Mount Diablo coal mines near San Francisco. In 1870 he was a candidate for Superintendent of Public Instruction for the State of Nevada. In 1878 he came to Arizona, lived in Tucson, and showed up in Tombstone where he mined for a while.

low and we will have to be careful. Ash and Watts much pleased with diet here. Its fine for a Mexican town. Had the luxury of a cot tonight. The population sleeps on the ground.

Friday, July 28, 1882: After receiving numerous directives, we left for Cumpas this a.m. I returned to town just after starting for grub and was told to get some pinole, but upon seeing the stuff, supposed some mistake had been made and didn't take it. I didn't know until later that it was used as a drink or mush on the road. It is parched wheat or corn, ground and such mealy looking stuff I didn't see any use for it on our journey, but it is very nutritious and that and jerky are about all the soldiers here use.* After wandering over the country and not finding the trail, we returned to town after a 25 mile ride, rather disgusted with things in general and Mexicans in particular, who had given us no less than three different directions to find the trail. Arriving at Bacuachi we found several parties going on the trail a few miles tomorrow, so we'll go with them. Watts nervous about Indians outside of town and didn't want to talk aloud. Comfortable night and good sleep. Mescal.

Saturday, July 29, 1882: With O'Brien and the Italian, we got away this a.m. and found the blind wagon trail, the Italian taking it with his wagon. Accompanied them 10 or 15 miles when we continued and they turned to the right, having a few miles to go to their camp. O'B very pleasant fellow, well provided with mescal. Lots of sweet acorns on the road. A big business done in them in the Mexican cities. They are money. They act as an astringent. Passed through a very wild and romantic country today and this afternoon were caught in a terrible rain storm in the head of the Cumpas river. Had to stop and take it, horses turning tail to it. Camped early and no water except the soaking which was enough for the stock. Watts excited over a shot I made at a rabbit. Better not to have made the noise I suppose. Good feed for stock. Ate our sardines and crackers and about dark were treated to the wildest kind of a rain storm accompanied by startling thunder and lightning. We stood up and took it the greater part of the night. The lightning was blinding and once we looked at each other to see if harm had been done. Being in an Indian country too, we were startled at times—took one or two scouts during the night. Kept watch by turns. How we did long for morning, standing shivering under the small oak, taking the pelting, driving rain—a regular tropical storm— and keeping close watch all of the time for Indians, fearing all about us and at times startled by unusual sounds or sights. Watts's black burro though was as good as a watch dog. All finally got a little sleep by turns.

Sunday, July 30, 1882: Made a good start this a.m. and after going a few miles stopped and finished our grub. Wild desolate country. Very hot and

*Pinole was the staple diet of Mexican travelers and soldiers. It was made of corn, roasted and crushed and slightly sweetened with panoche, a crude sugar. Pinole was prepared by putting a few teaspoonfuls in a cup of water, letting it stand until the grains had settled and swollen. It was then sweetened to taste.

horses felt it. Trail a fair one. Finally about two to three o'clock in the afternoon we struck what we supposed was Cumpas but which proved to be a small town or ranch called "Ojo de Agua." Here were assembled in the main street numbers of men and women who regarded us with curiosity. Population evidently disturbed about something which we soon discerned to be the loss of a young woman from Cumpas, three miles distant, who was supposed to be captured by Apaches. While going the three miles though, word was brought of her recovery, so her fate was not so sad as we thought. At last we entered Cumpas and found Adams's place and put up. Cumpas is larger than Bacuachi and quite a town. Houses, of course, all built the same way with corral in rear which you enter by going in the front and only door through the sleeping and eating room—all the same. Horses, dogs and all, I was going to say, held things in common, but it isn't as bad as that. All hands though just tumble down where they want to [eat] and sleep—no beds but mats of straw and a species of wood strung together in lengths which one throws down to suit himself if possessed of one; if not, your blanket must answer. The doorway is usual place for sleeping in this weather, right in the draft, if any. Geo. Adams and Jeff Dickerton, Ash's partners, and a miner, McDonald, seemed to run the place and to be cared for by a buxom señora who provided us with a splendid dinner in a little while of deer meat, eggs and cheese to which we did ample justice and being nearly starved, having but two small boxes of sardines and a few crackers since the day before.

Looked at the town later and ate some watermelons and drank mescal. All these old Mexican towns I guess are the same. This has the usual large plaza with church, half in ruins, facing south and the whole place has the usual tumble-down decayed appearance. Were very glad to get here though after our fearsome ride of 65 miles from Bacuachi over an uninhabited country. Watered horses about dark in the Cumpas river and our burro was much remarked about by the natives. He is a very extraordinary animal, black as the ace of spades, of unusually large size and with ears of wonderful size and length. One could hardly look at him without laughing. A party named Jackson, running the San Pedro mine near Ash's, invited us to stay night at his place so we took blankets there, as rain was more plentiful, and spread them on the ground under the roof at edge of corral where we could get all the air there was, as this is a fearfully hot country. This evening I pumped Jackson pretty well about the country, laws, business, resources, boundaries, etc., and got much useful information. Daniels, [J. H.] White's brother-in-law of Contention, and several others here at Jackson's. River is rily at present and little holes are dug by the women in the sand alongside, into which the water comes after filtering through the sand. It's a funny sight to see the women with the regular shawl over their heads file down to the river with ollas on their cushioned heads, each one scratching in the sand for clear water. A strong race—shiftless, hand-to-mouth folks.

Monday, July 31, 1882: Well, we started for Tobaccochi mine this a.m., about 15 miles west and got there about noon. I rode a mule to rest my horse. Very pretty country, wild and picturesque. Saw palm trees for the first time since leaving Florida. Quite a tropical country, very hot and tremendous rains. A very steep ascent to the mine. Had a bite at mouth of tunnel, then took candles and went through the 210 foot tunnel to where it cut the ledge on an incline from above. This is one of the old mines famed in bygone days for its richness and is said to have produced much bullion. As far as worked, it has been literally gouged out and all of the waste left with no dead work done. The whole formation is porphorytic [porphyritic] with no walls but the clay seams and the ore is rich—of high grade all of it and varies from two to six inches in width. Never saw anything like this before. Ascended to top of hill when through with the tunnel and descended the incline. Marks of the gambesinos [gambosinos] or robbers were apparent everywhere. Ash should have plenty of ore below these workings and his winze from the tunnel will probably catch it. In this locality is the "San Juan," "San Pedro" and one or two other old and valuable properties too. Returning [we] were caught in a tremendous rain storm. Rubber coat and heavy broad brimmed sombero do good service these days.

Indians bad in these parts and one has to be wary. People excited over the Apaches stealing a lot of stock close to town the other day. One bold Apache came into town, tying his mule outside, and after taking observations probably for stock, lit out. One man was killed the other day and about 20 of them [Apaches] killed and ate a mule at one of the ranches nearby. The women locked themselves up or rather barricade themselves, as locks are unknown, and were not molested. The simple name "Apache" is enough to scar the wits out of a Mexican. They are deathly afraid of them and have a right to be. They have scourged this country for years and years and though they do not attack the towns now, they lie in wait on the outskirts and one has to be careful. On the road close to Cumpas are numerous evidence of slaughtered Mexicans in the way of piles of stones surmounted in some instances by a cross. In some places the road is fairly lined with them. At the mine we were a good 100 miles from my camp at the mill. Wild country and an old, old country, all of 200 years old, that is, the town of Cumpas.

Ash, Watts and I camped at Jackson's tonight but were disturbed by unexpected arrival of Daniels and partner, and vacated cots for the ground. They just from Oposura with tidings of soldiers coming this way after Indians, 500 strong, Genl [Morales Jesús] García commanding. About time. The Mexican soldier is an institution. Clad in almost nothing, with rawhide sandals to walk with, and pinole and jerky to eat, he goes after his terrible enemy and generally whips him.

Tuesday, August 1, 1882: This a.m. we bade farewell to the señora with the blue eyed child and head resembling "G. A.'s" (about which child though we asked no questions as it was too evident a case) and to our watermelons, peaches, figs, eggs, chicken, etc., for [we] had been living high (although it is said "you can't get anything to eat in Sonora—nothing but tortillas and frijoles") and left town. Quite a cavalcade, Ash, Jeff [Dickerson], Mac [McDonald] and I with pack mules. Unless one knows parties in this country he probably will not fare very well. One must know and be known. I add this in connection with one's eating.

On the edge of town one Mexican with a smattering of English tried to frighten us about the dreaded Apache again—the uppermost thing in their mind at present—saying they were about Bacuachi. Mac yelled "we'll trade horses with them then," and off we went having little fear of trouble. Winchesters and six-shooters with plenty of ammunition were strapped to ourselves and horses and we had little fear, certainly not much in an open fight. The only thing to fear is ambuscade or when you may be off your ground a moment. They don't care to run risks anymore than any one else. Rested and lunched before camping for the night. Mac suffering from a boil in a very inconvenient place but his spirits were not much dampened and he was constantly going for poor Jeff, the most mild mannered man in the world, about his terrible temper. Jeff thought Mac superstitious. Made good camp tonight and slept well. No rain.

Wednesday, August 2, 1882: Pinole is very hearty—the wheat pinole. Cakes or biscuits and eggs go well this trip. Sun terribly hot these days, unremittingly so. Just imagine riding horseback all day, day after day, under a tropical sun, for this is a tropical country and one can form a little idea what fine amusement this mine examining is. Now and then the clouds gather and make with tremendous force, creating water spouts and the rain descends in a manner unequalled elsewhere. It's lots of fun to lie out in it all night, afraid when the lightning strikes near you that your rifle, revolver, or knife may attract it still nearer; but you cannot put them away in an Indian country and feel safe. And when riding horseback what can you do but ride through the storm and take things as they come. I am used to all of this now and don't care or much mind it [at] all, having gradually accustomed myself to all of the unpleasantnesses of this wild life. "It's singular," Ash said the other night while he was lying under the pelting rain and shivering from cold wind, "what one can accustom himself to and not mind it." Nothing molested or made us afraid on the road and we reached Bacuachi in time for supper. A "Baile" was to be held tonight, and being anxious to see one, I went with Miller of Janarериche. The prettiest girl had been married that day and the dance was given in her honor. Some pretty figures. Staid till mescal was getting in its work pretty well and then went to Dominguez.

Thursday, August 3, 1882: Reached the mill this afternoon and killed a rattlesnake just before I got there. It had the prettiest skin I ever saw and I made a good shot from my horse's back with revolver, taking the snake's head clean off, not injuring skin a bit. Dragged it to camp by lariat;

skinned it and will have a pretty thing. River high, swelled by a water spout. Horse nearly went down with me in one place. He is pretty well used up. Hard trip of 200 miles or more. In saddle every day, riding 25 to 30 miles and more. Rested him one day though. Redfern got a piece of candle and read and wrote so late I slept out on the grass tonight.

Friday, August 4, 1882: Ash and party got away early. Was to send burro with them to Señor Elias but he was not there. Ash a fine fellow. We discussed business projects in Mexico and both thought a good banking business could be done in Hermosillo and that we might do well together. It is a matter to be looked into and other things. I think Ash and I could get along nicely together. Redfern away at Cananeas with Hohstadt to see about lumber when we arrived yesterday, but came later in evening. Can get all we want there on time. Cap it seems did not do much.

Saturday, August 5, 1882: Rain as usual. Tent leaks. Will be glad when the rainy season is over. Bob better. Things moving very slowly indeed.

Sunday, August 6, 1882: Hunted for burro this a.m. on R's horse but couldn't find him. R then started for the Cananeas with John Hohstadt to see about lumber again. It's provoking that R shouldn't care for borrowed property any more than he cared for the burro during my absence. Took a walk with Cap this afternoon and tried to find a place I was at about a month ago where there was some rich float, but failed to find it.

Monday, August 7, 1882: Hohstadt just down from his mine and at last has discharged Johnson. He has paid for his experience with him. Wrote Mrs. Redfern as requested by him in a letter recently received. Must write sisters tomorrow, though can't tell when letters will be taken to town. Had grand wash this afternoon of self and clothes. River running high. Doctored horse this afternoon. In a pretty bad way after the rough trip, but feeling better now. Quite a talk with Cap. R is hurting my interests.

Tuesday, August 8, 1882: Last morning or two have been delightfully cool and pleasant and possibly denote a permanent change of temperature in the mornings at least. I mean from five or six o'clock sun is powerful. Will now try to write sisters and Nathalie. R back today from the Cananeas. Lumber purchased 3247 feet of Genl [Ignacio] Pesqueira. The Genl treated R and John H well and offered them, or R more particularly, an old mining property known as the "Madiera." Must be looked into.

Wednesday, August 9, 1882: Lumber expected today but didn't arrive. Roads very bad. Frazer a terribly lazy good for nothing fellow. Has good brain but whiskey and women have ruined him. Can't stand him much longer. Was very fortunate yesterday. Just as my long letter to sisters was completed, along came Finch [who] took that and my other to Tombstone, so they may possibly be mailed tonight.

Thursday, August 10, 1882: Lumber arrived this a.m. and once more it looks like business about the mill. Three wagons to bring the 3247 feet, but then the roads are very bad and about 25 miles to haul, having to make a road some of the way. Pretty stiff price. $40 per m at mill and same for hauling—total $80 per m. Two months time given and another month if necessary, easy enough terms. Very good lumber. Too good almost.

Friday, August 11, 1882: Pulp tanks made today. Frazer too outrageous for anything, so I had a few words with him this evening.

Saturday, August 12, 1882: Frazer left this a.m. for Bacuachi with Romero and family on their wagon and didn't even say adios to me. Good riddance to bad rubbish. Had another talk with Louis about Cap and now things are going along smoothly and my two objects are pretty well accomplished—riddance of Frazer and amiability of Redfern and Cap.

Frame pretty well along by tonight. McGee arrived this evening with mail and I expect will take Finch's place. Two great surprises for me, a death and marriage. While hastily looking over the Tombstone papers I saw the telegraphic announcement of my good friend Judge Lake's death of heart disease. An envelope containing Miss Lizzie Collins cards—sad and pleasant news from my old home S.F. Took a hand at a little mining today and filled two holes and blasted them for grading. First time in nearly two years. How tempus does forget in this country. Were it not for this journal all track of dates and days would be lost. I have to refer to it to be certain. Eagerly devoured papers tonight, or news rather, having to make a blaze as we sport no candle nor lamp. Our only light we have when grease is plentiful, when we wrap a rag and stick it in the grease. Gives a good light. Tent stands rains now so things don't have to be taken out and sunned. Life is primitive. Hang the life, we want money and will have it.

Sunday, August 13, 1882. McGee got away this a.m. early. He had some Indian news not at all pleasing and Jeff and Mac arrived tonight with further Indian news, stating that a number were between Fronteras and Bacuachi and no one could tell where they were liable to go. Their route and trails are east of here though and I don't much fear them, but then one can't tell and the uncertainty is not pleasing. Things very quiet in Tombstone. Big strike in Contention reported. Strange I don't hear from father. Rattlesnake skin in fine order.

Monday, August 14, 1882: Another soaking deluger last night. Tent worked well. Mac and Jeff got off about day break. Their trip will not be so pleasant as ours, as they will have to look out more for Indians than we did. Hope they and the Mexicans will pull through. "Mexican George" told me some news this a.m. about a mining man from the east who would probably be at the mill tonight and who seems to know Louis and me. Much inquiry seems to be made by different parties about our mill. It excites interest. Wish some one would offer me $10,000 for my interest. Wagon driven by Geo. Berry arrived this evening. A Mr. Moyle of S.F. was the other occupant. Is out on a mine hunt I think. Moyle is an old timer and he and Cap had a great time tonight discussing '49 experiences. Quite a change in grub too, as they produced some canned goods and M luxuriated on canned codfish tonight. Our jerky got left, only meat we have now. We got a quarter of beef lately and jerked it. Meat won't keep 12 hours fresh. A miserable drizzling rain this afternoon and about all night, something like an eastern rain and very unlike Cal[ifornia] or Arizona rains which are quick, sharp and heavy. This was unusual for here too. Nails about gone, so roofing must be suspended a while. Hohstadt back tonight and to our surprise has managed [to convince] Johnson and partner to work again on his mine. H is a queer stick and very unreliable.

Tuesday, August 15, 1882: Redfern started to Bacuachi about noon and hopes to return with the burro of which we got track through Jesus. Moyle, and Berry left this a.m. after regaling us with some hard and tough old time California yarns about fellows walking through chimneys, tunneling under snow, etc. They may go as far as Hermosillo and in all probability will stay with us a day or so on their return. Had to start in on making bread again today. No trick at all though with sour milk. Cap and I had quite a confab tonight.

Wednesday, August 16, 1882: Rain has staid with us pretty well since Monday. Quartered other day and will stay I expect balance of month. Rain most of time, in showers though. Got smoke stack up and in place this a.m. and little remains now to be done. Miller and Stewart outfit broke down near our place and repaired yesterday and today. Horse getting along well. Got him up today. We must go to Tombstone next week and get stuff. Query, how is stuff to be had? Ways and Means Committee must be immediately formed. Suppose I'll have to be that Committee as all of such matters finally come to me—problems to be solved. Have pulled through thus far so must abide events.

Thursday, August 17, 1882: No Redfern today. If he doesn't show up by tomorrow I must get an animal and hunt him up. Pump frame up and in place today and little now remains to be done. Johnson and pal back and seem to be reinstated much to our disgust. H a queer man. Quite a talk with John Hohstadt [Jr.] this evening about cattle at the tent. He will start out for himself, enlarge in some way, and R & I propose starting him if possible with a hundred cows, he to furnish a ranch he has leased in the Basochucas, and the necessary bulls. $1500 from R and me will buy cows and start things and John to have one third of all cattle and take milk for expenses. Big money in this eventually and a quite safe investment. Cattle are in demand and will be high priced after a while when the railroads are in. Five years will have money. I am in on the "Sierra Madre" mine given R and John by [Ignacio] Pesqueira and I should be as I would have gone to the mill if horse had been in condition. That mine must be looked after and secured very shortly. Rain tonight and no supper.

Friday, August 18, 1882: Louis back about noon almost played out, having been caught by the floods below and obliged to camp out all night. Had to swim his horse in one place. Dangerous work in these swollen rushing streams. Little-Daniel's wagon capsized in the water and Giant Powder, 25 lbs, and money swept away. Hard luck. Burro found but could not be brought up. Very bad rains. Hohstadt told us some of Frazer's yarns today.

I thought he would lie about us and so he has. Said he was lying awake one night and overheard R and me say that if H's rock went $300 we would fix things so that he shouldn't get more than $150 out of it. I didn't think F was quite so low down and would go so far in his lying. Hope I shall never see him again as I do not want any trouble with such cattle and might have it in that event. I feel hot.

Saturday, August 19, 1882: Roof all on before noon today and we can bid defiance to the rains now so far as machinery is concerned. Rain most of the time now. Clear in mornings till almost noon when clouds come; lightning and thunder start in and down comes the fluid lasting most of night and afternoon. Rather tough on us cooking. Have to cook between showers or enough to last a while. Wind and rain rather uncomfortable in tent as we cannot very well close it and both ends stand open. As soon as darkness comes we smoke and talk lying on beds till sleepy and then roll roll up for the night and let her rip. No light of any kind. No candles, lantern or nothing. Comprised a candle with grease and rag when we had the grease but that is now gone and rather expensive light at 50 cents per pound. We do a terrible lot of reminiscing. Florida now fails me. Am tackling Spanish in earnest and have progressed well the past few days. Will not be satisfied till I can read, write and talk Spanish.

Sunday, August 20, 1882: A terribly disagreeable day. Rain all day and for all the world like one of these miserable eastern rainy days which I had well nigh forgotten. Cap went to "La Mina" this a.m. with H to show him how to work his mine. H is coming to his senses I hope at last.

Monday, August 21, 1882: Saw some rich rock from the great M mine close to Chihuahua to day. Durand and Barron had it. Quite a confab with D tonight at camp fire.

Tuesday, August 22, 1882: Mill will soon be in running order and something has to be done to raise means for running her. Talk with Hohstadt today. Wants $30 to go in for us and will not abate a cent. Roads very bad. Rains though letting up a little and river going down rapidly.

Wednesday, Augsut 23, 1882: Some more confabbing today and I expect we'll have to give H $30 and let him go in with two yoke of oxen. Will have probably nearly a ton of freight. I shall go ahead and raise some money on the mill, $200 or $300, enough to start us up. Will start Friday a.m. and will ride Redfern's horse in, mine not being in condition and have things ready to begin again by Wednesday when H and R should arrive. Hohstadt started in today grading road by the mill. We will have to ditch our water three-quarters of a mile. Felt hot today, but cooled down subsequently. It's enough to provoke one to death.

Thursday, August 24, 1882: Pleasanter weather now. Tom Moore and Walter Harvey rode into camp today and after eating left for Bacuachi. Made list of things wanted today and hope to get off tomorrow a.m.

Friday, August 25, 1882: Got breakfast early and took cup of coffee with the Godfreys when I started on Redfern's horse which I got up yesterday afternoon after a five mile chase and an exasperating one. Pleasant ride. Studied Spanish on the road and near Custom House killed a rattlesnake and carried back of saddle with skin, leaving the rattles on. Had considerable fun with Mrs. A Conier and Mrs Elias over it at C.H. Mrs. AC made me a good cot bed and I was in clover.

Saturday, August 26, 1882: Thirty-two years old today and still a wanderer it would seem. How long must this last? My next birthday must see me differently situated. I hope I am not throwing away the best years of my life but sometimes feel that I am. I am in my maker's hands and hope I do not work against his will. Off soon after day break and stopped at Crystal Springs at 9:30 for breakfast—half way to Tombstone from the CH, 20 miles from latter place. Good grass for horse here and rested till nearly noon. [E. R.] Howe and [Tom] Ewing passed here on way to Los Delecias mine. Exchanged compliments and was about starting when stage from Bisbee arrived and I was much surprised to see Heine on board, fresh from New York. Rode with cavalry some distance and then crossed by a trail of mine and in early afternoon stopped at Mrs. R to see about state of things. Reached town in good time and found house occupied by a Mr. Howe who had permission, but whom I never met; traveling student and very pleasant fellow. Made several visits and ended at Clapp's, receiving hearty welcome and congratulations. Rev. Bagnall present. Strange coincidence in his birthday and mine occurring today, he 25 and I 32. Pleasant evening.

Sunday, August 27, 1882: Pleasant day. Good sermon this a.m. by Bagnall. Stain glass windows just in and add greatly to the appearance of things. Very neat little church and being gradually nicely appointed. Saw Mrs. Goodfellow a while and dined with Clapps at Jakey's about six p.m. Nice dinner. Attended Presbyterian Church this evening and heard good sermon by Dr. Robertson. A treat to get to church once more and worship my creator in the old accustomed manner.

Monday, August 28, 1882: Hard time today. Thought I wouldn't have much trouble in getting $300 on the mill for supplies, but couldn't raise it. Had J. V. Vickers been home would have gotten it, but he was east. Clapp rather provoked me by his shortness. Had to take father's balance and get time on balance owed. Will see that he gets the one eighth interest in the mining properties as stipulated for before. This money was to be used for development but must now be used this way and put into mines out of first mill returns. About as broad as it is long. He has interest now though. Shoes and dies not cast, but were started on today.

Tuesday, August 29, 1882: Finished purchases today and got things in readiness. Indian around again and I felt uneasy for Redfern and old man Hohstadt until they arrived at house about nine o'clock this evening. Made fine time with oxen—only 2½ days—fine travelers. Unable to get a dollar and much disgusted. When flush I let my money go and now that I want a favor it can't be done. Money is very tight, Tombstone very dull.

Wednesday, Augsut 30, 1882: Rustled around lively today and got wagon loaded and off by five o'clock this afternoon. Hard time to get Hohstadt away from newspapermen. Indians reported raiding upper Sonora which means my locality. Am troubled. Spent evening at Earle's and Clapp's. Bonillas at Clapp's; very clever fellow. Have good letter from him to Señor Flores at C.H. Friends don't want me to go, but I must now.

Thursday, August 31, 1882: Terrible excitement this a.m. Tom Johnson was killed on Monday by Apaches on the Sonora road about 20 miles from the C.H. while trying to catch up with Redfern who was not far ahead, and who with Hohstadt, passed by the red devils as they laid in the long grass concealed, but who didn't want oxen but horses. Poor Johnson. He was a pleasant fellow; lived four to five miles from us.* Bad times, and I don't care to travel, but it is necessary and I never back down. Found wagon at Charleston damaged today, but we got off this afternoon. Out of Charleston a few miles Berridge caught us horseback and I had to saddle horse and return to Charleston to sign a paper in ink relating to Bassett mine. After fixing things in Charleston I followed up the road and found oxen stalled in mud hole and [in] a bad fix. Camped and passed night by mud hole near Blair's. Laid with head next to Redfern's and in the night fired revolver at a pole cat near wagon without awakening Redfern. No fire longer than necessary. Caution being required these days. Bought rifle for mill and fixings this a.m. Had to have one to travel with anyway, having left mine with Godfrey who asked for it.

Friday, September 1, 1882: Partly unloaded this a.m. and dug out. Made fair time getting as far as Ochoaville.** Hunted the prairie dogs which caused a larger expenditure of cartridges to all passing the locality between Hereford and Ochoaville and got one. They are very hard to get and I was fortunate. At Hereford Hohstadt got a letter from the ranch stating that they were all O.K. thus far. Death of two of his boys by Indians was reported. The latter were numerous, requiring constant vigilance. They had not yet done anything more than kill and maim some cattle so John wrote. At Ochoaville met Tom Moore and Walter Harvey on their return to Tombstone full of stories about the Indians. Now they seemed to be running Bacuachi. On top of the Apache trouble come numerous reports of a revolution in Sonora. Genl [Luis Emeterio] Torres is reported march-

*According to the Tucson *Weekly Citizen* of September 10, 1882, Apaches, concealed in the willows, shot Tom Johnson in the back on the right side of the spine, riddled him with buckshot and then broke his leg and beat in his skull. Friends retrieved his body and buried it near the Sonoran Custom House.

**Ochoaville had its inception when Estaban Ochoa established a sheep ranch on the Elias Land Grant two miles from Camp Huachuca, and twenty miles south of Charleston. Because of its proximity to mines in the Huachuca and Mule mountains it grew in importance as a supply center. The town's principal merchant, J. N. Acuña, stood the expense of mail delivery from Charleston. In September 1880 about 500 people were dependent on Ochoaville for supplies and mail delivery.

ing against the present governor Ortiz and the grand result is to be the dispossession of and driving out of all Americans within the dead line, or 60 mile limit, in which we are. All leases are to be abrogated and the devil is to pay in general. Cummings seems to be full of importance on the matter, but I don't go a cent on him. We cannot be harmed very well. We'll stay with the mill anyway. Very cold nights on this San Pedro river. Will be glad when we strike the Sonora. Boys all glad they got through O.K. and very sorry for us as we have to face it all and the worst is to come.

Saturday, September 2, 1882: Good start this a.m., but were stuck just after crossing San Pedro in front of Ochoaville. Very bad time. Had to partly unload and carry things up the hill after getting oxen up with the balance. No joke carrying up the castings, 100 to 200 lbs to the carry. At last we got off and from now on had to keep sharp lookout for Apaches. Very lonely country. Met few men running out of Sonora, all badly scared. Numerous killings reported, some bodies stinking by the trails. Boys will probably meet and escort us down. Oxen made a bad break for water near Custom House and could not be controlled. Ran over an embankment and nearly capsized wagon. Load all or mostly in bottom only reason we didn't go over. As it was, the wagon wheels left the ground once on the up hill side and I was sure all was gone but fortunately balance was regained. R and I jumped but the old man was caught in the mud and water and had to be lively to escape bodily harm. Oxen very bronco and badly broken I believe. I'd shoot one of them if mine. He is a mean devil. Well, had some more unloading and reloading, digging, etc. Quite enough work for one day when we finally reached the Custom House or Aduana, and hauled up. Presented a letter to Señor Flores, temporary collector, I had from Bonillas and we were well received, having main office to stop in and whiskey bottle set out for us.

Friday, September 3, 1882: Papers were made out for us today and it was arranged that we should have the quicksilver upon payment of $40. $60 was asked last evening but I supposed they thought we were pretty good fellows and they would throw off something. Duties on stuff with papers amounted to more than I had, so R and I had to return to Tombstone to raise more money. Had quite a confab with collector and expressed myself in plain terms through Hohstadt about arbitrary way of doing things. The CH is a curse to Sonora and is operating against all parties wishing to enter Mexico. It drives away rather than encourages capital. Miller's wagon came in this a.m. under guard for an irregularity. About two a.m. they had a skirmish with Indians about head of the canyon. Fired some shots and had quite an excitement; no harm done. R and I had a horse of Curry's he left with us at Crystal Springs when half a dozen of the boys passed us on the way down, well armed and mounted to render assistance—Geo W, Bush, Curry, and Bill Murray. R and I started about two or three o'clock in afternoon. Rested at Crystal Springs and finally reached Tombstone at 11 o'clock at night. Pretty tired. Ate and slept well. On Burleigh road had to be careful as several Indians were reported seen on the road the day I left. Didn't place any reliance on truth of report though and went out the road a mile or two after the wagon, but not finding tracks, cut across the Charleston where I found it with the broken bolster. Lonely ride over that B road and once we pulled up short but it was a false alarm and we reached town O.K., a long 40-42 miles.

Monday, September 4, 1882: Finally got the money, $200 necessary, from Hudson & Co. by Clapp's accepting draft on R's aunts or one of them. Charged pretty well though, $2^1/_2\%$. Received letter from Consul Willard at Guaymas today relating to the quicksilver, and much to our surprise, a bill for services rendered by Consul, lawyer, etc., was enclosed for $58. Didn't look for any charge in the matter and didn't like it, but had to swallow the bitter pill and forward amount out of R's money. Tough, very. We're getting it on all sides. Wonder when there'll be a let up—revolution business seems to be going on. We're in for it now and must take our chances, but I must say that I am getting heartily sick of all of this excitement and risk. Wouldn't care though if it will only pay. Friends seemed to think we were going from them for the last time. We made a start this afternoon about five o'clock and our good friend Ashman accompanies us on the road a ways. Reached Crystal Springs, 20 miles distant, between eight and nine o'clock and got supper and then laid in our blankets till after moonrise, one or two o'clock, when we saddled up and were off. Came across one or two outfits on the road and my horse jumped from under one man ostensibly on guard I suppose, both badly frightened. Santa María outfit well guarded. Saw Chase in Tombstone who stated that he expected to have to pay a fine of $4,000 at C House simply because of a difference between the Mexican Consul in S.F. & CH officers, one side fighting the other about the papers. Pretty state of things in any government. Mexico better take care or she will lose Sonora. Left Ochoaville as day was about to break and got back to Custom House not long after sunrise. Long 80 miles to and from CH.

Tuesday, September 5, 1882: Shortly after reaching CH a number of shots were heard in direction we had just traveled and Apaches were first thoughts. Proved though to be a good sized black bear causing the excitement and which gave much sport. Just our luck to have passed the fellow without seeing him. Too bad we couldn't have had the sport. I want a good skin and so does R. Cold or cool weather will be better though. Fixed matters today and got possession of the quicksilver by paying at last $25 on the quicksilver and $7 on oil. Terrible value, but we had to have it. Road unsafe. Moyle we saw Sunday at CH, who reported 15 killed between Cananeas and Baccanochi. One Indian at last killed by two Americans before they went under. Fifty tried to take Pesqueira's horses from corral and although he is said to have 60 peons, they wouldn't come out and fight. P[esqueira] building a fort at Baccanochi [Bacanuchi].* Ben Williams of Bisbee** and nine men reported killed in the Mule Mountains [a false report] and six in Huachucas and still our imbecile government takes no action while the Mexican government seems paralyzed at the late audacity of the Indians as it has been seven or eight years since. They have been known to raid the upper Sonora before. Company of soldiers came in from Fronteras, Col. Torres commanding 21 in all and armed to escort us down but went another way this a.m. Some excitement today at CH over arrest and examination of a supposed Apache Indian and presumable spy. But evidence was not sufficient. Cleaned out with some suspicious looking Mexicans, one or two of whom had their eyes on me while I was paying custom dues. Jumped and left when I confronted them and all left in a hurry. Will look out for them. Didn't deem it safe to leave until some of [the] boys arrived, and this afternoon three or four of them came along armed to the teeth and stated they had not seen Indians and they thought road all O.K. Were going inside so we were independent and didn't ask them to stay.

Wednesday, September 6, 1882: No rain since night R left Tombstone with wagon. Made good start this a.m. First though saw some races between Mexicans horseback. Well, we started out with an extra man, Geo. Dormer, who wanted to accompany us and kept good watch all day. When passing place where poor Johnson was shot and killed the odor from his killed horse was unpleasantly perceptible. Watched the country well— were ready for a fight at any time. Came across a band of burros on the San Pedro evidently gotten away from the Indians. One of the tires got loose this afternoon and we had a great time trying to keep it on. No mud or water anywhere. Finally had to camp and we were in a nice fix with a broken down wagon in an Indian infested country and far away from any conveniences. Rather trying situation. Had to make the best of it. All old man H's fault. R wanted him to fix things when he could, but no, he must stand and talk and lie all day with this, that, and the other person, disgusting all. I have no patience with the old man. He is good enough in his way but it is a poor way generally and he is a complete ignoramus while having great pretensions to accuracy in his different foolish statements. He is kindhearted, but I am afraid that is all. His yarns are tremendous, just so long. They are the same, year in and year out, and number just the same words in their relating. Had to stand guard tonight all but the old man and he was sorry, etc. Pshaw. Confound such stuff as comprises him. I have no patience with him but wouldn't hurt him for the world. His wife wears the

*The rancho of Sonoran autocrat Ignacio Pesqueira at Bacanuchi had all the characteristics of a fortress, being a substantial one-story adobe building with an interior court or patio. All windows were iron-barred. It was the headquarters of an immense estate twenty-four miles square, and an adjoining tract called the Cananea estate. The consolidated estates were stock with 15,000 head of cattle.

**Ben Williams and his brother Lewis were in charge of developing the Copper Queen Mine and smelter at Bisbee.

pants and its well she does. She's a rustler. I admire her. During my watch tonight, between one and two o'clock, I heard a thundering noise of horses apparently charging down upon us and grabbed R, awakening him. We slept under wagon. Proved to be the band of burros which had followed us up during the night and came down upon us like an Apache charge.

Thursday, September 7, 1882: Road not traveled at all. Met no one going or coming. Bad thing for Sonora. Saddled horse early and corraled burros, then corraled oxen, cutting hobbles while one of the boys guarded on hill top. Bad time for Indians is early in the morning and just before dark and I examined the long grass quite thoroughly while riding through it. By dint of much hard labor and constant nudging, we got wagon a quarter of a mile further to first water, which was very slim but sufficient, and then we prepared to set the tire. R scouted through grass and bushes meanwhile, and we soon had hot fire—cut a boot leg to fill up with and were successful in clapping it on quite tight. Terribly rough through canyon, particularly one half mile. Just below Woodward's oxen made another bad break and I got into the mire waist deep. Wanted to kill "Red." Good luck till going down hill at Frenchman's, when my rifle went overboard and wheel passed over it, breaking the stock—in keeping with our general luck. Were stuck again while passing through river bed and here the oxen did their hardest pulling and took us out after the old man said we must unload. I was disgusted until the pull. Oxen ran away again within a mile of home and this time fixed things—breaking the tongue. R and I went home, and during the day wagon arrived and stuff at last reached destination. Found Bob saluated [sic] by a quack doctor in passing and Cap sick in bed with fever and all troubled about Indians as some had been close to house in night. All glad to see us again safe and sound. All eager for flour. It is very scarce, but we have to look out for ourselves and can't supply the whole country.

Friday, September 8, 1882: Stopped at Janarerachi last night where were a lot of the boys well armed and looking after cattle. Pushed on this a.m. and were stalled again, or broken down. Got unloaded and settled this evening. Tent in bad place for Indians, and in evening and after or about dawn, I am watchful—not pleasant, this continuous vigilance and state of insecurity. The lines are certainly not being drawn in very pleasant places for Louis and me. I wonder when the end is to be—not this Indian trouble and revolution business altogether, but this mill money matter. The future is very mixed indeed to me. Hope for the best but the worst presents itself continually and I fear greatly at times for the success of our enterprise. How I do long for a good legitimate business once more, and a settling down in civilization. No lights safe at night.

Saturday, September 9, 1882: My horse not around and am afraid the Indians have him. Hunted for him today unsuccessfully. First time I haven't been able to find him. Cap seems pretty bad. Looks like chills and fever.

Much sport today tying up strange bull and cutting his tail—lively getting animal, lassoing, etc.

Sunday, September 10, 1882: Redfern and I today hunted all over for my horse on horseback but did not find him. He may possibly be back in the hills. Cap doesn't seem to get any better. Walker turned up today all O.K. Reported killed. Glad to see him safe.

Monday, September 11, 1882: Cap worse this a.m. and R and I started off for quinine but had to go to Custom House and got there just before dark. Found Miller and party with cattle at Springs. Took señors [Gonzalo] Carranza and Carrera's cards. Former gone back to City of Mexico.

Wednesday, September 12, 1882: Carranza a very pleasant fellow and a perfect gentleman. Hoped to see us in City of Mexico and didn't want us to judge Mexico by what we saw here. Knows Americanos—R's friends. All inclined to be very friendly at CH to us now. Carranza kindly gave some plaster and oil of peppermint for Cap while Mrs. Elias gave me the quinine, so we did not have to go further. After supper we went out where grass was good half a mile or so and camped with Curry and John Hohstadt. This a.m. early we were up and off for home in a hurry. River bottoms very cold. Twenty miles away we met Charlie Smith and partner and Mitchell who had been traveling by night, as in fact, all traveling seems to be done by night now. Mitchell was to go with us, having been with us a day or two, but preferred traveling by night with Charlie and presented the spectacle of a very cowardly man we thought. Looked like a regular back down which we both thought our sisters would not have been guilty of. Examined place where poor Tom Johnson was killed and saw remains of fire in the willows and grass cut to lie on. Thought about the locality in the long grass with rifle ready for instant use. Also found what seemed to be a pair of drawers, evidently Johnson's, torn with bullet or buck-shot holes through them. Reached camp about two or three o'clock, found Cap apparently worse. Gave him medicine and did all we could.

Wednesday, September 13, 1882: Don't know what to make of Cap—we think he is playing off for some purpose. He rather denounced me for riding his horse on the 80 mile trip to get him medicine—as though the danger and hardship were what I liked. I'll tackle him later. He won't eat, is stubborn as a mule and acts queerly. Pulse regular and no fever. He won't eat and is consequently as weak as a cat.

Thursday, September 14, 1882: Forgot to say that yesterday Capt. Guiager (sounds so in English at least), the best Indian fighter the Mexicans have here, something like Genl Crook, rode into camp and we had quite a talk in broken English and broken Spanish. He was quite pleasant and has 28 men with him. Will scout around us to Cananeas and back near the mines so that now we feel quite safe. Apaches no aqui for some time I guess, if ever again. I had a great time with Cap last night. Made my bed near him to look after him as no one else would. Didn't sleep all night from his groans and the chiggers. Had a tough night—scratching, smoking, growling, and wishing for morning. Cap got up in night and fell to the ground in a faint. Had a big lift to get him back, 180 lbs. or more. Another time during night he arose with my assistance, and while I was holding him up on his feet, he lost himself again and I thought perhaps [he] was dead. Held him up to see if life would return till pretty well exhausted and then dragged him into his bed during which operation he came to. Seemed to suffer much if one might judge from the way he went on. No bones were broken though and I lost all patience with him. He will not do anything to get strength; senses he is dying; wants a will made which I started, but he wouldn't finish and says R and I are leaving him to die when we do all in our power for him, and but for us I don't know how he would get along exactly. He is terribly childish I think which must account for his actions and speech. He hasn't the courage of the feeblest invalid at death's door. I never saw such an old hulk. All vestige of manhood seems to have left him, if he ever had any. I am sick of him. I will do anything in the world for any person who will at least try to help himself.

Friday, September 15, 1882: R and Rankin looked after Cap last night but had no trouble. I seem to catch it all. Clouds gathered today and rain fell as heavy as we have yet had. Before the storm came we moved Cap on a stretcher to Mr. Hohstadt's and he is now safely housed. A hard strain on us and old man H had to squeal worse than any of us much to our gratification—he is such an old blow-hard. Cap very billious; liver out of order probably. He is turning yellow as though he had the jaundice. Godfrey seemed to think today that he would pass in his checks, but I don't think so, although his stomach ought to be pretty well eaten away by this time by rot gut. Out after horse today and got very wet not looking for rain. Scared up deer but couldn't get a shot. Storm was heavy tonight—came through tent and I was in a sad plight sitting in middle of tent while she poured torrents, lightning and thunder. Had a job to get to and find tent; struck match thinking I was near hole in front of Cap's rookery and there I was on brink. Another step and I would have gone in. Oh, these are sweet and precious times—take them altogether—kind of a secured job affair. Hope change will come ere long. R and Rankin went to Janarerachi this morning, or night rather, after medicine and all bunked in the tent.

Saturday, September 16, 1882: Rainy and sun shiny today. Equinoctial probably with change of weather. Storms for a week or two I guess and then clear weather. Cap Guiager back from scout and reports no Indians now, so will have a rest I hope. R found one of H's cows lanced with poison lance probably. Work on mill completed today, ditch now.

Sunday, September 17, 1882: Rain all of the time now. Every night now, half of the night with Cap while R and Rankin takes turns on the other half, or rather, Rankin helped one night. Cap disturbed no one tonight and R and I took his regular breathing for a good sign and expected to find him greatly improved in the morning. Fleas terrible at Hohstadt's. Nights cold especially my part of them, the last half. Horse am afraid has been taken by the Indians.

Monday, September 18, 1882: About nine o'clock this a.m. we were rather taken aback by Cap's appearance and presently heard the death-rattle and at 9:30 he died. I took possession of his papers, Redfern and Godfrey thinking I was the proper person to assume charge. His death was a great surprise to us all and something entirely unlooked for by me. It seemed to me though that he is dead and has died respectfully, so to speak. Whiskey must have killed him.

I was handed his papers today in Redfern's presence and discovered some very strange facts and during the day was possessed of information that would probably have separated him and me had he lived. Capt Hanson was a worthless man seeming to be utterly and entirely devoid of all the essentials of manhood—his being dead and just dying alters not the case. He has gone to his God with a guilty conscience I am afraid. We set to work digging a grave and after blasting several times had to give up that place and tried one or two more before finding a suitable spot where we could get down. R and I took turns sitting up with the body tonight. Body turned quite yellow before dying—liver probably.

Tuesday, September 19, 1882: Godfrey made box yesterday and this a.m. Redfern, who was up from Bacuachi, and I dressed the body, and K and I at the head, John Rankin and Rocus next and then Godfrey and old man Hohstadt, carried it to the prepared grave followed by Mrs. H and G and the children and R. The odor at the head was very unpleasant and I had to stop and go away at times. At the grave I officiated, reading in order as follows: 1st Corithians 15th Chap., 12th to 26th verses inclusive; Revelations Chap. 7, 13th verse to end of chapter; Revelations Chap. 14, 13th verse; Revelations 22nd Chap., 10th to 12th verses inclusive; Romans Chap. 8, 1, 2, 6, 7, 8, 24, 25, 32, 38, 39 verses. I picked this from my little testament trying to impress upon my hearers the truths therein contained, and I then prayed for the first time before such a number that this lesson might be heeded by us, that we should remember that in the midst of life we are in death, that this life is merely a probation, a fitting for a life to come, that we should improve the passing hours and at death be able to lie down with good consciences towards God with expectation of gaining his favor in the world to come. I had a chance to do good and I tried to do it with this people here who seem to have very little of the fear of God before their eyes or of his love.

This afternoon we started at the ditch, it being necessary to hurry things, and worked hard till evening. Will have to ditch nearly or about three-quarters of a mile. Cap's work of no avail. Money and time thrown away. It was strange ignorance on his part. John Gird and Gorman were here last night and went on their way this a.m.

Wednesday, September 20, 1882: Came to find out old man Hohstadt mistrusted Cap and the whole truth about him is coming out in a decidedly bad manner. The fact of a man being in his grave is no reason to my mind that I should not speak my mind plainly especially as he was such a poor specimen of a man and tried to injure me. I hope his God will not judge him too severely. Hard at work today on ditch. Didn't expect to come down to pick and shovel again, but here I am.

Thursday, September 21, 1882: Sun very hot and work terribly hard, but am in for it now till ditch is all right. Rather discouraging at times. I wonder how I will come out on this enterprise. I have very little faith in it now and count on nothing. I plod along though with as much heart as possible and do the best I can. One deserves something after so much hardship, privation and danger, not fancied but real. The best thing one can say about Cap is that he contracted his death by exposure nights while helping to guard camp against the Apaches. Ore shipment began today from the Manzanel to mill by 17 burros—one ton, 600 lbs.

Friday, September 22, 1882: R got hold of Rocus for a couple of days and we dug well today but have changed too much by advice of others as this work is new to us all. Tired out at night. Santa María trains on hand today—two tons received today.

Saturday, September 23, 1882: Put in good day's work. Fixed dam. Hard work this afternoon to save part of ditch. Gopher holes bad. Stripped to waist and worked late. Cutler came tonight and left package of mail for us at OK Corral. Very loud talker. Quite cold nights and very hot in day. Two tons, 400 lbs. today.

Sunday, September 24, 1882: Cutler off early. Rest very acceptable today. Ore came today—two tons, 52 1/2 lbs. Old man H and Casus went to Cananeas yesterday to interview Pesqueira on this recent agitation and movement which seemed to be directed against what few cattle men there [are] on the upper Sonora. Back today with good reports but I have my doubts. P's cattle range is becoming too limited. Geo Woodward on hand tonight. Had pleasant talk with him and learned some news. He and John went back to Bacuachi tonight on their way to Oposura.

Monday, September 25, 1882: At the confounded ditch again today, terribly hard job. No meat in camp now and we feel the want of it working so. H's rock looks very well and will probably mill well. Gorman and Gird back tonight from Arispe.

Tuesday, September 26, 1882: Worked this a.m., and this p.m. With shotgun and rifle, and old Bill, I started for large and small game and had a rough time of it, returning some time after dark with nothing. Saw only a pole-cat. Deer and quail both near tent.

Wednesday, September 27, 1882: Tiff with R this a.m. and quit work till he has gone at least. He left for Tombstone this afternoon intending to stop at Cañon Ancho tonight and Ochoaville tomorrow night. Wrote father and [E. A.] Schlaet. Very cold nights and blankets scarce.

Thursday, September 28, 1882: Worked on ditch today and we made good headway. Lache getting scarce. Bad way of handling the vacas. Gave the old man a deal on it.

Friday, September 29, 1882: Jeff and Mac, with a Col Henderson, arrived this a.m. in a buckboard. Failed reaching our camp last night on account of breakdown. Repaired at our blacksmith shop and the Col and I had a talk. He is just returned from Guaymas and the interior and there is nothing in the revolution business. After several pulls at what I understand to be the Col's favorite, they went off happy. Worked hard on ditch today and are over worst of it now.

Saturday, September 30, 1882: Put in a good day's work. The burro train stopped hauling yesterday, and brought exactly seventeen ton, 663 lbs. (17.663). H a terribly poor calculator. Elias and I agreed and the old man finally succumbed, seeming to be inextricably mixed. Can't afford to start up on that. Good wash in river tonight. Much work just now after ditching with breadmaking, cooking, washing dishes, etc., for Bob and myself. Can't sleep much on account of cold and fleas—the latter are a terrible pest and annoy me day and night.

Sunday, October 1, 1882: After making bread and doing necessary chores I hunted Bill with most exasperating experience. [I] walked and ran several hours when my patience was exhausted and I shot at him but revolver missed, strange to say, as I drew full bead and was bent on killing such a devil of a horse. Finally corralled him and ran him five or six miles to H's house near the mine. I wished to see and look at our's so as to be improved if R returned with any one contemplating taking hold with us. Rocus kindly showed me Geo W's and I then knew ours and after he left I went over a small portion of the ledge taking samples which made me feel very good. Stumbled onto a deer returning but wasn't quick enough and we badly need meat. Home about dark—lonely at tent and not particularly safe perhaps, but I have little fear of Indians at present. Godfrey suggested my sleeping at his house but see no reason for changing simply because Redfern is away. Bad spot for a surprise though. I might be killed and no one know it till late. Hope we can soon have an adobe house and some comforts and conveniences of civilized life. Must curb my temper more. I came nearly doing bad work today with revolver in my wrath. Cap's grave disturbed by coyotes or wild animals which pawed down several feet or more. Must place some rocks on top I think.

Monday, October 2, 1882. Weighed 1000 lbs. of ore Mr. H brought down Saturday from Frenchman's where it had been dumped, being too heavy to haul to Boston Mill at time; he took some to be milled and this afternoon weighed 1600 lbs. more which he brought today from Janarerachi, being part of lot dumped there for transportation to Boston Mill. Total 2600 lbs. and more to follow. Several tons or so, but we cannot start up on less than the 50 tons promised. Turned in water and fixed ditch. Bueno so far. Fleas and cold terrible. Sleep very little. Hope flea powder will soon be had.

Tuesday, October 3, 1882: I wonder how long this is to last. Everything is so uncertain and one has to stand so much. I feel more encouraged though since seeing that property of ours the other day. I hope relief to mind and body is not far off. If something sure and certain would only present itself no matter how remote I would not care. My father is growing old and should have rest and my sisters and brother I must look after. This all is not pleasant in the face of existing circumstances adding to my earnest wish to marry. I am tortured at times and am sorely tried on many points I cannot detail here. I hope and trust my three years experience in Arizona and here will not count as nothing. Oh well, I should not go on this way. I say often to myself, "Let her rip George old boy and keep a stiff upper lip," and I do and will. It's all right after all if Apaches and revolutionists and mill debt and money stolen probably and horse stolen and cold and fleas and chiggers and nothing to eat half of the time and scorching rides under an almost tropical sun of hundreds of miles and uncongenial people and family matters at home and private matters and a hundred and one things to worry [about]. I keep my usual trust in Almight God and whatever happens takes place for the best. It's tough at times this deprivation and hardship incident to a frontier life and I long, oh so earnestly, for a little change. Hope is a great thing amd I have a large stock. So now I'll stop a little; sorry I turned loose in this way for I seldom after all allow myself to think of these things too much. Another hard day's work on the ditch.

Wednesday, October 4, 1882: At it again today; good headway. Redfern and John Rankin came tonight. Mexican Geo arrived this a.m. stating Louis would be here this evening. Last of the ore came today, making grand total of 20 twenty tons, 753 lbs., rather different from the 50 tons promised. Will have to charge more than the price agreed for 50 or 60 tons which was $107 per ton. R full of news. No grub though. G got fooled at Palominas. Let contract today to cut Black Oak for mill to two Mexicans at $2^1/$_2$ per cord, paying Mexican coin will make it about $2^1/$_4$ which is cheap enough for the kind of work. Things are gradually approaching a finish.

Thursday, October 5, 1882: John R helped us today and R part of the day and we sailed along well. Am mighty glad things are so near the finish. Old man's cattle playing hot with ditch and I had talk with him today and he will build bridges or promises to. Very cold nights, days cooler.

Friday, October 6, 1882: Brought in ditch to well by noon and water will follow as soon as gravelly soil is sufficiently soaked. Cleansed in river this afternoon, the two Rs and I went to Janarerachi and got some things "Pinto" and helped Charley home with cattle and practiced lassoing horseback. Caught a calf by leg and scraped left hand, not getting to pommel in time. Bill tried to throw me as I picked something from the ground but didn't succeed. Wrote letter to father today, explaining more in detail about the rascally Hanson and suggesting several matters to him. Tomorrow H and I will probably go to the Cananeas to see Genl Pesqueira's roundup. R has failed in pecuniary promises to Godfrey and he threatens a lien by next Tuesday—just as we are ready for a start now comes this blow. I hope the thing will blow over and am now exercising my wits to cover this bad point in some way. Too bad; first one thing and then another. Hunted for my $50 or $45 again today without avail and now I haven't got $15 to my name. We were reported to be standing off the Indians in Tombstone, and R was implored not to leave for there but arrived with two 44s this time—brace of colts and rifle now. Indians disarmed finally at San Carlos and all with rifles or cartridges are now [considered] hostiles and can be killed; thank goodness. I entertained a stranger Tuesday night whom John R claimed was an Apache agent buying arms and ammunition for them. I am very positive he is mistaken.

Saturday, October 7, 1882: Succeeded in smoothing our matters this a.m. with Godfrey, but later on he overheard R talking to me and saying that G could fire ahead, etc., and then again there was trouble and G threatens anew. My patience is getting pretty well exhausted and I feel like letting matters take their own course as I will probably have to do any how. I hardly think G will do as he says. It will be to his interest to be calm and wait, though I must confess he has had much to contend against. Well full today and water a success. Much more in fact than we want and John R put in a waste gate today. R and I were to go to Cananeas today with H but John H and Geo W arrived and J said Pesqueira was still at Baccanochi so R and JH started for Palominas for flour and quicksilver. Am afraid my money has been disinterred by some animal other than human and carried off. It seems as though it was gone. All hands at Hohstadt's pretty well starved out. No flour, ours very low. Fine country for provender. Tom, a cowboy, and companion, went down the road today. Trouble with [Pete] Spence [Spencer] whose crowd threaten shooting. This country will not be an asylum for these desperados very long. Well, I wonder what the next few weeks will produce?

Sunday, October 8, 1882: Horse appeared today, this a.m., and I went over to his camp on the road and found Olcott, Supt. of St. Helena, Los Delicias outfit, and Tom Ewing. Very pleasant chat and drank ochata or some such name, made of starchy part of wheat and sugar. Treated to some pears grown on Co's property too. O very clever fellow. A fellow badly scared about Indians came into my camp and wanted to know how it was as Mexicans had said Indians were very bad. I reassured him and he went on. Wakeen [Joaquin] and Frenchman rode up stating that quick[silver] was at their place and they wanted me to get H to take up a rig from here for them and no charge would be made for carting quicksilver down from CH. Got H to agree to go up tomorrow with the boar and bring down quick for $2. Great feast today on turnips and turnip tops. Boiled nearly all day and very bueno. Got in some solid reading today and tonight from *Observer*, splendid paper. Cold nights, disagreeably so. Very comfortable in tent. Terrible skunk flavor tonight. Got pistol nearly on him when he lit out.

Monday, October 9, 1882: Warm days still but very cold nights. Few ducks flying today along river. Must be hard up for water to seek this country when one can jump across all streams. Fine tussel with boar this a.m. getting him into wagon. Pumped water into tank today to fill boiler. Tomorrow I expect the whistle will blow and awake the echos in these hills for the first time in their existence. H arrived tonight at last with the quick[silver].

Tuesday, October 10, 1882: About noon today this part of the world heard a steam whistle for the first time. Engine worked well. Small pump leaks and eccentric rod little noisy. Belts O.K. Was glad to see the old engine at work once more. Looks like a success. Wood choppers arrived today and started in. Have one of the ancient two wheeled wooden carts with oxen to haul. Close to business now. No R yet, should be back today.

Wednesday, October 11, 1882: Two ancient carts at work or on hand for hauling wood. I made old man Hohstadt commit himself this a.m. to two pieces of rock which he considered one his best, and the other about average, and will retain them for assaying in case of any possible trouble which there is likely to be, he is such an ignoramus on the subject of mines in particular and mining in general. Godfrey tried to have him bet on some rock but while H talks tremendously he will never come to time. Redfern came today with packed burro, so once more we are flush of flour and in no danger of having to ramage immediately for grub. Burro tricky and kicked R's spur, breaking it, and knocked off a tapidera from the stirrup. Bush came with R, so now we have a camp full. Some more talk tonight over Godfrey's $500 owing, but R seems disinclined to do anything. The old ignoramous Hohstadt much provoked me today in R's and my talk with him for more than $17, as he has not complied with contract.

Thursday, October 12, 1882: Am hearing something new most every day now about the old rascal Hanson. The latest is his statement that I broke my father up east and that he chased me away from home and I dare not return. This, and his statement that my father changed his interest from $1/3$ to $1/6$, his other stories about me, etc., are an evident plot to seize the mill and chase R and me away because on foreign soil, and his plot to have our claims jumped and recorded to him, only form part of a long story of rascality committed and other attempted on his part. Had he not died he would probably got a bullet or belly full of buckshot from me or R, or both of us, and died with his boots on. Tis well as it is. G determined to put on a lien and I don't blame him and told him so. Have done the best I can to stay matters but a crisis has come, so tomorrow some action will probably be taken in Bacuachi.

Friday, October 13, 1882: Well, today I agreed to sign a mortgage or paper placing mill as security for $515.35 to Chas. Godfrey and old man H, and R proceeded to Bacuachi to interpret and sign. I was not in a pleasant frame of mind and preferred traveling the 25 miles alone. I started about an hour before sundown, and in deep part of cañon picked up a good coat belonging evidently to an American. Dark and lonely ride in good keeping with my thoughts, but when I neared Bacuachi I kept a sharp ear and lost no time getting through the trees and bushes with Rand, often on a wagon as horse, often jumped affrighted at something. Indians, however, not troublesome lately.

Saturday, October 14, 1882: Found Con Cutler at Domingo Dunone's last evening and after supper had quite a talk and some good beer; said he was going to call me at four a.m. to see the comet but no Cutler appeared, though he said he called me somewhere around two o'clock I guess it was in the night. Domingo awakened me, asking if I was afraid of anyone, as several men were after me. I said "no," and he let in G, Bush, and John into corral. Kind of him to look out for me. Paper, simple enough in character, was drawn up and signed by R and me, but no stamps could be found, stamps being the great thing. Stamps seem to carry an immense power in this country and would seem to take the place of notaries, commissioners, etc. The man having the stamps was off branding cattle and we waited all day for him to return. Fine sample of Mexican business. Finally late in afternoon it was discerned that it was not necessary for me to remain, so Bush, John, R and I started back but being tired camped in big cañon for the night.

Sunday, October 15, 1882: Ten miles to mill and got there in good season. Seems balance started and camped few miles below us. R sick and had to camp. Made two good shots at hawks with six shooter, winging one and killing another. Thought one was an eagle and hunted him, in fact, we thought both were. Being obliged to go to Tombstone tomorrow, I had to go over to claim this afternoon and get some rock which I did and got some fine specimens of croppings well chlorided besides finding several of Hanson's claims the old rascal had kept from us.

Monday, October 16, 1882: Well, I started once more on the long ride this a.m., driving burro before me. Was sorry not to be able to be on hand for starting up tomorrow a.m., but that is impossible and it is better for some reasons that I should be away. Rode old Sam to take him to Heyne. First time in some months he had been saddled. Carranza at C.H. wanted me to wait over but I was anxious to reach Palominas and couldn't stop. Met Tom Ewing in cañon, other party near springs. Reassured all about Indians. Had rifle in readiness near the willows but everything was calm and serene. Guess Apaches have lit out. Not particularly pleasant traveling alone, one has to keep a very sharp lookout. At CH left burro and pretty well loaded with rock, I went on to Palominas and by dint of much spurring, berating, and pulling, I got Sam to the settlement. Was afraid he would fail me in the bushes but he struggled through and made the 50 miles by dark. Good supper and came pretty nearly getting between sheets for first time in nearly three years, but there was but one. Was treated nicely and slept in a good tight house. No winds and cold tonight. Enjoyed novelty of change.

Tuesday, October 17, 1882: Good breakfast and Sam felt all O.K. this a.m.

Very cold this a.m. on the river. Chills and fever all over country on San Pedro and Sonora rivers. Most all had a touch at our place but me, all owing probably to standing water and decaying vegetation since close of rainy season.

At Lewis Springs I met one of Arizona's fair daughters with "Rock," the hunter, fishing catching suckers. First time in all my tramps I had ever met a woman. She was cow-woman if not cow-boy, or cow-girl I should say, and kept a sharp eye on some cattle near[by], telling her little sister to jump on her horse and do this and that once in a while and away she would go. It was a funny sight and one quite novel. Rock seemed to be standing guard. Had an invitation to come and see them and then passed on and reached Tombstone between three and four o'clock, making the 32 miles in pretty fair time. Rode up 5th Street and then met Mr. Davis whom I had come in to see and his friend Mr. Britton. They gazed at me in wonder and astonishment. In my broad brimmed sombrero, armed and equipped for a long trip and any encounter, Davis would not have known me. Britton, a clever old gentleman of the firm of Britton & Ray, lithographers in S.F., said he would like to have a sketch of me just as I entered town. They looked and examined some time. A crowd of friends got around and I withdrew and dressed for dinner party at Judge Berry's at five p.m. No time to lose. On hand in time and exchanged a hearty welcome. Had a royal good dinner topped off with champagne and I had to tell about Sonora, Indians, etc. All swore I'll be killed yet. Passed a very pleasant evening and am in for it tomorrow. Mr. Davis's birthday today and we all congratulated him. Clapp's tomorrow night.

Wednesday, October 18, 1882: Saw my friends about town today and tonight dined at Milton's and we all had a jolly good time. Heyne just gone from town today. Went to Bisbee, so didn't see him. Did some more affidavitting today for Brigham and helped Judge [B. L.] Peel in his Bassett matter, straightening that out and dictating telegrams to [W. P.] Stanley. Stange mistake of records—a $1/10$ interest recorded, $1/6$ leaving $1/15$ in Poage still. Another error is certain in Sullivan matter of record. Name certainly not indexed right as properties were recorded. Judge [Henry] Dibble, the Louisiana carpet bagger, was disinclined for some strange reason to recognize a friendly salutation at first. He was picked up on the affront by me and was different. Next time and after this we meet as strangers,

Thursday, October 19, 1882: Fine weather. Considerable running around today on this thing and that. Tonight the jollification took place at Eccleston's and all had a good time. Good dinner and later the old bucks, as I term them, turned themselves loose and all joined in. Davis and Britton are two good ones. They're jolly as two school boys.

Friday, October 20, 1882: No dining out tonight but the usual jollification, meeting at Clapp's Prof. [John] Church, Geo Rice, Rev. Bagnall, in addition to usual number. Church told me our camp was not so dull as others he had visited of late. Whole country quiet; state elections possibly. Up town later and watched D and B play billiards till very late or early. Looked in at B.C.

Saturday, October 21, 1882: Today about noon at Milton's invitation I accompanied him D and B to Post Huachuca. Vehicle broke down several miles out and Milton and I returned and got another. Pleasant ride out. Got there almost dark. Good supper and bed, and cards in evening. First time between sheets since leaving S.F. February 4th three years ago this coming February. Didn't like them at all and didn't sleep well. Too slippery, and my pants hung in such a position that I frequently kicked them during the night when out would drop a piece of money, making quite a noise on the board floor. Milton got his pistol ready to shoot the robber. A bad time in camp and a scare tonight. Some Mexicans gave the Indian scouts whiskey and a shot and much loud talk was the result. Soldiers corralled the gang and stopped the business. Last time I was here direct from Tombstone there was a bad time too, when I sold the Indians my horse.

Sunday, October 22, 1882: Good breakfast and walk this a.m. looking at the new buildings going up. I called on Dr. Gardiner and staid a while. About noon we lunched and then started to go home, but one horse seemed to be founder[ing] and we couldn't get away until I hunted up a Huachuca acquaintance named Hill, who put in his horse and went with us. Quartermaster [Edward] Hubbard we thought might do something after his propose offers to Milton who had done him some favor, but the Capt. was found wanting. Balky horse., great time starting. Made Tombstone about dark and all had a grand good dinner at Jakey's—oysters, omelettes, wines, etc. Milton's last to his friends. He is very gracious. I was just in time to contribute at church.

Monday, October 23, 1882: Well, today Miss Davis and Britton got away. Milton and Mrs. C drove them to Contention. Mrs. Goodfellow and Miss Bascum also left for S.F. by stage. I called Friday and saw Miss B who goes to Bartlett's on the way home for a visit. I lunched with the ladies and related Sonora experiences. So now all jollifications are over and I must settle down to life's stern realities once more and prepare for Sonora again. Expect R about Wednesday. Called on Miss Peel tonight where was Rev. Bagnall. Both I think are in love with each other. Later attended the grand ratification meeting at Schieffelin Hall and heard Judge Carter and local nominees, all friends and acquaintances.

Tuesday, October 24, 1882: Showed rock around today trying to enlist some one for an advance and interest. Tombstone isn't what it used to be. Times terribly bad. Will know about things in the future as soon as mines are tried below water level.* Went around to a Mr. Smith's rooms this evening with E. R. Howe to see his collection. Pretty good one.

*The encounter of water on the 500 foot level of the Sulphuret mine in March of 1881 came as no surprise. Mining men expected to hit water, but most thought it would be at about 1000 feet. Because water is associated with secondary enrichment, the event sustained confidence "in the permanency of the veins." By April 1882, however, the flow had become serious

Wednesday, October 25, 1882: Am now rather wishing to get out and away. Finally caught Heyne this afternoon and had a talk over his usual beer. Called on and saw Mrs. and Miss Colby this evening. Tom Ewing in town. Had bad scrimmage near Bacuachi with guards, presumably one of his men being killed. After exhausting all of his ammunition, he lit out and finally reached our camp through the woods, where he got a horse of John's and came in. Reported mill running nicely, only one shift though, which surprise me as that is a waste. Wish I could get back now.

Thursday, October 26, 1882: Got Heyne to cabin at last this a.m. and showed him my copper and other rock and he will visit us possibly next week. Seemed pleased. Invited to go on excursion today to Helm's ranch with H. G. and E. R. Howe and Mrs. H and Mrs. Robertson and sister Miss Mayers, but didn't go, being limited now and business the thing. Went off in good style this a.m. with four horses, Brigham driving. An old acquaintance of mine named Johnson, who helped me guard Reilly's house one night in the troublous times, seemed quite surprised to see me in the flesh today, stating that he had heard the Apaches had gotten me in Mexico. I said "not much" although they got my horse. My good friends all warn me to be careful. I don't need their admonition and don't think any more danger is to be found, certainly not for the winter. One cannot tell though about the cursed fiends. Genl Crook I truly hope will bring about the needed reform. Called on Mrs. Chapin and Mrs. Berry tonight and saw Miss Santee a while.

Friday, October 27, 1882: No Redfern yet and I am wondering at his delay. It may be that the repeal act is so near that all are waiting for Nov. 1st. I hope to have someone interested with us before long. Have Judge [O. O.] Trantum, [George] Pridham and Heyne on a string. Spent evening at Clapp's. All full of Florida. Gov. [A. P. K.] Safford warm friend of Milton's and it wouldn't surprise me if he made a change of base within a year, that is, Milton, and it is among the possibilities that I may share some good fortune myself. Wouldn't object to old Florida again, though it would seem strange if my wanderings, which began there, should end in the good old state.

Saturday, October 28, 1882: Strallus [George's sister Alice] is ten days from Liverpool today on the *S.S. England* and I hope to get telegram of her safe arrival in a day or two when I will feel easy again about her. Am glad she is so soon to be home again. Bill Miller in town today and says they're running two shifts and R was to be here some days ago. Must be the bullion repeal act detaining them.

Sunday, October 29, 1882: Attended church this a.m. Bagnall good. Rather rapid delivery. Dined at Milton's and in evening all hands attended Methodist Church to hear new minister, Rev. [David] McFawn. [Joseph P.]

enough to curtail sinking of the Grand Central shaft, and that property was the first to install pumping equipment. Encountering of water also led to the erection of reduction works near the mines and abandonment of mills on the San Pedro River.

McIntyre married Miss Moses tonight and leaves for East shortly. So all scandal is at an end. Am sorry for Mac [McIntyre]. Such terrible straight-lacedness as he professed I don't believe in. There must be a vent to youth but it needn't take the form of evil. Innocent things are made evil of. I believe in cards, champagne, the theatre, dancing, etc., in the right way. I don't believe any robust, healthy person full of strength and life will accept the hell fire talk so many like McIntyre indulge in respecting these things. I don't believe in giving good things and things innocent of themselves to the devil and don't propose to.

Monday, October 30, 1882: Went out to Gentle Belle this a.m. with Tom Sorin, I believe, to see about letting contract. He bid 11¹/₂ feet. Think this evening that Howe and I had pleasant time at Robertson's with Mrs. R and Miss Mayers.

Tuesday, October 31, 1882: If I mistake not I went out to the GB ground today again with Fisher, this time who bid 12 feet and took the contract. This evening an election of trustee for church took place. I was asked if I would remain here but said no. Carr and Ingersoll were elected. Believe I dined again at Clapp's.

Wednesday, November 1, 1882: No R yet, suppose he will wait till after first. Letter though by Wells Spicer states trouble at mill. No quick[silver].Very unpleasant news. Godfrey incompetent as a mill man. Sociable at courtroom tonight for Episcopal Church, dancing, refreshments, etc.

Thursday, November 2, 1882: One of two things must be done with the mill. We must either sell out or incorporate east, which will probably necessitate my going there provided I can get there. This state of things has lasted long enough. Whist tonight in J V [Vickers'] office.

Friday, November 3, 1882: Election day approaches and excitement prevails. Nothing of any movement occurred today.

Saturday, November 4, 1882: Redfern at last came in tonight and had a tale to tell. Godfrey incompetent as a mill man. I told R we must sell or incorporate and I should go East. He thought as I and now wants me to get off as soon as possible. He is to learn assaying.

Sunday, November 5, 1882: Church morning and evening and R and I dined at Milton's. It seems very odd to me this going East business after so long a stay in the far west and I can hardly realize that we are proposing the thing precisely and earnestly for the good of the mill and mines. One thing is sure, we cannot go along in this pinching manner any longer and it is better to risk a few hundred dollars on any endeavor there than to sell out. Something must be done immediately and before there is a lose. What a grand thought for me to get home once more and see the dear ones. There is a dameselle I must see and I can't wait much longer. Nathalie shall see this child before long now. It *must* be done.

Monday, November 6, 1882: J. V. [Vickers] goes East day after tomorrow and wants me to go along, offering to pay a little of the expense. I was excited enough to think of the thing favorably for a while but I abandoned the idea. Impossible to go before returning first to Sonora. Must clean up down there and fix matters before leaving. We need all of $3000 cash to go ahead on and it is losing money to try to do anything situated as we are. Had some more cards in JV's tonight. Trouble at GB by Ben Maynard and I had to go to Randolph and have him go over. Just as I expected—shifted work and things I hope will go on better now.

Tuesday, November 7, 1882: The eventful day at hand. About 1750 votes cast in Tombstone City—just 1758. Lively times but only one man shot and he accidentally it was claimed. [Dave] Neagle and [M. E.] Joice [Joyce] had a skirmish.* It was [not] anything to rat Neagle and thinking to do it by voting Democratic. Mine was a badly scratched ticket, in fact, all tickets were badly scratched with few exceptions. Ward ahead tonight. Great time nearly all night at Clapp's.

Wednesday, November 8, 1882: No solution to the election problem yet. East though Democrats seem to be gaining heavily and old Ben Butler has finally got Massachusetts. Went out to GB today. Ledge looks well and is almost 30 inches wide. [Jerome L.] Ward elected Sheriff and [Joseph] Tasker and Wiley all O.K. Democrats got about half.

Thursday, November 9, 1882: In saddle all day. Went down on San Pedro river after Bush's horse but Curry wouldn't deliver him up. Ate antelope with boys and got to town in time for dinner. Very unpleasant ride— windy and dusty—too long out of the saddle.

Friday, November 10, 1882: Am to have Walter and Ralph's horse as soon as brought in. Hope to get off tomorrow a.m. Attended skating rink to-night and tried the roller skates. Rather different from ice skates. Didn't do as well as I thought I would. Great times. Went over to GB today and posted notice of work being done for year.

Saturday, November 11, 1882: Roller skating all the go now and Milton and wife and I went around tonight. M's corporosity [corpulence] some-thing frightful. Couldn't buckle his skates. Must trim down. Mrs. Clapp did nicely. I don't see very much sport in them. No horse today so now will wait till Monday.

Sunday, November 12, 1882: Attended church morning and evening and dined at [Robert] Eccleston's where I met Judge and Mrs. John Haynes. Bagnall very good in matter. To hurried in manner. Is improving. I like his discourses exceedingly; is an earnest man.

---

*The contention between Milton Joyce and Dave Neagle stemmed from the latter's bid for the Democratic candidacy to the office of Sheriff of Cochise County. When he failed to poll enough support on September 16, 1882, and Larkin Carr got the nomination, Neagle ran on his own, splitting the party and losing the election for the Democrats to J. L. Ward. Neagle's action created harsh feelings that were vented violently in some cases. The conflict between Joyce and Neagle followed a dispute that arose out of a challenge to a voter as a repeater. See Stacy Osgood, The Life and Times of David Neagle," *The Westerners Brand Book* (Chicago), Vol. XIX, No. 2, April 1962.

Monday, November 13, 1882: Journal reversed. [Filling one side of his journal, Parsons flops it and begins writing on the reverse side.] Wonder if present unhappy fortune will be reversed by the time this [journal] is ended. We shall see. Well, no horse yet and I am very anxious, it being four weeks now since I left. Won't get stuck this way again. Court opened today, Judge [James G.] Howard presiding only for a day though, when Judge Pinnie [Daniel H. Pinney] succeeds him. Lively times. Ed Williams, Ziegler's murder caught; good. No horse yet and I'm getting desperate. Spent evening at [James S.] Robertson's. Rather breezy, cold now.

Tuesday, November 14, 1882: Have decided to go alone tomorrow on R's horse, when late in afternoon word came of ranch horse's arrival, so will get off tomorrow. Frank Leslie was to go with us and may yet if he is not detained in killing matter of this morning, he ought not to be. He shot and killed the notorious Kid [William] Claiborne this a.m. at 7:30, making as pretty a center shot on the Kid as one could wish to. The Kid threatened and laid for him near the Oriental [Saloon] with a Winchester, but Frank got the drop on him, being quick as lightning and used to killing men, and the Kid has gone to Hell.* I say so because if such a place exists and is for bad men, he is there as he was a notoriously bad egg and has innocent blood on his head. I state facts. Frank has done the County a service and for that reason it is well that we did not get away sooner. Horse came today. If it came yesterday or when expected, the Kid would have been alive. God Almighty works in mysterious ways. I have contributed to the Kid's death. Frank didn't lose the light of his cigarette during the encounter. Wonderfully cool man.

Wednesday, November 15, 1882: Got off this a.m. about ten but Frank couldn't be found. Stopped at Hemming's and saw the boys a while and then traveled as far as Palominas. Good supper but uncomfortable night as I slept close to the table which was spread after I turned in for several late comers. Talked and smoked later with Eaton.

Thursday, November 16, 1882: Tiresome day's ride to Cañon Ancho where we stopped. Only Murray at home. Played cards later with him and several smugglers. Lunched with Santa María outfit on the road.

Friday, November 17, 1882: Got to camp by or before noon and found things quiet. Later though all quiet was disturbed. After all of my talk with Redfern and his acknowledging receipt of Godfrey's money, he still

---

*William Claiborne was thick with Cochise County's so-called cowboy element, being a friend of Johnny Ringo, the Clantons and McLaurys. On the morning of November 14 he wandered into the Oriental Saloon and butted into a conversation between patrons at the bar. Politely telling the cowboy to mind his own business, Leslie escorted him from the bar. Thereupon, Claiborne threatened to "get even." Told that Billy was laying for him in the street, Leslie merely stepped out the saloon's side door (Fifth Street entrance) and surprised Claiborne who was waiting near Nick Noble's fruit stand. As Billy's rifle came up, Leslie fired his revolver, hitting the cowboy in the chest. A new twist to this incident is Parsons' comment of having contributed to Claiborne's death.

offered G but $250, saying he didn't have the rest. G hot of course. Worried so, I couldn't sleep for some time. R is tricky.

Saturday, November 18, 1882: Poor Bob is without grub or money. I could not keep eyes clear of water while considering his situation, but am nearly strapped myself. Wonder what's going to become of things. The outlook is very discouraging. R snaps his fingers in face of creditors and spends money sent for business at Bird Cage and similarly. I have hard luck. G will go to extremes on the paper given by me and R I am afraid. Bad, bad state of things. R pulled out this a.m., saying he would go to Tombstone for G's money. I went over to claim and worked hard great part of day in getting specimens. Tonight I started well loaded, not knowing whether I should ever see the camp again. Too unpleasant to remain. Left after dark. Lonely ride to Frenchman's.

Sunday, November 19, 1882: My feelings rather down. Found R camped at Frenchman's and stopped there. Cold night. Long day's ride. Elias with two of Hohstadt's cows went with us till we left them. H in a bad way too. Just before reaching Palominas met Carranza and several others, also Carrera, believed full as a tick. Ochoaville about dark—good dinner—immensely hungry. Long talk with [Epitaco] Paredes tonight on Mexico's laws, 20 league zone, etc. Elicited considerable and valuable information.

Monday, November 20, 1882: Reached town about five o'clock or 4:30. Skinner of Deadwood invited us to dinner and we had a good one at Jakey's. R telegraphed on his business. Called at Clapp's and staid awhile.

Tuesday, November 21, 1882: No letter stating sister's coming. Was afraid I might be hardly in good time. Spent pleasant evening at [Warner] Earll's. Mrs. E a very pleasant and delightful little lady, full of church.

Wednesday, November 22, 1882: No telegram for Redfern today. [A. H.] Stebbins very kindly has granted R and me the use of the new Cochise Club rooms for two weeks. Very cozy, comfortable quarters. Met Miss Mayers at Robertson's P.O. and took her to the skating rink a while this evening. Tried skating a few minutes. Don't compare with ice and very different.

Thursday, November 23, 1882: No telegram yet and I am anxious. Went to Shakespeare reading tonight at Miss Santee's but didn't enjoy [it]. Left after a while. Vizina blacksmith shop and hoisting works caught fire tonight and seemed to be all gone at one time, but Huachuca Water was finally turned on and the powerful stream soon squelched the flames.

Friday, November 24, 1882: Lowering skies. In a bad frame of mind owing to R's actions and non-fulfillment of promise to me when I signed away my interest in mill—in matter of the mortgage. He don't seem to care how things go. A disagreeable day with rain and muddy streets. Quite unusual for this time of the year. Dined at Milton's tonight, a Mr. Hoble of Marysville being present. Later went to Cochise Club with the gents and played Milton a game of billiards. First I've played since leaving S.F.

Saturday, November 25, 1882: Col. Lewis in town again. E. R. Howe, my roommate, left today for the "Minas Prietas" near Hermosillo. Sorry to have him go, but he may have a good thing at the mine. Goes as assayer. Unable to find Redfern till tonight—at club—No word yet about his telegrams. Told him how worried I was and he said he was satisfied that everything would be all right and in any event that I should be well paid for my loss if things went by the board. Told him we wouldn't lose.

Sunday, November 26, 1882: Attended church morning and evening. Trouble again in choir. Volunteers disbands today. Too bad, always trouble of some kind. Dined at Mrs. Clapp's. She's keeping quite well now I'm happy to say. We have considerable talk about Nathalie. Mrs. Clapp said she'll be a gray haired bride.

Monday, November 27, 1882: Geo. Woodward and Bush in town, also Godfrey, who is very [annoyed] with Redfern and returns in a few days to go for the mill if something isn't done at once. R still has no word. I doubt if he telegraphed. Tonight I followed him up till about two a.m., when he must have "*tried.*" At Bird Cage all of the time—champagne and women. I saw enough tonight to satisfy me about the way R's funds have gone. Too bad, too bad. Am in bad luck these days.

Tuesday, November 28, 1882: Had long talk with R this a.m. on his cause and actions. Doctor [N. S.] Giberson invited me to ride over beyond the Dragoons with him to see a patient, 30 miles or so distant, and we started about 2:30; spanking train and fine roads, horses went finely about nine miles an hour and made distance [in] about 3 1/2 hours. Several armed men on road told us to look out for a drunken cowboy on ahead as they nearly came to it with him, he pulling his rifle. So when we caught up to him I held my Winchester in readiness. He rode up to me and after a good square look on both sides he concluded to vamose. I had the drop. Crossed RR track about dark and finally reached house with aid of lantern and firing my rifle.

Wednesday, November 29, 1882: Mr. Griffin, the patient, was treated last night after good supper by Mrs. Wright and attentions by her spouse, and we slept in some hay in stable with one of the horses. Good warm bed, though Doc was afraid of Maggie walking on us in the night. Had to go to Russelville so were up before daylight and off soon after. Wildest country I've seen yet. Boulders of gigantic size were tumbled promiscuously about in all manner of queer shapes, while others took form of ruined cathedral peaks—all presenting a most wonderful appearance. Russelville a young but promising camp. Smelting ore and the Peabody Mine doing well.*

*Russellville, often spelled Russelville in early newspapers, located in the Cochise Mining District four miles north of Dragoon Summit, sprung to life in summer of 1879. The Peabody Mine, owned by the Russell Gold and Silver Mining Co., was the pride of the camp. By fall of 1881 the mine had accumulated considerable copper carbonate on its dump, and its Philadelphia owners installed a Rankin & Brayton 30-ton water-jacket furnace, manufactured by the Pacific Iron Works of San Francisco. The furnace began operations in May 1882.

Saw freight train at Summit Station and wanted to get on it. Strange sight for me, [first] time in nearly three years. Pleasant ride returning and reached Tombstone about 12:30 or one. Dr. G a very entertaining, brilliant and intellectual man. Most excellent company. Dined with him tonight at Aztec House.*

Went for Redfern and he handed me a note containing a confession of his misdeeds, turning matters over to me and asking me to write his aunts and not talk to him on the subject. Was surprised at his gambling, he preached so against it. Women, wine and cards will ruin any man physically, financially and morally. Am very sorry for him and hope now he'll stop. Saw Godfrey at R's request and he will wait until I can communicate East. It seems as though my troubles would never end. I hope the end is near. I think I've been quite patient thus far. How matters will go now I don't know but I hope for the best and trust that everything will not be lost. Am getting very sick of things here. Hope M will make Florida racket stick, for there will probably be a good chance for me.

Thursday, November 30, 1882: Thanksgiving Day. Went with Milton to race track this afternoon and saw the Tombstone and Tucson nines play base ball. Quite exciting. Our boys badly beaten. Horse race—Dankee's mare ran. Harness broke on way home, no serious damage, though there might have been. Pleasant entertainment at Schieffelin Hall tonight by Methodist Church. Broom brigade did well, drilled finely. Eat turkey at Milton's, Mrs. Berry on hand. She was taken sick at table and Dr. was called immediately and pronounced her a very severe case of pneumonia. Turkey splendidly cooked and dinner a fine one—all overloaded. Very unfortunate termination in Mrs. B's illness. Judge away on a visit to Hermosillo and Guaymas.

Friday, December 1, 1882: Letter from Strallus [Alice, George's sister] this a.m. stating that sister would probably start tomorrow. What a grand time we'll have in the hour or two I hope to see her. Wrote and copied a long letter to Miss M. E. Redfern, Washington, D.C., and sent it today. I gave a pretty full history of mill doings and debt. I asked leniency for R. Spent pleasant evening at Robertson's with Pinney, Miss Mayers exhausted.

Saturday, December 2, 1882: Expect sister [Emeline] may have left yesterday on special train, papers stated [she] was to leave Boston and did leave for Cal. We'll see her soon. Worked on Bazaar matters some today.

Sunday, December 3, 1882: Went to church this a.m. as usual. Bagnall is improving all of the time very perceptibly—good sermon. Good sermon this evening too.

Monday, December 4, 1882: Howard Herring and I saw [L. W.] Blinn and had promises of lumber Saturday. Got it today and prepared it for use to-

*The Aztec House, also known as the Bachelors' House, was located on the northeast corner of Fremont and Third streets.

morrow. Some little work getting stuff ready. Sister left Thanksgiving Day on Boston special train and I shall see her on Friday next. Spent yesterday in Chicago. What a time we'll have.

Tuesday, December 5, 1882: Up early and hard at work this a.m. before breakfast some time. Got lumber thrown in almost before any one came. Bagnall next, soon came Fred Thomas and we got the booths up by two o'clock working pretty lively. Decorators started in and by five o'clock the hall looked well—very pretty indeed. Used about 1000 ft. of lumber. All worked hard today and things all O.K. by night. Japanese, French, Swiss, German, Turkey, and Iceland booths all dressed in respective colors and presided over by ladies in costume representing the different countries. Good crowd tonight and thing passed off very nicely.

Wednesday, December 6, 1882: Some fixing around to do today. Tried the parlor skates a while this afternoon. Tonight good crowd. Aphgan made by Mrs. Davis raffled off and Milton's mother got it, he taking chance for her. Great times tonight, lively, Japanese ours, Clapp and Stebbins furnished it.

Thursday, December 7, 1882: Great times today tearing down and removing the debris. Worked hard and got things to rights by early afternoon. Hard work. Felt good to be busy. Bade Mrs. and Miss Colby goodbye tonight, they leave tomorrow for Deming and probably go to Kingston. Arranged tonight to drive over to Summit Station with Pinney and Redfern—tomorrow some joy for a while.

Friday, December 8, 1882: Redfern couldn't go for some reason best known to himself and I was late getting off horseback. Didn't lose any time though going the 27 miles to Dragoon Summit Station and went beyond a few miles to Dan Strong and Mayers camp where I dined. Strong returning with me to take charge of my horse.

We reached station some time ahead of train and were on our horses when she hoved in sight. Saw sister on front platform of a pullman, and dug spur into horse, and was alongside and off in a second. She was almost as quick as I. Dr. Strong came rushing out declaring his intention of staying by her till he could deliver up his charge. I handed over belt, pistol, spurs to Dan and jumping on the train, we were off. In the car had a great time meeting so many all mighty clever people and all so fond of sister. Had quite an audience as I told of the country we were passing through—Tombstone, mines, Indians, cowboys—great times and lively ones till Tucson was reached and then at Porter's Hotel dinner was served. Sister is changed some for the better and was in quite good health, surprisingly so. Goodbyes had to be said presently and I jumped off the cars into darkness of night and thoughts like a dream. This rush into and glimpse of civilized beings, refinement, and pretty girls—kaleidoscopic in the extreme.

Groped around, and finally after getting directions from [L. C.] Hughes, I camped at Arizona Lodging House and strangely enough close to [where] John, Milton and I spent our first few nights. Tucson wonderfully improved in three years. No wonder I didn't know it. First time I've been on a railroad train in nearly three years. New times and experiences seem to be coming over the spirit of my dreams.

Saturday, December 9, 1882: Showed up this a.m. and met quite a number of Tombstoners—Mr. [Charles] Hudson wined and dined me at his elegant home this evening. Met Hoblitezall and put up at Cosmopolitan. Attended *Pinafore* rehearsal tonight at Opera House. Home with Fryes, Hawkins disagreeable as usual.

Sunday, December 10, 1882: Attended Episcopal Church in Masonic Hall—Fair minister. Bull fight this afternoon and think I might never have a like chance, I thought I better improve it and went in. Rather tame affair though. Little exciting at times. Called on Miss Pomeroy this evening and staid till about church time. Walked part way home with Hudsons—Mr., Mrs. and Miss. Bade Hoblitezall a final farewell.

Monday, December 11, 1882: Expected to leave today noon but unfortunately trains didn't connect. Met Carranza at hotel tonight and had quite a talk with him. He was excited over the killing of two men only a short distance from his Custom House. Pleasant fellow. Went about some with Frank Lord this a.m., he being just in from a mine his father is working. We used to be good friends here, but I am rather done on him for two things and am afraid in addition that he is very shoddy. I was a little short of money but could have gotten all I wanted of Mr. Hudson, or any one at the bank, but got a couple of dollars from Frank, who later brought up the matter before his mother in my presence, remarking, "Take what you want for your expenses," he having given me money to give someone in Tombstone ($50) and showing all lack of politeness and good manners in that remark. He was sorry too that I could not remain over to dine at his house, he said, and after I found I couldn't go till tomorrow, he never opened his mouth again about dinner, allowing Ed Hudson to invite me to dine at his house. These things show the man. Pleasant evening at Ed Hudson's. His wife a great conversationalist. Her friend Miss Boynton, from the East, a pleasant young lady. Later, Mrs. and Miss Hudson arrived and I accompanied them and Miss B, the latter more particularly, to see *Pinafore* at Opera House. A full and fine house socially and financially too, I should think. Battle march new one called "Battle of Cibicu" dedicated to Genl [Eugene Asa] Carr was rendered. Carr present. Frye had bad cold and Hawkins very bad cold. Get off early in a.m.

Tuesday, December 12, 1882: Up early and took train about 6:30 I think. Met Ben Block on cars who first spoke to me in Tucson, seeing me talking with Carranza. [George] Hearst on the cars. Disagreeable stage ride. Found money telegraphed me ($1400) from Miss M. E. Redfern to pay off mill obligations, so that matter will be fixed this week.

Wednesday, December 13, 1882: Much waiting to do and business to fix before I leave. Met Noxen and Thomas at [Francis G.] Burke's today in Genl Ewing's behalf, but they were obstinate and hoggish.

Thursday, December 14, 1882: Made arrangements today for leaving for Sonora tomorrow. Pinney will go with me for a taste of roughing it and Sonora life ala Mexican. He will probably get all he wants and more too.

Friday, December 15, 1882: Was very careful in getting and packing money on my horse this morning as I don't care to be followed or have any trouble which is so common nowadays. The two poor fellows just killed had much less than I. I had to pack almost $450 in dobies and $127 currency. Heavy weight, 30 or 40 lbs. I guess. Made Ochoaville about dark and put up for the night.

Saturday, December 16, 1882: P a little chaffed last night and we went only 32 miles. Had a pull of it today. Thought of putting up at Woodward's but they were all gone and locked up there, so we had to push on and make the mill, 50 mile ride. Found a fine state of things—old man H, Bob and Bush gone to Arispe to attach. Pinney pretty badly played out.

Sunday, December 17, 1882: Found paper in Spanish on the mill telling us to be at Bacuachi in a certain time. Went to Bacuachi today, John R[ankin] going with us. Wood choppers came for me as soon as I struck town and I paid them off, $137.50, and was glad to get rid of the money which was a burden and anxiety. Buried $250 in the rocks today. Pesqueira with lumber at the mill. The three worthies were expected back today from Arispe but didn't come. Saw Saylee and gave him a N.Y. paper which he seemed crazy to get and eagerly devoured.

Monday, December 18, 1882: Waited all day in Bacuachi for my parties, being assured of their coming but they didn't appear and I was in a quandry as to what to do. P very anxious to return to mill and wait there.

Tuesday, December 19, 1882: I considered this a.m. that best thing for me to do was to push on for Arispe, about 40 miles distant, and so informed boys who kicked but started with me. Very rough trail over the mountains and they played out after going about ten miles and left me to continue my journey alone which I did with feelings of misgiving when I learned on the road that my parties were still in Arispe. Hard road from Chinape to Arispe in river and sand. In a distance of 15 miles S told me he counted 52 crossings and then gave it up. Buena Vista is passed on road about half way I should think between C&A. Entered town about dusk and after rambling about struck Bush and the crowd and found a place to put up at. Attachment out that day and all three very obdurate.

Wednesday, December 20, 1882: Put up with a clever old fellow named Elias, a connection of my C.H. friends. He put out his mescal bottle, gave me a cot in a large adobe building which was being fixed up for some kind of a celebration on the morrow and had a fair supper. My feelings last night can better be imagined than described. There I was seemingly at the complete mercy of the men who contemplated seizure of mill—no friends, ignorant of Mexican law and with scarcely any knowledge of the language. I was hard pushed—I never want to pass another such night of anxiety and mental strain. All night in my sleep and dreams I was arguing and arranging matters and worried terribly. Everything against me and the law upon me in a foreign country and seemingly all opposed to me. Saw Bob and Bush separately and did my best, but all to no avail, as the law favored them and they were going for all they could get in damages for waiting. I told how I sent word of my coming at certain time to settle and had kept my word but to no avail. Their claims amounted to $200 or $300, more than amount claimed for services. A providential interference now happened in my behalf. It was a God send—I spied Ben Block, my Tucson acquaintance, who happened to be in Arispe that day on business and who volunteered his assistance after I explained matters. "I'll stay by you," he said, "and see you though," and stay he did. We went to see the Judge of the First Instance and explained matters to him, Block speaking the language like a native. He was favorable to us I thought. The others came in presently and we had a grand pow-wow, but to no good except to appoint a meeting at their lawyer's house about 11 o'clock I think it was.

At lawyer's, a pleasant Spaniard, Block turned himself loose, narrating his experiences in law in Sonora, how it cost and was never ending, etc., argued in Spanish and English. Took lawyer out and talked in private with him and took my part so strongly that finally my figures were accepted and later we repaired to the Judge's court and I settled by money and checks, taking receipts in full for all claim against mill for Miss Redfern, with Ben Block as witness. I paid the lawyer's bill of $50 and costs of $10.50 and was mighty glad to get off as well as I did having to pay Block only his expenses for the day of $4. How happy I was. Block and mescal did the work. I made my points and turned the tables. What a change from the morning. B did me a good service. They probably do not owe him any good will. Indeed I learned later that his presence kept them out of $500 that they would never have gotten. John appeared about noon—first time he met his father since their row. Looked about Arispe some. Found it pretty much the same as all Mexican towns—tumbled down and thriftless. Six stores in the place and one or two Americans, half Spanish themselves. About 1000 people I am told. Used to be a place of importance and the capital of three or four states. Good climate. Saw some red, ripe oranges on fine trees and ate sugar cane, first since leaving Florida, John and I together. He didn't care much for society of others. To-night the festival, or whatever it was, took place, and the hall where I slept was crowded with women and children singing on their knees, their musical twang disagreeable. They're all great on a long strain at close of a sentence or line. Slept in old man's room tonight. Hard up for water in night but sugar cane satisfied my thirst.

Thursday, December 21, 1882: Kept the circus going all night. Something in connection with Xmas. Ignacio tried to explain but I couldn't understand him. Pretty señorita at table last night with the two señors and several soñoras. Dogs numerous and a burro brushed past me as I sat at seat of honor [at] head of table. Old Dr. McKinney gave me a great game about his troubles with Shugart and Miller at Ignacius's store. An Irishman named Kane stuck to me pretty close thus a.m. to go with me as I was well armed and he was not at all. So after a present of sugar cane and adios all around, we got away from the dismal place, old man H having further business in town, I not caring to be in his company anyhow. Only a cup of coffee and two tamales this a.m., served on corn husks and we had a hard, cold ride to Bacuachi. He not knowing the trail, I lost it twice, once in the mountains, but found it again all O.K. and we reached Bacuachi about dark, thankful to get there. After good supper and thawing out, as it was very cold along the river bottoms especially after sundown, and some mescal, we felt better and had good rest. Passed a mescal ranch today and I was quite interested in watching the proceedings.

Friday, December 22, 1882: Set out for mill this a.m. On the way saw some deer, and a Mexican and I hunted them a while afoot, getting one, part of which we took along. Quite exciting sport. Thousands of game now—deer, turkey, and smaller game. Arrived at mill in season to take down tent and pack everything away. Made everything as secure as I could. Found some quicksilver flasks and buried them on edge of ditch close to the rocks thrown out of the well, distant from mouth of ditch about two feet I should think, on right side going towards Hohstadts. P and S buried that and the amalgam after dark, placing latter in a hole on tailing ground 17 paces from corner of pump on line with large tree.

Saturday, December 23, 1882: Cold last night. Took tent and hammocks and mattresses to Mrs. H's and packed away stuff under mill flooring. Got Louis to agree to go up around mill several times a week and see that everything was all right. Didn't sleep very well although the tamed deer didn't lick my face this time as it did before. Got away quite early, P, John and Kane accompanying. At CH Carranza opened a bottle of champagne for me and it did taste mighty good after the long 40 mile ride. Pressed on to Ochoaville, P and I, and got there about dark. He has enough of roughing it—50 mile rides he didn't count on and having to be on the *qui vive* most of the time to guard against surprises. Rather bad country to travel now, rustlers and Indians loose again.

Sunday, December 24, 1882: Worked along comfortably today and struck town in the afternoon. Xmas eve and glad to get back, more so than from any of my other trips. Dined at Milton's and attended church later, but was too tired to stand.

Monday, December 25, 1882: Xmas day. Service this a.m. which I attended. Church prettily decorated. Sorry I wasn't back in time to assist but am in luck to be back today at all. Splendid music at church, best outside of San Francisco I'll bet. Letters, presents, and congratulations. My dear good Nathalie remembered me too. Sister sent on my pipe which is a little beauty, and some other things useful and ornamental. Splendid dinner at

Clapp's. Good time. Hard work to get Nathalie's present, it seemed to be mislaid. Robbers entered P.O. last night and I was afraid had taken it.

Tuesday, December 26, 1882: Trouble again today. R had a good chance to send horse to ranch but found him attached by Tuttle—a piece of perverse spite. I released horse, borrowing $28 from Vickers for R and we got the horse off and laid for Tuttle. Found that R's saddle had been repeatedly rented by the old fraud and was out when we demanded it. Shot off my mouth at him and wanted to maul him but let matters go by. He's a good one. Took hold of him but he wouldn't resist. Was pretty hot. Xmas tree at church today and I helped Bagnell distribute gifts; pleasant time.

Wednesday, December 27, 1882: Telegram from Miss R to me sending $125 for Lewis to get off with, but he wouldn't budge for less than $300, and so telegraphed. Have to stay by him pretty close. Miss R telegraphing me to if possible.

Thursday, December 28, 1882: No money yet, but promise of it and I want to get R off. He's troublesome. Bought his pistol out of hock and now the horse and pistol are free. Vick said, "Well George you stay with him pretty well,"—stay by all friends and these with whom I am associated in business, but I'm getting tired now. Xmas tree tonight, I think it was at Methodist. Went with Milton and wife.

Friday, December 29, 1882: Well, at last funds came today and R proposed to leave in the morning. Kept track of him today, but he fooled me tonight after I left him in bed about 11 o'clock. Am sorry for that. Ed Suman seems to have switched off from a proper life, laying it in the smallness of his makeup to McIntyre's curse. Reasoned with him some times. He seems bound to go to the devil like several others.

Saturday, December 30, 1882: R finally got off this a.m. thanks to his good aunts. Poage left for California yesterday with a proposition from me to work up there. R will prepare the way for Nick Stanton who I hope will follow to Chicago in a few days. I hope now to do something within the next 60 days. Am getting desperate. Shall soon make a break of some kind.

Sunday, December 31, 1882: Last day of the year and not a pretty respectable one either. Attended church as usual in the a.m. and in evening went to S[unday] s[chool] celebration at Methodist Church after dining with Milton and wife, and good old Mrs. Richardson. Harry spoke his piece well. Considerable noise at the usual time. Wrote Nathalie today, last letter this year, thanking her. Schlaet sent me box of cigars and home folks many things useful and ornamental.

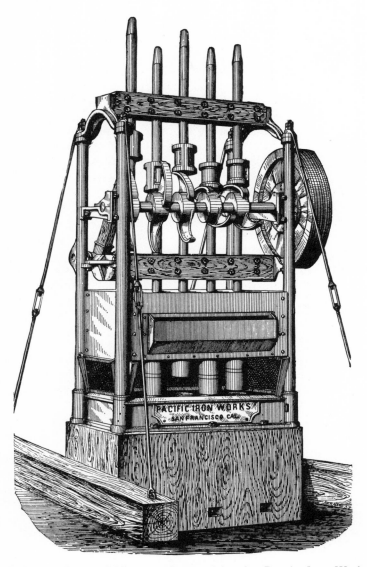

The Reliance Quartz Mill, manufactured by the Pacific Iron Works of San Francisco, was popular in Mexico because of its iron frame. It was produced with 750- and 500-pound stamps, and was effective on gold or silver ores with either wet or dry crushing. Although not iron-framed, the quartz mill of Parsons and Redfern was similar in design to this crusher.

1883

Monday, January 1, 1883: Wrote Nathalie today, my first letter this year. Bagnall and [M. M.] Sherman dragged me off calling, but I switched off to see fire parade after we called on Mrs. Berry. I then called on Mrs. Reppy and Ward, Pridham and Miss Brown, Eccleston, Santee, and Mayers, Miss Wallace and Mrs. McCoy. Dined at Milton's. Looked in at Fireman's ball tonight a while and was forced into an unpleasant experience with N and wife. He and she having considerable trouble. Did what I could.

Tuesday, January 2, 1883: Unpleasant weather. Bad Indian business again close to town, two men killed. Straying bucks probably going to Sonora after getting their squaws from San Carlos. Bad, very bad. Crook is damned now up hill and down. County certainly receiving set backs. Had full length photograph taken today in Sonora rig, arms, etc., to send Nathalie and sisters. Good negative. Spent evening, or part of it at Miss Santee's.

Wednesday, January 3, 1883: Rain last night and today. Mountains covered with snow. Met [G. G.] Gates today for first time. Letter to him from Tompkins. Got letter other day from father which had been cut open, a nice job, along with others and thrown into a street in Terra Haute, Indiana; the postal car being robbed there. At Milton's tonight. Little Harry wrote and sent his first letter tonight. It was to his grandmother in S.F. and a good beginning.

Thursday, January 4, 1883: Called on Miss Peel tonight I think it was, and met Mexican consul there.

Friday, January 5, 1883: Writing letters my preoccupation at present preparing way for mill matters. Played whist this evening till late at Dick's.

Saturday, January 6, 1883: Got my photos today and sent one each to Nathalie, sister and Strallus. Called on Mrs. Berry tonight with Pinney and we whisted. Head hurt me and I stopped game. Gave Mrs. Clapp remaining picture.

Sunday, January 7, 1883: Attended church as usual this a.m. Walked home with Miss Mayer and saw Mrs. R and the "Kid" for first time since birth. Lunched with them. Mrs. Clapp and Mrs. Richardson honored my humble abode with a visit this afternoon; first time. Got it cleaned out just in time. Dined at Clapp's and went to church in evening. All of us ate sugar cane this afternoon I brought from Arispe.

Monday, January 8, 1883: Fine weather these days. Walked over hills to-day with Major Earle, went through his mine, the "Luck Sun." Fine look-ing property; manganese will probably predominate. Walked over to [A. H.] Bayless' new find on the "Anchor" and found a good looking prospect.

Tuesday, January 9, 1883: Sister's birthday and I sent her a card of con-gratulations. Vick called me in today as witness to Councilman's [James J.] Nash's proposition to pay 5% commission on sales of city bonds he may make. Nash authorized to make proposition. Wrote Genl Ewing yesterday and McCormick of Chicago today. Went to Miss Peel's tonight for Spanish lesson, but it was delayed until tomorrow night.

Wednesday, January 10, 1883: Snow is melting on mountains. They look beautiful in their white mantle. Had first lesson in Spanish tonight. Pinney, Frank Earle and Harry Castle in class. Good progress.

Thursday, January 11, 1883: Wish I could get Nick off. John R in town to-day. Sent R photo today. Spent evening at Clapp's. Opera and music with Mrs. C.

Friday, January 12, 1883: Finally closed mill business today. Paid [J. P.] McAllister and [George] Pridham and sent these receipts and an explana-tory letter about other matters to Miss Redfern, Washington, D.C. Spent part of evening at Mrs. Robertson's and balance at Pinney's going over our experiences and times at Flushing and in Cal. Am selected to inspect County books by Supervisors, and Vick and I will soon tackle them.

Saturday, January 13, 1883: Beautiful weather. Letter from R insisting that I should go on, but how can I. Long talk with Nick and wrote R and Poage, making several propositions. Something's got to be done very shortly. R unable to talk his mess there. Indians at it again on upper Son-ora, stole horses from the Frenchman. Guess coast will be clear when I have to go below again. Can't tell for how long though. Took Spanish les-son tonight and was greatly encouraged by Miss Peel.

Sunday, January 14, 1883: Very unpleasant day. Indians below reported to have killed one or two men near the mill. Hope they'll let the mill alone. Church morning and evening. Am thinking of being confirmed in Febru-ary. Sang a little at Milton's tonight. Had to positively refuse a request severeal times to sing a secular song, but request was made in all inno-cence by Milton's wife. Mexican Consul Prieto present and sang sweetly. At last we have a genuine social scandal in what is termed high circles. Dr. Giberson and Mrs. L. Price figuring in the matter. P it is stated tried to shoot Doc and has applied for divorce. G told me he just had his papers from a wife 22 years older than himself.

Monday, January 15, 1883: Cloudy day. Have consent for inspecting County books at $10 per day; being paid in warrants though will reduce amount one quarter. Pretty good thing on me a Sunday or two ago. A lady a newcomer, saw the top of my white hat by church window outside and was much alarmed. Thinking the cowboys, of which I was undoubtedly one, were coming in to have some sport and was in much trepidation even after I went inside and took a seat. Spent evening at Pridham's.

Tuesday, January 16, 1883: Commenced on County Treasurer's books today and found several errors. Had to wait on Ben Goodrich some time before getting them. Had some Spanish after dinner with Pinney at his house and then went to Milton's and spent the evening

Wednesday, January 17, 1883: Very cold again, snow on mountains makes it so. Company of cavalry came from Huachuca and went this a.m. over to Dragoons on an Indian hunt, Indians reported in some force over there. At last something is done. Castle was appointed by supervisors to assist me and began this a.m. We found some curious things. Cannot get Sheriff's books and Co Treas[surer] for 1881. Will be a great time I guess from present appearances. Letter from J. R. this a.m. wanting me to go on. I cannot. His folks have gone back on him he writes. About time I think.

Thursday, January 18, 1883: Letter and draft from Genl Ewing at last. Wrote father, enclosing letter from Eaton introducing me to Parker in N.Y. Must do something with that mill. It's making and keeping me poor. Found many errors and some striking ones. Several warrants, if not forged, were paid with knowledge of parties. Showed Supervisor [L. W.] Blinn glaring doings. Treas[urer] anxious to make good deficiencies. Is to morgage property. Between $3000 and $4000 thus far. This is strictly private.

Friday, January 19, 1883: Cold, ice and lots of it. Hard work on the books. Studied Spanish at office till late, Prof. [M. M.] Sherman helping me.

Saturday, January 20, 1883: Coldest night I've known in a long time. Snow blew in on my clothes and covered table. Helped Mrs. Clapp this afternoon and at noon helped move piano from McCoy's to Scheffelin Hall for affair tonight. Took Mrs. Clapp, Mrs. Richardson and Harry around to the entertainment tonight and we all had a good time. Milton came later. Trouble to get seats at first, others occupying them. Brooks capital. Play, part of cast—Mrs. McCoy gave mad scene from Article 47. Don't like such things. Dancing later and I indulged till 12 o'clock. Had Spanish lesson tonight—P and I.

Sunday, January 21, 1883: Pleasanter day. Church this a.m. Dined at Milton's and in evening heard Miss Holyoke at M.E. Church on temperance. Good speaker. Don't believe in her methods.

Monday, January 22, 1883: Hard at work now day and night. D[unbar] reported to be thinking of suicide. Bad business—20,000 and over. There'll be a circus soon. Went to S Hall tonight with Clapps and Mrs. R to see vanity play—fair.

Tuesday, January, 23, 1883: Supervisors and [Edward R.] Monk in today and fun is ahead—mixed, terribly mixed. Worked tonight for Vick and now between nine and 10 must go at Spanish for over an hour or two.

Wednesday, January 24, 1883: At work as usual. Think I spent this evening at Mrs. Clapp's. The town is pretty well awakened now, lively times ahead. Forged warrant, first one we found—sprung on [Milton] Joyce. Spanish tonight. Got guitar after much trouble and Prieto sang for us.

Thursday, January 25, 1883: We worked till about midnight, Judge [William] Herring being in a hurry for final results. C and I seem to be in good graces of all who tell us to fire ahead. J[oyce] sullen and threatening. He better look out for a rope. I do not fear anything but lookout sharply.

Friday, January 26, 1883: J's in court and Castle on stand to simply press entry. Bad case for J but I see what his defense will be. Am afraid D[unbar] will have to stand it all. Bad, bad state of things. Tombstone quite aroused now.* A good sentiment is growing. Put them through they say, meaning the ring. Their fun is over. The day of reckoning is at hand.

Saturday, January 27, 1883: At last [a letter] from Nathalie. She acknowledges receipt of photo, etc. My future certainly is vague and uncertain. I don't think though that she means what some might possibly infer. She's a good, true, noble woman and straight forward as can be. Well, I'm being used pretty roughly anyway—my luck though. I propose to leave this cursed mining business and go into something where I will have some show for what I undergo. I have the name of rustler and hard worker and many wish me well and hope I'll succeed, saying I deserve this, that and the other thing. A change is upon me and I feel it keenly. I must have business and very quickly too. No time to lose either. Good legitimate business and nothing else. I'm going to make a break. Nathalie is very dear to me and I'm through building air castles. Spanish class tonight.

Sunday, January 28, 1883: Have written ultimatum East to those interested in mill. Something must be done immediately or I will have to drop things and go to work. I think I will be told to go East very shortly, probably next week. Church in morning. Dined at Clapp's and in evening C and I met Judge Herring at his house and went over statement with him. Was entrusted with important mission this evening by H and Supervisor Blinn. D was about to skip and I accomplished purpose.

Monday, January 29, 1883: At it again, but work is over now, the most important part of it. Have arranged so that I will not be detained in this County matter as witness in a long standing trial. Am using my precaution so as not to be caught. There is but one thing for those east to do and that is to have me go East. That's dead certain and to protect interests I will be sent for probably.

Tuesday, January 30, 1883: Beautiful weather all of the time. Crow and Stanley examined books today for defendant who was around himself considerably. Don't see how deficit is to be made good by their plan.

*As a result of Parsons' audit, Milton Joyce, ex-chairman of Cochise County Supervisors, and ex-county treasurer J. O. Dunbar were arrested and charged with raising a county warrant. See Tucson *Daily Star*, January 27, 1883.

Broom Brigade drilled tonight at new Court House by Capt. Belle Mayers—capital. Played some cards afterwards with Snyder of insurance fame, Prof. and Nick, and pretty late returned and had a dance with the fair captain, taking her home. Dancing said to have been prohibited by the Methodists but I didn't know so till too late.

Wednesday, January 31, 1883: Well, I got word this a.m. from Washington to draw $250 traveling expenses East and go on. So it seems I am to go. Must await arrival of letter and note their effect. I want at least $100 more before starting. It quite takes my breath away to think of seeing house and N once more and be in civilization. A change is ahead. Castle on stand today in D case.

Thursday, February 1, 1883: John Rankin brought horses in today and I must go with him tomorrow to Huachucas, having promised to go and see several copper claims. At it as usual today. Case only too clear against J. and D. Wrote sisters, Nathalie and Stanley tonight of my proposed trip East. Doc Ingersoll had a pass issued to Giberson, gotten by Johnston, and proposed selling it to me for half fare. It is limited though.

Friday, February 2, 1883: Well, finally got off this a.m. in the face of hard, strong and steady wind, making traveling very disagreeable indeed. Met Gates beyond Lewis Springs. Left Sonora road near the hay stack and went over hills a mile or two to the boys camp, Miller, Bush, and John, where they had a lot of cattle. Miller in Sonora on a drive up. Another party named Merrill, a hand. While eating Phinn Clanton* rode up and staid a while. First time I had ever talked with this notorious cowboy and Earp hunter. John and I started for Ash Canyon at south end of Huachucas after a bite, and about 200 yards from camp on the prairie amongest some mesquite bushes, John showed me what was left of the body of a Mexican—what the coyotes had left. All J would say was that he was probably riding some horse not belonging to him. John intimated that a careful search might show one or two more. Its the only way. Find wind across prairie—never faced a harder nor steadier [one]. Finally reached Hutchison's camp and was provided with good cot at Black Bear Co.'s house.

Saturday, February 3, 1883: Up and off early afoot up the steep mountain and a hard tramp it was to the summit in snow part of the distance. Grand sight from the crest, which was a narrow ledge, giving magnificent views east and west. Ash Canyon is almost opposite Hereford. A very pretty part of the Huachucas. Down the west side we went on a fair trail to "Gray Eagle," thence the best way we could to "Grand Fraud" claim, from which some fine peacock copper is taken. After examining this we descended the mountain and after a long pull reached the "Little Maud," a small pros-

*Phineas Fay Clanton was born in 1845, the second son of "Old Man" Newman Haynes Clanton. The Clantons were notorious rustlers and Phineas was no exception. In 1887 he was convicted of grand larceny in Graham County, but unlike his father and brothers Billy and Ike, Phin Clanton died of natural causes at his home in Globe, Arizona, on January 5, 1905.

pect. All of this is in Copper Canyon. Now began the fun; climbing back another and steeper way, and not having exerted myself in so long a time, before it went hard with me. I'll never forget that pull up that mountain side through snow which came through my dilapidated and worn out boots. Not expecting such a tramp, I was unprepared. Saw the Mountain Chief and Edith on the way up, former having a little native copper. At last summit was reached and I was never more thankful in my life, having to stop every few yards and rest. Rifle and coat had to be lugged too. Now a struggle began to reach the bottom in safety. The fork of canyon we went down led past the Grand Slide, a claim I was to see, but we became separated, having no trail to follow and getting down as best we could, sliding on snow. Tumbling and falling about, I slid part way by sitting down and catching bushes. Now and then I'd fill up with soft snow and have a time. This 20 mile tramp I'll never forget.

Sunday, February 4, 1883: Up early and off for Grand Slide mine which I missed last night. Liked it fairly well and think there may be a chance for something good; advantageously situated. Brought away good specimens. Got away from camp about nine o'clock. Dr. Jerrold superintendent now of B Bear. Sixty ton smelter partly up. Discouraging for them thus far. Pleasant ride across prairie to camp and John and I discussed a cattle proposition which is certainly a very feasible one and in which there is money. I consider Bill Miller and John Rankin good square cattlemen and shall do what I can East. John agreed with me as to danger of doing anything so near the border. It's a fine proposition 300 miles north. Found Bush at camp. Boys joke rather much about dead Mexican—six bullet holes through him. No coroner business in this, mum's the word. Life and property have to be protected on the frontier. Several shooting rackets lately occurred. Tiresome ride to town from the camp and had to work my passage, horse being played. Looked at "Stanton" on the way, but couldn't find anything worth speaking about. Am afraid of a fraud there; much disappointed. Reached town pretty well played out after ride of 70 miles. Attended church tonight. Wrote Johnston for pass. Supped at Vickers'. Very pleasant family.

Monday, February 5, 1883: At work on County matters today with Castle, but completed things today for present at least. Have a job for Walker a day or two and then I hope to be able to go East. Bishop Dunlop* around today and a reception was held this evening at the old Court House at which there was a goodly number. Had quite a talk with Mrs. Stevens at reception about Lewis Lee who is married to a pretty girl, and is cashier of

*Bishop George Kelly Dunlop, of Kirkwood, Missouri, was appointed by the Episcopal Conference to the diocese of New Mexico and Arizona in 1880, but did not arrive in southern Arizona until February 1882. Thereafter he was in and out of Tombstone until his death in February 1888.

the bank in which he was bookkeeper. So my oldest friend is fixed. When shall I be? Danced considerable and a few of us had a rollicking good time.

Tuesday, February 6, 1883: At work today for Frank Walker on Sycamore Water Co.'s books. Called on Mrs. Berry and Clapp this evening.

Wednesday, February 7, 1883: Little cold again. Worked Water books part of day and balance of it helped Castle prepare warrant statement for Joyce. Bought trinket for Nathalie today after much trouble. Pendant of filagree Mexican silver and very pretty, a cross. No church, Bishop and Bagnall at Bisbee. A ball through Vick's office this afternoon nearly took Williams in the leg; accidental discharge. Spent pleasant evening at Earle's. Bob up from below. Gave him $3 to pay Mrs. Hohstadt on his return below, amount I promised her for Pinney's board.

Thursday, February 8, 1883: Gloomy day. Finished Joyce business today and made out bill. Also gave bill to Supervisors for $170. It will be passed next session. Proposition on hand to fund the $106,000 indebtedness and take it up with Co[unty] bonds—good scheme and money in it. The cost to County now is double by discount of 50% or more on County warrants general fund. Gave John Rankin my rifle last night until my return from the East. He reports another dead man near their camp.

Friday, February 9, 1883: Got trial balance today for Walker and $20. Also collected Joyce's $15 and paid Vick half for Castle. Too much to do to get off tomorrow a.m. and rainy tonight so will delay a day. Gave bill for services in County matters, $170, and am to pay Vick 10% on it. He takes care of it for me. Visited Duke and R Cloud properties today and took samples for General Ewing. Saw Mitchell tonight. Have to visit "Pluto" at Total Wreck district.

Saturday, February 10, 1883: Intensely disagreeable last night and couldn't possibly get away. Met Bishop and Rev. H[endley] of Tucson at Milton's last night. *Daily Republican* thought it wonderful that I should *ride* out of town and result was I was joked continuously all day. Packed trunk and borrowed satchel tonight. Took traps down town and stopped at American House for the night as stage wouldn't come to mine in dark. Church consecrated tonight by Bishop Dunlop and Bagnall ordained priest. Hendley of Tucson helped. Meeting at Court House tonight to decide issuance of County bonds for redemption of outstanding warrants. Finally decided to issue $100,000 — I knocked proposed amendment of $120,000 through city attorney, suggesting the probably settlement as an offset to that.

Sunday, February 11, 1883: Up early and by P's invitation went to Oriental for cocktail. Had a fine one—champagne and bottle to take off of good stuff. Fine ride this a.m. Took top of stage. Air soft and nice. Thorn proposes joining me at Contention or Benson rather tonight. Left baggage at Benson and continued to Pantano. At Contention I met Shillian, formerly of Tombstone, who skipped the place I think. He is in Jalisco, Mexico, I believe. Expected stage at P but there was none. A nine [mile] run to Total Wreck,* so I telephoned Marsch, supt. of Pluto, and he came over for me with buckboard; seven miles. Long time to wait and important to return in evening. Train station agent's wife's face familiar and discovered her to be Judge O'Meliveny's daughter, whom I met in Los Angeles 6 $^1/_2$ years ago. She is now Mrs. Safford. Pleasant chat. Finally reached Empire district. Was astonished to find the good foundation there for a large camp. About 5000 tons of ore on the dump; free milling and this had to be taken out in sinking shaft and running levels. Fine $100,000, 20 stamp mill. No stoping yet. Fine property. Found better things at Pluto then I expected. Good wide ledge between porphyritic lime, contact vein with good ore, four to six inches wide. Conditions all favorable for good thing. Third south extension of Total Wreck, Major Miram's properties, seem to be worked out. [Rest of entry is illegible.]

Monday, February 12, 1883: Up and off early this a.m. Decided to take second class ticket, $77.55. Took too much time to get it ready, so had to delay a day at Benson. Mc and Bishop D and Rev H at Depot. Chism told me at Bloek's store that Indians were very bad below. C found body of one poor fellow just killed and B had his horses taken on road at the Frenchman's. Hendley and I had long walk and talk today and he treated to cigars and beer. First rate fellow. I like these Episcopal ministers. They are ministers in every sense of the word and teach and preach a manly religion. Making a man of a man by allowing him to be the judge in matters the church should have nothing to do with whatever.

Got Rev. H interested in Pluto and gave him eastern address. [Charles] Reppy came down this afternoon and Thompson, R going to look over the field at Lordsburg. Roomed at Virginia and retired early. Some interesting conversation in the next room by couple evidently not married.

Tuesday, February 13, 1883: On hand in lots of time for ticket this a.m. Cost $77.55 and I must squeeze through to N.Y. on remaining ten dollars. Off at last about nine and about a dozen Tombstoners on train. Had to talk County matters some time. Have quite a reputation now and my opinion is well received—seem to have a name in Mexico and S.E. Arizona I wasn't aware of until just now. I get on the outside a little. Am plainly on the road now and can scarcely realize it. Liked looks of Lordsburg where most Tombstoners got off. Clifton Copper mines, 90 miles distant, and a narrow gauge road is being built there by Scotch company [the Arizona Copper Company] who seem to be buying up everything in the way of copper. Would like to get into it. Met Bishop Dunlop on train and we had a long and pleasant chat. Parted at Deming. While dining at Deming was pleas-

*The Total Wreck Mine in the Empire Mountains of Pima County was discovered by cowboy John T. Dillon, who described its location on a boulder strewn hillside as a total wreck. He sold the location to the Empire Mining and Development Company, and a fairly large mining community developed around the workings.

antly surprised by the Colbys and had a pleasant time with them later. The judge expected me last night by the papers, and arranged to go up road a piece with me, but I was not there, and he had to go alone. Bishop had stopover so was deprived of his company.

Wednesday, February 14, 1883: L. Rosenbaum, a pleasant little fellow, is my traveling companion. Made myself very comfortable last night. Take meals at lunch counter at great saving. Can't eat much on the cars. At Raton this evening two engines helped us up the 185 foot grade. Scenery said to be grand, but very disappointing to me after what I have seen. One place somewhat resembled the horseshoe curve on Pennsylvania Central but not so short; 2000 foot tunnel at summit. This is a spur of the Rockies. Not as cold thus far as I expected. Gave what encouragement we could to a consumptive—advising California and Florida. He was nearly killed last night. Car wheel grazed his foot after he fell, close call. Las Vegas quite a town; house cars. Hot springs the attraction. Great resort for syphilitics. Does rheumatism great good too. Tall hats and good clothes appeared here for the first time. Look with much interest at a lady in furs. Broken bridge delayed us awhile today.

Thursday, February 15, 1883: Rate of speed very slow until today, 18 miles an hour. Now make better time. Am now past Arizona, New Mexico and Colorado and am now in the great grass hopper and prohibition state— Kansas, and I have only a dime left. Should have exercised more fore-thought. Don't see much to admire so far. Prefer Arizona for grass and cattle aside from its mines. Stock though said to be doing pretty well here.

[Editor's Note: For the sake of brevity and to save production costs on this book, the account of George Parsons' two month sojourn on the East coast has been dispensed with. From the standpoint of generating interest in his mill and mining schemes the trip was a failure. On the train, in Chicago, New York, and in Washington, D.C., Parsons cornered people whom he thought might be interested in Arizona and Sonoran mining projects. With the exception of enlisting some continued support in the mill by Louis Redfern's aunt in Washington, D.C., he experienced bad luck at every turn. As George put it, some people "wouldn't take" to his schemes, others would not see him, most made no response at all. In New York City he found it "hard to do anything." In Cleveland he found his contacts "very ignorant of mining" and suspicious of people in Tombstone. Easterners were interested more in "land, large tracts in the far west and old Mexico."

George had better luck with his family, spending enjoyable moments renewing acquaintances with relatives, and seeing his father and sister in Brooklyn, and brother Sam in Derry, New Hampshire. Above all, he looked forward to seeing Nathalie, the girl he longed to marry. But that fantasy forever crashed in New York. Although he found her "the same girl in appearance, not a whit changed," there was someone in the parlor. His anger flaired, "confound the some one," he wrote in his diary. Their second scheduled meeting never took place. Instead he received a letter "which was not an agreeable one." When they next met Nathalie was cool, and she stood him up on their last meeting. After waiting an hour he left. "Am afraid she's not the girl I thought . . .," he wrote in his diary. So much for years of fantasy.

George fared better in Chicago. There he met Tombstone mining acquaintances who took him to the City's Board of Trade, which he found as bad as the New York stock exchange. Some Chicagoans, however, viewed him as a distinguished and knowledgeable visitor, and on April 7 a Chicago *Tribune* reporter questioned him regarding Arizona's Indian troubles. This was Parsons' chance to vent his feelings regarding United States military policy toward the Apache Indians; which he did with great freedom. That lengthy interview appeared the next day, April 8, 1883, and is reproduced in its entirety below.

Mr. George W. Parsons, of Tombstone, Ari., who is now stopping in this city, was called upon yesterday by a reporter to learn something about the present Indian outbreak in that part of the Southwest. Mr. Parsons has spent about three years in the Territory and the neighboring State of Sonora, Mexico, and is thoroughly conversant with the country, its resources and wants.

He describes Arizona as being wonderfully rich in deposits of the precious metals. Several bonanza mines have already been opened, and the attention of capitalists has been called to others which promise to be equally rich, but the troubles with the Indians are proving a serious drawback to the development of the Territory. This last outbreak, he says, has put Arizona back another year and frightened away people who were preparing to settle there and make permanent investments.

"The difficulties now," says the gentleman, "are with the Indians, the outlaws who infested this region having nearly all been driven away or overcome. The mining camp is situated between the San Carlos Agency on the north and the Sierra Madre Mountains in Old Mexico. Between the agency Indians and those in Old Mexico there is constant communication, and they are continually inciting each other to commit depredations. Those living south of the border line cross over into United States Territory and the San Carlos Indians go over into Mexico, committing all sorts of atrocities while on the warpath. Gen. Crook tagged the agency Indians, and one of them was killed a short time ago, which proves beyond a doubt that all the hostile Indians do not live south of the border line. Since I came north several of my most intimate friends have been killed by these savages.

Have you not soldiers and Gen. Crook to protect the country?

"We are supposed to have four companies of United States troops at Fort Huachuca, a six-company post twenty-five miles west of Tombstone. These soldiers are always about twenty-four hours behind time in following up a band of savages. The Indians make sallies, murder the whites, and are back safe and sound in their mountain retreats long before the troops are ready to follow them. A short time ago five men were killed by the savages only seven miles from the post. Four companies of soldiers were ordered to start in pursuit at 5 o'clock in the morning, and it was 3 o'clock in the afternoon when they reached the scene of the massacre. Of course all the Indians had escaped. Gen. Crook does not seem to be doing any better than his predecessors. He has never subjugated the Chiricahua Apaches, who live in Old Mexico and are continually making hostile incursions into Arizona, keeping up a steady communication with the Indians on the agency. The latter are well provided with guns and ammunition. It has been the custom to have about twenty-five Indian scouts at the different posts. These devils are kept a few months, till they have been drilled in our ways, and then they are sent back to the agency, and a new lot taken on. They steal our guns and ammunition, and then turn against us, and supply their neighbors. The officers would rather not have Indians for fighting men, because they are so treacherous, but they are taken and drilled in accordance with orders from the Government. Two or three of those supposed to be the most reliable are employed as trailers. The savage nature of these Indians is illustrated by the horrible deed committed by one of their scouts. He agreed with some of the officers at the post that if they would give him a certain number of cartridges he would bring in his own father's head. He went, and soon came back with the head, and then offered to bring in the old woman's, his mother's, if they would give him more cartridges. This is a specimen of the sort of soldiers these red devils make."

Why do not the soldiers protect the people? ·

"I do not know. It is generally believed that money is being made out of the agencies. If the United States Government would only withdraw all the troops in Arizona, and tell the settlers there to take care of themselves, they would soon settle this Indian question. These bands of hostiles are small in number, and they could soon be disposed of, but so long as the soldiers remain, the people naturally look to them for protection. The Mexican Government is willing to co-operate with ours in the subjugation of these savages, and if Mexico was like some of the great Powers she would bring in big and just claims against our Government for damages and depredations committed within her territory by our agency Indians."

"Arizona," remarked Mr. Parsons, "has a beautiful climate, and is one of the finest mineral countries. She will soon have ample railroad communication with the outside world. All that is needed now to develop her resources is protection against the Indians. The failure of the Government to subjugate these hostile tribes is a serious drawback to the welfare of the Territory."]

Thursday, April 19, 1883: Arrived at Deming this a.m. about seven o'clock and I stopped over. Short of funds, got $10 from Lon Huians, Blinn lumber Co. man, friend of mine and took room at RR hotel. Dined at Colby's and spent the evening there. Deming I'm afraid is not destined to be much of a place. The A&P when running from Albuquerque to Mojan will carry through passengers and freight in all probability on the north and on the south the probable road from El Paso to Pacific south of Guaymas will probably hurt it more. Wouldn't surprise me if rails were taken up.

Friday, April 20, 1883: It seems my interview in Chicago *Tribune* was copied into Tombstone paper and is well received everywhere. Indian troubles common here. Saw picture of poor little Charlie McComas carried off after death of his father and mother.* Terrible thing. At Willcox [J. D.] Hooker of S.F. [brother of H. C. Hooker] got on the cars and we had a good deal to say about Dakota and chances there. He proposes to go up there soon and investigate. Also had some talk about a ranch. He's down on the present state of affairs and denounces the soldiers. Said the [Tombstone] Rangers were at his place when he left. Was highly pleased at my interview in Chicago. Met boys at Benson and all along the road, the first words almost being how glad they were I had put things in the way I did in my Chicago *Tribune* interview. At Tombstone Vick and Truman met me and Vick took me off to supper or dinner at a new place. Made me stop at the office and P and I played whist against Vick and M[aurice] Clark. Went home with Pinney.

Saturday, April 21, 1883: Had a great time cleaning house this a.m. and getting things to right. Then stopped at Mrs. Clapp's and went with her and Mrs. R to bank and saw Milton. Great times today shaking hands, talking East, mines, Indians, etc. Dined at Clapp's, of course, and had good time. All hands seem to think I struck the nail squarely on the head in that interview and I'm glad it gave such satisfaction.

Sunday, April 22, 1883: They think I'm pretty swell. Well I won't be tomorrow. Church this a.m. and met many friends of course. Dined at Stewart's early, then went to Judge Herring's and delivered packages and messages. Warmly welcomed home. I seem to have made quite a reputation for myself by the famous interview. Went to Methodist this evening with Mrs. R, Mrs. B, Mrs. C, M and H.

Monday, April 23, 1883: Well, I'm back again in my rough flannel shirt and the boys say they know me once more. Returned loan to Blinn & Co.

*The killing of Judge Hamilton C. McComas and wife Juniatta, and the kidnapping of their six-year-old son, Charlie, by Apaches led by Chatto, shocked the southwest. The incident occurred on March 27, 1883, along a desolate stretch of road between Silver City and Lordsburg in the southwest corner of New Mexico. Although a sizeable reward was offered for his recovery, Charlie McComas was never found.

this a.m. of $10. Telegram from Nick [Stanton] asking me if I had sold mill. Replied tonight to go ahead and do what he could, that I had not done anything definite. Indians bad yet. Want to go to Sonora as soon as possible with [Maurice] Clark. Dined at Milton's tonight. Wrote Miss Redfern today, suggesting payment of some money on Louis's note to me.

Tuesday, April 24, 1883: Met Woods of Girard Mill today by appointment and had satisfactory talk with him about renting mill, if not sold. Very clever fellow. Must do something as soon as reasonably safe to return to Sonora. Everybody gone from mill and it's at mercy of anyone. Hohstadt and crowd at Custom House. Bad times. Old man threatening as I expected. I'll put a quietus on him some day if he isn't careful and attempts any more funny business. Spent pleasant evening at Pridham's playing whist; all well. Wrote Nick today, Chicago—description of mill and mines.

Wednesday, April 25, 1883: Weather not warm yet, but soon will be. Am now waiting for something to turn up. Can't wait long though. Spent a very pleasant evening at Capt. [W. H.] Seamans [clerk of District Court], Pinney and I; Mrs. S and I played whist against Capt. and P. Very pleasant people indeed.

Thursday, April 26, 1883: Met Godfrey today and had some hot talk over gun, etc. This mill business makes me sick. Dined at Clapp's and met the two consuls, [Joaquin Diaz] Prieto and Pimlio, or something like that, of Tucson.

Friday, April 27, 1883: Wouldn't wonder if mill was attached again from hints Godfrey threw out. It wouldn't be a bad idea to have old Hohstadt scalped. He's a bad egg. I certainly am not going to Sonora in the present state of affairs. Went to Old Guard today with Sumner [Vickers]. Looks as well as ever. Called to see Clark tonight, P, SV and I. Not home.

Saturday, April 28, 1883: Was to go to Hereford today to discharge some freighting men for Vick, but other arrangements were made. Country south of line reported unsafe by correspondent from Oposura, who warns people to be on the lookout now that hostilities are commenced on both sides [of] the line. I propose to retain my scalp yet a while.

Sunday, April 29, 1883: Went to church this morning. Dined at Eccleston's. Church again tonight.

Monday, April 30, 1883: So much time has elapsed that I don't remember much for this week and certainly don't for today. Don't have anything of much importance. I believe that this evening Pinney and I called at Capt. Seaman's to bid the madame goodbye.

Tuesday, May 1, 1883: Mrs. Seamans started for the East. Want Strallus to see her. Miss Brown went to Roty's [Rurty] ranch near Camp Rucker, also this a.m.

Wednesday, May 2, 1883: This evening Pinney, Sumner V and I spent with Clark at his house and had a good time till quite late. Indian news rather discouraging for a Sonora trip at present.

Thursday, May 3, 1883: I wrote Culver about a Sonora land proposition of 150,000 acres. Whist most every night.

Friday, May, 4, 1883: Weather delightful; sprinkly. Street contract expired and its very dusty at times. Shade trees are being planted; cottonwoods mostly—a good idea and one started during the last two months during my absence. About 200 already planted.

Saturday, May 5, 1883: Warm today. TP and I tried revolvers this afternoon in front of my house in gulch. Have got my hand in again pretty well. Dined at Clapp's where were two Misses Herring, Howe and Gladwin and Mr. and Mrs. Fenler—merry dinner party being about three hours at the table. Attended Prompter stock assessment sale today and bid against Knipoly, working things very acceptably to interested parties.

Sunday, May 6, 1883: Church morning and evening. Church matters flourish. Cushions now. Have most all of the modern Christian luxuries. Pleasant call on Miss Peel this afternoon and arranged for Spanish lesson.

Monday, May 7, 1883: Genl Crook is on the right tack at last. Country dangerous though now. Must try to get down there next week. Am afraid Indians have been broken up into small bunches of four and five or more. Sumner Vickers and I took our first Spanish lessons tonight from Miss Peel. I have begun again.

Tuesday, May 8, 1883: A long tramp over the hills today to relocated a piece of property, 540 long by 40 wide, next to Ruby; good ledge running through part of it. Lost the Cedarberg but circumstances were such that I was given option of the small piece and for this services, etc., am to get 3000 shares Ruby mining stock and notes for $450 to pay possible and probable assessments in future. Two or three properties to be consolidated with the Ruby. Ruby a good showing—good mineral there—may make some money. Lewis kindly disposed towards me. Arranged for Clapp to have 1000 shares of the stock. I had no real rights except what were given me and am quite fortunate. Recorded the "Pearl" this afternoon.

Wednesday, May 9, 1883: Large swimming tank being built foot of 5th St. 85 x 13 ft., 13 ft. water. Just in my hand. Some fun ahead. Pring's enterprise. Called on Herrings tonight with Sumner.

Thursday, May 10, 1883: Spanish lesson tonight. Good start—H.H. belongs—Late commencing. Cards as usual later. Father seems desirous I should go to C[entral] America. Possibly I may. S[umner] V may go with me. Must then do something with mill at once. Clark, S and I were jumped for jurors today at office. Special venue in Kinsman-Woodman murder case. My name not on the list of jurors and Capt. S[eamans] found me by not calling my name. Completing list before hand, taking in S and C. It is miserable to be on good terms with the powerful in the land.

Friday, May 11, 1883: Boils started on me again. Couldn't sleep much last night. Hoped to get off for Sonora next week, but Capt Thorndike accosted me today and said a large party of Indians were close to the mill the other day so I won't go Sonoraward yet. Signal fires on Whetstones and Santa Ritas or Mustangs tonight. Hostiles on their way north. They are broken into small bands below probably, and now is time to look out. Spent pleasant hour at [Albert] Springer's tonight. Mrs. S very bright. Deeded over the Pearl today to Ruby G & S Mining Co. Sent $25 draft to Father tonight in payment of difference to him.

Saturday, May 12, 1883: Court opened at 8:30 and I was on hand and heard all of the arguments by Herring and Smith for the people and B Goodrich and Stanford for defense in Kinsman-Woodman murder. First case of kind in Arizona, I believe. Kinsman and father were Milton's and my first tenants in Tombstone. Great interest manifested. Verdict of manslaughter brought in by jury in half an hour.* Dick was foreman. Mark did finely as district attorney. Milton, Judge H, Mark S and H went to Hereford to spend night and Sunday. Invited to go but refused, boil too much. Received 3000 shares of Ruby G & S Mining Co today and notes for $450 yesterday in settlement of recent mining matters between Lewis [and] me. At Clapp's a while tonight and spent balance of evening as usual—cards.

Sunday, May 13, 1883: Took Mrs. C and Mrs. R to church this a.m. and dined with them this evening, taking the old man's place. Mrs. R seems quite serious about bringing about an acquaintance between some wealthy girls, friends of hers and myself. Had much sport over it. Church tonight. Boil very bad. Long talk with John Rankin this afternoon about northern Arizona.

Monday, May 14, 1883: Quiet day. Letters from Culver and Johnston today. Commenced taking sulphur and cream of tartar this a.m. for my blood. John R thinks I shouldn't attempt going to Sonora yet. Indians too bad. Liable to be bad though all summer. Crook and Garcia and Torres will split them all up. John was one of the Tombstone Rangers** and said that my letter [*Tribune* interview] was read aloud to the men in the field and

---

*In front of the Oriental Saloon on the morning of February 23, 1883, Bill Kinsman, "a local sporting man," was shot and killed by May Woodman, apparently for good reason. May had been living with the abusive Kinsman, who according to testimony, had caused her pregnancy. She was sentenced to five years for manslaughter. It was not the first case in Arizona where a woman stood trial for murder, as Parsons asserts. According to the *Arizona Weekly Star* of May 17, 1883, "four or five years ago a woman named Gallegher killed a soldier at Yuma by stabbing him. She was tried for murder, convicted of manslaughter."

**The Tombstone Rangers, a paramilitary group, may have had its inception in September of 1881 when John Clum, Parsons, John Behan, the Earps and others were sloshing across muddy Sulphur Spring Valley in pursuit of marauding Apaches. The group, however, was not sanctioned by gobernatorial action. Official sponsorship came in spring of 1883 when Governor Frederick Tritle authorized formation of militia companies. Tombstoners were quick to respond. At the prompting of county supervisor Theodore White, Judge B. L. Peel, and businessman L. W. Blinn a militia force of sixty men was formed, captained by Milton Joyce. While Captain John Bourke implied that the Rangers did their fighting in the saloons of Tombstone, some did accompany Crook into the Sierra Madres, while others patrolled Cochise County.

that Thurston and Joyce, the Capt, remarked "George gave it to them pretty straight. He hit the nail squarely on its head." Spanish tonight.

Tuesday, May 15, 1883: Dined at Milton's tonight. Attention is being now directed to our part of northern Sonora and the time may soon come when capital will flow in. I hope I may have something before I leave for Central America, as events are shaping themselves for me in that direction. Guess I'll say goodbye to this old journal which has seen so much with me in Sonora and this shall constitute my Sonora journal as I don't think much more remains for me in that portion of the land of mañana and I hope never to go through with so much again with so little to reward me for all I have done and risked.

Wednesday, May 16, 1883: I now begin a new page in a new book and hope its finis will see me more prosperous and I have faith to believe it will. My experiences though hard are not profitless. Now though we want and must have the money—the funds so long fought for. Terrific old boil and it cinches me fearfully. Geo Woodward in town again. Thinks my horse is in Bacuachi. Cards every night. Whist now at Vick's in the evening. Big suit of Copper Prince and Queen on hand now. Rain today.

Thursday, May 17, 1883: Very cool. Pleasant musical entertainment tonight at the Herrings. Went with Clapps, taking Miss Richardson. Milton seriously entertaining Florida proposition. Rock from Central America from father. He's in it now sure. With that and my two land schemes, and other things, I may make some money. Pluto looking well—big thing there I think.

Friday, May 18, 1883: Studied Spanish faithfully today with Howard Herring, and I think we'll tie together on it. He's very bright. Placer gold excitement in Lower Cal[ifornia] exciting attention; some going from here.*

Saturday, May 19, 1883: Cool yet. Johnny Hohstadt on hand today and had a long and satisfactory talk with him. He's a good fellow. May be able to get my horse; gave him brand. Johnny Rankin also on hand and I sent another letter to Davenport. Played casino at the Rector's this evening.

Sunday, May 20, 1883: Church in the a.m. Called on Miss Santee later and gave her pic[ture]. Dined at Clapp's where were Mrs. Earl and son, and in evening churched again and Prof went home with me and we talked political economy, politics, emigration, the South, and Chinese question till nearly midnight.

Monday, May 21, 1883: Lower Cal[ifornia] excitement seems to grow. Many going. Have just gotten more full length pictures struck off and sent them to Mrs. W, Mr. Kip, Sam and Schlaet today. Studied Spanish hard with H H this a.m. Had lesson tonight. Spent evening at [Albert]

*The word of rich gold placers in Lower California between Calmalli and Mission Santa Gertrudis, 450 miles south of the border at Santa Diego, was spread by newspapers in Guaymas and southern California. The result was a minor rush from California and southern Arizona. Tombstoners Nellie Cashman, Milton Joyce, and Jack Ciunin organized one expedition in mid-May 1883.

Springer's where were Mexican Consul Prieto and little girl who sang sweetly.

Tuesday, May 22, 1883: Getting warm at last. Grand nights now. Governor Tritle in town. Milton drove him to Contention for his train today noon and I went to his house and helped get away with a gorgeous repast gotten up for the Gov, but of which he was unable to partake. Cards till quite late in Dick's room.

Wednesday, May 23, 1883: Copper Queen and Copper Prince case argued today. Campbell went for Prof [W. P.] Blake pretty mightily.* Dined at Herrings and later took Mrs. Richardson to Peel's and spent a pleasant evening.

Thursday, May 24, 1883: My prospects heightening. Redfern writes of some one coming with Nick to see mill property—to buy, and father writes flatteringly of Central American prospects, wanting me to go there and take hold and Col Lewis and Bob wants me to see them about assuming charge at Arivaca. So I guess there's a change ahead for me very soon. Had lesson tonight. Am making good headway. Studied with Howard this afternoon and later held his head while Ingersoll pulled a tooth. Stopped in a few minutes at Clapp's and met Cap Seamans and Judge Pinney. Latter rather uncouth, former a perfect gentleman. Went up to Castles to meet Peacock Club, but a reading was in progress when I arrived and not caring to distract it, withdrew. Copper Prince now and Heyne is elevated—appeal though may be advised.

Friday, May 25, 1883: Nick Stanton is back and says he has a buyer for the mill. We'll soon see. Studied as usual with Howard Herring this afternoon. Dined at Milton's.

Saturday, May 26, 1883: Quite warm now, 92, not unpleasantly so. Am to have one of Sycamore Co.'s horses for Sonora trip; so that's fixed. Attended [A. J.] Felter's Court today with Howard to study Spanish as the Consul was being sued on an attachment. Studied later some time, letting dinner go till very late. Am in earnest about this Spanish business and propose to know it in two months more. Called at Clark's to bid Miss Locker goodbye, and then went to Lerridge's for Mrs. Clapp and Mrs. Richardson, where I took then. Cards later with Dick and [A. H.] Bayless.

Sunday, May 27, 1883: Warm. Flies bad in church this a.m. Took Mrs. C and R there. Church in evening and later talked at Mrs. Berry's, bidding her goodbye, as he goes to Cal tomorrow.

---

*Bisbee of the early 1880s was the scene of a legal battle between its two principal mining companies, the Copper Queen and Copper Prince. It happened this way. The Copper Prince had tapped a lense of copper carbonate on the same horizon as the Copper Queen orebody. When it became apparent that the two deposits were related the law of extra-lateral rights, or Law of the Apex, was invoked. Lawyers representing the Copper Prince claimed the apex of the deposit was on their client's land, thus permitting them to follow the ore into Copper Queen property. The Apex Law was upheld in court and the Prince extracted ore from the Copper Queen lode. The controversy was finally resolved when the Copper Queen purchased the Copper Prince.

Monday, May 28, 1883: Spanish lesson tonight and Mrs. Richardson was on hand. Spent evening and took her home. Had quite a Florida talk.

Tuesday, May 29, 1883: Boil business about over I'm happy to say. Must now prepare for Sonora. Must get off Friday or Monday as suits Clark best. Walker gone to Bisbee and I am in office till he returns tomorrow night. Spent evening at Herring's with Mrs. R playing euchre and having a good time till quite late. Went to Fairbanks [sic, Fairbank] this a.m. for Jim Eccleston. Good horse and nice drive. First time there.

Wednesday, May 30, 1883: Decoration Day and observed. Capt Seamans Commander of GAR Post and appropriate and interesting exercises were held at K of Prussia. In W Co. office today working on Eccleston's books for error in April balance sheet. Took Mrs. R to Mrs. Blinn's this evening.

Thursday, May 31, 1883: Well am to start Monday morning with Clark for Sonora, so that's fixed. He proposed a wagon but I preferred horseback, being better in case we were jumped by Indians. Saw a wreck of a youth today I knew in S.F. Thought he'd get to the devil there pretty soon, too bad. Bayless goes tomorrow. Spanish tonight.

Friday, June 1, 1883: Went out to G Hog this am. Examined B Top shaft, risky thing. Bad Indian news again from below. Hope it won't deter us from going. A great time at the camp fire tonight of the GAR Post. Burnside post capt., Seamans commanding. Seamans resigned and Earle elected as Commander. Dined at Milton's this evening, Judge Berry and I.

Saturday, June 2, 1883: I was dished again. Clark is sorry that press of business would prevent going Monday, but Aleck says he talked Indians to him. It seems as though I was fated never to go below again.

Sunday, June 3, 1883: Flies very bad in church this a.m. Took Mrs. R this evening. Wood's man will not go now, so unless Walter will go my trip will have to be abandoned.

Monday, June 4, 1883: Well, I'm dished. No one to go with. Walter unable and I shall not go alone. Cannot go next week as is proposed by a party—Fuller, Berry, J S and Mr. Clark. Walker says I must be on hand for him every day. Too bad and I'm much put out, but cannot help it. Must earn grub for myself here and can't wait on other parties forever.

Tuesday, June 5, 1883: Clark suddenly made up his mind this morning to go to the mill immediately with me as I couldn't go later and wished to get off this afternoon, but later, decided on tomorrow morning, so we'll go then. I can get back Sunday night and Walker will be delayed one day.

Wednesday, June 6, 1883: Well, arose early and once again donned my overalls, put on sombrero and accoutered myself as formerly for the Sonora trip. Friends tried to dissuade me from going as the Indian business was still bad, but I decided to be guided by information at the Custom House, so this was a chance not to be lost for doing something with the mill and was with some risk. Got off about ten a.m. and made Ochoaville in good season. Some changes since I was last here. Found Manuel here. He is superintending several properties in the San Joses nearby which promise well. I was surprised to find that Clark was a first rate Spanish scholar and spoke the Castillian quite well and so were the señoras Korner and Peterson, the former exclaiming about his pronunciation "muy perfecto." After supper Mrs. P played on La Guitarra and sang sweetly and Clark surprised us all again in that line. Todina was also good. Good beds, worn though. Didn't sleep much, not being broken to saddle yet.

Thursday, June 7, 1883: Made a good start this a.m. and in a little while reached the Custom House. Carranza was so glad to see me that he embraced me, Spanish style, and immediately spoke about the newspaper interview I had in Chicago, and how truthful it all was. I sent him a copy as I had something about Mexico I wanted him to see. He was much pleased and considers me a good friend to Mexico. From him I learned that the road was all right, no Indians having been seen lately, but he advised us to look out for them in the grass and be on our guard. A rather tiresome ride to the Frenchman's where were the Hohstadts — all hands, as shiftless, lazy and good for nothing as ever, excepting the hardworking mother. Old man plumb full of gas as usual—is about moving back. Clark and I had good bed in the hay in a shed.

Friday, June 8, 1883: Well, made a good start and got to the mill at last. Was surprised to find everything in good order and pretty much as I had left it. Bob at the house. He seemed well satisfied with the mill, and so expressed himself. I offered in writing just before leaving, one half of mill and mines for $4000, half cash and balance 60 or 90 days and he to supply working capital—our half to be a lien on property. Hard trip into the hills. Claims seemed to please him. Looked at three and returned to Frenchman's by Janarerachi trail after a hard day of it.

Saturday, June 9, 1883: Two prospectors, Morehouse and Hank Purcell, camped at Frenchman's last night. They've been in the hills back of mill but say they haven't got anything. We'll see. M E and I slept on the ground last night with a pup on either side to signal danger. Indians stole some horses out of corral a while ago, but they'd had a good job doing so last night. About midnight a fellow rode into camp from below, Gavilan south of Oposura, and reported Crook as having had a fight one week ago last Tuesday. Number of Indians got away—bad. Bears around this a.m. and I wanted to go on a hunt but we were left with M and P and the other fellow and had a rather pleasant ride to C.H. At Woodward's I dismounted and went into the house. Indians had fired through the key hole, breaking the lock, and the ball went into the opposite wall. At the Springs, 12 miles from the C.H., was camped a large party of New Yorkers; several congressmen, etc. They took especial pains to tell us of the special car they came in to Fairbank. Their fire water was very good and well relished after our long ride. One of their guards, head man I guess, asked about the roads, Indians, etc., and said they were like a parcel of old women and scared to death. Were waiting now for an escort of 21 Mexican soldiers. Col. Cutler's and Jackson's command probably, J was with them. Met Col C, Hawkins, and Tom Farish near the CH, they being obliged to stay behind and fix matters.* C was in a damning mood and I guess they had trouble. A bottle of beer by Carranza made ME, C and me happy. Mrs. Elias, to whom I introduced C, treated us well. Fine mescal, etc. C's fame had preceded us and Mrs. Elias was quite happy. [Reached] Ochoaville about sun down.

Sunday, June 10, 1883: Well, Clark expressed himself as quite well pleased and his willingness to take hold, but wants me with him. Perhaps I can be with him a while. Took a note for him today and letter for Emanuel and left for home while C went off with Emanuel expecting his father and several others this evening on their way to Providencia, fifteen miles west of us over mountains. Made home about 4:30. Eccleston provoked me exceedingly by his disagreeable manners and want of feeling with respect to persons, friends of mine lately killed in Mexico by the Indians, and we had quite a sharp spat. He is very unpopular. I am through with him I think. Stopped at Clark's and gave them the news. Dined at Milton's and got to church late.

Monday, June 11, 1883: Up early and to the tanks on the hill where Walker showed me about the gauges, supplies, etc. With him all day into the night fixing things as he leaves tomorrow for the East to began 40 holidays. No time for Spanish class tonight. Clark on hand this a.m. and leaves tomorrow a.m. for Sonora again, his party being delayed.

Tuesday, June 12, 1883: Walker off this morning. Things went all O.K. today. Mr. and Mrs. Clapp's eighth wedding anniversary today and I sent around a pair of vases. Bagnall and I dined with them.

Wednesday, June 13, 1883: Frank Leslie came in last night or the night before with private dispatches from Genl Crook and a full report of his recent doings. Frank gave me some private information upon my word and honor as a gentleman not to reveal it. He [Crook] is camped [at] Silver

*This is the same Thomas Farish who was Arizona state historian for nearly seven years and the author of an eight volume history of the state. Thomas Edwin Farish was born at Macon, Tennessee, on June 4, 1837, the son of Adam Thomas and Mary Wren (Prather). Thomas at age fifteen, his mother and siblings, followed the gold seeking Adam to California, where he had acquired a store at Marysville. Thomas worked in San Francisco for eighteen months and in 1856 engaged in gold mining along the Feather River and other spots in northern California with younger brother William. In the 1860s Thomas took part in the political affairs of California. As a member of the legislature in 1867-68, he authored a bill which saved to San Francisco thousands of acres of tideland about the bay, and introduced another bill to create a school for the deaf and dumb, and he supported creation of the University of California. In 1879 he and other San Francisco investors purchased the Yellow Jacket and Head Centre claims at Tombstone and formed the Head Centre Consolidated Mining Company, and he came to Arizona as its superintendent. When mining at Tombstone waned Farish went to Phoenix and later took charge of the old Vulture Mine. Farish also engaged in public service, serving as Governor Zulick's personal secretary in 1888, as well as that governor's immigration commissioner. He served in the sixteenth territorial legislature and during the administration of Governor B. J. Franklin served as territorial treasurer. It was during this period that Farish imbarked upon a writing career. In 1904 he published a book of reminiscences, *The Gold Hunters of California*. In 1913 he was appointed state historian and set about compiling a history. That work grew in size, reaching fourteen volumes, which he revised to eight for publication. In 1918 he was striken with an intestinal obstruction (probably cancer) and on October 29, 1919, died in Los Angeles following surgery. He left a wife, Margaret (his second), and two sons, William and Thomas, Jr. For additional details see *Arizona Republic*, October 31, 1919.

Creek, 60 miles east, with several hundred Indian prisoners, all women and children, excepting three dozen bucks, so I don't see where the big victory comes in that is claimed for him, although the imprisonment of the squaws may bring the fighting bucks to terms, as they do all the work.* The fighting men are left in Sonora and situation not much changed it seems to me. No use to return now as rains would impede his progress. There will probably be a rest till fall and some more big killings by Indians—some of those venturesome Sonora rustlers will be picked off yet.

Well, the deuce is to pay—some one having a spite against Walker or me, or possibly one of the opposition Co's men, cut off our supply last night and result was that this morning there wasn't a drop coming into the tanks on hill. Sent out a man over the line who found a plug pulled about a mile out and some rivets taken off, furthermore. Fine state of things. Possibly J[oyce] and D[unbar]'s work, revenge for my assistance in bringing him forward as a dishonest official in recent county matters. He's down on me I know. Went around town in a hurry getting people to let up on water as much as possible, and had breaks repaired, and by noon water was coming in again. Up on the hill a number of times today. Hard work, pressure weak. Fine thing this—just at this time. One party suspected an old employee. Dined at Milton's and went to Schieffelin Hall with Milton, wife, and Harry to see our friends play the *Octoroon*. Very well done as a whole.

Thursday, June 14, 1883: Warm now. Morehouse and Hank Smith got off this a.m., saying they were going south in Mexico, below Gavilan, to see a copper property. Saw them off. Jack Ray on hand and I'm afraid will be a bleeder. Must look out for the Huachuca boys though. Pressure improving and tanks in good condition this a.m., so I feel better; must have more pressure though—only 21, should be 42. Must now go up there again. Took Miss Richardson to Herring's from Miss Peel's and had euchre.

Friday, June 15, 1883: Signs of rain, but none yet. Will be glad when it comes for my tanks and water supply. Pressure back again today. A meter broken last night—so they're at it yet. Well, I'll wear them out if I can't catch them. At Mrs. Blinn's tonight with Mrs. Richardson and Mrs. Herring, euchre. Schools closed today and exercises were held at Schieffelin Hall. Harry did very nicely indeed. I took little Lillian Vickers with me. She's a cute, pretty little thing, very bright. Spanish this a.m. at 10:30.

Saturday, June 16, 1883: Cool and pleasant. Water very low in tanks and I don't like it. Have to follow customers up pretty sharp about wastage and look after several holes. Caught a big leak at Mrs. Hawkins. Stopped a moment at Mrs. Clark's where also was Mrs. Stevens. Mrs. C was alarmed at action of Miss Daisy's horse on the mesa in the distance and wished me to go after her. Rode a new Colorado horse, finest saddle animal in the

*During Crook's campaign in summer of 1883 Frank Leslie was employed by the army to carry dispatches back and forth between the camp on Silver Creek and Tombstone, a distance of ninety miles. His pay was $50.

county, and soon returned with the daughter, all O.K., and one of Prof. James's daughters.

Sunday, June 17, 1883: Miss Santee left this a.m. for Silver City, N.M. From there she goes home to Clinton, Iowa. Bade her adios yesterday. Hot on the hill regulating valves today. Church this a.m. and p.m. Took Mrs. C and Mrs. R this a.m. Milton at Johnson the new mining town at Peabody mine. Returned this p.m., David with them. Clarks and Judge Berry back from Providencia. Warm, wish the rains would begin for my tanks and supply. Reservior cleaned and water coming in. Hope to have full pressure soon. Long talk with Prof [Church] tonight at cabin—religion, evolution, etc. Very intelligent man, but a little off in orthodoxy.

Monday, June 18, 1883: Got draft for $395 Friday from Prof. [John] Church on Walker's road contract. Got c/d [certificate of deposit] for $385 paying 10% on Mrs. Burnett's ac[count]. Cannot use Walker's name at bank so am obliged to take c/d [certificate of deposit] for fear of having to [put] out more on the road account and make this statement in case anything happens to me and c/d is found in my name. Bagnall and a lot of us went up town, B went up with me on the hill and attended to tanks.

Tuesday, June 19, 1883: Very hot day. Was greatly worried today about the water supply. It's getting frightfully low. Hoped ardently for rain, but clouds are not sufficiently heavy yet. Swimming tank or natatorium inaugurated today by Mitchell and Pring. Milton and I tried it, Harry too. Very exhausting. *Octoroon* tonight and I went in late and took Mrs. Walker home.

Wednesday, June 20, 1883: I have ignored the gauges, finding that the S[an Diego] Smelter was satisfied with the flow there and shall do all I can to increase flow into town. Hope rains will soon come. Have a hard time of it looking after wastage and keeping things straight. Hot and exhausting work and I earn my $180 a month with all of this responsibility. It's too big a contract, running this smelter too and its a bad time to have any shortage or to get caught on supply as negotiations may be pending looking towards a sale to the Huachuca Water Co. Today I had a hot time of it giving the city the most of the water and trying to satisfy the smelter too. They got after me this afternoon, but I was just ahead of them. Got my bridle back today at last. Cost $5 to put it and sheath in good order.

Thursday, June 21, 1883: Rains will be along in a few days I think. I hope so, at least skies responding. Had some Spanish this a.m. with H.H. Breakfasted with Mrs. Walker and Franky. Flow better and increasing. Went to the Peacock Club meeting tonight after Spanish. Smelter shut down today for three weeks.

Friday, June 22, 1883: Water increasing and I am correspondingly happy. Worst seems to be over. Spanished this a.m. with H.H. Dined at Clapp's tonight. Mrs. C under the weather again. Fourteen years today since my dear mother passed and went to heaven.

Saturday, June 23, 1883: Water gaining all of the time, buena. Rifle newly sighted and fixed and Charlie Smith and I tried it today and found it shot splendidly. Had to move the sight a very little. At Herring's a while this evening and about ten o'clock Aleck and I tried the baths. They're well patronized—12 feet deep. Good dining, etc.

Sunday, June 24, 1883: Water fine now. Lots of it. Paid Judge Peel $30 on Bassett patent matters today on order of Stanley, my proportion. Church this a.m. Dined at Milton's and staid all evening. Mrs. C down again tonight rather under the weather. Miss R going away in a few days.

Monday, June 25, 1883: Water and pressure all O.K. now. Clouds threatening. Letter from Benson of Cleveland tonight with P.O. order, $5 enclosed "for luck," as he put it, in examination of Blue Top shaft. I refused to make a charge. Spanish tonight and spent evening at Miss Peel's.

Tuesday, June 26, 1883: Hot, 106 and perhaps more. Takes a long time for rain to come. Lots of clouds, wind and signs, but no fluid yet. Dined at Milton's and we all went riding later. Put in new valve at 4th and Fremont Sts tonight. Water lively. Cards at Herring's tonight. Met Miss Peel at store and took her there and home. Mrs R later.

Wednesday, June 27, 1883: Worked on the County bonds this a.m. by request of Supervisor Blinn at his office and at noon $80,000 worth were expressed to California. Lively times getting them ready. Hope County warrants will now soon be worth something near par. Co. I, 6th Cavalry, part of Crook's command, just from the Sierra Madres and the campaign in Mexico came in town today and rested at Dunbar's Corral. Had quite a talk with some of the boys. They had a hard time of it and looked it. Were afraid of the scouts more than once. Had a hard time and a rough one.

Thursday, June 28, 2883: Spanish tonight. A man named Martin wants to lease the mill. Times not what I should like them to be there. Am getting tired of all of this and will pull out at a sacrifice. Expect I'll have to rent the mill at modest figure to avoid probable trouble with H and Hackinson.

Friday, June 29, 1883: Made out bills and worked at the office today till late as I go to the Dragoons tomorrow. Our first heavy rain this evening— hail and wind, a rattler. Went to the Mary A mine today with Deputy Sheriff [Bob] Hatch to purchase on for Clapp and the bank. Pleasant ride on a good mule. Magnificent view from top of mountains where mine is located. Had to climb up mountain on foot about a mile after leaving animals. Stopped at springs and reservoir—all O.K. Tel[egram] from Walker today stating probable transfer of Sycamore property to the Huachuca Company.

Sunday, July 1, 1883: Pleasant day. Attended church a.m. and p.m. Hudson and daughter here with a Miss Culver, also of Tucson, a pretty girl. Dined at Clapp's. Mrs. Berry, with niece Annette, came today.

Monday, July 2, 1883: Started in collecting today and had a race of it all day. Got along better than I expected. Chinamen hard to find. Spanish tonight. I'm the only pupil now. Took Mrs. R to H's a while this evening.

Tuesday, July 3, 1883: Telegraphed Redfern today that he could have my Sonora interests for $300, that I was going to Oregon with Vickers or something to that effect. V wants me to go with him and I will if I can. Am sick of Sonora and will sacrifice to get out. I haven't any more money nor time to fool away there, nor do I propose to risk my life there any more. Indian business far from settled. May be worse than ever. Spent a delightful evening at Herring's. Quite a number present. Dancing, music, etc., in honor of Miss Culver, Hudson, and C, I suppose.

Wednesday, July 4, 1883: The glorious 4th. Tel[elgram] from Walker this a.m. that trade was consummated, or rather, that came yesterday and another today to stop wagon. There'll be some howling now. Milton and I billiarded this a.m., and this afternoon after the storm was nearly over, Prof [M. M.] Sherman and I started for Kendall's grove just beyond Fairbank, where a picnic was in progress. Arrived about time they were breaking up, but had lots of fun on the road home via Boston Mill. I rode a little mule, a funny little fellow and gave the others lots of sport. Once while picking up dirt from the saddle to throw into a buggy ahead, the saddle turned but I landed on my feet. That sight was the occasion of much joy. I rode in the middle entering town and caused much merriment. Milton had a lot of fireworks and I helped him set them off tonight. Quite a display. No public action by City authorities, but the citizens took matters in hand as individuals and did well.

Thursday, July 5, 1883: Pushed collecting lively today Am anxious to get in all I can before fact of sale becomes generally known. Called on Mrs. Goodfellow and later stopped a while at Peacock Club.

Friday, July 6, 1883: At it again lively today with good results—some considerable kicking about wagon being taken off. Church social tonight at old Court House, very pleasant affair; rather sultry though. $77 taken in and a little over $40 cleared. Took Mrs. Reppy home. Danced considerably and had otherwise good time. Quite a number out.

Saturday, July 7, 1883: The old fraud Hohstadt in town, I suppose to see what's to be done. I'll have to rent mill to Martin I guess to preserve peace in the family. Old man as crazy as ever about his mine. It would be a good thing for him and his family could the Indians catch him. Wish I could never see or hear of him again. Spent evening with Mrs. R at Supervisor Blinn's. Milton and wife called but didn't stay. Col. [J. S.] and Mrs. Clark and Judge and Mrs. Herring on hand, cards, euchre and cribbage. Fire at Blue Stone [& Reduction] Works today; damage slight, insured. Good swim this afternoon; rather exhausting.

Sunday, July 8, 1883: No morning service at any of the churches. Breakfasted at Clapp's. Dined there also. Church this evening slim attendance.

Monday, July 9, 1883: Getting collections well in hand. Mr. Davis arrived today from the East. Called at house and we all had a good time.

Tuesday, July 10, 1883: Have leased mill to Martin to January 1, 1884, at $100 per month and other agreements. Am sick of this whole thing. Feel better now that trouble is obviated below by Martin's working the old fraud's rock and Hackinson's. This is a good stroke as a law suit for damages was impending and everything might have been lost.

Wednesday, July 11, 1883: Spent a very delightful evening last evening. Mrs. Clapp invited some 40 or 50 of Mrs. Richardson's and her own friends to meet at Judge Berry's house—cards, singing, dancing and a general circus at the end were had. Milton and I, with Bagnall, were left on the kissing business. I don't go much on that kind of thing. Prof. Church, Supervisor [Theodore] White and Major Earle on hand. Hunted Reppy till late but couldn't find him. Good swim this afternoon.

Thursday, July 12, 1883: Showery. Mrs. Richardson, good, clever old soul, and Mr. Davis left today for San Francisco. Mrs. R leaves behind a multitude of friends who will miss her. Mrs. Clapp especially will miss her. Spanish lesson tonight and spent evening at Peel's.

Friday, July 13, 1883: Rain once in a while, cleaning atmosphere. Commenced on books today, not much of a job. Short week's work. More Indian deviltry below, worse than ever. Crook has failed. Met Señora Elias and Señorita O and madre at Peel's this evening where I went to get Miss P to translate into Spanish a letter I wished to give S[umner] V[ickers] and Prof. Sherman who goes to Sonora tomorrow. Called first at Miss B[essie] Brown's. Good collection today of school bill, $256, through Judge Herring.

Saturday, July 14, 1883: Dug Grey left for Denver today as our Commissioner to mining exposition. Sumner and Sherman left this a.m. About noon I got a saddle horse and went to see the baseball match. Red, our boys, against Grand Central's. Quite a number present. Our fellows ahead when I left with the Clarks. Rode home in their carriage and let Locker have my horse. Good swim this afternoon. Dined with Milton and in evening went to Goodriches, meeting his wife and self there, also Judge and Mrs. Berry, Annette, Col. and Mrs. Clark and Miss D.C. Little Cora Goodrich recited for us and it was the most wonderful thing I ever saw or heard for one so young. She's a remarkably interesting child.

Sunday, July 15, 1883: Warm day. Dined at Milton's after writing a lot of letters, and we called on Mrs. Reppy later, and I went to church. Saw Mrs. and Miss [Daisy] Clark home and staid a while.

Monday, July 16, 1883: Want rain again now. Studied Spanish three hours this a.m. and now have the auxiliary and regulars very well. Must now go for the irregulars. Took my first every day lesson this a.m. and shall now push ahead all I can. Spent evening at Miss Peel's as Major Earle goes East tomorrow a.m. Stopped first at Herring's a while. Bade Dr. and Mrs. Robertson farewell who also leave tomorrow.

Tuesday, July 17, 1883: Was invited by Professor [J. A.] Church of the Tombstone Mill & Mining Co. to dine with him this evening and Bagnall being also invited. We reached there about six p.m. and presently along came Judge and Miss Peel. Didn't rise from the table till nearly nine o'clock and had a very delightful evening. After Miss Peel and father left, Professor and I beat Bagnall and Pennington at whist. Pennington a very clever and nice fellow indeed. Prof a man of remarkable vigor of intellect; very agreeable and not pedantic with all of his knowledge.

Wednesday, July 18, 1883: Study every morning now and am doing all I can to succeed in Spanish. President of the two companies coming and I have some entertaining and wire pulling to do. Books journalized. Not much bookkeeping. Billiarded this afternoon with Clapp and this evening was spent at Mrs. Clapp's.

Thursday, July 19, 1883: Estudiare español as usual this morning. Tel from FW this a.m. to sell work horses at $300. Called on Mrs. Goodfellow this evening, later at Castle's, and ended at Herrings, where I talked Florida till 11:30. Beautiful nights these—cannot be beaten in the world anywhere.

Friday, July 20, 1883: Spanish as usual this morning. Its confounded hard work but I'll stick to it now. Wrote up books so as to be in shape for the president when he arrives. Rain this afternoon. Dined at Clapp's. Croquet and music and home and bed very early. First time I've been to bed at ten o'clock in many months. Usually 11:30 to 12 and one. Too late but nights too glorious and people don't seem to care to go [to] bed these times.

Saturday, July 21, 1883: No president yet. Binnet back with stolen horse. Good job. Charley off with team for the Huachucas; contract job. My good friend from the Mexican Custom House on the San Pedro in town. Carranza and I will try to return some favors. Later Carranza dined with me and we had a pleasant time together; clever fellow.

Sunday, July 22, 1883: Took things quite easy. At Spanish part of morning. Dined at Clapp's as usual. Church later, good attendance tonight.

Monday, July 23, 1883: Spanish as usual this a.m. Spent evening at Pridham's, Miss B not home. Fine weather; showery at times.

Tuesday, July 24, 1883: Everything quiet. Letter from Sec of Co tonight telling me to keep accounts apart after June—rather late. Spanish this evening. Evening at Miss Peel's. Miss Herring there.

Wednesday, July 25, 1883: Things still in status quo. Invitation from Prof Church to afternoon party or kettle drum Friday afternoon at four p.m. At office on business, Frank's wood contract, and Prof took me to one side and proposed a manganese ore scheme in connection with a mine here, which I am to work up for our mutual benefit. Tonight, or afternoon rather, Milton and I played some billiards and I dined with him. No we didn't play—I watched him and Judge Herring.

Thursday, July 26, 1883: Well, time is hurrying us all along. It skips along at a pretty lively rate. Milton's 35 today—opened some champagne at his office in bank in honor of the event and was bathed with it pretty well. Went off too soon.

Friday, July 27, 1883: A day of dissipation. Attended Prof Church's kettle drum this afternoon and church social in the evening. We were all made happy. Quite a crowd at Churches. Pennington put up a job on me at whist. Lively times. Well, this evening closed festivities at the old Court House. Danced and carried on till midnight.

Saturday, July 28, 1883: Spent evening at Clark's where I had been invited. Invited to dine there tomorrow but must go to Mrs. Clapp's instead. Miss Daisy Clark plays well. With singing by ME, playing by his sister— champagne, etc., we all had a jolly good time.

Sunday, July 29, 1883: Services twice a day again. Took a plunge at Natatorium this a.m., just a block from my house. Bagnall's brother dying of consumption and he starts East tomorrow a.m. It wouldn't surprise me if he and Miss Peel arranged things to his satisfaction, to say the least, tonight. She's a lively girl and should marry so that she would have an easier time in life than she has had or would have with Bagnall. Women are still very queer beings though to date. Dined as usual at Clapp's.

Monday, July 30, 1883: Walker arrives tonight. Will send carriage for him. Tel[egram] this a.m. I will get $300 out of the Co. if nothing; that's pretty good. Paid Church contract of $15 yesterday and am happy. Spanish I think as usual tonight. Maurice Clark gave the girls leaving an entertainment at his house this evening. Quite a number present, music, dancing.

Tuesday, July 31, 1883: I saw Mr. Hale before Walker this a.m. Is the great piano manufacturer of N.Y. City said to be worth $15,000,000. Had a little talk with him but didn't like him very well. Walker looks well indeed and had considerable to say. He and Hale get along well together. Guess I am to collect next month, so may be able to squeeze out two months.

Wednesday, August 1, 1883: Am working ahead still, not doing much of anything. Spent evening pleasantly at Miss Peel's; Miss Herring on hand. Prieto and Josephina spent part of evening, singing, etc. Carranza in town again and very anxious to get the mill for Señor Flores, offered me $200 per month rent for it, but of course I couldn't do anything having rented it to Martin till Jan. 1 at $100. Seems just my luck. Offered to sell for $6500 subject to lease. Wish I could get a few hundred or a thousand out of it. Dined at Clapp's and croqueted later till dark.

Thursday, August 2, 1883: Was to meet Carranza at eight o'clock, but he misunderstood hour and didn't appear. He will be soon back from the Aduana and I will go for him. Spent this evening also at Miss Peel's— whist—Miss Herring and I beat. Judge arrived during evening—didn't like because we couldn't have ice cream.

Friday, August 3, 1883: Hale went to S.F. yesterday. Will be gone about a week or ten days. Am still on deck, but nothing much to do. Some whist tonight at Vick's. ME and I beat. Later went with Sherman to do some electioneering as Catholics are working to get the school monies by tomorrow's election. Was asked to help and carriage placed at my disposal for tomorrow. Must do what I can.

Saturday, August 4, 1883: A very exciting day. Walker had to go out of town on business and wished me to start in on collections and get in all I could. Worked till about noon and then I couldn't help pitching in and working for the old beard Clark. Hudson and Hartmann against Springer, Levan (alias Allen) and Joe Pascholy. The last two disreputable characters and anxious to handle the monies just received by sale of school bonds. Ladies could vote and I went for all I knew of—dragged down some of the fellows—changed some tickets at door and ran in the last voter, a Mexican girl. Lots of fun though. Much hard work. A good feeling was raised this afternoon and it didn't take much persuasion to have votes cast the right way and save the honor and credit of our town. Total vote 776 to 96. Four and a fraction more to one, a big victory. No more attempts by priests and thieves will be made I think to get at the public monies. Dined at Milton's and took Miss Reppy home later.

Sunday, August 5, 1883: Breakfasted at Milton's. Bagnall East but services were held as usual. I was wanted to read the services but not being familiar with them, was afraid of making mistakes. I did, however, read the lessons and greater continuous part of the service, Frank Earle reading the rest. Trying to one's voice to read so long, continuously—slim attendance. Beauty of Episcopal service being able to have a church without any minister. Sermon skipped but services occupied an hour. No services tonight. Spent evening at Herring and dined there.

Monday, August 6, 1883: Collected pretty lively today. Markle in today and Pinney and I talked Spanish with him. Had lesson tonight and showed Miss Peel some pictures, giving her one of mine.

Tuesday, August 7, 1883: Collecting again today. Lesson with Markle again, conversation. Bought a sombrero today, a $20 hat for $10, souvenir of Mexico. Quite elegant. Dined with Milton and Mrs. C.

Wednesday, Augst 8, 1883: Walker back. At it collecting today. Time nearly up now. Jumping today.

Thursday, August 9, 1883: Rather stiff today from jumping yesterday. Head out of order too. Felt rather badly.

Friday, August 10, 1883: My two months up today. Unable to read, write or do anything today on account of my head and eyes. In a bad way. Been applying myself too much studying Spanish.

Saturday, August 11, 1883: John Davis arrived today to take Ralph's place in the bank. Miss Peel, Frank and I spent evening at Miss Herring's. Found Major Earle home from the East on our return.

Sunday, August 12, 1883: French Price back and he read service. I helped in the choir. Mrs. Robertson, Pennington and I sang while Judge Mitchell played. Dined at Clapp's and then tried Maurice Clark's horse, a magnificent animal, finest in this part of the country. Felt very good and ran some distance, I having only plain bit by mistake and not a curb—were gran caballo y un magnifico caballo. HH makes me tired.

Monday, August 13, 1883: Well, I close up things today and tomorrow and then will end the old Sycamore Springs Water Co., $57,000 is a good price and stockholders should feel good. I took Miss Daisy Clark out this afternoon by request of her mother horseback riding and we had a delightful ride. She is a very remarkable girl for her age, just 13. Is very remarkable indeed. Is accomplished in music and languages, rides finely, talks wonderfully well and is very attractive. A truly remarkable girl and one calculated to make a stir in the world. Is seven years or more ahead. A man rode up to us in a great hurry, asking if a party had passed us with several horses, he saying they had been stolen from him and dashed on. Thinking there might be shooting we turned back.

Tuesday, August 14, 1883: Spanish tonight and spent evening at Miss Peel's. Am not studying enough.

Wednesday, August 15, 1883: Made trial balance today and came out right to a cent the first time. Felt pretty good. Have made $372 out of the Co. in two months and two days, so have done pretty well. [J. S.] Clark is catching it all around and is so unpopular that he will probably leave and Walker take his place—looks that way. Can go in myself then I suppose. Rather fine ride with Miss Clark this afternoon.

Thursday, August 16, 1883: Finished matters today with SW Co. and it is a thing of the past. ME, C got back today and I was invited to dinner at Clark's in honor of Miss Daisy's birthday. Kadish, the Misses James and Miss Rouse present and we all had a jolly time of it.

Friday, August 17, 1883: Co. matters still hang on—something to do every day. Methodist dinner tonight at Court House and a lot of us went. Not much of a dinner, but a good time. Entertainment in evening not much fun.

Saturday, August 18, 1883: Studied pretty well today and had lesson tonight. Played euchre later.

Sunday, August 19, 1883: Church this a.m. French Price read service. After dinner rode with Maurice Clark on his sister's horse and stopped at house a while, where were the Rouses. Am wanted to join Maurice, C and Kadish on a trip through Mexico. Thunder and lightning; lightning bad. Prostrated Mrs. Stephens and [W. K.] Meade at Merrimac House and shocked Prof Church and Mrs. Cheyney at Charleston. Milton and wife returned today from short visit there. Sister just arrived in San Francisco. Impossible for me to go, am very sorry.

Monday, August 20, 1883. No lesson tonight. Miss Peel away at Charleston. Called on Mrs. Goodfellow this evening.

Tuesday, August 21, 1883: Spanish tonight and Clapp's later where were the Goodriches.

Wednesday, August 22, 1883: Am a late bird in mornings now. Fence carried away again. I'll lay for them tomorrow—makes me pretty hot. Quite a time at Clark's tonight. A lot of us gave another entertainment to the young ladies, the balance going away in a few days to school again. That is, a few of them. I'm at the time of life now when I run with young, old, and find both congenial. I can never grow old and take as much and keen on enjoyment as ever in games and sport of all kind, and enjoy as much questions of the day and their discussion with old heads. I am enjoying life quite well, but wish to be fixed. Don't believe I ever will be unless marriage does it. I think more of a certain young lady now than of anyone else outside of my family, a noble character and direct descendant of a famous English barrister. Wonder what the result will be. It is in God's hands.

Thursday, August 23, 1883: Studied well today, several of us. I had a good swim today, nice fresh water. After Spanish tonight I took Miss P to Herring's by appointment and we had a good time playing cards. Am getting along very well now in Spanish and can see progress.

Friday, August 24, 1883: A little warm. Am wanted to join a party going to Judge Gray's in the Huachucas [Parsons errors here. Gray's ranch was located at old Camp Rucker at southern end of the Chiricahua Mountains] to be gone a week. Am considering. Spanish lesson tonight.

Saturday, August 25, 1883: Maurice Clark rode around this a.m. before I'd left the house and said that his mother would not go unless I went as she was afraid of Indians and thought I was. Well, everyone should be in case of any engagement—so that settled it. I wished to wait till Monday as tomorrow is my birthday, and Sunday too, but arrangements ordained otherwise. Maurice tried the four in hand and things were gotten ready. Spanish tonight and Miss Peel and I went to Herring's a few minutes and then ice creamed.

Sunday, August 26, 1883: Thirty-three years old today. Am trotting along pretty lively now. Walking hitherto. Times seems to go faster and faster the older I grow. Well, I arose early and took cup of coffee at Aleck's and about 6:30 or 6:45 we got away. A fine four in hand driven by Maurice, a capital whip. Miss Daisy in first with him while in back seats were Mrs. Clark and Mrs. Robertson and baby and Bela Kadish and myself. Fine drive by Turquoise to [G. W.] Sanderson's [at Soldiers Hole], 25 miles, where we stopped and refreshed man and beast. J. V. Vickers and family drive up about same time or little later and we had quite a party.

After fine lunch here we drove on and when about 18 miles further our right leader fagged out and we were in a fix. Close to Linderman's, but no help there, so I saddled the other leader, and with Miss Daisy mounted on her horse Dilly which we were leading behind, but which was not a driving animal, pushed on to Cavil's a mile or two ahead for assistance. Found him but he had no horses except one saddle animal, so on we pushed to Gray's while Cavil went to the ambulance to tell them. Lonely road and ride through a deep cañon and Miss Daisy was rather nervous about Indians. Hard work to pacify her. Finally after much shouting and noise the dogs at Gray's set up a howl and we found our way there. House off the road and not on it as Cavil said. After something to eat, I started back thinking that Mrs. Clark might be worried. As black as Egypt threatening rain, thundering and lightning and my horse lost the road. Finally found it again but went wrong direction. Knew by lay of country that I must be wrong and was about turning back when a light ahead appeared which startled me as I didn't think there another ranch nearabouts. Thinking it might be Sonora Apaches returning to reservation, as soldiers were awaiting them here some time, and also thinking it might be robbers, I pulled six shooter and rode up. Discovered that it was the hermit's place, old Dr. Munroe's. He put me on the back track and in course of time I reached the gate. Thought my trouble was now over, but horse again left the road, and after much wandering about over hills and through the dark woods, I was about to get off and crawl into some hole or under a tree or bush till morning when I stumbled into the road again and there 200 yards ahead was a light, my destination. All hands were safe at Cavil's and in a little while beds were fixed. Cavil and Kadish slept in wagon while Mrs. Clark slept on floor of the one room house, Miss Robertson and infant on the bed and Maurice and I together on the floor.

Monday, August 27, 1883: Break[enridge] came down with fresh horses this a.m., accompanied by Miss Daisy horseback, and Maurice went back for the sick leader, returning pretty soon with news that he had died. Rather bad. Finally reached Gray's all right. Camp Rucker, Judge Gray's place, is a beautiful spot in the Chiricahua Mountains, delightfully situated. An old government post, fine adobe houses, plenty of water. A very desireable spot.* Slept on floor. Good bath, swim in fact in quite a deep pool.

Tuesday, August 28, 1883: All hands visited the hermit's today and had quite a talk with old Munroe, who claims to be a descendant of the president. Is 71 years old and in his day probably was a man of some local reputation. He has a tunnel through a hill 128 feet long with gates and houses on either side at each end. Object of tunnel was, he told me, to try and find coarse gold as he thought he would cross an old river or gravel bed. Old man disconnected in his talk and a great talker.

Kept on up the cañon to saw mill, which much to my surprise, proved to be the old Tanner and Hayes outfit which was in the Huachucas close to our quartz mill two years ago. Saw Tanner and had quite a talk. Music, quitar, singing, talk, etc., made the evening pass pleasantly. Gray's household consists of himself and most estimable wife, a lively character; daughter Mrs. Hall engaged to Cavil. Adopted daughter, Miss Emma Fish, and John Gray at present in San Francisco. The old lady is as fresh and young as possible though 56 and accomplished an immense amount of work in a very quiet way. All are very kind and attentive.

*Michael Gray acquired title to Camp Rucker in December 1882, upon its abandonment by the army, and turned the site into a working ranching, stocking it with a few hundred head of cattle obtained from John Chisum. The Gray ranch was also known for its luscious peach and almond trees.

Wednesday, August 29, 1883: Maurice and I visited old Munroe today and had a chat with him. A pretty good walk. Drank some sulphur water from his sulphur spring and brought away some corn and melons, the latter not very ripe. Wild pigeons numerous. Eat them every day.

Thursday, August 30, 1883: Great time with a bronco mustang today which threw Cavil and nearly broke his neck. Mounted him successfully twice although he plunged and carried on. Last time I was not so quick and landed behind saddle. Was chucked off but not hurt and it took several hours to catch him. Ladies implored me not to remount, and Maurice didn't want me to. Mrs. Rob implored in name of my sister who was coming to see me and there was a great time. I would have either mounted or killed him. The judge blindfolded him and I landed in saddle all right. Didn't stir; quite a joke. Let him go through the woods after blind was taken off and gave him all he wanted a few minutes. Bad on the road some of time, but a dose of spurring fixed him. Examined a place of Munroe's which he wanted Maurice to go in with him on. Small spring on hill side and some good bottom land. Music again tonight. Tomorrow we go.

Friday, August 31, 1883: Up at day break and hunted horses all morning—all hands of us, vaquero and all. At last I found and brought them up and at 12:30 we bade farewell to our kind host and hostess and left with "Billy" in the wheel and he worked very well. Too late to go though, so we camped at Sanderson's. Mrs. C and daughter slept in wagon while we fellows camped on the porch. Soldiers Hole about as I saw it two years ago, when with the Earps, I was after Indians.

Saturday, September 1, 1883: Reached town about noon. Pants badly gone and I had to handle myself carefully. Nothing new except Aleck tearing around and raising old Ned. Good swim this afternoon. Dined at Milton's. Visited with Dunbar this evening about the horse and got him to believe that it was all right. A well sound horse would have stood the trip O.K.

Sunday, September 2, 1883: French read the morning service as usual. Very few present. Day slipped away quickly. Dined at Milton's. Was given a champagne dinner in honor of my birthday, which I was to have a week ago. Hard time tonight with Aleck. Got him home finally, then Maurice and Bela stopped at my house till late.

Monday, September 3, 1883: Wish I was in San Francisco with sister, but can't very well help myself. Must do something with the mill now. Reppy got it on me pretty bad. A paragraph in the *Epitaph* yesterday read, "It is said that Geo. Parsons went to Capt. Gray's ranch to break colts, but one bronco caballo came nearly breaking Geo." Result was that about everybody in town went for me unmercifully. Aleck got off today with Dr. Willis for the Chiricahuas to bring back his wife. Will have to run the store somehow.

Tuesday, September 4, 1883: Things very quiet. Went to theatre tonight to see Nellie Boyd. Miss Daisy, Miss Rouse, Maurice, Kadish and I. Too small an audience for profit, money returned. Spent evening at Rouse's.

Wednesday, September 5, 1883: Expect to go to the Chiricahuas soon. Dined at Clark's tonight. Miss Rouse there. Judge and Mrs. Dibble called.

Thursday, September 6, 1883: Aleck and wife back last night and the County is now safe. Saw one of the boys from mill who said that Hohstadt will be here with bullion Saturday night.

Friday, September 7, 1883: Dined at Milton's and later played him some billiards.

Saturday, September 8, 1883: Quite a tramp over the hills today with Kadish. Visited Ground Hog, Bassett, Eucalyptus, Ruby, Prompter and Luckson. Pretty good pull afoot. Pleasant talk with Streidinger this evening. Very pleasant fellow. Told me I was one of most popular men in town. Pleasant to hear but don't see any money in it.

Sunday, September 9, 1883: Cavil and Mrs. Hall came to town Saturday afternoon and were privately married by Judge Peel at Occidental. Cavil told me aside that he forgot to bring in a single thing of a bundle he had prepared to bring in of goodly wedding apparel and didn't have even a clean pair of socks. Pretty good. Quite a talk with J. S. Clark yesterday who wants me to join Maurice in a trip to Chihuahua, Durango, etc., after lands and mines. Don't know. Fine music this a.m. Bagnall back; good attendance; attended tonight. Called on Mrs. Goodfellow later.

Monday, September 10, 1883: Maurice after me to go to Chiricahuas. Must wait till I hear from bullion and Flores at Nogales. Hohstadt in town today saying that no bullion would come until first of month. He lied though, as I learned later on having brought some himself. I wish I was clear of him. Letter from Nogales; nothing there.

Tuesday, September 11, 1883: No Chiricahuas at present. Clark goes to Sonora with Rountree rather unexpectedly and I decided to do the Huachucas as I can have the use of Maurice's horse, George.

Wednesday, September 12, 1883: Kadish got horse and went with me. We left and returned one and two o'clock. Met Joe Rayenard (French Joe) on the road. Several miles this side of Charleston I got off horse to shoot as he wouldn't stand and he got loose. We all chased him an hour or more and at last the boys had to drive him to Charleston while I walked. Got a lift with Burns. Took quite a number to catch him. Corraled him at Carr's. Geo very frisky. Had a time mounting him at T. Made Tanner's Canyon after dark and camped.

Thursday, September 13, 1883: Went to Ramsey's Canyon and over the mountains to west side. Hard climb. Stopped at Preston's saw mill a while on east side and at Mores on other side, where we rested and had a bite. Queer old fellow, More—good hearted and hospitable. Terribly rough descent. We would have to slide in places and pull horses down same way. Left Joe at foot and went to Sunny South Mine. Got fine specimens and continued. In middle of woods met Hart with two others who had been to examine a mine—strange meeting in this out of the way part of country. We camped at Pat Maloney's. Slept in wagon. Strange as to coldness on this side and warmth on other side of mountains. North and east side should be coldest. Great time spinning yarns. Indians gave Pat close shave at time they killed Billy Murray.

Friday, September 14, 1883: Went to old mill site this a.m. Window frames gone, houses standing. Not a drop of water coming into tank. Never saw water so scarce in Arizona before, canyons comparatively dry. Crossed by way of Tanner's and went to Miller's Canyon to find [Ed] Stump's camp which we finally reached after tiresome pull up mountains a mile along the reservoir, for it is in this canyon where the main reservoir is supplying Tombstone with water. Well received by Ed and Mottier and had a fine supply. Hard picking for caballos up steep mountain side. All shut in at Stumps. Fine large pines, bracing air and we slept well under the trees.

Saturday, September 15, 1883: Visted Stumps lead and free milling properties. Best I've seen in Huachucas. Hard climb to them. They're making adobes for a smelter. Stopped at reservoir on way down and for first time used telephone* and asked for Clapp after talking with Clark at office on Allen St., city. Fred Smith responded, Fulton having left for the post as I expected. Great invention; talking 30 miles and understanding and distinguishing voices. Crossed mountains into Hunter's Canyon afoot, passing Douglas's place and were soon at Mustang's in Ash Canyon were was Miss Sarah and Birdie Herring. The latter though was sick. After dinner Miss Herring and I practiced with my six shooter and we all gathered corn for us to take and roast at Tanner's tonight where we were to camp. Left late in afternoon carrying a present to Miss Peel, an emblem of extraordinary honesty, small ear of corn which was first plucked. Upon reaching the only house on the road running along base of mountains at a point nearly opposite Ramsey's, we heard loud voices at the house in a gulch and riding to top of hill in a minute saw a man shoot another with a rifle, killing him instantly and then apparently go towards a woman to kill her. We were at a terrible disadvantage, having only six shooters and no rifles, but decided to act and break for him if the woman was to be attacked. A few seconds though showed us that there was no such intention and we wheeled off to one side to await developments as there seemed to be more yet to come, other parties being around. We rode a short distance and then were called to return which we did.

I then told Kadish to stay behind and I would ride up and find out what I could from the shooter. I rode to within about 50 feet of him when he cornered me, halting me, saying not to come any nearer, that he was well fixed, was not a bad man and had to do it. I replied, I only wanted to shake hands and see how things were but he wouldn't have it. [He] sat there near body of fellow just killed with two rifles, ordered his horse and spurs from another and mounting, rode away across the plains to R Canyon with the rifles on pommel of saddle, first though telling us to stop until he passed. I hollered out we'd give him a show and away he went. Jones, cattle man, killed James. Think I knew James in Sonora. Didn't recognize

*The telephone line between Tombstone and the reservoir in Miller Canyon was completed in April 1882. *Mining and Scientific Press*, April 8, 1882.

one another. Aggravated case. Didn't stop at Tanner's, thinking that our horses might be wanted in the night, so pushed on to the post and got there about nine. Clapps there. Good sleep in corral in the hay.

Sunday, September 16, 1883: Roasted our corn up canyon and it went pretty well. Saddled Kadish's horse and Mrs. C rode on Nance's saddle, Harry behind her about three miles up canyon while Milton, John Davis, K and I walked. Took a few shots there with Milton's rifle and I plugged the bulls eye. Returned in time for lunch. Lunched and dined with Milton and started homewards about six, I riding my horse and K in carriage leading his. Beautiful moonlight night and nice riding. My stirrup broke and at Charleston I got in carriage and K rode his horse. No news of killing in Huachucas until we brought it. Another killing by rustlers or Indians at Antelope Springs of Ward, for whom we all brought in a letter when passing there coming home from Chiricahuas. We were asked if we had seen Indians as they seemed to be at it again, but we had not.

Monday, September 17, 1883: Took things easy today. Social tonight and I took Miss Daisy and Miss B[essie] B[rown] by request, except latter there. I had to. I make it a point not to take girls out so far. Pleasant time.

Tuesday, September 18, 1883: Maurice returned today and is desirous of my accompanying him to Sonora about 50 miles from Guaymas where are some plumbago or graphite and marble properties, offering me a $^1/_{15}$ interest or $^1/_5$ of his $^1/_3$ if he takes hold. Must write East immediately to see about California. Started in to do collecting today for Eccleston (Jim) on Carr's account. Heavy collections. Some Spanish tonight—Pinney and I together. Billiard later with Milton and Maurice and then the latter and I stopped at CP few minutes. Benefit night, very tiresome.

Wednesday, September 19, 1883: Collecting again today. Wrote East, very busy. Took short ride with Maurice this afternoon. Lesson tonight.

Thursday, September 20, 1883: Collecting still holds out. Clark quite in earnest about Sonora. Must find out something definite from father.

Friday, September 21, 1883: Wrote Redfern. He must come instantly and take my place in the mill racket. Dined at Clapp's tonight. Billiards later with Milton and Maurice.

Saturday, September 22, 1883: Spanish tonight after a break of a few days. With Pinney part of evening; he goes East shortly. Then to JE's room where a grand time was being had. Music and we serenaded Pinney's later and he pulled two revolvers on us. Tried to get away and two of the boys chased me back—out ran them the second time.

Sunday, September 23, 1883: Service this a.m. Good sermon by Bagnall. Dined at Clapp's about five or six where were Judge Dibble and wife, and Rouse, wife and daughter. Champagne dinner and a very pleasant time.

Monday, September 24, 1883: Lots of people just in from Sonora. Yellow fever very bad in Guaymas and Hermosillo.* Don't fear it much here.

*Outbreak of yellow fever at Guaymas was at first denied, the contagion being blamed on "a very malignant type of malarial fever." Whatever it was, according to the Tucson *Weekly Citizen* of September 22, 1883, it claimed 1,000 to 1,500 lives between August 16 and September 20, 1883.

Wonderful how facts become distorted back East. The papers there an-nounce killing of poor Ward by Indians jumping a stage seven miles from Tombstone, or rather jumping on it. They don't seem to know the differ-ence between jumping and jumping on. Bad state of things below. Capt. Seamans and wife arrived tonight, also Judge Berry. Mrs. Colby here from Deming.

Tuesday, September 25, 1883: Bob Darrah back, so my job is done. Bade the Dibbles goodbye this evening, they go to S.F. to reside.

Wednesday, September 26, 1883: Drove to Benson with Maurice today. He had light buggy and Billy was one horse; 25 miles, 3½ hours, good time. San Pedro Valley wonderfully changed since I last rode through it 3½ years ago or more. Bottom lands all taken up and some fine ranches are on the river. Were welcomed by Mr. Saulsberry [Monroe Salisbury], owner of the smelter, and later by Mr. and Mrs. Sweeney, former, nephew of Rouse, and capital fellow. Maurice came down to see about a batch of ore sent down to be smelted from the Way Up. Benson pretty well destroyed by a late disastrous fire. No accommodations to speak of. Dined with the Sweeneys at Salisbury's and were made comfortable on the porch where we camped for the night after spending a very pleasant evening in the Sweeneys' cozy little home and looking at the smelter in operation in the night time, a pretty sight. Terrible sickening smell in night, the smoke be-ing blown in our direction. The arsenic in the smoke was very bad.*

Thursday, September 27, 1883: Up early. After breakfast examined smel-ter. Mr. Sweeney, who is running the whole thing, a Frieburg man, kindly explaining everything. Saw eastern bound train arrive and depart and met some Tombstoners, among them Diss who had a long story to tell, his side of his shooting matter. Wound similar to Garfield's. Wonder he didn't die. Had on some pants with mark of one of the shots in the leg. Left in season to arrive at Tombstone in time for six o'clock dinner at Clark's. Called at Rouse's and spent part of evening. Morey there of Louisiana.

Friday, September 28, 1883: Martin and Colyer in here from the mill with small bar of bullion. Seem to keep away from me. Wish I was rid of this business. It distances me fearfully. I've had my share of it and more too. At Springer's a while tonight and Peel's, Clapp's and I. A Mr. and Mrs. Hurlbert of Hermosillo there, refugees from the yellow fever scourge; 50 deaths in one day there or Guaymas, don't remember.

Saturday, September 29, 1883: Had long talk with Colyer, but of no avail, for money, as they were short and laid out everything for supplies. Well,

*The smelter of the Benson Mining and Smelting Company was blown in on September 28, 1882. Managed by Monroe Salisbury of the well known stage line of Gilmer & Salisbury, the refinery operated on custom ore from the Empire Mining District and mining localities as far away as Chloride in the northwest corner of the territory. The *Mining and Scientific Press*, January 19, 1884. The Benson fire, supposedly arson, occurred on the night of September 18. It burned the entire block opposite the depot, which was the site of the town's major hotels, the Virginia and Benson, as well as all the saloons. Damage was estimated at $40,000. See Tucson *Weekly Citizen*, September 22, 1883 for additional details.

can't help myself. Long account in *Epitaph* yesterday or day before, about mill and mines. Carranza a pleasant fellow, says he'll help me in Spanish. Had lesson tonight. Took a guitar lesson today, first one, from Dan O'Connor. Got a fine guitar for $15 other day, and am anxious to learn to play it, being fond of the music. Spanish tonight.

Sunday, September 30, 1883: Fine day. Church a.m. and p.m. Lunched with Mrs. Clapp, Milton having to go to Huachuca on business, and this evening I took Mrs. C, Harry and John to dinner at the Grand.

Monday, October 1, 1883: Yellow fever still very bad. Spanish tonight.

Tuesday, October 2, 1883: Helped Doc Goodfellow today to straighten out some of his matters. Heavy county bill of $3600 due. Dined at Milton's and Spanished later.

Wednesday, October 3, 1883: Bad murder and suicide business today. Black Jack, stage driver for Sandy Bob, cut throat of Mexican woman and then his own.* Studied Spanish a little with Carranza today. He wants English and I want Spanish. Wrote Miss Redfern that I propose to sell mill to Carranza and Flores for $4500—$500 cash January 1st when lease expires, $2000 six months and balance in a year with interest at 1% per month. Spent evening with Mrs. Clark and Miss Daisy.

Thursday, October 4, 1883: Agreed to go to Chiricahuas tomorrow with Maurice. Some more work for Doc today. Making some appreciable headway at last in Spanish. Old Collector Wiggins presented me a bill today of $50 or more which was to be sued if not paid—old Hayes & Tanner lumber bill which I paid two years ago. Told him to fire ahead. Found my receipts, check and bill receipted. Shows importance of preserving old receipts.

Friday, October 5, 1883: Got Kadish to take hold of Doctor's bills and work them up on commission. Won't get off to mountains before next week.

Saturday, October 6, 1883: Cost too much money here in town.

Sunday, October 7, 1883: Were going to Chiricahuas tomorrow but Callender Minstral Show is in town and must take that in so will wait till Tuesday. Church in morning. Dined at Clark's.

Monday, October 8, 1883: Went with Maurice, mother, Miss Daisy to Minstral Show tonight and had a jolly time. Billy Kersands is immense. Everybody there. Mrs. Clapp eyed me sharply and I'm in for a tease now. Miss D is a wonderfully bright, active girl. Letter from father tonight stating that Sam was on the road to California and he would be here Saturday probably—very sudden move, occasioned by his bad health.

Tuesday, October 9, 1883: Couldn't get started till about noon or one

---

*According to the *Arizona Weekly Star* of October 4, 1883, stage driver Jack Standiford cut the throat of his paramour, María Contreras, and then slit his own throat. Standiford who was known as Black Jack was well known, having driven stages in California, Idaho and Montana. At the time of the murder-suicide he was employed by Robert Crouch. For additional details see Prescott *Courier*, October 6, 1883.

o'clock, driving Billy and George; buckboard. At Sanderson's where we rested Geo tried to find Maurice with his hind legs, but M tumbled a double back summersalt over the tongue and got out of the way. Rode till midnight and it was very cold. Stopped at Cavil's. He seemed excited about recent Indian news, saying the soldiers were hot after the Apache just below. Camped on piazza after warning at five and slept well.

Wednesday, October 10, 1883: Up early and breakfasted at Gray's. Warmly welcomed. Mrs. Cavil now living with her husband, leaves Miss Emma Fish alone, the adopted daughter; bright, nice lively girl.

Thursday, October 11, 1883: An Indian scare. Some seen up the canyon. Maurice and I took sack of flour to the old doctor's and then escorted Miss Emma to Cavil's. Near the house Maurice made quite a racket—up the canyon a piece and scared them at the house, they thinking it Indians. Burke of Tombstone, just arrived with another party, jumped behind Mrs. C and then ran behind the house. I was ahead and found him white as a ghost and trumbling like an aspen. Sickness added to his nervousness. Some music at Gray's this evening by Burke and Miss Emma.

Friday, October 12, 1883: Am practicing guitar so as to be able to play some few simple things and sing them. Walked around after deer today but didn't run across any. Hunted horses today but didn't find them; bad fix. Just before retiring found horses. Mighty fortunate.

Saturday, October 13, 1883: Got good start and arrived in town about 5:30 or 5:45. Came new road and saved some [time]. Not an antelope or deer in sight. Dined at Clark's and put up nags and blankets later. Telegram from Sam [George's younger brother] that he would arrive tomorrow.

Sunday, October 14, 1883: Church this a.m. Dined at Clapp's, and Arthur arrived on noon stage to escort Mrs. Clapp to San Francisco. Milton, Arthur and John helped me to welcome Sam tonight upon his arrival. Looked well and enjoyed his trip. Got him good room at Occidental after dining and seeing some of the town—gambling, etc., and left him to sleep. Stage driver told him usual Indian and stage robbery stories and filling him full, seeing he was a tenderfoot.

Monday, October 15, 1883: Sam had to break off college and all desires that way as his health gave out and he is now doing the very best thing in going to Cal[ifornia] to ranch it. Will join sister and with combined help of Heins and B's will do well. Showed Sam about today and this evening we dined at Milton's. Adjoined next door to Berry's later, where was Mrs. Berry, and all had good time, dancing, singing, etc.

Tuesday, October 16, 1883: Showed Sam about today and this evening Milton drove us down with Arthur to Charleston, where we saw the mill and smelter in operation and Sam was greatly interested. Cheyney took us in tow and was very kind. Showed us where poor [M. R.] Peel was killed; bullet holes still visible. Cheyney very pleasant, nice fellow.*

*George W. Cheyney arrived in Tombstone in 1882 to manage the mill of the Grand Central and Toughnut mines at Contention, and ended up as managing director of the Tombstone

Wednesday, October 17, 1883: Started for Bisbee about eight a.m., Milton taking Arthur, Sam and me and didn't arrive till two p.m., 28 miles, about 30. Fine [toll] road over mountains into the camp, cost $30,000. Typical mining camp, collection of tents and wooden buildings in center of a deep, narrow canyon, and things generally quite primitive. Mr. Lew [Lewis] Williams took charge of us and we put up at his house. Ben Williams away with Judge and Miss Peel, Mrs. W and Bagnall at the Cananeas. Went all over the great Copper Queen mine, one of the best copper bullion producers in the world and were highly interested. Down 400 feet to water. Grand sight at the great cut where operations were first commenced.* Some native copper at bottom. Office constructed of slag moulded into bricks; fire proof. Fine dinner at which was Father [Patrick] Gallagher, Catholic priest here. Billiards later and a good time till bed time.

Thursday, October 18, 1883: Up and off by 4:30 as Milton had to get back to open safe. Fine ride over mountains but we wandered from the right road a few miles and were delayed in reaching town, arriving about 11 a.m., or 11:30. Very pleasant trip indeed and much enjoyed by all hands. Dined at Clapp's in evening where were Misses Rouse and Bessie Brown. Jolly good time singing, etc. Dinner was for Tuesday or Wednesday evening but I forgot. Bisbee relations and their ladies had to be told to come another time. Rather awkward, stupid on my part.

Friday, October 19, 1883: Sam didn't care to visit the Huachucas so that trip proposed by Clapp is off. Calling this evening.

Saturday, October 20, 1883: Milton and Arthur went to the Huachucas this a.m. Calling as usual tonight.

Sunday, October 21, 1883: Church morning and evening. Dined at Clapp's, where Rev. Bagnall and Dr. Millar, an old Tombstoner just returned from S.F. where he had been under medical treatment some time. Sam much pleased with our church, minister, etc.

Monday, October 22, 1883: Dined with Maurice and Miss Daisy tonight. Fine time. Adjoined to Mrs. Berry's later where we had music, etc. Great fun amongst a certain few in a "Dorty" business they've sprung on me. I might surprise them all some day.

Tuesday, October 23, 1883: Went through Grand Central mine this a.m. with Arthur, John and Sam, and later through Girard mill. This afternoon

Mining and Milling Company which absorbed the properties. He quickly expanded his mining properties, acquiring prospects at Oro Blanco near Arivaca. With decline of mining in Tombstone he and his wife Annie Neal, and four daughters, moved to Tucson in 1892, where he served as postmaster for four years, as well as superintendent of public instruction. He died at Tucson in August 1902.

*The Copper Queen mine was in trouble at this time. The original deposit, mined through an open cut and two shallow vertical shafts, was nearing exhaustion, and the company was preparing to explore the neighboring Atlanta claim. A year later, when funds were all but exhausted, the great Atlanta orebody was struck, and Phelps, Dodge, and Company was propelled into a major copper producing firm.

went to the Bassett, horseback. Maurice kindly offered his horses and he, Sam and I went. Dined at Judge Berry's tonight. Mrs. Clapp being present, going to her departure on Saturday. Great time.

Wednesday, October 24, 1883: Went through the Court House, jail, etc. today. Wells was reading to some women. He recognized me first and stopped; painful to think of him. His misdeeds have probably ruined him for life. Am glad he stopped and thus avoided my noticing him much.

Thursday, October 25, 1883: Gloomy day. Sam having good time. Horse back riding and lawn tennis today for him. Thinks the people here grand, but doesn't like the country. Rather rough to one unused to it. Reppy has got it on me again. Mrs. C and a few others started calling me Dordy or Dandy, the significance is a deep one as they plague me much about [Daisy Clark,] a very young but very bright and brainy girl here and they go for me. *Epitaph* this a.m. had the nerve herewith pict on this page—cut out of the paper. Grand racket today over it. I'm Major Dandy and Geo now. Made several calls and spent balance of evening at Mrs. Clark's. I like her, also her daughter, in fact the whole family.

Friday, October 26, 1883: Sam got off at noon today and Arthur too, the latter to spend a day in Tucson and join Mrs. Clapp there tomorrow for S.F. Sam may stop over too. Long talk with Sam last night. Level headed boy. A little fresh though. Needs some hard knocks. We'll all be westerners ere long. Spent evening at Clapp's. Smoked pipe with Maurice at Castle's.

Saturday, October 27, 1883: Cold and very windy. Mrs. Clapp left about one. Milton going to Tucson with her. Sorry to have her go. We are warm friends. Their house is like a home to me. It's delightful in a place like this particularly to have such true warm friends as the Clapps.

Sunday, October 28, 1883: Milton back today. Sam stopped over at Tucson with Arthur and had a good time and they all went on together. Am glad. Sam just in time for grand time in Tucson. Ed Hudson took them in charge. Church morning and evening. Went home with Miss Peel and others going to her house and later with Bagnall to his house where we discussed religious subjects until midnight. B a capital fellow.

Monday, October 29, 1883: Awaiting developments. Hope something will soon break. Must now devote myself to Spanish and guitar. Studied well today and had lesson tonight after lapse of a few weeks.

Tuesday, October 30, 1883: Took guitar lesson this a.m. and practiced much, and studied Spanish. Had tooth filled. Teeth in fine order. Lesson tonight. Oriental [Saloon] wall, side of house, fell in with a crash tonight few minute after I passed. Fell out rather. No one hurt. Whist tonight.

Wednesday, October 31, 1883: Townspeople this a.m. wanted to know if I was underneath last night. Fellows jumping me this a.m., remembering my experience of a year and a half ago. Poor Arthur Hayne died in S.F. other day. An example of a man who killed himself by careless habits. He wrote a letter of warning some time since to some of the boys here telling them to take warning by him. Sorry to know that he had to go; he was a fine fellow. This evening we all had a jolly and sociable time at Miss Peel's.

Thursday, November 1, 1883: Maurice very desirous for me to join him in a general agency and mining business here with headquarters at the adobe on Fremont Street. Must do something pretty quickly. Sent father several letters lately, one I think today wishing to know positively and at once about C[entral] A[merica] matters.

Friday, November 2, 1883: Times rather slow. Spanish tonight.

Saturday, November 3, 1883: Was routed out of bed this a.m. by Heyne who had some very important copying to be done in the matter of Copper Prince vs Copper Queen and wished me to do it as he wanted someone in whom he had confidence, so I started in today. Wrote late till two a.m. Expecting Flores today to settle mill sale preliminaries—didn't arrive.

Sunday, November 4, 1883: Church morning and evening. Dined at Clapp's. Mary's invitation, she runs mess now. Fine dinner. Copied some this afternoon, it being quite necessary. Good attendance today.

Monday, November 5, 1883: Hard at it today. Copying 20 and folio. Pretty good pay. Spent pleasant evening at Herring's. Court opened this afternoon; all looks busy again.

Tuesday, November 6, 1883: Seems to be lots to do copying and getting jurors affidavits. Very pleasant evening at Major Earl's; cards, games, etc.

Wednesday, November 7, 1883: Made statement before grand jury this a.m. as to killing in the Huachucas. All of us subpoenaed. Jones said to be in Idaho. Grand time tonight, Episcopal social. We got the Hermosillo Mexican band of five pieces which recently ran from the yellow fever and all had a jolly good time. Not so many turned out as we had hoped. Billiards till late.

Thursday, November 8, 1883: Still at copying and getting affidavits. Very tired tonight and went home comparatively early. Rountree and Miller here from Sonora and report my rifle lost, for which I am very sorry, more for sake of old associations than other reason.

Friday, November 9, 1883: May be deputized to go to Huachucas so as to be with Maurice's party he is expecting to take over. No go at present.

Saturday, November 10, 1883: Don't recall anything of special interest today. Presume I had usual copying to do.

Sunday, November 11, 1883: Church morning as usual. Maurice and I dined with Milton this evening; capital dinner. Believe Maurice and I went to hear Rev. Mr. [G. H.] Adams* this evening. Fine speaker. Went to Maurice's house this afternoon with Maurice horseback and saw Mrs. Stevens.

Monday, November 12, 1883: At it again today. Copying pays pretty well at 20 cents a hundred words. Called at Clark's I think.

*Reverend G. H. Adams arrived in Arizona in September 1879 and visited Tombstone in October before assuming the welfare of Prescott's Methodist congregation. From there he moved on to Tucson, back to Tombstone, and on to other Arizona mining camps until his name was "a household word all over Arizona."

Tuesday, November 13, 1883: Party given at the old Court House this evening. Attended and had pretty good time. Some few objectionable characters present. Considerable kicking about one or two committee names.

Wednesday, Novemebr 14, 1883: Some copying off and on. Expect to join Maurice in general mining business shortly as Central American matters are off at present on account of yellow fever there.

Thursday, November 15, 1883: A little send off for Trenchard Price this evening at Herring's. Went there after bidding the Rouses goodbye who leave tomorrow for New Orleans. Quite a time—Miss Rouse too there; she's quite pretty and very quick and lively. Quite a time at the feast.

Friday, November 16, 1883: Rouses left this a.m.; Maurice drove them down. Compared today, tiresome work. Been at it some little time. Don't think as highly of Prof Blake from what I've read.

Saturday, November 17, 1883: Maurice took his mother and sister today on our trip to the Dragoon foothills to see the old Royal Arch, now Arcade property. Ferris went in a buggy to show the ground. Found a good looking prospect. A good example of difference in prices in two years—$2000 now; $15,000 then. Pleasant day of it. Breakfasted and dined at Clark's.

Sunday, November 18, 1883: Fine day. Mr. Umstetler of Pittsburgh here, owner of Ground Hog, with Fisher. Church morning and evening. Dined with Mrs. Walker on hill. Attended Bible class just formed with Maurice Clark, we were the only persons present.

Monday, November 19, 1883: Finished testimony comparing today. Arranged to go with Nick tomorrow. Will start general mining agency business, doing any and everything in that line with Maurice shortly. Anything else too. Will lead to something perhaps. No R this time. Lent Carranza $30 today; goes to Chihuahua. Also R $40, and Nick has $85.

Tuesday, November 20, 1883: Off this a.m. Maurice and I with Nick to a spot about 35 miles distant, north and other side railroad track to see a property of his. Got there in time to examine it and reach the cabin at old Russelville before a wind and rain storm caught us. About six of us in little cabin. No room to spare when stretched out on floor—an example of decay of mining towns here.* More houses than people. Nick has good, though doubtful, property in lime.

Wednesday, November 21, 1883: Pleasant ride in. Dined with Milton tonight and with him this evening. Not getting blankets, staid all night.

Thursday, November 22, 1883: Breakfasted with M. Finished some copying today. Much interest taken in the Dunbar forgery case—very old matter of last February. Court room packed tonight. Milton and I went and heard old Southard. Stopped taking Spanish lessons with Miss Peel and

*After attaining a population of about 300, Russellville began to decline when the Russell Gold and Silver Mining Company was purchased by Kansas City men represented by George J. Johnson. He moved the Russellville smelter to within a 150 feet of the Peabody mine, eliminating a three mile haul of ore, ordered yet another 30-ton furnace, and a new town, called Johnson, sprouted within a half mile of the reduction site.

settled up. She said $17, but I paid $20. Two months. Have done pretty well for time I've studied.

Friday, November 23, 1883: Maurice putting in gas and getting things ready for business. Confusion most confounded.

Saturday, November 24, 1883: Don't recall anything of interest today.

Sunday, November 25, 1883:Church in a.m. and dined at Clark's. Pleasant evening.

Monday, November 26, 1883: Too far back to remember much of what takes place from day to day. Must do better in the future.

Tuesday, November 27, 1883: Am going out now and spending evening.

Wednesday, November 28, 1883: Am not through copying yet. Affidavits hold out pretty well.

Thursday, November 29, 1883: Thanksgiving Day. Had a good time. A dozen of us got a four in hand and drove over to Cochise Stronghold. Maurice driving. Dined at Clark's, pleasant time. Jim and Miss Barrett dumped out by the roadside; fortunately ahead of us; king bolt came out.

Friday, November 30, 1883: Mill men in town and have been unsettling hard with them, got $10. Am very much disgusted and wish some one would take the matter off of my hands. Am troubling myself too much for other people when there's no money in it. Everything has been shoved over on to me.

Saturday, December 1, 1883: Winter is here. Well, nothing new today.

Sunday, December 2, 1883: Church in the morning. Walk with Milton in afternoon. Dined there. Boys in evening; club.

Monday, December 3, 1883: Crystal wedding at Howes tonight, 15 years. Gave them a handsome sea green [paper] weight to match ink stand. Music and a good time till quite late. Went for music for Miss Peel and later saw her there.

Tuesday, December 4, 1883; Cap. Seamans made me go home with him to dinner tonight, rough shirt and all, and we had a jolly good time.

Wednesday, December 5, 1883: Qualified today as Notary Public; Milton and Maurice as bondsmen. Al Jones charged me half price. Cards in *Epitaph* and *Republican* and think almost in full blast—Clark and Parsons, Mines-mining, and R.E. French, German and Spanish spoken. Bela Kadish's assay office same place and etc. Maurice and I dined tonight. Called at Earl's and Milton and I played cards there a while. Bought a good seal today from Cap. Seamans, only $3.50.

Thursday, December 6, 1883: Worked at Williams's office today, copying, etc. Took first signing—Heyne's affidavit in Copper Queen fight. Dined at Clark's, taking Miss B Brown by request, a send off to Rountree, who goes to New Mexico with family. Champagne dinner. Miss Barrett, Miss BB and Miss D C, Milton and son OH. Pleasant evening singing, joking, etc. Cold these nights. Am getting house tightened some.

Friday, December 7, 1883: Fine day at last after a very surprising rain of several days. Cold and disagreeable. A fellow killed himself today, Campbell. More killings lately. Scott and Bennett wounded by Apaches. Carrie Jones Scott died recently in NY; her first child.

Saturday, December 8, 1883: Cold. House fixed some to keep out cold. First time in nearly three years. Nothing new today. No business yet.

Sunday, December 9, 1883: Terrible news from Bisbee this morning. Rustlers raided the town—Castaneda's store. More particularly and wantonly shot at everybody, women and all, killing outright poor Tappiner and D. T. Smith.* A posse went out, but will probably return with the usual result. A shooting epidemic again lately. Scott and Bennett shot just over the line, train ditched and robbed and one or two killings done near Deming at Gage. Campbell kills himself and now this bloody work. The things seems to move in cycles.

Monday, December 10, 1883: Posse returned as I expected, nothing accomplished. Maurice teaches me some Spanish now. Called at Miss Peel's tonight to restore shawl left at church today at Smith's funeral. I sang, also other day at other killing. Sad times. Cold.

Tuesday, December 11, 1883: Clear day. Wrote Bidwell today. Posse didn't do any good.

Wednesday, December 12, 1883: Business very quiet in town and generally. Pumps will start soon and decide the fate of Tombstone. Six months time will be enough. Some singing tonight—Clapp's stories.

Thursday, December 13, 1883: Helped Milton today at his request in matter of obtaining subscriptions to reward for capture or killing of Bisbee robbers. About $7500. [See p. 267 for additional details] Hard work. Bachelors' Club social tonight. Was not going, but certain conditions being complied with, I went taking Mrs. Berry and Annette. Good time, oysters later.

Friday, December 14, 1883: Fine weather. Got the sign up—Clark and Parsons. We exercise now quite regularly. Maurice has quite a gymnasium in the back yard. Sad news for the Clarks. Their old S.F. friend Mr. Laughlin,

*The most tragic event in the history of outlawry at the copper camp, the Bisbee Massacre happened at seven o'clock on the evening of December 8, 1883, when five men wearing heavy coats and masks attempted to rob the Goldwater and Castaneda Store, which received monthly $7,000 in gold to meet the Copper Queen mine payroll. While two men stood guard outside the store, three men with guns drawn, held up customers inside, and demanded Joe Goldwater open the safe. He complied, but there was only $120 in the safe. The bandits shook down customers, took $700 in coin from A. A. Castañeda, and pilfered miscellaneous pieces of jewelry. The heist netted no more than $3,000. Meanwhile, the two bandits outside the store became nervous and reacted with deadly violence when approached by people on the street. Before the five bandits made their escape, they left two men dead, assayer John Tappiner and D. Tom Smith, a stage driver and deputy sheriff from New Mexico. Two others were mortally wounded, expectant mother Annie Roberts and J. A. "Tex" Nolly. Indian Joe, a bystander, received a minor wound. Two posses led by Billy Daniels and Sheriff J. L. Ward took up pursuit. All the bandits, including their leader John Heith, were caught within forty-five days.

Maurice's godfather, worth several millions or more, was shot dead on account of decision of state supreme court in his favor by the loser.

Saturday, December 15, 1883: Not so pleasant. In court half a day for Col. Clark. Cases prior to April 9, 1880, against and those later for him. Good hot bath and exercise this afternoon—makes one feel good.

Sunday, december 16, 1883: Church in a.m. Dined at Milton's. Church in evening late. Mild weather again.

Monday, December 17, 1883: Gymnasium in back yard great thing. Does one much good. Business very light. Think I called at Clark's tonight.

Tuesday, December 18, 1883: Weather still mild. Probably will have most of Bisbee murders soon. Think it was this afternoon I drove to Grand Central mill with Milton who went to insure it. My mill matters off for present by letter from Flores on account of cursed Apaches; too bad. Dined with Milton; late dinner.

Wednesday, December 19, 1883: Helped [G. R.] Williams half a day on Bon Ton mining case, compiling assessment and no one testimony, separating it. Cohen's suit vs Emanuel. Social Ladies Aid Society tonight and crazy quilt raffle. Miss C a wonderfully bright and charming girl. Can't help it if she is young. She's very attractive to me. Must be careful. Must not hurt her feelings or mine. Must bide ourself.

Thursday, December 20, 1883: Hard at work today on BT matter. Called at Herring's with Milton. Good whist with Miss Sarah Pastuer.

Friday, December 21, 1883: Concluded Bon Ton matter today. While Williams argued, I selected testimony for him. Won, motion denied for new trial. Dined at Clark's and took Mrs. C's acknowledgement.

Saturday, December 22, 1883: Copper Queen and Copper Prince up today. Nothing though for me to do. Williams left for S.F. at noon, almost stepping from court room into carriage. Hope to get much business from him. Received from father last night a fine Spanish and English dictionary, just what I wanted. Also church book of common prayer from Strallus and a novel. Bisbee murders, two jailed here [Red Sample and Tex Howard, captured in Graham County and delivered to Sheriff Ward]. No violence yet; can't tell though. Vick's brother [Sumner] here from NY. Trust deed of ME C and other today. Court adjourned till last of January. G Belle work progressing. Caples stuck for funds. Am trying to help him out. Bachelor Club meeting here tonight.

Sunday, December 23, 1883: Deeming it my best interest to do so, I went this a.m. with Col. Clark, Col. Stanford, Fred S., Mr. Taylor and Maurice to Cochise Pass, Dragoons, to see a promising mining property there called the Flora Culver or something like that. Four horses and stage. Col. C quite sick going out. Looks like a good thing with that property. Dined at Clark's; church late.

Monday, December 24, 1883: Great times today. Very busy helping arrange church and collecting $50 purse for Bagnall. Pleasant time at church this evening. Children happy. With a few remarks I gave Bagnall the purse and we, that is, Maurice, Miss Daisy and I repaired to Mrs. Clark's house where a table was spread and presents laid out. I gave Mrs. C and Miss D each a pretty Xmas card and Maurice a handsome amber cigarette holder. He gave me a pretty alarm clock and Mrs. C a very handsome pocket diary for '84. A pleasant time, quite like a Xmas. Gave Matilda a lace shawl.

Tuesday, December 25, 1883; Xmas Day. Beautifiul day. Attended service. Church very pretty in greens and handsome cut flowers sent by Miss Peel from Los Angeles. No music though, too bad. I received today by mail a very pretty riding whip, broken though, but can be repaired. From whom it came is a mystery to be unraveled in time if possible. Billiards this afternoon and about 5:30 a fine dinner at the mess. Went by Mary's invitation. Great time later, singing,. Repaired finally to office and finished there.

Wednesday, December 26, 1883: Things a little slow today after yesterday. An unchristmasing day. Trying to work up the Dragoon mine racket. Something there I think. The heavy indications do not go for nothing. Went out to Gentle Belle today and measured ground. Big assessment work due.

Thursday, December 27, 1883: Am helping Maurice some on his stable he is building back of the house. Caples is wrestling with hard luck still. Am doing what I can. Maurice and I are to have our heads smashed, so report goes, by Bracken and Kennedy, opposing parties on G Belle. Let them start in. It'll be kind of interesting. Mr. Fitzgerald , a N.Y. gentleman, friend of Clark, spent evening with us. Milton on hand. Good time.

Friday, December 28, 1883: Business very slow indeed. Trying to work the Dragoon racket. Assays average $88, $47, $94, and $123. Called at boys and girls. Six handed euchre.

Saturday, December 29, 1883: Some good affidavit work today. Caples still hanging on. Stable finished today, and Nick, the finest horse in the country, stabled. Called at Clark's tonight. Pleasant time.

Sunday, December 30, 1883: Church this a.m. Rode Dandy, Major Earle's fine horse, this afternoon. Maurice had Nick out; fine horse. Milton at office this evening so didn't go to church.

Monday, December 31, 1883: Last day of old year. Wrote several sketches of Maurice and myself today for tomorrow's big issue of *Epitaph*. Big thing. Fireman's ball tonight. Milton, Maurice and I attended. Great times. Kept it up all night. Last for me. Will now retire this journal to keep company with the other just like it. Will use now the diary and book good Mrs. Clark gave me on Xmas day. It's plenty big enough. I have been journalizing for many years, 15 I think, and gradually contracting [condensing] all of the time until now I can put into a few words all I wish to say. So farewell journal. I shall now pursue the C idea and follow in new path.

1884

Tuesday, January 1, 1884: New Year's day and a cold and disagreeable one. Election day as well. Made about 50 calls with Maurice. Attended Fireman's ball last night with Milton and Maurice and all had a great time. Didn't get home and to bed till between five and six. Rather poor condition for calling. Maurice and I breakfasted with Milton about 10 a.m. M got me up about eight, precious little sleep. Mrs. Adam received at Mrs. Clark's. All, particularly Miss D, looked well. Lots of fun. Returns declare Carr reelected. Expect next time there'll be some fun. May take a hand myself. Pretty tired tonight. Huachuca main burst so cold. No water. Bad times. Milton went to S.F. today on his vacation.

Wednesday, January 2, 1884: Cold snap still on. Letter from father to hold myself in readiness for a California trip to inspect a gold mine near Nevada City. Gymnasium nearly ready. Have increased chest $^3/_4$ inch in two weeks, moderate exercising. Also gained $3^3/_4$ lbs and dimensions of thigh and upper arm. Dec. 29, chest 36 inches, waist 32, upper arm $12^3/_4$, forearm $11^1/_4$; thigh $20^1/_2$, calf 13. Weight without clothes 144 lbs. Height 5 ft, $8^1/_4$ inches without shoes; increase in 2 weeks—chest $^3/_4$ inch, waist $1^1/_4$ inches, upper arm $^1/_4$ inch; f arm $^1/_2$ inch, thigh $^3/_4$ inch, weight 4 lbs. Irregular exercise too. Can make big change and will do it.

Thursday, January 3, 1884: Weather moderating. Business looking up a little. Parties desirous of having Sonora properties examined. Big card in New Year's edition of *Epitaph*. Rather cheeky everything considered. Exercised Major Earle's horse Dandy this afternoon. He is a Dandy. So full he couldn't contain himself. Need exercise badly. Dined at Clark's. Some music later. Must now leave out what I am having to say. It's strange, but fate has so decreed. Honored by Cap Seamans offering me charge of his office during his Cal trip. Am considering tonight. Telegraphed East about the Cal mine trip. Am afraid it isn't a go at office.

Friday, January 4, 1884: Mild, strange weather. Completed to decline charge of County Clerk's office as Maurice may go to Sonora on business and I to Cal. Men working mill arrested, may cause my presence. Dragoon racket still on and it is quite impossible to tie down for six weeks. Declined with thanks. Letter in Spanish from Flores stating $30 loan to Carranza enroute. Was not fooled in them. Think I can tell human nature pretty well, though some persons think they know better.

Saturday, January 5, 1884: Weather mild. Business slow. Exercised at gymnasium this afternoon, Maurice and I. Lots of fun. Dined at Clark's and acknowledged several deeds there. Called on Mrs. Seamans, M & I, to say goodbye. [Dan] Dowd, another of the Bisbee murders, brought in by Davies tonight, who followed him into the Sierra Madres and caught him there.* Think it was today that Maurice and I gave Caples $40 for 11.350 shares of Gentle Belle stock.

Sunday, January 6, 1884: Maurice and I drove Capt. and Mrs. Seamans to the train this afternoon at Fairbank. Had to leave church early to do so. Very windy and dusty, disagreeably so. They go to California. Lost dogs on return. Church late this evening.

Monday, January 7, 1884: Nice weather. Up early, practiced at gymnasium at 7:30 till 8:30. Business improving some. Arranged for Dragoon Summit trip today for tomorrow. Had our first Spanish tonight under the new course; Maurice teacher, Miss D and I pupils. She is wonderfully bright. New pronunciation, Castillian. Will become better later.

Tuesday, January 8, 1884: Weather fine. Ran for stage and had to wait half hour. Dark as Egypt at six a.m. Cool ride on top. Quite a talk with Col. Lewis on train. Milton looked fine. Mrs. Clapp a little worn but otherwise seemed well. Train on time. Rode to Summit with them, spending a pleasant hour. Harry left in S.F. Nick came in good time and about one o'clock I started back. Fine horse, Major Earle's "Dandy," took me back in four hours. Haven't been on such a stepper since I've been in the country. Rather tired tonight, 70 miles, 8 stage, 36 cars, 26 horseback.

Wednesday, January 9, 1884: Sister's birthday, must write and congratulate her. Sent off some *Epitaphs* today all over country with our New Years card. Spanish tonight and a pleasant and profitable time. Called later on Earles; Herrings, Maurice and I then billiarded. Sad dog experience today. Watch dog jumped a sheep and killed it, and being a general nuisance, he was put to death—axed as Miss D says. I wasn't an expert at the business and office resembled a slaughter house when through. Dog got in by mistake.

Thursday, January 10, 1884: Tiff with cross grained Dr. Willis today about pail. Maurice took his mother and sister to the old Royal Arch today to show it to Bela. We're trying to get him to take hold and work it. Disagreeable day for them. Break down, bird killing and bad time generally.

Friday, January 11, 1884: Worked some today on horse raffle tickets.

*Billy Daniels and two other deputies doggedly trailed Dan Dowd and Billy Delaney into northern Mexico. Daniels captured Dowd at the Corralitos Mine and smuggled the killer across the border in a freight wagon to avoid time-consuming and costly extradition. Meanwhile, Deputy Cesario Lucero pursued Billy Delaney 300 miles into Sonora, and found him in jail at Minas Prietas. Mexican authorities looked the other way, while Lucero spirited the criminal across the border.

Maurice proposes getting two more serviceable horses with proceeds. Tickets $3, 100 chances. Exercise at gymnasium at noon now. Too cold in early a.m. and too little vitality. Spanish tonight; doing very well. Maurice and I took Miss Daisy to Judge Berry's where she staid the night.

Saturday, January 12, 1884: Fine bath and exercise this a.m. Maurice went to Prompter mine today with Bob Lewis to examine it. Reppy's birthday. Tumbled into a surprise party at Berry's and joined it. Lots of fun.

Sunday, January 13, 1884: Church morning and evening. This afternoon went over horseback to see the "Tom Thumb." Dined at Clapp's. helped Miss Peel sing in Sunday school matter.

Monday, January 14, 1884: Worked today with Mrs. Clark in getting a surprise party ready for Maurice tomorrow evening, his birthday. Exercised as usual at gymnasium. Spanish lesson tonight; progressing.

Tuesday, January 15, 1884: Went out of town this afternoon on "Dandy" to examine the T Thumb and Toledo claims which are put to us very low indeed. Helped further on surprise party. Dined at Clark's and made the surprise quite a success. Quite a company present and all went off well.

Wednesday, January 16, 1884: Bela left today for N. Mexico; will locate there for the present. Rustling around in Toledo and other business. Carlyn and Leman in from Sonora and the mill. Bad times with the rascal Hohstadt. Will jump on him myself now. Time has arrived when I can strike back after waiting a year. Spanish tonight. A right hard lesson.

Thursday, January 17, 1884: Some snow, very wet, and rain last night. Fixed the Sonora boys this a.m. with affidavit, sworn bill and necessary papers to warn old H with. Rustling today on the mine matters. We must get, if possible, $1/2$ of Dixie, $1/2$ of Toledo, $1/3$ of Bourbon, Broken Letter and the Tom Thumb. Farish furniture came today, enough for three or four homes here.

Friday, January 18, 1884: Went out on "Dandy" to Prompter and arranged with John Haley, half owner in Star King formerly Dixie, to be a $1/3$ owner instead of $1/2$, we to do assessment work for this year provided we bought Cogdill's interests. He assented. Rustled around doing some heavy talking. Wrestled with Cogdill a long time, finally reducing amount to $150. Borrowed $150 of G. R. Williams for Maurice, he giving some notes but I'm responsible all the same. Used but part for this. I furnished my half, $75. Guess there's money for us in this purchase.

Saturday, January 19, 1884: Col., Mrs. Clark, Miss Daisy, Maurice and I drove over to the properties today and had a pleasant time of it. Lost the Col but he turned up O.K. Returned via Maurice's house. Tom Thumb a valuable piece of property. We can sell to Recorder Al Jones now this one thing for the whole cost and more I think. He wants to chloride it badly.*

Sunday, January 20, 1884: Church a.m and p.m. Maurice and I had quite a horseback ride this p.m. looking at Star King.

*Chloriding was the extraction of profitable ore without development, usually by lessees. The term originated at Silver Reef, Utah, where rich silver-chloride in sandstone was worked.

Monday, January 21, 1884: Business increasing, will make some money ere long. Spanish tonight. Reading the second reader; getting along nicely. Miss Daisy very bright, doesn't have to study much, acquires quickly. M and I called at Herring's tonight.

Tuesday, January 22, 1884: We made about $25 today; guess we'll get along. Called on Miss Peel this evening. Exercised at gymnasium quite regularly and feel much better for it. Long discussion with ME tonight.

Wednesday, January 23, 1884: Farishes [probably William] at last here. Bought in some property for Col. yesterday, $925.75 and $506.80 Examined at some length into placer claim rights to cover land. Judge [J. S.] Robinson assisted me to come to a conclusion which I formed for [George] Ward of Antelope Spring ranch. Processed some letters of Walter Locker's in Chihuahua properties with view to sending reports to Chicago.

Thursday, January 24, 1884: Saw [Bill] Delaney, the last of the Bisbee murderers, this a.m. Just brought in. Davies, Deputy Sheriff, on stand. Received $30 from Flores of Nogales for account of Carranza today. My confidence was not misplaced no matter what stories some will tell. Called at Hudson's this evening, not home. First though M and I took Miss Daisy home from the Farish's. Called later at Goodfellow's and saw Mrs. G.

Frday, January 25, 1884: Bones sore from jumping yesterday. Spanish tonight. Rainy and cold. Surprise party at Mrs. Eccleston's tonight. Successful, a great many present.

Saturday, January 26, 1884. This evening M and I played Bagnall and Sherman some whist, according to Cavendish on our side. Rules worked well.

Sunday, January 27, 1884: Church a.m. and p.m. Helped Sunday school singing with Miss Peel. Dined at the mess with John D and after church was at Berry's a while. Stebbins back, glad to see him. Good ride this afternoon; Dandy felt fine.

Monday, January 28, 1884: No business. Took horses to race track and tried them a while this afternoon. Practiced stiff walking and some running at 100 and 200 yards with Maurice. He's racing one; is a fine runner himself with good European record; uses spiked shoes. Must practice the points. Later a pleasant gathering at Mrs. Clark's of elderly people.

Tuesday, January 29, 1884: Fine weather. No business today; not feeling well. Jim E drove me to track today and I tried his trotter, fine horse. Old rascal H in town. Now for some developments I suppose.

Wednesday, January 30, 1884: Some Spanish tonight and later quite a gathering at Clark's. Card party, music, etc. Pleasant evening.

Thursday, January 31, 1884: Fairly pleasant weather. Great preparations going on today for the Leap Year party tonight by the Spinsters to the Bachelors. Invited by Miss Haines, a convenience matter and all had a good time. Large attendance. Fellows waited on by the girls. Lots of fun.

Good supper. Maurice and I spent an hour or two this afternoon pulling chocolate for them. M and I discussed matters till a very late hour.

Friday, February 1, 1884: Old H and I don't meet and probably will not. I don't care to come in contact with the old rascal. More trouble again down below I hear. Figured up accounts and balanced them tonight. Showing not so bad. California racket still hanging, fine. I had an interview with some of the city fathers who want me to run the city water works.

Saturday, February 2, 1884: Milton and wife arrive tomorrow from Florida. Will be glad to welcome them back. Chock full of business today. Lots of folks on hand. Acuña, a Sonora gent, on hand with securities to borrow on.

Sunday, February 3, 1884: Rain night and day. Church this morning. John and I drove down for Milton and wife this afternoon. Train a little late. Due at 5:05 RR time, half an hour or $^3/_4$ slower than ours. Arrived in fair health and good spirits. Fine time but rather disappointed in Florida. Cold there. Mrs. C bad cold. Lots to tell.

Monday, February 4, 1884: Sun at last. Nearly four nights and three days of rain. Beats the record. Mrs. Clapp showed me some of her finery and nice things they brought home with them this a.m. Has some elegant diamonds from her father. Practiced minuet tonight at Mrs. Earle's for Washington's birthday party. Miss Peel and I partners. Called for and took Miss Bessie [Brown] by request. Spanish lesson first.

Tuesday, February 5, 1884: Still rainy, beats all, this weather; steam and telegraph probably agencies. Wish it would let up. Dined at Clapp's tonight and was presented by them with three handsome scarfs and pin. They are very kind indeed to me. Played cards with Prof this evening. Terrible in the minuet business. Am trying to keep out of it. Milton gave me good rubber coat, having two; mine lost or stolen.

Wednesday, February 6, 1884: Raining as I write. Lesson tonight, exercise as usual. Ed Williams wrestling match with Dick Rule exciting considerable attention.

Thursday, February 7, 1884: Weather better. Rubber coats still necessary though. Business slow again. Another racket with me today. Am afraid of too much bull headedness in the future. Minuet drill tonight. Good progress. Three sets now. Took Miss Peel home and staid some time singing. Am wanted by school trustees to lecture at school house for pupils and parents. Guess I've got cheek enough to never back out of anything.

Friday, February 8, 1884: Pleasant once more. No Spanish tonight. Col. Clark going East Sunday and too much on hand. Sincerely hope he may accomplish his purpose. M inclined to blues at times. Have been there. Practiced in back yard today jumping. Tripped twice over a cot, breaking it the last time and breaking up the two Ms, Milton and Maurice, who nearly laughed their heads off. Dined at Milton's tonight.

Saturday, February 9, 1884: Weather pleasant. Good exercise this afternoon. Arms and upper part of body in fine condition. Must devote time now to legs and thighs, calf, etc. Lots of fun tonight. Wrestling match to a fine house. Milton, M and I on stage. Williams second. Gates, the San Pedro wrestler, selected me to keep time, but Maurice had a stop watch and I deferred to him. Exciting. Two throws in hour to be made by Wilson, one throw in 21 minutes, rest of 15. Couldn't get another. Dick looked well, but he and Ed lacked wind. Fine thing and exciting and Gates wanted to show me a throw at Elite later, place being packed and I went over his head, he on top, but I got on top of him. Lots of sport.

Sunday, February 10, 1884: Church this morning; rather late though, as Fisher came in to talk Eden Lass and show a $1900 assay of GH. Splendid chance to make some money, but am afraid it will have to go. Have written Stanley. Got Prince Albert coat and vest today. Too small; have expanded very much. Dined at Clark's and churched later. Col left this a.m. for New York and Washington.

Monday, February 11, 1884: Rain again. Climate certainly changing. Wonder if it isn't time that steam electricity and civilization doesn't bring rain. Minuet practice again today. Raffle for the horse came off tonight. My number 26 lasted pretty well. When the last two were reached, #10 and #53 held by Dan O'Connor and D McCarty. Maurice offered $50 to Dan O'C and was the fortunate man. Last one drew $135 offered at auction but I bid him in for M. So M is ahead $200, and the horse. Good sport. M commenced teaching his sister and Miss M French today.

Tuesday, February 12, 1884: Pleasant weather, fearful wind though. Went horseback to the Ground Hog and through it with Fisher. Very fine showing. Lost hat returning. A squall struck me and the hat went to Sonora I guess. Hunted unsuccessfully a half hour or more. Rode to Prompter bareheaded and John Haley lent me one to go to town with. Was to meet Hoag at Hidden Treasure but he didn't appear. Had some Spanish tonight.

Wednesday, February 13, 1884: Cold. Walked over to the Prompter in 25 minutes, thence to Silver Plume and again hunted hat but it was non est. Very strange. Coyotes though probably have it now. Belongs to M. Quite a tramp. Returned via Mrs. Walker's and dined there. Miss Santee and Dunshee brothers board with her now. Spanish again tonight. Some cribbage later with Mrs. Clark and then letters to Benson and Stanley about Eden Lass and Ground Hog.

Thursday, February 14, 1884: Wrote sister and Redfern this a.m. Valentine's Day. Believe we practiced the Minuet tonight.

Friday, February 15, 1884: Threatenings of bad weather, rain at times.

Saturday, February 16, 1884: Rainy. Nasty, nasty weather as the English say. Guess the California project is up. Mrs. Davis came tonight with Harry and looks well. Mrs. Herring's two sisters, Mrs. Battin and Miss Inslee, also came tonight and the Blinns last night, so there's quite a town full. Col Watts, a friend of Farish's who knows it all, at office some time today or yesterday. Looked at North Point mine today.

Sunday, February 17, 1884: Church in morning and late in evening, after which went to Miss Peel to see how she was. Dined at Milton's. Mrs. Davis's birthday. Got some pretty flowers for her. Bishop comes this week, confirmation next Sunday. Will be confirmed. Rather short notice.

Monday, February 18, 1884: Still rainy. At Bisbee bandit court business this a.m. All will hang I think; motion denied. Helped Maurice get up a horizontal bar today. Guess the gymnasium won't be any go, not interest enough taken. Minuet rehearsal tonight. Went for Miss Peel but her ankle was still lame so staid a while and she taught me the Spanish Fandango on guitar. Later billiards with Judge Herring and Maurice. Oysters later. Judge kept us young till long after midnight.

Tuesday, February 19, 1884: At last a fine day. Up rather late in consequence of last night's dissipation. Judge Herring a remarkably strong, vigorous man. Up most of night and this a.m. in court arguing for Heith, trying to save him from the gallows before crowded courtroom. Interesting arguments. Heard conclusion this afternoon and Mark Smith for prosecution. Mark did well. Was afraid of crowd he thought, but he soon forgot the people and sailed in well. Minuet drill tonight.

Wednesday, February 20, 1884: Jury brought in an outrageous verdict of murder in second degree last evening. Everyone incensed. Later called at Herring's with Maurice, a pleasant evening. Mrs. Battin and Miss Inslee very pleasant. Telegram to go to California. Washouts will delay.

Thurday, February 21, 1884: Heith sentenced today. Imprisonment for life at Yuma; pretty cheap; too much so. Not over yet. Dress rehearsal tonight at theatre. Bishop Dunlop arrives tomorrow for my confirmation next Sunday. Rather anxious outlook tonight for H, M and I took hot scotch together and rather think there'll be a necktie party tonight. Must start on Monday, I think, for S.F. and Nevada City.

Friday, February 22, 1884: Fine weather. Heith taken from jail this a.m. about eight, and hung to telegraph pole on Toughnut near 1st. Very grave; no noise or confusion. Saw his body lowered and carted off. Rush for pieces of rope. Humorous verdict, no dissenters.* Pity hanging wasn't begun three years ago. Great time collecting records. Appointed by Co. Treas. to collect Bisbee subscriptions; good success. The social this evening was a great success. Minuet well and gracefully done. Miss Peel looked

---

*The mastermind of the Bisbee Massacre, John Heith, or Heath, got only a life sentence, while his five accomplices received the death penalty at their trial on February 19, 1884. Bisbee citizens considered this a miscarriage of justice and corrected the situation. The humorous verdict, penned by Dr. George Goodfellow, was also adopted by the coroner's jury: "We, the jury, find that John Heath came to his death from emphysema of the lungs, a disease very common at high altitudes. In this case the disease was superinduced by strangulation, self-inflicted or otherwise."

lovely. Herring in a.m., and dancing p.m., good combination. Bed very late. Dined at Clapp's.

Saturday, February 23, 1884: Weather fine. Finished collecting today. About all in, $3512. Good work, 1% drew on SMP for $200 today. Signed draft. Business look up again. Bishop reception this evening at Prof Church's. Attended and had a good time. Pennington went down town with me later and we had some billiards.

Sunday, February 24, 1884: Large congregation in morning and immense one in evening. Many of my friends to see me confirmed probably. Dined at Clark's and sat with them. Only one confirmed. Impressive; first confirmation in Tombstone. I have now done my duty and our family are invited on the most important question today, one in my age. May God help me to do my duty. My friends glad to see me come forward, particularly Stebbins, who was with me till 12 o'clock. Bishop preached a very broad service in evening.

Monday, February 25, 1884: Weather fine. Bob Lewis, mother and sister here. Will leave tomorrow thinking I can get through. Steamer connection probably anyhow. Now for a change of life again. Very busy today. Went out of town with a Mr. Shedd—M and I to see our properties. He thought well of them. Simpson surprised me by saying he was glad to see me come forward as I did last night. I spoke seriously to him a few minutes. Our influence is a wide one in this world. My Sonora picture sent to S.F. by an insurance man and exhibited there as Big Dan Dowd.

Tuesday, February 26, 1884: No bed last night till 2:30. Breakfasted with Maurice. Late for stage and nearly forgot money. Mark and Steb went as far as Benson. Luben [Pardu] convicting witness on train. Told us much about the notorious five. He says that he and others heard them at Buckles ranch in middle of night, before they went to Gray's.* McSurgan on same train going through too. Got a tourist booth tonight. Slept fairly well.

Wednesday, February 27, 1884: Weather good. God's country again— green fields presenting beautiful contrast to snow capped mountains. Terrible floods, especially bad between Colton and L.A. Saw one house carried away by the water [of the] Santa Anna river. Very bad times. Stopped with McS at Pico House. Los Angeles mightily changed. $6^{1}/_{2}$ years since last here. Few old landmarks left. My judgement was good about remaining. Met numbers of Americans. Fine negro music tonight at hotel by the darkies. City full of transients. Steamer only way to get through.

---

*Luben Pardu, an old prospector who lived in the foothills of the Chiricahua Mountains, testified that Red Sample, Bill Delaney, Dan Kelly, Dan Dowd, and Tex Howard were at his place a week previous to the Bisbee Massacre, at which time they met another man whom he identified as John Heith. Pardu was also at Frank Buckle's ranch in the Sulphur Spring Valley where the murders stopped to divide their loot. For a detailed discussion of the Bisbee Massacre see George M. Ellis, "Sheriff Jerome L. Ward and the Bisbee Massacre of 1883," *The Journal of Arizona History*, Vol. 35, No. 3, Autumn 1994, pp. 315-342.

[Editor's note: Again for the sake of economy, I have omitted Parsons' journey to California. The trip had little to do with his Arizona experiences as he went there to inspect the Spanish Mine, a gold mine at Nevada City that his father was considering investing in. While he deemed it a "fine chance for good legitimate mining," the operation appeared rather dilapidated, and George felt his father did not have money enough to work it. The trip, however, was rewarding in other respects. In his usual gadfly manner, he renewed acquaintances in San Francisco, Alameda and Oakland, seeing Schlaet, the Goodfellows, and an assortment of prominent people from his banking days, both male and female. He stayed at the Baldwin Hotel and ran into Milton Joyce and Jim Vizina, and attended the Patti Opera, and a Greco-Roman wrestling match between Muldoon and Whistler. And on March 25, he experienced an earthquake, the worst since 1868 according to the San Francisco *Chronicle*. On his return, George stopped over in Orange County to visit his sister Emeline and brother Sam, the latter having acquired land which he planted to grapes and fruit trees. He left Los Angeles on April 11, and despite recent heavy rains which sent the Santa Ana River over its banks and threatened to wash out the Southern Pacific tracks, George made it back to Arizona in fine shape. "Have left kind friends and fine country not for a great while I think," he commented in his diary. "Wouldn't surprise me if I got back to California soon."]

Saturday, April 12, 1884: Dry country again. Reached Benson about 2 or 2:30. Made connections with Sonora train all right. Met Mr. and Mrs. Pridham going East. They took my train. Met Moore on Sonora train and very quickly accepted his kind invitation to ride up, he having driven Ps down. Horribly dusty. Heartily welcomed by the whole town it seemed to me. Dined at Clark's, where also was Bob Lewis. Orange blossoms I brought kept very well. Saw Clapps later.

Sunday, April 13, 1884. Windy. Easter Sunday. Church full. Took my first communion this a.m. and am now entirely enlisted in God's army and have done outwardly what had been done inwardly a long time. May God help me to work now more faithfully for thine, and make myself of more use and benefit to him and the world at large. My good friend Stebbins knelt with me. Dined at Clapp's and of course had lots to tell. Church again in evening and long talk with Bagnall at his house till midnight.

Monday, April 14, 1884: About with the boys this a.m. Great times. Have mill and ranch business on the taps at present. Watched Milton and Maurice box a little this afternoon and this evening. Made a few calls upon the bride [Bessie Brown] and groom MacNeil. Mrs. Corella at Peels and Herrings. Considerable fun at Herrings. Boys and girls, old dog Tray, etc. Quite a talk with W[illiam] Farish.

Tuesday, April 15, 1884: Weather pleasant. Chance at Clifton for business probably if I want it, but cannot very well leave here for present. Things frightfully quiet, CG and C will be shut down all summer. Drove down to Charleston this afternoon with Jimmy Eccleston at his invitation. Mrs. Cheyney kindly invited us to supper and we staid. Mrs. C very pleasant. Had a delightful visit and returned at 8:30.

Wednesday, April 16, 1884: Proposed a long letter today and evening to Redfern about Antelope Springs ranch; full particulars. Also wrote Señor Flores and Miss Redfern with reference to the mill. Principal mines will shut down this summer for pump machinery and in effort to reduce wages to $3. Things will be dreadfully quiet till fall or winter and then they will boom. Miss Annie Lake to be married today. Attended confirmation lecture tonight.

Thursday, April 17, 1884: Cool for time of year; good. Ed Smith left today; sorry to see him go, genial, clever fellow. Bank business light for force at work. Called on Mrs. Clark tonight and then spent evening at Bagnall's. Whist. Maurice and Frank E there. Pleasant evening. Must rustle around and see about some money; funds going.

Friday, April 18, 1884: Weather fine. Maurice training for foot race on May 1st. Am exercising again. Have fallen off in measurements about $2^1/_2$ inches all told. Take egg and sherry about eight and we then exercise. Times getting calky, nothing doing. Young Crocker here from Cleveland. Says Ruby will be valuable. Mines will close down and times dull here till next year. Contention tired of doing all of the pumping.

Saturday, April 19, 1884: Bad times for the Clarks. Hope they may come out yet ahead; will do all I can to help but am afraid it can't amount to much. Pleasant social at Earle's tonight. Took Miss Peel. Miss Santee appeared tonight fresh from Silver City after Ed Smith who left other day. Strange doings between them. Consulted with and consoled Miss S a while. Seems at times she was non compos mentis. Maurice and I located Tom Thumb #2 adjoining TT; small.

Sunday, April 20, 1884: Church as usual this a.m. Dined at Clark's. Mrs. C, Miss Daisy and Maurice and I went to ME Church and heard Rev. Adams; not so good as usual. At Bagnall's a while tonight having a talk. Miss Sioux, as she styles herself, left this a.m. and I think for good and hope so for her own good. Called upon Miss Barrett this afternoon and there met Jimmy and a Miss Matt; Mr. Hudson also on hand at Eccleston's.

Monday, April 21, 1884: Some fellows want me to help them to start a new camp near Gila Bend. They say they have gold rock running $25 to $230. Pleasant evening at Earle's. The two brides, Mrs. MacNeil and Mrs. Tom Moore, were entertained and we had lots of fun. Two more probable brides in the near future there—JE and Miss B and MS and Miss P. Miss A Lake's announcement of marriage received today, Mrs. Townsend now.

Tuesday, April 22, 1884: Maurice went to Dragoon Summit Station today and met his father driving him back. I saw Mrs. C at M's request this a.m.

and told her of WU being saved. Very close call though George probably gone though. Dined at Clapp's. Called later at several places. Caples got in from Dragoons tonight and says he's got a big thing. Wrote Poage tonight that I could sell 1500 Prompter [shares] at $2^1/_2$.

Wednesday, April 23, 1884: Exercised this a.m., alone though.

Thursday, April 24, 1884: Things dull and getting more so. Mines will probably shut down the first. Dined at Clark's tonight and fixed deed business for them.

Friday, April 25, 1884: Nothing new. Am trying to interest some one in [Joseph] Dougherty's proposition 200 miles below here in Gila Bend country. Everybody seems dead broke. First horseback ride this afternoon with Mrs. Battin, Miss Inslee, Misses S & M Herring. HH and I went to Sycamore Springs and beyond a short distance. Dined at Herring's and spent part of evening; balance at Milton's.

Saturday, April 26, 1884: Dull times ahead, but I believe camp will be better than ever next year. Is to be a $3 camp. At Clapp's late. Champagne, etc., in honor of Mrs. Batten and Miss Inslee. Muldoon in town, the wrestler. Magnificent specimen of physical culture.

Sunday, April 27, 1884: Attended church as usual a.m. and p.m. Dined at Milton's. Quite a talk with [Rev. David] McFawn and Bagnall tonight. Muldoon-Wilson wrestling match tonight. Wilson very easily handled. Wanted to see it but of course couldn't go Sunday night.

Monday, April 28, 1884: Weather fine. Am trying to get some one to take hold of the Dougherty scheme. Hard work though. I rustle like thunder. At Herring's tonight to have farewell cut up as the aunts leave tomorrow a.m. Great times; cards, dancing, singing. They're jolly aunts. Walked to race track today with M. He's training for $^1/_4$ mile and 100 yards races.

Wednesday, April 30, 1884: Took Bruce about today. Went down the Grand Central with Mr. [C. W.] Leach. Last chance for a time as mines will probably shut down tomorrow. Not much excitement yet over the $3 business and I think there won't be much. Visited Huachuca reservoir later, stopped at TM&M office and had quite a tramp. Dined at Clark's this evening and had pleasant time. Music, etc. Bruce a very clever, nice fellow.

Thursday, May 1, 1884: Everything was race today. Bagnall, Brewster and I walked to track this afternoon. Quite a crowd. Maurice here as usual. Brown only ran part of the quarter, claiming swelled ankles. M ran 100 yards alone for medal in $10^1/_2$. Track somewhat fast. Fine time. He also beat Bob Lewis handicap 100 yards race, giving Bob 15 feet. Dan O'Connor and Bob had good race, Dan beating. Bob wild. Wanted to know what was matter. J Haly thought he couldn't race fast enough. Poor consolations to the mother and sisters. Slight sprinkling of rain tonight.

Friday, May 2, 1884: Rain early, clear later. Bruce left on stage rather strangely this a.m., not stating last night his intention. Didn't of course see him again. Still wrestling with Dougherty and his Gila Bend proposition, trying to induce some one to take hold. Everybody broke. Nothing bad yet about reduction of wages here. Miners hold meetings every day. No developments yet. Dined at Milton's tonight and later saw Mrs. Seamans with them. She goes East tomorrow. Won't live long probably.

Saturday, May 3, 1884: Bade Cap and Mrs. Seamans adios this a.m.; Mrs. S probably for the last time. Rustled hard today and finally got Billy Howard and Bob Upton interested. They will take hold for a half interest. Will get outfit and start by wagon from here. Am glad to have been successful in so far as I can go. Will now hope for good results. Called on Mrs. Goodfellow tonight.

Sunday, May 4, 1884: Church as usual a.m. and p.m. Communion this a.m. Walked part way to Church's with Mrs. Cheyney who told me of an engagement between the Prof. and Miss Peel and probable marriage next month. I communicated suspicions to Mrs. Clapp recently and now they're confirmed. Took Miss P home from church and congratulated her. Am very glad for her. She'll fill the position in every way and Church is a most fortunate man. Dined at Clapp's and walked around to Herring's a while, later.

Monday, May 5, 1884: Dougherty went to New Mexico this a.m. on sudden business, will return in a few days when they'll go off on the Gila Bend racket. Miners Union interviewed the superintendents this a.m. [E. B.] Gage nervous. Went to meeting later and heard Swayne. Cigars and beer free by Summerfield. Reports make miners rather arbitrary. Don't think there'll be serious trouble though.* Summoned to grand jury duty this a.m., but judge absent and court adjourned till tomorrow. Mr. and Mrs. Clapp and I dined at Clarks tonight. Music, etc., in evening.

Tuesday, May 6, 1884: Court opened at 10 a.m. and a lot of us serve as grand jurors. Stebbins, Meade, Taylor, Hartman; quite a gang of the boys. M foreman. Was notified last night to be in readiness and have wagons in order as trouble might ensue. So lively times may come again. Told F I was one of them and to count on me every time. I hope the Union will have better sense than to do or attempt harm and bodily injury. Am at the front every time on law and order business. No business this a.m. at GJ. This p.m. though we did considerable and the murder case I'm interested [in] was up. Pleasant horseback ride tonight. I with Mrs. More and Maurice with his sister. Beautiful, moonlight night; saw Mrs. Walker.

Wednesday, May 7, 1884: Getting warm now. Fine exercise this a.m. Lively times today. At our mutual protection meeting this evening word

*According to the *Mining and Scientific Press* of May 10, 1884, Tombstone mining companies faced two other problems besides the threat of flooding: a reduction in the price of silver to below a dollar an ounce, and decline in the grade of ore, all of which resulted in an operational loss for the town's major producers during the first four months of 1884. As a result, miners' wages were cut twenty-five percent, from four dollars to three dollars a day. A union was formed, the miners paraded with brass bands, and refused to accept the reduction; a strike was called on May 1, 1884. Mine owners responded with a lockout.

came that Grand Central hoist was to be attacked. [Tom] Farish called for volunteers and I responded, first man, and went for a carriage at Col. Clark's suggestion. The Col, Farish, Robertson and I rode up in a hurry. False alarm. Guards posted, watch word given and we returned. Guns and ammunition gotten tonight. Up late discussing situation and advising. Lively times ahead probably. Signal agreed upon and steam to be kept up continually. Organized tonight. I made motion to have chair appoint committee to select officers and battalion captain, and Earle and Farish were elected.

Thursday, May 8, 1884: A bad undercurrent of feeling. No outbreaks yet but they're anticipated most any night. Nice ride this evening, Mrs. Fitzhenry and Miss Daisy, Maurice and I. Grand Jury business still engaging me. Some fine experiences. Nothing of a fiery nature today but the air is full of rumors. Patrolling begun.

Friday, May 9, 1884: Still Grand Jurying at a hard rate. Old Huachuca murder case up again. Stood guard on Grand Central hill tonight to protect hoist. Maurice joined me at midnight. We went home between two and three a.m. At Herring's a while I believe. Not much sleep these times. Miners cooling off I think. Milton and Mrs. C at Herring's. Left them about 10 and Milton thought I was getting more than my share of Grand Jury duty.

Saturday, May 10, 1884: Weather fine. Intense excitement this a.m. Slept late of course and on way up town learned that Hudson & Co. had suspended and that Milton had hurried to Tucson. A wild place. Hurried to Grand Jury room. People thought that Clapp had skipped with a lot of money and wished a warrant sworn out immediately and officers sent for him before train could be reached.* I headed this off by having Jimmy E sent for, knowing Milton had done nothing of the sort and he verified that everything was intact. Mrs. C standing the thing bravely. Good thing for M, his leaving. Somebody would have him killed otherwise. Shortly after Jury met this afternoon word came that the mob was preparing to break into Bank's offices, as officers were too few. Twenty deputies ordered, and

---

*On the morning of May 10 Safford, Hudson Bank of Tucson suspended operations of its branch in Tombstone. With $50,000 to $150,000 owing depositors, cashier Milton Clapp immediately headed for Tucson to learn the cause of the closure. Meanwhile, Tombstone's out-of-work miners vented their fear in a wave of hysteria. Shortly after the institution closed its doors, the street in front of the bank was crowded with excited men clamoring for admittance and demanding to know the whereabouts of Clapp. Finding him gone, the crowd dispersed.

Bitterness nevertheless prevailed. Judge Southard expressed the sentiment of a great many citizens when he remarked that he "believed the failure was a damned swindle and that the depositors had simply been robbed." Charges and counter charges were leveled, townspeople accusing the bank of bad speculation, the bank blaming the debacle on closure of the mines. Nevertheless, many miners "lost their little all," and local authorities feared that the bank would be destroyed. An investigation promoted by a federal judge and local citizens, backed by swearing in of deputies by Sheriff Ward, and the arrival of a company of soldiers from Fort Huachuca, calmed the situation.

we marched to mob in a hurry and read them, partially restoring confidence. Exciting times a while. I nominated bank committee which will help assignee. Was appointed committee of one tonight on special bank business. City distraught tonight and carefully patrolled. Fight expected on mesa but nothing came of it. We were ready. Slept at M's house tonight.

Sunday, May 11, 1884: Took Mrs. Clapp to church this a.m. Bishop on hand. Have no money. Eat at friends till arrangements for them are made. My few dollars are in bank. All kinds of rumors and reports afloat. A few of us, and very few they are too, making strenuous efforts to convince people that Clapp is all O.K. and that things are better than they seem. I wrote statement for *Epitaph* which appeared as Bank attorney's, Major Earle, Trantum and I are doing all we can. Confirmation service tonight. Three confirmed. Dined at Berry's. On guard tonight. Bed about three a.m. House threatened. Money supposed to be there. Mrs. C comes in for a good show of abuse; makes me hot. May get a row yet. Rope around bank cut. No damage however. Air thick yet.

Monday, May 12, 1884: John Davis and I took turns guarding house tonight. I don't propose letting anyone in. Fine lot of hypocritical friends here where C has done much for and who now berate him. Col H and Judge B, and Frank K amongst others. "All, all most honorable gentlemen." I told Mrs. C this a.m. that in view of threats and very bad state of affairs so that one couldn't tell what a day might bring forth, she better go at once to S.F. as M had gone and I was afraid to have her stay and was afraid even for Harry's safety. T and Major E concurred with me. Mrs. C at once packed with assistance of Mrs. Earle and friends and was all ready tonight. Did all I could all day and night when off jury and got things in readiness for tomorrow. Miss Peel arranged to go to instead of a day later. Jimmy E back late last night feeling good. Special engine. Conference all around between one and two a.m. T scared. It was suggested today that I had $60,000 hidden. Some people idiots, those not crazy. Pleasant times at Herring's a while tonight in honor of Miss Peel's departure tomorrow.

Tuesday, May 13, 1884: Scratched M B Clapp off of one trunk and got all off on stage and then drove Mrs. C, Miss Peel, Harry and John to Fairbank this a.m. Miss Sarah H and Pennington accompanied us. Pleasant ride. Miss C in quite fair spirits considering Miss P will return later as Mrs. Church. Confoundedly glad to get Mrs. C off without trouble. People cooling off some. Most of guards discharged. Jimmy, Bob and John prepared statement yesterday from books and I insisted that Ben Goodrich should state books correct and in good condition in tonight's paper. Took the slip to paper myself with assets and liabilities, nothing detailed however. No guarding tonight. Can't tell how statements will be received.

Wednesday, May 14, 1884: Jury duty still. Tried bulling bank stock today with good effect. Terrible news from the East on top of all of these troubles. A dozen banks said to have suspended and another panic imminent similar to '73 and '74. Feeling blue for father tonight. Am afraid he's caught, he's so venturesome. Nothing but an earthquake left for us now. First good sleep last night in a good while. Was appointed special deputy sheriff other day.

Thursday, May 15, 1884: Committee work today on Recorder's office and Supervisors. Some disagreeable facts in all of the offices. There'll be some jumping stiff legged tomorrow night. Down to cases but will get Jury certificates tomorrow as we adjourn. Some billiards with Stebbins till quite late. Dined at Clark's tonight. Bank business straightening out some and things look better.

Friday, May 16, 1884: Weather fine. Grand Jury adjourned about noon today. Some wrangling towards last. I drew resolutions thanking foreman, clerk and District Attorney which were adopted. Report in tonight's paper and a bad time between two parties. We spared nobody on account of position but have reported without fear or favor. Maurice went to Nacosari today with W. Farish's party guarding treasure. Hopes to get hold of something there. With all of our rackets we should do something. Mrs. C all right at Los Angeles.

Saturday, May 17, 1884: Very busy this a.m. corralling Grand Jury certificates at 80 cents. Made good wages. Have some money once more. Staid at Maurice's house tonight and had good bath. Bad scrapping match tonight between M and Mark. I thought the GJ report would cause trouble. I went for Recorder's office. Haven't seen Al Jones yet.

Sunday, May 18, 1884: Weather good, windy. Church a.m. and p.m. Sang in choir; only male singer. Poor attendance and collections. Hard times now. Dined at Clark's. Bagnall stopped at Clapp's tonight with me.

Monday, May 19, 1884: Cool. Things getting slow again. J. E. back from Tucson tonight with rather encouraging news. If people will only keep their shirts on they will come out all right. Judge Rountree got in last night from Carlisle and reports things satisfactory with him. Kadish is with him or rather, has a painting contract he got for him. Sent some *Epitaphs* off today at Milton's request.

Tuesday, May 20, 1884: Talked Antelope ranch with Taylor this a.m. The Cornishmen in to see me too. Palmer talks mill, leasing though. No business in town to speak of. Bob Kenny and I had good exercise this a.m. Believe I had some whist this evening. [T. L.] Stiles, assignee, around today or last night. Mrs. C frightened about Col tonight. Had to force office and found him asleep. Great time.

Wednesday, May 21, 1884: Depositors' meeting called this a.m. by Stiles and committee appointed to examine into matters with him. He talked well and only repeated my line of argument here for the past week or two. They hopeful. Foment against Milton and I am advised to keep him away from here. Guess he won't be around for a while. Dougherty expected tonight but didn't come. Dined at Clark's. Spent evening at Bagnall's. Cribbage and casino.

Thursday, May 22, 1884. Weather pleasant. Began Spanish with Prieto today. Valued some property today to testify about in court tomorrow. Lawyer Adams quite wild. Depositors committee reported tonight at Court House. Heard rumors of bad state of things and that Milton was to be charged with forgery, etc., and was on hand for him. Co. Treas. and Sheriff had taken out about $7000 since grand jury court but put it back at Stiles persuasion, although they probably was secured by M. Was glad things passed off so smoothly. Packed house and some bad talk but nothing serious. M not dragged in. Long talk with JE tonight, who told me much and talked with me as he said he would with Hudson or Clapp.

Friday, May 23, 1884: Weather fine. Exercised as usual this a.m., but cut my arm deeply and may be laid up a while. Testified in court today as to value on certain term RE. Preferred conditions paid today. Must now write Spanish composition for lesson tomorrow. A very nice and characteristic letter tonight from Mrs. Clapp. Am glad I could be of service to her. Witnessed a marriage this evening at Occidental by request of Rev. Bagnall. A. Shakly of Bisbee married Ella Green of Amador, Cal.

Saturday, May 24, 1884: No news yet of J.D. Guess he'll come along though. Got Mrs. Clapp's box out of bank this a.m. and will forward it soon. Spanish lesson today. Water turned off. Must attend to that; garden will die. Stiles gone to Tucson. Genl W told me tonight to warn MBC against coming here a while yet and gave me two parties names who would attempt to get away with him. G & L. Billiarded with Judge T and home with him later to see Tel from M who is now at Pinal for Anglo Cal.

Sunday, May 25, 1884: Church a.m. and p.m. and took up collection for first time as Major Earle was away in Sonora. Also sung in choir with Mrs. R and helped children sing at S. school this afternoon. Pretty busy. Dined at Clark's and took Mrs. Farish some flowers.

Monday, May 26, 1884: [Joseph] Dougherty at last on hand and he and Bob Upton and Billy Howard preparing to get off in a day or two. Took Joe D to cabin and gave him some things for trip. At last my efforts seem to be about rewarded as to getting things under way. Now we'll see what there is in the new country. Had Spanish lesson today and in evening called on Mrs. Pridham where I had a warm talk with MacNeil about Milton and later called on Mrs. Adam and was treated to mint julip.

Tuesday, May 27, 1884: Letter from Milton this a.m. [He's] at Pinal a while on bus[iness] for Anglo Cal. Quite a time packing Mrs. Clapp's tin box and ladle in another. Shipped it to H.L.D.S.F. Dined at Clark's lately. Water turned on again so I can have garden all O.K. Little notary business today for a change. Fixed Joe D off with various articles for the trip to the new country. Am in calling mood now. Went to Springer's and Reppy's tonight. Bank matters in status quo.

Wednesday, May 28, 1884: Joe got off this a.m. about nine with Bob Upton and a fellow whose name I didn't learn. Bob and Joe drive and other fellow rides. Good heavy wagon well supplied with everything for good testing and examination. Will be gone probably two months. Joe will look out for us and see there is fair play. So at last my part of the program is carried out after great rustling and it remains to be seen what will come of it all. With ranch matter with Nick Stanton, Sonora with Maurice and Gila business with Joe, some money should be made. Spanish today.

Thursday, May 29, 1884: Things quiet. Chloriders [mine lessors] stopped by the Miners Union. About 50 men it is said compelled to stop. Doing some work for Col Clark at Sheriff's office. Called at Herring's tonight.

Friday, May 30, 1884: Decoration Day. Commemorative exercises held at Schieffelin Hall. Talk by Judge [W. H.] Stilwell. More work for Col. today. Met Con Cutler, goes to Sonora tomorrow and I think I'll go with him if I can get off. Grand chance to try to clinch mill racket. Called on Mrs. Caples tonight and we had some music. Howard and I billiarded later; beat him two games.

Saturday, May 31, 1884: Wrote letters and prepared to get off to Sonora, Nacosari cañon, with Cutler. Expect to leave about three p.m. or thereabouts. Here it is the 9th of June and I am at Nacosari. Got off at 3:30 and reached Palominas about dark. Muchas cambias at Palominas. Very little packing on my part. Buckboard and good pair of mules.

Sunday, June 1, 1884: Staid at store today. Cutler getting some goods to send off. In afternoon got off to Custom House. Made pleasant acquaintance there; young official from Ures. Drank some chocolate with him. Beer and quite a talk with Don José Elias.

Monday, June 2, 1884: Long ride today. Started at 5:30 a.m. sharp. Met Jim Handley just from Suisquipe as we were leaving. Drove 67 miles according to Cutler and reached Fronteras before sun down. A lively ride. Cutler is a slasher. Stopped at Don Cuyatano Silva's. Smaller place than Bacucachi. Mucho mescal. Quite tired. Good thing we are with Cutler. They walled him in.

Tuesday, June 3, 1884: Walked up on hill and saw old bells at church ruins. Off about seven. Rather pretty country. Old orchards standing one hundred years and more. Many teams on road all for Nacosori cañon. Saw remains of load blown up by Indians fews months since at bad place in rocks where Bennett was killed and Scott wounded. Cutler a lively driver and talker. Many points of interest along road. Places were many killings took place, old ruins, etc. Reached camp in mountains before dark and found all hands well. Pretty place. Lots of friends.

Wednesday, June 4, 1884: Pretty spot in mountains. Good grub and a large and coming camp. Maurice fat, Hunt and Shaw well. Lon Ashman here in charge of company's store, pleasant fellow. Manard Adams in charge of smelter. He, Maurice and I drive about three miles below Cutler's and had grand wash in a water hole. Started up some deer. Sleep well nights.

Thursday, June 5, 1884: Off today on a long and tedious horse back ride to San Pedro mine. William Farish and I returned by way of the Rosario and had a tough climb of it getting to the property. To other old properties worked ages ago bid fair to be good with development.

Friday, June 6, 1884: Another pull today over to El Dorado mine, 15 miles distant over the roughest trail I ever knew. Wonderfully well mineralized country. Deep cañons with step walls. Terrific climbing at times. W. Farish had narrow escape with horse. Seven men killed at mine by Indians. Danger little now, though one cannot tell anything about them. Like old times. Made some pancakes. Hard trip; old gold workings; separated once. Shots found me; horses played. Mucho mescal for entertainment.

Saturday, June 7, 1884: Did some heavy loafing today. In good condition for it. Things moving very slowly. No, I forgot, I climbed Nacosari Mountain and found [E. R.] Howe 6300 ft. up. Hard climb afoot. Visited La Fortuna and Cobresa. Water just struck in tunnel. Hot walk. Trouble at mine other day and G. Adams nearly killed by Mexicans; stoned. Bad times. Charley Watts married a Mexican in camp.

Sunday, June 8, 1884: Trouble again. Miners struck for $2.50. New store just completed and goods moved in. Quite a nice one for the country. Lon has his hands full. Passed day very quietly. Maurice and Howe returned Tuesday and I may go south further with Farish.

Monday, June 9, 1884: New developments today. Lon hot about something and charge of store offered me at $125 and board, dinero Americano. Rather abrupt proceeding. I accepted though and Maurice will probably find something here. We're busted and must get something ahead to operate upon. Wrote letters today, six or seven, and tomorrow will pitch in. M and I drove to the rocks this afternoon and had good wash.

Tuesday, June 10, 1884: Started in this a.m. Confusion most confounded. Goods just in and a great time. Lon is just in the store. Very lively times exchanging provisions por los dobes. Number of men in and grub had to be furnished them. Rather poor business giving credit in advance. Seems to be a great lack of system generally. Maurice and Howe started for Tombstone this afternoon. Maurice will return to work for the company. We must rustle now awhile.

Wednesday, June 11, 1884: Up early and at it today. Fine work. Probably about $20,000 worth of stock carried. An immense amount of business done. Will keep me hopping. Am getting along well enough. The Mexicans seem too lazy to speak out their own language. Difficult to make them out, ear lacks cultivation. Have grammar all O.K., but must train ear. Reading and talking two different things. Great rush in evenings. Rorner, Young, Richards, and Smith arrived today. Tired nights, very.

Thursday, June 12, 1884: Prepared a sign today reading "Se cerrara la tienda a las once todos los Domingos y durante y media de la noche." Am glad to have store shut Sundays though have to work part of day. Indians reported out again and Crook after them, but they hardly come in here. Things in embryo here and badly mixed. Will straighten out later. Meals now in new adobe house saving walk of a mile. Have a cot now and things in good style.

Frday, June 13, 1884: Weather warm. Gradually getting stock to rights. We fellows entered in a mescal contract today. I didn't know it was against Farish's orders to have it here. Must get rid of it now. Terribly rushed last night. No fun with a store packed full of Mexicans all jabbering away and preserving no order whatever. They don't half speak out and with localisms its hard work. Pretty good sales per day. I issue paper money of my own for change when I can make it.

Saturday, June 14, 1884: Things gradually being righted. Two boys with me now, neither able to speak English. Can't see how we will be able to supply 200 or 300 men here when they start in. Hard to get flour even now. Men had to go out and [fight] fire today, coming up canyon pretty lively.

Sunday, June 15, 1884: Closed doors at 11 a.m. Big business though beforehand. Mighty glad of chance for a rest, enjoyed it immensely being well tired out. Good wash this afternoon in creek up road half a mile. Clean once more.

Monday, June 16, 1884: Things lively today especially tonight when the store was jammed and Lon Ashman and I were kept busy constantly for an hour and a half. Hardest night yet. Flour all out. Sold 300 lbs. tonight in dabs. After closing store at 8:30 we went over to Charley Watts and after mescal heard some music a while, guitar and violin, by Mexicans.

Tuesday, June 17, 1884: Things moving along. Books at office behind and mixed I guess. My hands full about all of the time. Bill Farish with Streeter started below today for a week or ten days. Not such a rush today. Some casino this evening. Some good yarns told about Yaqui Indians.

Wednesday, June 18, 1884: One story of Yaquis is that they cut their mouths on each side while eating with knives first time. Another that they carried wheelbarrows and all the first time they saw them, not knowing enough to wheel their loads. Nothing new these times.

Thursday, June 19, 1884: Regular machine work now. Up at six, at it all day and at night rushed to death several hours.

Friday, June 20, 1884: Rain before long. Very monotonous this kind of life. Have a battle every night with the Mexicans. Most of them here seem just a little removed from the Australian bushman. Pretty well played at night. Store jammed and the jargon terrible. Lightning a while.

Saturday, June 21, 1884: Lon Ashman has swung clear and I ran things entirely myself now. Have Don José María Torres's boy, Lorenzo, and Don José Mesa's boy, Manuel, to break in, and William Thomas, the butcher, to do the work. Señor Martinez, my Spanish assistant, arrived tonight along with Liborio Vasquez, the prieto for this district. Seems a very gentlemanly fellow; M's family. Rush tonight. Mail tonight and I received 13 letters and postals. Sister gone East much to my surprise.

Sunday, June 22, 1884: Hot weather. Closed at 11 a.m., not feeling at all well. Good bath this afternoon. Went up canyon on Farish's horse to get it. Also had a time with large rattlesnake. Beautiful color. Sorry I didn't have my knife along to get skin. No vegetables. Wrote several letters tonight and got them off.

Monday, June 23, 1884: Great times with the boys, betting on flies the newest thing. Each fellow takes one lump of sugar, places it on table and first lump of sugar with fly on it wins. Lively tonight, very. Irishman at mine says its a great country when they spell meat Kearney (carne) and rope McCarty (mecorte).

Tuesday, June 24, 1884: A hot day and hotter night as the woods are on fire about us. Fine sight tonight. A little uneasy about three a.m. Could hear fire plainly and seemed to be coming for us. Large amount of black and Giant powder on hand. Dressed and kept an eye open. Adams went to smelter. Had a curtain rigged up today in room. A little better.

Wednesday, June 25, 1884: Thermometer in sun 122. Nearly about 100 probably in shade. Very little business through day and evening. Lightest evening yet. Terribly uncomfortable day. Good bath in tanks tonight. They were fine. Shaw and I indulged. Just deep enough to dive into with care.

Thursday, June 26, 1884: Maurice arrived today, bringing hack and a lot of stuff. Had a rather hard trip. A Mr. Foushay and young fellow named Fitch along with their own conveyance. Going below further. Guitar and good music tonight. Rainy season commenced today or night rather. Quite a rain. Freshened up things. Good sleep tonight.

Friday, June 27, 1884: Maurice started right in today I believe working for the company. Will probably assay for the smelter. Rain again tonight, thunder and lightning. Must have Giant powder removed.

Saturday, June 28, 1884: Cloudy in afternoon, but no rain. Unpleasantly warm and flies bad. Little to do at present and store stock very low.

Sunday, June 30, 1884: Closed at 11 a.m. as usual. First trouble this morning. An insolent drunken Mexican caused the trouble. I took hold of him first and then Thomas, the Negro I have to run butcher shop and assist in store, fired the man bodily. Thomas, or Boas as Farish calls him, measures 45 inches around the chest and is probably the most powerful man here. The man came in a second time and Thomas literally fired him through the air and thumped him well. Others gathered and a row was imminent but didn't come off. Good bath this evening at creek. More Tombstoners on hand.

Monday, June, 30, 1884: Over 10,000 lbs. flour received. So there's enough of that for the present. Excitement over about row yesterday and guess everything's lovely again.

Tuesday, July 1, 1884: Very hot. Very little clothing does us now.

Wednesday, July 2, 1884: Same old thing all the time. Time steps away very rapidly indeed. Shaw and I commenced studying with Martinez today once more Spanish, but I don't consider him very much of a teacher.

Thursday, July 3, 1884: Everything goes along in the same old way. No exercise for me. I feel the need of it. This is a dog's life. None of life's amenities whatever. One might as well be in the store and have the long hours for aught of any place to go or anything to do, else.

Friday, July 4, 1884: Explosions of Giant powder awoke us early this a.m. in keeping of the glorious 4th. Had pistol shooting later and I came out ahead with my old colt .44-40. I've got her down fine. Some Mexicans serenaded us in afternoon and we engaged them for the evening and had a great time then. Closed store early and gave ourselves up to a good time. Mescal flowed freely and dancing (stag) mucho. Americans and natives exchange songs and celebrated till quite late having done all we knew how.

Saturday, July 5, 1884: Frightfully busy day. At work in store and office. Things badly mixed in office in books and Shaw rather inexperienced. Money lost by bad bookkeeping heretofore. Maurice helping.

Sunday, July 6, 1884: Closed as usual at 11 a.m. Some goods in today and more tomorrow. Will have lively times. Good bath this afternoon.

Monday, July 7, 1884: Have rather lost the run of the days. Great monotony.

Tuesday, July 8, 1884: Mucho calor. Hace mucho calor estos dias. Me no gusto este tiempo. Es muy malo. Estoy mucho ocupado ahora con nuevo negocios. Los canos ha venido con provisiones y hay mucho hacer. Una larga cuenta se had recibido y contene muchos articulos. No hay descanso para los mal hombre.

Wednesday, July 9, 1884: Hot all the time. Bath today. W. Farish left for Tombstone and NY today. Brown accompanied to Tombstone to return with his wife.

Thusday, July 10, 1884: Nothing new. Hot with rains every now and then.

Friday, July 11, 1884: Things vey stale. Close and hot also. Am getting goods out and priced. The cost is heavy. Added to cost of goods must be reckoned frieght per lb. and cost of Custom House papers which I estimated at 4%, then 15% added to make Mexican money to which are added the duty and last a second or additional duty of 5% on value of first duty. An immense amount of figuring for small packages.

Saturday, July 12, 1884: Nothing new today. Maurice and I arranged to go off tomorrow into the mountains to see the Esperanza and Plomosa.

Sunday, July 13, 1884: Closed as usual at 11 and at 1:30 started horseback, Maurice and I with a Mexican, to see the Esperanza and Plomosa. Rode Donovan's horse, a scary bucking animal, who has killed several people. Pleasant ride to the "E." Fair prospect. Thence to the P on top of a mountain. Great time getting there. Rain. Went to buttom nearly 200 ft. by Mexican ladders, a curious substitute for giving better. Examined and sampled. Fine time getting horse in rain, mud and dark woods. Branches whipping me all of the time. Lead most of distance, calling directions. Home about 9:30 or ten. Fine time from corral to the house.

Monday, July 14, 1884: Business lively today. Smith and Richards with Mrs. T. E. Farish arrived today and I suppose there'll be an overhauling now. New boom business. Yesterday a.m. quite a few of the notables were on hand, the heavy merchant of Valencia, Durango, the heavy military man, Col. Torres, and one or two more. Supposing my room was vacated by them for good, we took what mescal was left, but learning they were to return, replaced it with water and left. There was a great scene as detailed to us later. All billed at the old man's invitation, and with bien salud, drank off the water. Explanations had to follow.

Tuesday, July 15, 1884: Mercury 94 yesterday. Warmer by two degrees than before. They say Gringos bring changes. Another racket with Charley today on hand. Have a good man now in place of Thomas, called Joe or Frenchy. Have store well stocked, shelves full and things looking and going well now. Two men and two boys, assistants, and I do the overseeing and managing part, helping customers too at times, fix prices, order goods, etc.

Wednesday, July 16, 1884: Sisters and father together on the Hudson in a pretty home of their own. Things going well there. Hope they'll continue. Rumors growing about changes. Farish has turned our affairs here, store purchasing, accounts, etc., [over] to Smith and I may be bounced and probably will be as Lon Ashman is thick with the new crowd. I'll gamble though on there being some way on the stock now. They can't fire me out bodily though. I won't go. Good bath in creek today and helped Joe corral steer and staid through the killing by rifle.

Thursday, July 17, 1884: Maurice surveying today, a change from steady assaying. He is jumped about pretty well. The New Jersey gang* are beginning to run things; am told unofficially that Rolly is to run books, LA the store. He was very politic in leaving when he did to curry favor under a new regime and escape if possible past troubles. Busy trying for balances today. Things will pop next three months. Don't believe A wants to run smelter much, patent reasons.

Friday, July 18, 1884: Well, this evening I received the grand bounce but am to stay my month out for which I contended and which is certainly my just due. Smith told me this evening that LA would take charge tomorrow. The N.J. crowd are in and have full swing. Smith's birthday—a serenade by Torres tonight. Great times. Troubadour songs into which I was

---

*Parsons is referring to the New Jersey and Sonora Mining Company, which according to *Arizona Weekly Citizen* of August 30, 1884, had just installed two thirty-ton Rankin, Brayton water-jacket furnaces to smelt copper mined from their vast properties at Nacosari.

brought by the natives as the storekeeper and caratel keeper. Much joy and much mescal. Torres floored early in the fray; drank Smith's health at his invite. People kissed my hand and todos estaban buenos amigos.

Saturday, July 19, 1884: Rain. Felt a little off today. Too much joy last night. Good bath this afternoon. Will take things easier now than Lon Ashman takes back the control. Must do some rustling too between now and the 10th of next month.

Sunday, July 20, 1884: Closed at 11 and Lon A and Richards took stock bal of day. They went through warehouse yesterday. Joe, my good Frenchman, was fired this a.m. Rather rough on him. Called up on the hill at Farish's this afternoon and met the madame.

Monday, July 21, 1884: Things going along as usual. Flies outrageously bad. Will not be sorry when I am out of the store.

Tuesday, July 22, 1884: All the time hot. Chinaman cook had another row today I think it was and as usual I was present at the thumping. Matters askew on the hill again. Miller and Mexicans don't get along at all. Furnace started again today; pretty sight at night. Turning out pretty good mat[te] for shipment to Wales.

Wednesday, July 23, 1884: No mail this time for me. A fellow misses it away out of the world as this place is. Arranged today for a trip to Shaw's gold mining properties with him tomorrow. If representations are correct we have a good thing, Maurice and I.

Thursday, July 24, 1884: Started pretty early with Shaw riding Robley's horse, a nice one. A hard pull. After reaching country where boys were hunting gold it took some time to find them. Took freshest trail and got there after a while. Good prospects for placer diggings. Moulton has great faith in ultimate results. Will reach bed rock at about 20 or 25 ft. probably. Easy digging. Collett helping. Later, we three went to the gold quartz mines. A hard pull but magnificent sight. Best thing I've seen since mining. Surest possible scheme. Perhaps a good fortune awaits me now. Wouldn't sell my quarter interest for $2500. Two fine rich ledges, sampled them well. Hard time over mountains home; rough country.

Friday, July 25, 1884: A little sore today after the exceedingly rough pull yesterday. Had to slide down in some places and horse slide after me. Found a new gold lead though while tumbling about in the rocks which may amount to something. Couldn't get a rougher trip I think, but we explored considerable country. I really think that at last I have found a stake. Shaw, Moulton, Maurice and I will be, and are partners, and if present placer work is successful will take up all land we can. Some Mexicans are making money nearby.

Saturday, July 26, 1884: Better day than for sometime. Rain this afternoon, a little. Needed badly here and at placers. Gorman and W. Gird arrived from town today, Tombstone, bringing lots of news. Mrs. Pridham dead is saddest. Some rain tonight. Looks like a dry season.

Sunday, July 27, 1884: Good wash today. Fine dinner tonight mostly by the two Gs. Canned stuff—lobster, oysters, and wine until I for one got too much in my diaphragm. First square meal in a good while and I made the best of it. Music tonight at Maurice's. He has moved to new assay office.

Monday, July 28, 1884: Nothing new particularly. Mrs. Farish bitten by a tarantula this evening. Supposed to be rather; nothing serious.

Tuesday, July 29, 1884: Gold assay of $90 and $45 oz. silver, better than last assay, so Maurice and I will join Moulton and Shaw and try for gold. We have some fine property and ought to make some money. Will cost M and I $61.34 Mex money to come in apiece and Moulton, Shaw, M and I will have $1/4$ each. This is the best thing yet. Guess we'll have to call the company the New Discovery. Gird and Gorman got off early this a.m.

Wednesday, July 30, 1884: Yellow Jack at Cumpas next town and guess we'll have it here but I don't fear it. Time slipping away fast. Am to see Farish tonight, guess he wants me at the mines, an agreeable change from store. Good wash at creek today.

Thursday, July 31, 1884: Farish wants me to go to mine first of mouth and keep account of material, work time, etc., at $150 per month. Boys think it a good chance for me to go to our gold mine and work it. My month is up the 9th and I'll probably remain here until that time at store and then probably go up the mountains to mine for Farish. More roaring at boarding house. This time Bob was thumped and Howard put out.

Friday, August 1, 1884: Nothing new. We're nearly starving to death. Rain again. No sleeping out of doors tonight. Liable to be bad times here within the next ten days from all accounts. I'm ready for anything, guns, etc.

Saturday, August 2, 1884: Rather early this a.m. while I was working in the store office, Maurice rushed in and called to me to get my rifle quick and not stop to question. Jumped for my rifle and six shooter expecting every minute that the store was at point of being attacked as it was about time and we were settling affairs, and immediately conjectured it was another Bisbee. Shaw thought Indians had jumped the camp. Soon discovered though that poor Neil McLeod had been shot and killed by a half breed named Revers, whose head he had punched the night before at Milt Sweeny's wedding celebration for speaking disrespectfully of his (McLeod's) wife. Dick Watts and McLeod were leading their horses along when Revers jumped them and killed poor Neil. McLeod was the best boxer in Arizona and had the belt a while and was not a quarrelsome man at all. Maurice was interferred with by Hermudas while trying to discover if life was extinct. M attempted to assert authority by drawing pistol but was shut up pretty quickly. Funeral this evening. M had service from prayer book.

Sunday, August 3, 1884: Open till 11 a.m. Shaw and Dorment stage rolled in about 1:30 for first time in history of this part of Sonora. Good stage and four mules, good ones too. Five passengers and mail along. Letters for all hands. Bad things home on the Hudson. Fire, loss $2000, insurance $^1/_2$. Good bath. While talking with Maurice across the creek this evening a roar was heard and I crossed the gulch just in advance of a rush of water four feet deep which came along with great force carrying rocks and parts of trees before it. Heavy rains above. We've got it some in gold. Must get possession under Mexican law as soon as possible.

Monday, August 4, 1884: Getting stuff together. Pretty sight from bluff opposite at night. Mexican camp fires below, hills on either side, whole effect quite picturesque. Shaw likely to make money on stage line. Passengers $18 a piece Mex. + 15 Am. coin. Had I money might have joined him. Wrote several letters today including paper article on Neil McLeod's death.

Tuesday, August 5, 1884: Stage went out this morning, no passengers, however. My last week at store and can't say I'm sorry. Moved across the gulch today to the new office, two loads. Have everything clear now and distinct, liable to be misunderstandings otherwise. Slept there tonight. High and quiet but am afraid the pit and future oven smoke will be bad.

Wednesday, August 6, 1884: Moulton in today. No rain, consequently no ability to work placers successfully. He and Collett sunk 30 odd feet and drifted as much and got good showing but can't do anything without water. Not absolute bed rock. Expected water there but didn't get it. After considerable discussion, it was decided to push matters on the ledge and sink 30 to 50 feet. We'll have to blow in considerable but we have a good thing to work on. Natives becoming impatient as no dinero comes.

Thursday, August 7, 1884. I packed Moulton well and got him off today. Had big load, bellows, iron, steel box bucket, etc. Hope now for good things. A month will tell the tale. Hope to make a stake at last. No Smith yet and no dinero consequently. Will be the company's own fault if the smelter is damaged or anybody hurt. There's considerable growling and the natives are very mealy. A horse turned a couple somersaults this a.m. with his rider, neither hurt fortunately.

Friday, August 8, 1884: Had to scramble inside last night—rain. Pleasanter on other side of gulch. Water rushed down again today with great force. M and I had to cross on a wagon. I went here early as there was nothing doing at store and Shaw had to wade over knee deep. Quite a palaver tonight, Shaw, Maurice and I talked our mine matters over till quite late. Very slim attendance at store today.

Saturday, August 9, 1884: Gorman and Gird arrived from Cumpas today and left after dinner for Tombstone. Had racket at table about Clapp, taking his part. They were pretty rough. My last day. Time up tonight. May help in morning though till closing time.

Sunday, August 10, 1884: Helped Shaw or rather took his place at store office while he was at supt.'s office. Good wash as usual. Smith with Richards, two brothers, arrived today. Now that Manager Richards is here there will be new developments and a "quien sabe" case all around.

Monday, August 11, 1884: The newcomers inspected the mine today and are well pleased, exceedingly so. Leavenworth, in from mine, is much pleased with our prospects. Farish told me this a.m. that I am to run books, store, etc. Robley and Ashman both quitting. So I am chief now in those matters. Have my hands full and considerable responsibility. Will go it a while till funds are ahead. Have an eighth in "Plomosa" now with Maurice. "Make or break" is my motto. Some strange society here.

Tuesday, August 12, 1884: Newcomers bustling around and about. Developing some pictures every night most now which Doctor Richards took along the road. Mr. Randolph a hearty, jolly old gentleman; like him exceedingly. Stage arrived today bringing several passengers but little mail.

Wednesday, August 13, 1884: Nothing new particularly. The capitalists seem highly pleased with their mines here and propose going ahead which is good news for the country in general and possibly for M and me in particular. We are discussing the advisability of my leaving the company's employ and rustling on the outside. Don't like to lose $180 per month though.

Thursday, August 14, 1884: Stage went out this a.m. Richards and party went to "San Pedro" today and returned much pleased. A plant will be placed below here I think. Country will soon boom in all probability. Richards bros. and Randolph left today by the four horse team all in good spirits and seeming to be well pleased with prospects here.

Friday, August 15, 1884: A very bad time today and almost violence several times because there was no money to pay Mexican laborers with. They surrounded our office doors, windows and pay window, coming up with clubs, shouting dinero, dinero, etc. Very bad for us. Torres was sent for and fortunately arrived in time and finally Martinez was dispatched to Cumpas and Oposura for funds. Yellow fever at Guaymas where our banking is done is very bad, and place being quarantine, money can't be had for present. Bad state of affairs. Don't want any more of it myself. I am not paid fighting wages. Wish the capitalists could have been detained a day later. This kind of work won't do. Some of us cannot afford to prejudice our interests in mining properties here.

Saturday, August 16, 1884: Storm has blown over for a while but is liable to come again. I decided today to rustle on the outside and have equitable arrangement with Maurice. Will leave when mouth is up, Sept. 9th.

Sunday, August 17, 1884: Closed as usual at 11 a.m. Dined at Farish's and told Farish and Smith that I proposed to vacate Sept. 9th, and spoke for Fred Castle. Old man gave me a little taffy. Shaw is in with Maurice and me. They allow me at rate of $150 per month and we three divide all of my expenses. There is much for me to do in the country and I'll have a rough time of it but with our good connections and properties we can get hold of, we are in a fine way to make money. Maurice saying he would not care to sell his prespective opportunities for $25,000.

Monday, August 18, 1884: Grub teams got in Saturday and we're once more eating and saved from starvation. Were out of most everything including salt the last day or two and were in a bad way. Very little work for me nowadays. Domingo in from Sonora River and reports Hohstadt's mine doing well. They want to rent mill.

Wednesday, August 20, 1884: Fine cool pleasant day. Shaw in bed today. Moulton in today for powder and fuse. Reports mine opening up big and everything highly encouraging.

Thursday, August 21, 1884: Stage in today, also Don Jose with the long wished for money; so now we're all happy once more. Assays on Magurite still way up. Guess we've got it—$80 gold and about $30 silver. Am sick of this country and dog's life and want to leave it as soon as possible.

Friday, August 22, 1884: Got on to $222 coin today but had a time trying to conceal it. Money going fast. All hands feeling better again. Mexican gambling games going, mucho mescal and mucho dinero en todos los partes. Had a wild time today and night trying to settle with Mexicans old accounts, etc., and alone. Fine picnic. Rain today. Am talking mill hard to Farish. I leave next month on arrangement with boys. Am to receive salary and share expenses. I rustle while they work for company.

Saturday, August 23, 1884: Alone still and very busy. Stage off this a.m. Rodey came to office tonight with head tied up having received bad cut at mine from windless crank. A miracle he wasn't killed or mangled. All pitched in; I plastered him and we did him up in fine style.

Sunday, August 24, 1884: I suggested reading service to the boys and this evening made a beginning. Will have service every Sunday. Shaw is member of Baptist Church and Maurice and I belong to the Episcopal.

Monday, August 25, 1884: Much trouble. Adams has taken possession of smelter contrary to all he has said, pending payment of $15,000 to R[ankin] B[rayton] & Co. of S.F. when the NJ and Sonora R Co. has already paid $7,000 more than the plant here can be duplicated for. Duplicity on Adams part it seems to me and strange acting after the way he has talked. Hearing that Miller, the foreman, would be general boss of everything had been busy talking about me this a.m., I went for him and he crawled. I went for him for Maurice too, with same result. Maurice started for Oposura today horseback on company horse and Adams immediately followed.

Tuesday, August 26, 1884: Thirty-four years old today and still in the back ground. Will have money though next year, am confident. Necessary for me to go to Cumpas today to get $640 left there for company. Had good horse but too late to go further than the Ojo de Agua, where I stopped over night with Don José Mesa. Very nicely taken care of. Has quite a family; seven in all and tremendous wife.

Wednesday, August 27, 1884: Cutler and Col. Torres arrived before I got off on way to Nacosari. Reached Cumpas and Geo Adams all O.K. Just two years this month since I was last here. Apaches very bad then. There but little while when Maurice arrived from Oposura, 20 miles or 18 distant, and a little later along came Adams from same point. Couldn't find my man till night, usual way in Mexican towns, so had to remain over night and M went on. Hard work killing time. Lots of fruit and eggs.

Thursday, August 28, 1884: Very hot day, unusually so and I had heavy load of about 50 lbs. of Mexican dollars in saddle bags and three bottles of mescal. Great time getting off and keeping my money matters a secret. Lots of men wouldn't hesitate to go for me here if they knew what I had— ticklish business. Had Adams and a Mexican for company most of distance. Very hot ride of about 30 miles. Delivered everything safely. Dined at Farish's.

Friday, August 29, 1884: Back again to plain carne and frijoles after chicken, eggs and fruit. Very hard rain and wind storm tonight making things very lively a while. Water rushed down canyon in great force from above threatening serious results at times. We had to be carted over to meals and back. Wrote several letters tonight.

Saturday, August 30, 1884: Up at four a.m. to work on statement with Shaw which was usually gotten ready. Maurice left for Tombstone horseback about five a.m. on company and private business.

Sunday, August 31, 1884: Shaw went out to our mine today and returned with some rock. I wish the great uncertainty was over which attaches to the thing. At one time I feel finely about his assays and again down. Took an old Mexican, Jesus Ochoa, out this a.m., a good arrastra man and we will now soon find out what's in the thing. Dined at Farish's where also were Sam Brannan,* Con Cutler, Armstrong. Cutler went for me on the bathing question.

Monday, September 1, 1884: Bad news today. Jackson was shot and killed a few miles out from Cumpas enroute to the mine. Apache work reported

---

*It is hard to know which Sam Brannan Parsons is referring to, father or son; both were kicking around Sonora at this time, Sam, Jr., having mining interests at Oposura. If George is writing about the elder Brannan, then he dined with illustrious company. Sam Brannan, Sr., arrived at Yerba Buena (San Francisco) in 1846 with 200 Mormon colonists aboard the *Brooklyn*. He was one of those fortunate individuals who was at the right place at the right time, being in California on the eve of the Gold Rush. He made a fortune in the mercantile trade supplying miners with all sorts of necessities, and was a foremost figure in colonizing Sacramento. He built railroads, established vineyards, opened a bank and issued currency, and founded the San Francisco *Alta California*. As California's first millionaire, Brannan gave freely of his money, helping finance the Union against the Confederacy; his purchase of revolutionist bonds contributed to the overthrow of the French protectorate in Mexico, and he recruited, armed and trained Americans to reinforce Benito Juarez's forces. Mexico repaid Brannan for his services by granting him a large tract of land at the headwaters of the Yaqui River. At the time George Parsons encountered him, Brannan was sixty-five years old, working to recoup a fortune lost by intemperance by promoting a colonization scheme in Sonora and selling property in Guaymas. That dream, however, was dashed when he could not raise money to survey his Mexican tract. He died penniless in Escondido on May 6, 1889.

but seriously doubted. Revenge the motive. Jackson too free a cusser. Cowboys reported with Apaches, absurd. Cutler feeling badly indeed. Offered $1000 necessary to catch murderer or no man's life will be safe. Cutler went below tonight. I don't want any more traveling with money.

Tuesday, September 2, 1884: Pretty lively work settling with Greeks. New system works very nicely. Rates check well. Assays went about as usual.

Wednesday, September 3, 1884: Moulton and Palmer came in today from our mine. Shaft looking very fine indeed. A foot of rich gold rock and ledge growing. Shaft 32 feet deep, fine wall and things looking well. Ochoa at work on an arrastra* and we will soon know something. The old man worried some about Indians.

Thursday, September 4, 1884: Went around with Moulton today and got tenates and smithy he wished, a big load. We settled with Palmer and bought his horse, needing it for the arrastra with M's mule. Shaft cost between $5 and $6 per foot, cheap enough. Quicksilver is all we want now. Will soon be grinding and I think we'll get some money.

Friday, September 5, 1884: Pretty busy today. The prefect Aviso and a major, Emilio Kosterlitzky, in today. Took prefect to dinner, wined him and got certain information I needed on some points in mining in the country. Very pleasant man. It seems that Jackson was shot by his Mexican who rode behind on a burro. He'll be fixed. Kosterlitzky gave Delaney away, the Bisbee bandit. Stage in today and a flask of quicksilver for us. Now we'll soon know something.

Saturday, September 6, 1884: [A. J.] Huneke and Hawkins arrived on yesterday's stage, the latter to take my place or rather the position offered me at the store and office. Had quite a fight last night with him over respective merits of Doctors Goodfellow and Willis. The latter I don't go a cent on.

Sunday, September 7, 1884: Got Morris Hirsch's mule and went out to the mine today, taking 10 lbs. of quicksilver. A hard pull for the camp but finally got there. Arrastra nearly built. Took a new route home saving several miles. Jack went with me and was pretty well tuckered out. Met Robles on the main road. Home some time after dark. Had fine luck finding the mountain trails. Service tonight.

*The arrastra, or arrastre, was no more than a circular rock-lined pit in which broken ore was pulverized by stones attached to horizontal poles fastened in a central pillar and dragged around the pit. Mercury, copper sulphate, and salt was added to the pulp, and the mass was retorted to separate the precious metals. Because of its simple construction, the arrastra was called a "poor man's mill."

**Emilio Kosterlitzky was commander of the elite para-military police force known as the Rurales. He was born in Moscow in 1853, the son of a Cossack cavalry officer. He attended military school in St. Petersburg, but saw service in the Russian navy, which he hated. He jumped ship at Puerto Cabello, Venezuela, and made his way to Guaymas, Mexico. In 1880 he was commissioned a lieutenant in the Mexican army. Emilio's service against Apaches and Yaquis caught the eye of Porfirio Diaz, who put him in charge of a "hard-riding, fast shooting, and utterly ruthless constabulary." He became known as the "mailed fist of Porfirio Diaz."

Monday, September 8, 1884: Smelter running again under Schneider, turning out good matte slowly. My time is up today, but I shall remain if possible until next Sunday and Monday a.m., [and then] start off on my second account or that of our company's that composed by Maurice, Shaw and Myself. Hard trip yesterday, consequently very tired today.

Tuesday, September 9, 1884: Quite cold. Am talking mill to Huneke and hope now that we can start a mill company and move the mill over to the gold country. Some whist and casino tonight. Hawkins and Adams vs Huneke and myself. We were worsted. Mr. Pesqueira, Don Cayatano Silva, and Señor Corrella arrived today and we took care of them.

Wednesday, September 10, 1884: Did the courtesies last night and today to the Mexican gentlemen. Bonillas and Herbert arrived this a.m. too. Glad to see them. Had to leave almost immediately for our iron flux mine, 10 or 12 miles east in the mountains, and take a man, he afoot. Very hard trip, rough wild country. Trail too indistinct to follow. Had to course it and arrived on top of a mountain opposite to one pointed out as my destination. Cut trail though and met our Mexicans and were happy.

Thursday, September 11, 1884: Found Alberti short of grub. Rather bad. Had tortillas though and little panoche and tea and slept pretty well. Lots of game and bears plentiful. Mexicans and all seem to fear them. Deer plentiful too. Grand scenery; wild and magnificent. Donovan and Smith arrived today.

Friday, September 12, 1884: Maurice back today from Tombstone in advance of stage, Charlie Reed with him, buckboard. Town improving. No letters.

Saturday, September 13, 1884: Rain. Our's the only dry place. Have to cross dry gulch on wagon or wade knee deep. Some music tonight, guitar and violin. Reed a great musician.

Sunday, September 14, 1884: Pleasant weather. Everything quiet. Don Jose fortunately arrived with money so things will be O.K. tomorrow, pay day. I understand that my mill is being run by Bob. He is rather cheeky. First impulse was to jig the outfit, but I'm a gainer in several ways. Hope to soon dispose of the outfit and then I'll feel relieved of a great load.

Monday, September 15, 1884: Pay day and very busy time. Will leave tomorrow and take to the hills. Moulton in today with fresh samples. Another ledge, arrastra working nicely.

Tuesday, September 16, 1884: Great day for Mexico. Celebration of deliverance from Spain in 1810. Mescal flowed freely. Robley and Ashman left today and I disconnected myself with the concern and was to go hills with Huneke this afternoon but he couldn't get a horse. Got Moulton off and will follow tomorrow. Busy time getting him off.

Wednesday, September 17, 1884: Horse is all loaded and fixed and I am now off to see whether or not there is anything in our gold mine.

Thursday, September 18, 1884: Had a hard pull through mountains yesterday on a worthless horse. Tumbled onto a cactus once with horse on me or almost so. Came out O.K. Found arrastra going O.K. and the new horse working well. Leavenworth struck camp shortly after me with a young deer over his shoulders and we relished our supper. Interesting to watch arrastra. M thinks the Mexican doesn't use enough quicksilver. Seems to grind well.

Friday, September 19, 1884: Used more quicksilver today but with no better results. Can't seem to catch the gold. It seems free too. M very much disappointed. I am not. Quicksilver needs retorting for one thing and then other ingredients probably retards amalgamation. Nice looking rock and lots of it. The old Mexican has a claim I shall see which is probably a very good one. Centipedes and tarantulas around.

Saturday, September 20, 1884: Looked over claim today and decided that more work should immediately be done. A 50 foot shaft sunk; a tunnel to cut several ledges should also be run. No more arrastra business. Water too low anyhow. Must work our mine with machinery. Hopes are high and low. Hope this seesaw business will soon end. I shall see the thing though to its life or death. Left camp in early p.m. and arrived about six p.m. Found a young fellow named Hand on hand, friend of Huneke's. Pleasant. Two letters also—Howe and Milton.

Sunday, September 21, 1884: Hard rain storm last night and cloudy today. Creek up again. Fellows disappointed of course, but agree with me on the shaft business. We'll push things as rapidly as possible.

Monday, September 22, 1884: Mrs. F quite sick and I was to go to Cumpas today for medicine but found it here. Moulton and all hands came in today. Very little amalgam. Moulton feeling blue. I have not lost faith.

Tuesday, September 23, 1884: Settled with Ochoa. Mine is costing us something. Am to help Shaw a few days on books. Began today at noon. Hard rains, gulch so deep that I thought I couldn't get over for supper, but made it. Waist deep, but not for me. Three rows today. There'll be another killing before long.

Wednesday, September 24, 1884: Tried amalgam today and M got four pretty gold buttons which we will keep as mementos. M made good arrangement today. We are to send the company two tons of our gold ore for a flux at Schneider's request. More to follow probably. Will get about 60% of assay value. Good thing and quite unprecedented. Hope it will continue a while.

Thursday, September 25, 1884: Liborio Vasquez, the perito, came last night and now we're in for it, $125 or $150 to get possession. I took the perito and Maurice to where Moulton and Leavenworth were camped. They had made a fine trail. L returned with me and went later with two doz burros for our ore. I rode the bucking mule and whaled all the bucking out of him with M's quirt. M and the P back tonight. Everything satisfactory.

Friday, September 26, 1884: Ore arrived today, about two tons, fine looking stuff. Brun horned some out and got a big prospect of free gold. Sessler in today. Has another ledge we may take hold of near ours. Stage in today with mail for most all of us. Ike Patrick brought me two letters, he and Jim Davidson. One from Miss Ida Palachie in reply to my note of sympathy over her late horseback accident. A charming girl, must correspond if possible.

Saturday, September 27, 1884: Things very quiet. Smelter shut down again; Schneider unable to run it. Things greatly mismanaged. Hope Sweeney will take charge. Things generally going at a big loss.

Sunday, September 28, 1884: Brun in a sweat about our lines crossing a ledge he wanted. McLane and Maurice had some words. No bulldozing goes in this country and if any shotgun business is wanted or if necessary we're in for it strong. Shaw slipped off this a.m. against Farish's orders. Liable to be trouble. Am now to go to the Rosario with the perito. Went but couldn't find the necessary extension.

Monday, September 29, 1884: Had a hard scrabble over the hills today with Sessler. Inspected his two ledges and sampled them thoroughly. Visited our camp and found them working. Moulton found several small nuggets, very small though, and I brought one in. Thinks bottom of shaft richest. Packed in a lot of samples.

Tuesday, September 30, 1884: Weighed our ore brought in by burros the other day, 3,600 lbs. Each wheelbarrow sampled and all the samples mixed, and Hand assayed the business giving us $80 per ton; almost $60 gold, bal. silver. We now have possession of the "mina de oro," cost $161 for necessary papers. No work necessary for four months. Arranged by the perito, Liborio Vasquez.

Wednesday, October 1, 1884: Took Hand and Huneke to our gold mine today. Camp vacated; fellows probably hunting horses. Ate their grub and left a note. Then looked over claim and sampled. They were well pleased. On top of the main ridge we spied a huge bear and kicked ourselves all over for not having rifle. I sent a couple of pistol shots after him at 300 yds and couldn't tell effect. A hard rain storm to go home in. Thoroughly soaked. Letter unexpectedly tonight from Strallus.

Thursday, October 2, 1884: Johnny Hohstadt in camp with Mason. Johnny paid me $16 for stores sold last spring. Reported mill in good shape and running and greatly relieved my mind upon some points. Hope never again to be so worried by anything else as I have been by that confounded mill racket. Expected to go to Cumpas today but storm prevented. Hope to go to Sonora River with JH in a few days. Bought [M. T.] Donovan's saddle and bridle tonight; "Best saddle in country."

Friday, October 3, 1884: Didn't get off today either. Must leave tomorrow. Cleaned saddle and rifles and revolver today. Stage in this evening. More letters, one from Sioux, rather sad. Col. Henderson arrived tonight. Looks after properties below Smith and Clark. Hawkins is disgusted and has resigned. Huneke helping Shaw. Fine old circuses.

Saturday, October 4, 1884: Feast day at Cumpas, Saint San Xavier, I think. Fitch and I go together. Must now get mule saddled and be off. Here it is the 13th and I'm back from quite a trip. Hand, Fitch, Col. Jack Henderson, Frenchy and I reached Cumpas about dusk and put up at Geo Adam's. In evening several of us walked over to Tinadipse where the feast was in progress and took in the sights. A great crowd. Looked pretty all illuminated by candles. Lonely walk back.

Sunday, October 5, 1884: This afternoon Hand, Fitch and I went to the San Pedro mine, 22 miles distant, west from Cumpas. He forgot the trail although over it a number of times recently. I had been to the Tobacochi two years and more ago but managed to get our trail twice and reached SP after dark some time and camped. Jeff Bickerton came later. Mosquitoes quite bad; worse than I ever knew them in Mexico.

Monday, October 6, 1884: Looked San Pedro—scaly work. Old mine and hardly safe to enter. On back trail visited the San Luis, San Nicholas, Tobacochi and near Tobacochi had fine swim in a tank about 20 x 30 formed in a deep canyon. It was fine and very refreshing. Found Ochoa at the Consuelo, the property I came to inspect. Sampled it and looked at it but was not favorably impressed. Saw his four arrastras. Returned about dark. Mule I rode under the weather.

Tuesday, October 7, 1884: Mule sick so can't return on him. Went to Ojo de Aqua today and saw José Mesa. Wishes me to go with him to Nacosari; fears an attempt to rob, having been shadowed. Has company funds from Ures. If armed possibly will go with him. Visited feast again tonight, went with Martin. He and Frenchy had trouble other night. Bad feeling by some Mexicans against Americans. Carried my Colt six shooter in my boot leg. Lots of merriment tonight; gambling, dancing and drinking.

Wednesday, October 8, 1884: Had Geo Adams' horse this a.m. to go to Galeria today or yesterday, Frenchy's place. He still in Oposura with Henderson. Horses very scarce here in Cumpas. Frenchy a great case. Had a great time steering him and Dominque home from feast the other night. Can't seem to get away from Cumpas now.

Thursday, October 9, 1884: Liborio Vasquez, the perito, rode into town this afternoon and wanted me to go to Oposura with him. Fitch had to go so off we went, arriving about eight p.m., seven leagues distant. I rode Col. Torres' horse. Passed through Hickory, a pretty spot; numerous burial mounds. Passed to left of one spot where Liborio's father, mother and two sisters were killed by Apaches. He disliked very much even to pass near here, he said. I should think so. Seemed quite a town in the dark.

Friday, October 10, 1884. Interesting town; old church said to be 264 years old. Visited prefect Aviso, also post office, and brought quite a number away for Nacosari. Two señoritas called with guitar this afternoon while I was away and I kicked myself all over for it, as I had expressed the wish in the a.m. to hear and see the true Spanish business. People quite white here. Best town and people and society I've yet seen in Sonora, not excepting Arispe. Quite a talk with Franer and Henderson. Latter has very lively and active imagination.

Saturday, October 11, 1884: Liborio's wife very pleasant. Could get along fairly well with my knowledge of Spanish. Could I be here a month I could sling it all O.K. A talk and mescal with F & H again this a.m. about mill and other matters. Left about nine a.m. Met people returning from Magdalena along the road, women with heads tied up and one with white mask to protect from sun. Warm in a.m. Horse seemed to be off on his wind. Stopped to help him. Arrived at Cumpas in time for dinner and found horse; Maurice sent off on him about three p.m. Liborio's horse.

Sunday, October 12, 1884: Had a tough old pull of it last night, terribly tough. Didn't reach canyon till long after dark and the 10 or 12 mile walk with rain, water rushing down it from floods and frightened horse was a combination very disagreeable. Came near camping, it being difficult to keep trail but finally pushed her through after one of the most disagreeable rides on record. Had a hard time passing the falls. Good bath last night and rest today. Huneke, Hand and Cutler went below today.

Monday, October 13, 1884: Moved into Maurice's room today. Shaw nearly busted. Moulton in yesterday or day before. Rock changed to silver. Formation broken. All hands feeling rather blue. Trying hard to keep up courage. Nothing doing.

Tuesday, October 14, 1884: We have the blue horse in camp now and he's a good little fellow. Will pack me about. Will go off again tomorrow.

Wednesday, October 15, 1884: Saddled up this a.m. for a visit to M Hursch's camp to see a copper property of his. Farish though wished me to go to Tombstone on special business so I changed animals with him and started on his favorite mule, a finely gaited animal. M & I went first to the "Mina de Oro" and I struck out over mountains for Cumpas trail so as to pass the mill and see how things were there.

Thursday, October 16, 1884: Struck trail O.K., but mule got off in the dark and I had to bunk under a tree till morning. Found I was 10 or 12 miles from Bacuachi which I reached about nine and breakfasted. Traveled with Londeu and McDonald some distance. Reached mill in p.m. and found it running. Bob at mine so only saw Barker, assayer, and Louis H. Also saw Mrs. H, old H absent. Left Frenchman's about dark and pushed on to Custom House, arriving some time in middle of night. A pull of nearly 75 miles since a.m. Good sleep in p.m. Boys at B said I couldn't make it.

Friday, October 17, 1884: Bad time with the dogs last night. Some time before I could get a bed. Pushed on from CH about 7:30. Rather cool reception at Ochoaville. Understood it. Dined at Crystal Springs and rested and while there four horses and large carriage arrived with Col. Clark, B

McDonald and Lon Richards. Latter jumped out and I had few minutes talk when they pushed on to CH. I reached town just after dark and saw the Herrings the first ones. All laughed at my long hair and beard. Went to an entertainment at school house and saw many friends.

Saturday, October 18, 1884: Great time today getting clothes and things together. Couldn't find shirts. A hearty welcome back by my numerous friends and the two papers. Had pictures first taken for sisters and then was clipped. Was made quite respectable once more. Hard looking case when I arrived. Judge C. S. Clark and deputy sheriff [Billy] Daniels of Bisbee discussed me. D was asked by C who I was. He replied a Mexican from the Babocomari. C replied, "a wild looking one he is." Pretty good. Called at Cap. Seamans this evening and met his daughter, a very pleasant girl. A rousing political meeting tonight. Bean for congress spoke and well too. Went with Mrs. Earle and Judge and Mrs. Berry.

Sunday, October 19, 1884: Was glad to be able to go to church once more. Bagnall preached. He leaves Nov. 3rd. I am much disappointed and hurt at recent developments. The reflex influence will be very bad. Am more sorry for the cause of Christ than from any other consideration. Church again tonight and glad of the privilege to worship God the proper way. Dined at Herrings. Same old jolly family. Telegraphed Milton yesterday.

Monday, October 20, 1884: Lazed about and took things easy. A pretty good strain on man and beast, the ride I took. Dined at Sweeney's tonight. S and I later played some billiards and I introduced him to a number of gentlemen. Mrs. very pleasant. Has pretty baby. At Clark's house.

Tuesday, October 21, 1884: Town much livelier than when I left. Dined at McFawn's tonight with Bagnall. Nice dinner. Later Mr. Whyte, called the elocutionist, had considerable to say. Was in the Zulu war in Prince Albert Company, he says. Stage in tonight from Nacosari, but no orders for me. Saw Donovan. At Berry's a while, cards, then Herring's—same—sick of them [cards that is].

Wednesday, October 22, 1884: Got around some today. Exercised mule this p.m. Had talk with Ben Maynard, who said the recent assessment on the GB was a good big one and seemed well satisfied with it, and when it was done. Dined at Berry's, then called on Mrs. Tom Moore, who soon joins her husband at the Cananeas, then on to Mrs. Adam where the Genl and I differed about Blaine and ended at Herring's where a surprise party was being held. Danced only once, with Miss Mary Farish.

Thursday, October 23, 1884: Received orders this a.m. and sent telegram immediately for the Farish boys to come. Long letter from Maurice. Magnificent results of assays at Mina de Oro and once more my spirits are elevated. Has bought out Shaw for about $165 for both of us. Am glad he's out. Dined at Vickers' this p.m. where were the Herrings, that is Judge and Mrs. and Miss S. H. Hard rain tonight. Billiards later with Judge.

Friday, October 24, 1884: Lots of work buying things this afternoon. Went out to see Old Guard Mine with Vickers. Looking finely, horn silver and specks of native [silver]. Sixteen inches high grade ore. Letter from Milton saying would be here next week, so must wait over if possible. Dined at Reppy's. Pleasant evening. Called later at Springer's where met [L. M.] Jacobs of the Bank and Judge Stilwell. Later yet called with Donovan on Miss Shaw and Mrs. Castle. Lots of fun teasing Miss S about her brother.

Saturday, October 25, 1884: Dined at Sweeney's tonight and while S and I were doing some private smoking, Col. Clark and Richards arrived from Nacosari. Got some letters and exchanged news. Judge Berry and I went out to the new strike today near Great Eastern. Sampled the T.T.

Sunday, October 26, 1884. Church a.m. and p.m. Dined with Major and Mrs. Earle. Maj. got word from Milton tonight that he would arrive Tuesday night and for me to meet him. So will see the old fellow after all.

Monday, October 27, 1884: Looked after business today. Arranged with Frank Earle to go out tomorrow. [James H.] Toole, Hudson's partner, suicided at Trinidad. Recent developments show Hudson up in poor light. Will never be sure myself again.

Tuesday, October 28, 1884: Frank and I made an early start and examined the Mannie R ground and Bassett. I shall turn matters over to Frank as I shall be away. Major Earle drove down to Fairbank on business and returned with Milton, saving me the trip. Was glad to welcome him back. Looks well but thinner.

Wednesday, October 29, 1884: Milton breakfasted with me this a.m. Spent the day seeing friends and overhauling his things. He made me a present of his handsome Remington and Winchester rifles. Also of lot of articles he didn't care to take back. Dined at Berry's. My charges arrived tonight safe and sound. Turned them over to Mrs. Farish. Lunched with Bob K.

Thursday, October 30, 1884: Smith in town and trouble in the air; financial embarrassment. Major and Mrs. E and Mrs B drove Milton down while Annette and I followed horseback. Saw him off all O.K. Then hunted Smith. Rather unfortunate state of things at present but hope everything will soon be all O.K. Some bad talk against Milton here but nothing said or done. A new rope project was presented to him. May be something in it all around.

Friday, October 31, 1884: Things quiet. Must await developments a few days before returning, so cannot leave tomorrow. An old friend in a very bad way tonight. Judge B & I requested to look out for him, etc. Had laughable experience at Goodrich's other night. Report of man under Mrs. Thomas' bed next door. Joined the gang. Hauled out a ten year old boy at point of two revolvers.

Saturday, November 1, 1884: Matters still in the dark. Must wait a little longer for replies to telegrams sent. Judge B & I requested again tonight.

Sunday, November 2, 1884: Church a.m. and p.m. Music by the band (Hawkin's). Bagnall preached his farewell sermon tonight. Leaves Wednesday. Dined at Herring's. Quite a party. Spent evening with Bagnall having long and quite satisfactory talk. Gave him letter to father.

Monday, November 3, 1884: No news yet and I must stay. Dined at McFawn's. Col. still under the weather. Speeches, music and excitement tonight. Spent evening at Capt. Seamans' playing guitar, singing, etc.

Tuesday, November 4, 1884: Election Day. No presidential business here, but betting plenty Blaine will carry the day. Am to meet Mrs. Clark at Fairbank this afternoon. Met Mrs. Clark this afternoon, the Col. and I. Looking and feeling well. Dined there. Excitement high over election. [W. H.] Savage, the Rep candidate for Dist Atty, called me out of a crowd and went for me as he supposed I was working hard against him, seeing me mule back and in carriage. Think I made him feel cheap. Lost my vote not being here to register. Could have probably got Co Treas. office if here.

Wednesday, November 5, 1884: Still no news from the East. Bad, very bad. Wires too full of election business. Man killed last night. Rignat by Donohue. Talk of lynching D today. Bagnall left this a.m. for his home in Rhode Island. Saw and talked with Hohstadt. Gave me a request for money on note which I don't owe. Some more shenanigins. Met Surna, the perito for Arispe district. Am to visit him in Arispe this month. Blaine got it probably. We're to have ratification meeting.

Thursday, November 6, 1884: Still unable to get away. Writing letters and preparing to go. Am getting uneasy. Political situation shifting all of the time. First one side and then the other. Blaine pretty well assured tonight and I retired feeling better. Spend evenings at friends, Herring's and Seamans'.

Friday, November 7, 1884: Summoned on Grand Jury; was let off. Friends thought I made a pretty slick speech to the judge. Am ready to go to Mexico now and remain there some time. Blaine is defeated and times will be very bad. Confidence unsettled and the outlook poor. Am sorry for the country. Will leave tomorrow. Went the rounds tonight seeing friends and saying adios.

Saturday, November 8, 1884: Couldn't get off till nearly noon. Breakfasted with Col and Mrs. Clark. Reached Ochoaville about dark. Slept in the store. K & P not as friendly as formerly. I take along the presidental news, unwelcome as it is, of Cleveland's election and tell them all that Mexico is good enough for me now.

Sunday, November 9, 1884: Long ride. Passed Custom House O.K. Near Janarerachi met two Mexicans from Hohstadt's mine who came for a bottle of mescal from Bill Miller's. I followed them back and had a very hard time of it over the high country. The darkness was intense. Fortunately they had some small pieces of candle which helped the way. Found Bob and talked big in the a.m. Tarantula walked over my hand at five. Mexican struck it off. Slept in a rather hard place; animals of some kind kept me awake some time.

Monday, November 10, 1884: Rented Bob the mill at $75 per month this a.m. from Oct. 1st, all repairs to be and are paid for by previous use of mill. We arranged that his work on mill was all paid for to put it in running order by use of several weeks running prior to Oct. 1st, the rent of $75 per month to be commenced at that date and amount to be paid Maj. Earle for my account in Tombstone. At Hohstadt's arranged some business about wood and reached Bacuachi before sun down. Had to camp at Chacon's. Drunken Mexicans; hard time of it.

Tuesday, November 11, 1884: Was glad to find mule all O.K. and things undisturbed. Was apprehensive. Looked like a bad crowd to me. Long day's ride. Thought I was followed for some time by couple of Mexicans. Found water conveniently, deer plentiful. I bore too much to the east and was caught behind Nacosari mountains about sundown. Had a rough time of it crossing ridges and was about camping for the night when I stumbled into the old placer trail and after a hard ride reached Nacosari about nine.

Wednesday, November 12, 1884: Staid around pretty close today. Nothing new here. No one wished or seemed inclined to accept the presidential news except Farish and Cutler and they were jubilant.

Thursday, November 13, 1884: Expected to go to our camp today but didn't get started. Maurice went to Oposura yesterday to bring back prefect Aviso if possible, as serious trouble is anticipated on the 15th.

Friday, November 14, 1884: Went to camp today and took Mathison along, meeting him on the road. Met Moulton coming in. He went back. Bottom of shaft looks better than expected to find it. Moulton returned with us.

Saturday, November 15, 1884: Pay day and not the trouble feared. A great clearing out of the store though by Mexicans and those who feared they were not good. Special police appointed. I worked with Shaw helping him to settle. Pretty steady job of it.

Sunday, November 16, 1884: Started off for camp with Moulton this afternoon feeling rather out of sorts. Intend to do some prospecting. Must wait a little while to see how things will move.

Monday, November 17, 1884: Moulton and I didn't feel very sprightly and staid close to camp today.

Tuesday, November 18, 1884: Prospected around camp in vicinity. No results. Williams, who went with us, a Mormon probably, returned tonight with blankets for me. Cold nights in our camp.

Wednesday, November 19, 1884: This a.m. we all broke camp. M and I went north prospecting for water and mine, and this afternoon I fortunately discovered what may prove to be a very valuable mining property in bottom of a rough canyon—three feet or more of mineral on top with clay gangue next to hanging wall. Water being on claim. Both of us highly elated tonight. Camped near the discovery.

Thursday, November 20, 1884: Went to work on the discovery today and got variety of samples. I also found some nice looking quartz gold. Returned to camp today feeling good and building air castles. Game scarce hereabouts. Old man M the worst case I ever knew for losing things. Has lost three pipes I gave him.

Friday, November 21, 1884: Left camp this noon to return to N. Back of Nacosari mountains visited Londeu's copper prospect and camped beyond aways. Hunted this p.m. Want meat; no deer.

Saturday, November 22, 1884: A terribly hard pull, hanging on to side of Nacosari mountains. Thought the Huachucas were rough but this took the cake. Animals did well. Before sun down a while I shot and killed a fat buck with good horns. Made a fine center shot. Had a job with him; rolled down mountain side. Finally reached our pass and camped over summit a ways. Fortunately found several cups of water for M and me but poor animals had to suffer.

Sunday, November 23, 1884: A cold night. High wind and very disagreeable until Nacosari creek was reached. Reached home all O.K. Things the same. Had to hoof it many a mile, being loaded with deer and outfit. Good square meal. Fixed deer head and hope to present it in good shape. Good dinner this afternoon. Evening at Farish's. Read some later.

Monday, November 24, 1884: Took things easy today. Awaited Shaw now to have grand settlement and see how we all stand. M and I figured some today. Some music and a great game of whist tonight. Fitch and I partners.

Tuesday, November 25, 1884: Moulton fixing things for a stay at the Mina de Oro. Don't see anything else left for me to do but go out there and work. Had a trip today to see a new prospect; sampled it and prospected. Got into a hard piece of country and had a time getting out. Stage in tonight bringing Farish boys. News from home; all well and things apparently prosperous.

Wednesday, November 26, 1884: Gloomy and chilly. Hard times for the boys; were cheerful as possible though under circumstances. Maurice is caught for nearly $1000 and I in neighborhood of $100. Nothing doing; camp dead. Some fellows waiting for money. Cards in evening, some music tambien.

Thursday, November 27, 1884: Got the old man off this afternoon with both animals heavily packed. Took wheelbarrow along and boards for sluice box. Mose went off with him on way to his camp. We hired a Mexican at $1 a day and board to help Moulton. I shall go soon. Thanksgiving Day; nothing else but good health to be thankful for. Bad health would be strange here. Ain't growling though.

Friday, November 28, 1884: Hard at work today on accounts trying to get things straightened out. Maurice and I settled and came out about even. Strange after running along so many months. Am afraid the camp is gone in. Must get away and to camp as soon as possible. Fitch came in last night and left this a.m. for the line. Sent Xmas presents to sister, Strallus, and Sam, $5 ea. all around; all American money I had.

Saturday, November 29, 1884: Maurice started for Oposura today on mining business for us.

Sunday, November 30, 1884: Spent day quietly. Read service in evening. Not appreciated by third party.

Monday, December 1, 1884: Nothing new. Can now get burro, but unfinished business on hand will retain me until after stage arrival. Cards and guitar in evenings. On track of goods stolen other night.

Tuesday, December 2, 1884: Traded boots and shirts for some fine moccasins today. Long legged, fine ones. Got deed finally of Shaw's interest to MEC and me fixed up. Stage in early. Large mail for me, eight letters and one with a familiar handwriting, Nathalie's. Is to be married. I got a printed announcement in French of her engagement. So that is the grand wind up. We are widely apart I fear in more senses than one.

Wednesday, December 3, 1884: Loaded the burro this a.m. with plenty of blankets and some other stuff and hoofed it behind with the rifle in my new moccasins which come to my knees. Pretty long nine miles for moccasins first time. Found camp O.K. and arrastra going. Was started last Friday at noon. Mexican is a good man. He grabbed rifle and ran to Moulton's assistence other day when the first blast went off at the mine, thinking Apaches had attacked him. Mine nearly half mile from arrastra.

Thursday, December 4, 1884: Started in today to break myself in for hard manual labor once more. Hope the last adios to the class of work four years ago was final, but it seems not. It's all right though I can stand it and will fight it out on this line if it takes all winter until I know what I want to. Riffles work well. Great institution, an old California placer mining invention and introduces some good features into this primitive way of milling.* We calculate on working half a ton per day. Work horse and mule six hours each. Silverino breaks rock. After three or four feet deep we sampled the bottom and got a fine showing. Quite a lump of amalgam.

Friday, December 5, 1884: We are stripping the ledge Mexican style. Singular formation with seams running to vein at right angles, scaring us at times but they stop there and the ledge goes right along about its business as prettily as can be. Hard, hard work but my muscles are in good trim and I don't feel it as much as I thought I would. Great talks around camp fire nights. Mexican can't speak any English. Good thing for our Spanish. Nights cold, and with no shelter in this canyon, it's rather rough nights. Wind howls down canyon fiercely at night. Wish we had even a tent.

Saturday, December 6, 1884: Put in my first hole today since quitting time

*Parsons is wrong here. Riffles, or transverse bars in a cradle or sluice to trap coarse gold, tin, or other heavy minerals, was introduced into California gold mining by men who had used such hydraulic equipment in Georgia and other south Atlantic gold producing areas as early as the 1830s.

four years ago. Old times again. Hard work to get rock quickly enough for the arrastra. Old man rather set and queer, cranky but good-hearted. A hard worker and honest, a good partner. Great time trying to breathe and keep warm at same under the blankets. Have to cover up head and all. Hope we can get a shelter soon and we will if the rock will only pay.

Sunday, December 7, 1884: Moulton went to town for some stuff and returned late with burro loaded with boards for the second sluice. We've got to have some meat and I went over mountains today but didn't get it. A long tramp, fearfully cold one in hard wind. Rain started in this evening and we had hard work trying to keep dry. It caught me rather badly.

Monday, December 8, 1884: Rain all day and night. Took sample from Contention ledge and we got in half a day's work. Getting along fairly well on the ledge; are in 8 or 10 feet now. Will cross from foot wall to hanging. Tonight we had what the old man called a blizzard. First hail fell heavily and then came a regular cyclone. We hung on to the piece of tent which was partially lashed and kept it from going but it was a close shave.

Tuesday, December 9, 1884: Rain fitfully falls. Worked though till afternoon and then went to town, riding horse and driving burro, packed a deer part way for Marsh who killed two this a.m. with my rifle and gave us one. Fresh meat once more. Reached Nacosari about dark. Found all well. M on hand, everything status quo. Was last one to get a meal in boarding house; abolished. Fellows having to rustle for themselves now. No stage. Things getting down to cases.

Wednesday, December 10, 1884: Rain still. Seems as though it never would let up. Some teams in today delayed several months I think. Pesqueira is putting up. Stage in late tonight. No news. Shaw only one in luck. Letter with two passes to Cal. M made assays of gold rock today. Small but it's there. Arrastra has been running or was up to yesterday, now 10 days, probably five tons crushed.

Thursday, December 11, 1884: Disagreeable day but I pulled out with Sessler. Burro fairly loaded. Took new trail. Better yet, got haunch of venison at his camp. M not feeling good. Ledge seemed to be petering. Hard work reassuring. My confidence not shaken. Walls below too slick for me. Miserable night; wind and rain. Hard lives with not much shelter.

Friday, December 12, 1884: Another forlorn night. Got in half a day. Have to vibrate between shelter and fire in wind and rain to warm up. System of coals under cover helped. Can't have fire too near tent, too much wind. Fine existence this; fine picture three of us huddled up together, getting warm and wet at times. Wind howls. Too much fire for rain though. Big one. Hard work to be very merry.

Saturday, December 13, 1884: Still storm continues; unprecedented. Old yarns about played out. M tried bottom of gulches and found placer gold; quite rich; money there in rainy season. May try some in arrastra.

Sunday, December 14, 1884: No work. I shall stop that in future if possible. Strange thing this a.m. About 20 shots fired in gulch below us, probably three or four miles away. Indians, contrabandistas or quarrel of mining claim now that water is sufficient for placer mining. Uncertainty not pleasant. I incline to last theory. Will have to be very careful and keep arms at hand. Beauty of being isolated and not knowing occurrences outside. First ice last night. Sun out, chance to dry blankets at last after a week.

Monday, December 15, 1884: At work once more; old man terribly discouraged. I have the old faith. Nothing arguing against proposition yet in my estimation. Got out some big boulders today. S gave us a hand a while today. Hard day's work.

Tuesday, December 16, 1884: Maurice out today. Didn't like looks of things but I satisfied him later and we got some good looking samples from other ledges. Bottom of creek when panned gladdened his heart. He thought it all pretty tough for me and wanted me to come in and go to town and do something there but I'm going to stay with the thing now through thick and thin until it's demonstrated.

Wednesday, December 17, 1884: Got in another good day's work but have stopped stripping, having found how ledge lays. Not sufficient ore on top. Will now go for it below. Squirrels a nuisance and other animals; sad havoc with grub. Prospected ledge up hill this p.m. with good results. Got some fine samples.

Thursday, December 18, 1884: Got things together and started for Nacosari about noon; packed in fine specimen of ore to send to Tombstone. Some free gold visible. Hard time getting in; pack went overboard on a side hill and having no saddle blankets, slipped badly. Hard riding. No Pesqueira yet and no stage. Grub getting scarce. Comes tonight.

Friday, December 19, 1884: Skipped around today getting some matters attended to. Busy most all of time. The long looked for Augustin Pesqueira arrived today. Very much of a gentleman.

Saturday, December 20, 1884: Good weather and settled at last. Very busy getting traps together and helping M figure on his co-relations. He goes tomorrow to Tombstone to spend Xmas. Is retained by Co so will return. Mail came last night. So Sam seems to have been game and done it [got married] before his brother—go it old son.

Sunday, December 21, 1884: M got off this a.m. taking my deer head and horns and big sample of ore from our mine with free gold in it. I went out with a terribly bulky load on burro. Weight only 150 but bulky, 50 lbs Giant powder. Not comfortable to pack, but had to have it. Great time getting through. Took new trail. Old man shot deer but didn't get him, so we're out of meat again. Took dogs with me. Had quite a growl with M tonight and guess I set him thinking some. Must have a shelter.

Monday, December 22, 1884: Started drift 20 feet down shaft on good ore. Let Mexican cut stuff for hut part of day. Don't care to be caught in another storm without a shelter. Went over to other camp with mule early and Marsh went in and brought us some stuff with his which I forgot. Great time with dogs. They keep a fellow warm though. No meat for them. Beans, flour and mush all we have but that's pretty slick.

Tuesday, December 23, 1884: Hard day's work. Started arrastra once more this a.m. Have ore to work now. Each charge half a ton, estimated. Five tons already worked. Former ore not the best. This is good.

Wednesday, December 24, 1884: Another hard day's work. Some heavy windlassing. I am starting another cut or drift on surface into hill on $100 rock. Horse and mule grinding away. Xmas eve. Fine old situation for me. Thinking of happy times tonight, crowded stores, excitement, etc.

Thursday, December 25, 1884: Xmas Day. No use to kick, so put in extra hard day's work and didn't find any nuggets for presents either. Perhaps Dame Fortune will deal more kindly with me by this time next year. Fine weather anyhow. Wouldn't have worked today but old man is anxious, is hard up, has three or four children.

Friday, December 26, 1884: Still at it. Jumped some deer but Maurice's gun snapped twice and I didn't get my meat. Chased in moccasins later but they saw me first amongst boulders and oaks on top of mountain. Hut enough done to go into and I took blankets in tonight. Some more rain.

Saturday, December 27, 1884: Rain set in again. Worked all a.m. though in it and in afternoon started for camp at N as beans were about out and had to have some. Storm worse than ever as I started and I had an intensely disagreeable ride through rain, hail and wind. Canyon flooded but floundered through it O.K. A drink of mescal at coal camp made me feel better. Hard trip. Found dogs at office. They jumped all over me. Returned Xmas a.m. half famished. Great time trying to get dry tonight.

Sunday, December 28, 1884: Storm at it all day and gulch running a river of water with terrible force. Mustn't go out today. Stage in this afternoon. Letter from home; Xmas letter, package coming. Maurice lost my deer horns and I'm much put out about it. Would rather have lost $25. Must try to go to mine in a.m.

Monday, December 29, 1884: Rain still. Couldn't get out today. Must get off tomorrow. Roads in terrible condition.

Tuesday, December 30, 1884: Weather still dubious, but looks like clearing. I got off in good season for camp with provisions tied all over the horse. Got back in time to put in some good licks before dark.

Wednesday, December 31, 1884: Last day of the old year. A brilliant crispy night. Moon full; grand and gloomy in my mountain den. Got in good day's work. Well, I wonder what Dame Fortune has in store for the coming year. I said upon leaving California for Arizona I would try a mining life for five years and the five years are nearly up. I think that a little more perseverance will win me the day and I shall stay with the present mining enterprise to the bitter end and probably decide things by this test.

OUTLET

INLET

The 30-ton water jacket furnace, manufactured by the Pacific Iron Works, Rankin and Brayton Company of San Francisco, revolutionized the processing of lead and copper oxide and carbonate ores throughout the West and Mexico. Two of these furnaces were in operation during George Parsons' stay at Nacosari.

1885

Thursday, January 1, 1885: Here it is February 25 and I've a job to transcribe all of my scraps from Jan. 1, not having any journal and unable to get one in the mountains of Sonora. New Year's Day: worked hard all day. First time customary greeting was omitted. Moulton isn't accustomed to it from 30 years mining and I didn't waste it where I knew it wouldn't be appreciated and Siberino, our ojaque, wasn't sufficiently civilized for it. Thought of the good old times tonight and friends enjoying themselves in NY and San Francisco. Perhaps next year for me. Dogs keep a fellow warm, one on either side all night.

Friday, January 2, 1885: Much trouble with arrastra. Considerable clay which plasters quite hard the sides and bottom. Put in two extra stones today. Trifle heavier work for horse and mule. Horse is very provoking at times. Storm gathering again.

Saturday, January 3, 1885: Rain all day. Worked through and was thoroughly wet. Am almost barefooted. High wind. Wet and cold and very miserable all three of us tonight. Our piece of canvas is some protection on top but sides being open they catch it. Danced around the fire and ate our beans in a very uncomfortable manner tonight.

Sunday, January 4, 1885: Ledge widening in drift; pay ore almost one foot. Am satisfied that a little mill would pay us well. As regular and pretty a ledge as one could want. Can pan out big gold prospects—free gold. I accidentally discharged rifle alongside 50 lbs of Giant powder in the hut. Only damage a busted saw. Rather close business. 50 lbs. Giant would scatter me pretty well. Heavy wind, cold, snow.

Monday, January 5, 1885: Same old thing today. We worked in drift while I packed ore down on the burro and did outside matters. Cold nights. I read a little Spanish nights aloud by the fire when not too cold and there is a blaze sufficient. Wish I could have a month of steady application to it.

Tuesday, January 6, 1885: Siberiano finished work on a little casa for M today and now I discharged and paid him off, $28.50. M tried for a deer this p.m. but failed to kill one. I walked over to other camp this a.m. to get some lard and small piece of meat if possible. No one home. Found some and helped myself. Meat tasted good after not getting a smell in two weeks. Beans and bread only diet but they're pretty slick.

Wednesday, January 7, 1885: Siberiano left this a.m. Having trouble with rock. It cakes on sides and bottom of arrastra. Iron may make the matter more troublesome. Dosed well with salt today; will help it perhaps. Old man and I don't like one another very well. He's a terrible growler against his fate and childish. Its very trying indeed in the face of so much unpleasant and disagreeable ways to have to put up with his nonsense.

Thursday, January 8, 1885: Have discontinued work on shaft level. Face of drift shows finely; nearly, if not quite, a foot of high grade ore. Will drift on surface and get some lighter rock for arrastra. Took flying shot at two deer yesterday as they passed camp; no go. Old man anxious to clean up, so contrary to what I wished, which was to run at least 30 days, I consented. I estimate about $100. Old man is crazy I guess. Hard to get along with. Must have grease somehow. Beans and bread without it don't go well nor stick to the ribs.

Friday, January 9, 1885: Still pursuing the ever tenor of our way. Some strangers around placering our claim; rains bring them.

Saturday, January 10, 1885: Old man went hunting to other camp today and returned, stating that it was Sunday today and was so being observed at other camp in usual way of cleaning bodies and rifles. I insisted to contrary, but to no use. Old man observed three to one that it was Sunday. [He] started for Nacosari early in p.m. Found I was right upon reaching N. Wanted to bet me tobacco and I don't know what all. No stage. Good bath. Long talk. M seems to be acting strangely. I was a hard looking case on animal at N, bare footed almost and sore neck, generally dilapidated and broken up. Took cold somehow.

Sunday, January 11, 1885: Joe's wife died last night, poor woman in child birth, sad case. With medical attendance no serious results would have followed I think. She just bled to death. Had quite a wrestle with Windmiller for grub. Left at three p.m. with lard, panoche, etc., strung all over the mule. Stopped at M and S for supper. Mule got off track in dark and I had a devil of a time for a while.

Monday, January 12, 1885: Used horse and mule for last time on arrastra today. Clean up tomorrow. I made a big strike today in finding a new ledge on our claim giving big prospect in the pan every time tried. M also got big thing on hill, other end of claim. I'll be O.K. yet.

Tuesday, January 13, 1885: Commenced cleaning up today. An immense amount left for M to pan out while I scrape the bottom. Hard work. Looked dubious at first but improves as work progresses. Don't expect over $100 for the ten tons as 25% silver is lost, and cold and ice and wind prevent good amalgamation. Wish we had hill rock in. That's free and lots of it. We've a bonanza there.

Wednesday, January 14, 1885: Better luck today. Looks now as though we'd get two lbs. and perhaps more amalgam; $200 or more then. Cold work especially for M in panning. Couldn't find a fine bunch of amalgam which we saw a few days after starting. Several Mexicans prowling around. Am afraid of robbery.

Thursday, January 15, 1885: Colder today and very disagreeable. About all the dirt panned at dinner time. A difficult and cold job for Moulton. Bad enough scraping; my job.

Friday, January 16, 1885: Cleaned out shaft this a.m. Received note from the perito to come in today by a messenger to see him at N as soon as possible, so went in as soon as possible and found a great state of things. Perito office merged with the prefect's and Don Liborio out. Was afraid of sudden demands but L treated us well and liberally.

Saturday, January 17, 1885: Sent letter to Maurice along with title papers. Fixed those matters last night and this a.m. as Robles hadn't gone. Wrote home and to Davenport. No more stage and we're completely shut in from the outside world. No mail for about a month, and being at Xmas time, is doubly bad. Am going to see now as soon as possible what can be done about working our mine to a profit and sent off strong letter to Bidwell. My mind is now easy. No immediate money to pay, mine O.K. for four months and trip to Oposura unnecessary.

Sunday, January 18, 1885: Andy Brown in from Adam's with a fine yarn. Martinez detained by authorities. The devil to pay in general. Provisions very scarce; no flour at store and outlook very discouraging. I saw it all coming a few months since and fixed myself. Am all O.K. Got off at three p.m. and found old man at Sessler's. Camp O.K.

Monday, January 19, 1885: Old man and I went hunting today and saw no deer. Seem to have left the country. My moccasins are worn through and I'm in a bad fix.

Tuesday, January 20, 1885: Retorted amalgam today and got about three oz. gold. No more arrastra business for me. Never took any stock in it from the first. It's too bad after all of our hard work. We've got the development though. Confound it, I'm having a terrible streak of bad luck all of the time now. Wonder if the country isn't cursed. I shall stay with it though to the bitter end. Will make it yet. Old Man fearfully down in mouth. Much worse than no company.

Wednesday, January 21, 1885: Cold this a.m. Worked at my new find today. Old man trying the placers below. Simply awaiting Tombstone news now. I shall push our matters now vigorously in another direction and may have to go to Tombstone. Cut soles for moccasins from old boot tops today and got along right well. Marsh after meat with my rifle.

Thursday, January 22, 1885: Fellows in today with a buck and once more there's meat in camp and we're happy. Old man through with placers; nothing there for him he says. Will get some more development work now if possible.

Friday, January 23, 1885: We took animals and went over to the Flag mine today. Put in several shots. Got good specimens. Water running though where best showing was. A good mill site there and only one I think within reasonable distance of mine, half mile. Must get the mill there.

Saturday, January 24, 1885: Bad cold; better today. Morris Hirsch and several others on hand today and camped with us. Some Tombstone news.

Sunday, January 25, 1885: Went in today and changed clothes. Everything in status quo. Principals will show up this week probably. Late start but reached camp in good time. F., M., Hirsch, McSweeney and Hayes there and our precious meat gone. They came surely at a wrong time. M likes rock very much from the Flag mine.

Monday, January 26, 1885: Put in some licks today at surface drift and my find, so as to make as good a showing as possible before quiting.

Tuesday, January 27, 1885: Some more of same kind as yesterday today. Every shot shows better and better. Must try for some meat tomorrow.

Wednesday, January 28, 1885: From reports I'm afraid that Mrs. F[arish] has gone back to her former life. Was hoping for the best. Old man and I had a long and hard tramp today, probably nearly 20 miles. Deer very scarce. Moulton started a large doe. I was on a hill and couldn't render assistance. Very pretty sight to see pursuer and pursued. Our camp is some hundreds of feet above the placer country and foothills and its a terribly stiff climb after hard day's tramp especially.

Thursday, January 29, 1885: Made some finishing touches today to the drift. Have done all I can to make a good showing and have worked hard and undergone a great deal more than I ever hope to experience again. Now will see if I am to make any money. One part of programme is completed. First act is played. Now for the second.

Friday, January 30, 1885: Moulton went in today to see the lay of things, so I kept camp alone. Lonely at night; old Jack, the dog, is good company.

Saturday, January 31, 1885: M back today and still no letters. Am mighty anxious for some. No Clark and no nothing. Very bad; must do something decisive before long.

Sunday, February 1, 1885: Nothing new. M rigged up a rocker and was off most all day. Returned disgusted. Must go in tomorrow. Can't stand this sort of thing any longer.

Monday, February 2, 1885: Went in today. Everything the same. Finally traced a letter Robles brought me from Maurice. Has some scheme or other on hand and has sent off my Xmas letters and packages by a smuggling outfit. If they're taken in I'll probably never get my mail and be accused of smuggling in the bargain. I cannot understand why he hasn't improved various opportunities to send me my mail. Am afraid he's too indifferent. I never could have treated him so. Going on two months now and no word from home.

Tuesday, February 3, 1885: No Cutler and no news up to 4:20 and I started for camp. This is getting unbearable; suspense very disagreeable. Hope never again to be caught in a like fix. Found camp O.K. Moulton rocked some but there's not enough in it.

Wednesday, February 4, 1885: We went on a deer hunt today and camped in a frightfully wicked looking spot after dark, a place where Tom B refused to camp with Moulton some time previous, afraid of animals and Indians. Water was warm; a warm spring. Rather unpleasant. Wild cats and Mountain Lions around in the night. Their voices not particularly musical; in fact, quit the reverse. Unpleasant companions for close proximity. Had a great time hunting water and a camp.

Thursday, February 5, 1885: Early hunt. M's gun no good. My foot hurt and I'm not able to use it freely. Had to jump onto some rocks out of way of the fool horse yesterday in moccasins and hurt it. Quite a leap. I made good long range shot yesterday at deer. Forgot to allow for distance though, as glasses deceived me, and didn't get my meat. Long journey today through the foothills and reached camp about dark, both rather disgusted. No deer except in and near Cumpas wash. Siberiano and Pancho washing below camp. "Muy poquito oro," they say.

Friday, February 6, 1885: Old man pulled up stakes and left today very unceremoniously. Had a few words with him. So Jack and I were left alone tonight. Old man rather provoking, very cranky indeed.

Saturday, February 7, 1885: Alone last night. Left camp early for Nacosari and found old man at Sessler's. Rode into town ahead and remained all night. Old man in a rather bad fix financially as well as I. Over came my hard feelings towards him after a while and made up.

Sunday, February 8, 1885: Looks like a storm so Moulton and I rode out to camp and packed in our goods and chattels, not getting back until some time after dark. Hid tools in drift and took off the windlass rope and brought that in along with 40 lbs. of Giant powder. Pretty good loads. So the first act in the play is ended. Farewell to old camp for several months. Machinery the next thing and then —

Monday, February 9, 1885: Unpacked and stored things today. Sold powder to Patrick, flour to Sweeney, and thus realized a little money for the old man and myself. Ate at Tom Adam's with OM today, but must quit that. Will get along somehow. Will Farish arrived last night and brought me a letter from home thus easing my mind. First one in nearly two months. Last received about Dec. 20th I think. Now we'll see what can be and what is going to be done.

Tuesday, February 10, 1885: Robles' sister died this afternoon and I paid my respects tonight with Don Liborio Vasquez. The body was gaily decorated in bright colors and carefully dressed being fully exposed. I smoked cigarette with Col. Torres, Don José María and others in an adjoining room. Don Liborio told me to say "Soy con ud," which I did and smoked and mescalled frequently.

Wednesday, February 11, 1885: Am trying to get W. Farish over to the claim. Hard work. Will probably induce Mr. Havland to go. He's a friend of Judge Berry's. Both say we have a good thing if we have six inches and we have six to 10. It's very trying, this kind of business. Less hard work in anything else in the world probably. Shall keep digging away at them.

Thursday, February 12, 1885: I eat at Pancho's still; steady diet of tortillas and frijoles, eggs, no meat. Pretty fair. I don't want any of the Americana's grub. She's too close and mean and has too long a tongue. Leavenworth in today. Had some guitar music tonight. Am still struggling with Farish. Old man going to Sierra Madres on a final prospecting trip and I shall outfit him for Clark and myself. He shares equally with ME and myself.

Friday, February 13, 1885: Moulton and I visited the San Pedro today and had talk with Morris Hirsch about the Sierra Madres and probability of his going. Armstrong started for Tombstone today with Adam; Farish to have the poor boy's leg treated properly. A bad case of neglect. T. F. must be crazy. His indifference is astonishing. Sent letter home.

Saturday, February 14, 1885: Accepted Cutler's invitation to go with him on Monday, so will go that way instead of the Sonora River as originally intended. To stop at mill. Old "Blue Grass" would hardly pack me there and I don't care to be stuck on the trail 20 or 30 miles from nowhere. Moulton will take him and trade or sell him for burros for Sierra Madre trip.

Sunday, February 15, 1885: Things quiet today, nothing new. Got Maurice's things together and have contracted with Frank L to take the dogs and them up. Am getting pretty fair eating now at the mess started by Strickland, Sessler, Kennedy and others.

Monday, February 16, 1885: Cutler didn't get off as expected. Have packed all of Maurice's things and had quite a job. Will take Havland to see the "Mina de oro" tomorrow if we don't go to town.

Tuesday, February 17, 1885: Strange to say Cutler came up with Nightingale ready to go and we got off at 10 a.m. I rode on tail end of buckboard to Cachul ranch and then changed with Windmiller who was riding Pete and was rather sore. Pushed on to Fronteras, arriving after dark. Although late, Cutler rustled up some supper for us. Don Cayetano Silva hurt by a mule. Mescal and egg go well.

Wednesday, February 18, 1885: W sore and I rode Pete; uneventful day. Camped half way to Custom House, 30 or 35 miles from Fronteras and rustled for grub. Divided mind with Havland. W seemed well provided and got a good cussing for his disinclination to share grub. Shaughnessy, Dick Watts, Tom Devine and Havland were in one wagon and Cutler, N and W on buckboard while I rode mule. Cold night, very.

Thursday, February 19, 1885: Got a good start this a.m. and the rest brought me in to the CH by an hour or more, 30 miles or so and down grade. Cup of coffee from some Mexicans on road made me feel good. I rode mule into CH in time for good dinner, though late. Great things to night—Cutler feeling good and S made things howl later.

Friday, February 20, 1885: W wouldn't take mule any further as he looked gaunt and had small swelling on his back. Both of us therefore had to climb on behind and wrap ourselves around each other and thus hang on until Charleston was reached, 30 miles distant. Fine looking objects from the dust. I scraped off some of it and then went over to Cheyney's and found not only madame but her sister, Miss Neal, and a Miss Keith, new arrivals. Pleasant call and rode home on tail end of butcher cart.

Saturday, February 21, 1885: Arrived last night about eight p.m. and was a curious looking object to my friends. Chucked all bedding out of doors, beat it well and had good rest. Quite a job cleaning up this a.m. House unopened for 3½ months and much dust. It's good to get back amongst other things, to receive the exceedingly hearty welcome which always awaits me. I have a host of warm friends here. Trimmed today and got into some civilized clothes. Dined at Clark's, Maurice at Huachuca. Called at Herring's.

Sunday, February 22, 1885: Washington's Birthday. Was asked to read service but was late and Major E read. No minister yet for the little church. About six people present. Stormy weather. Called on Cheyneys and ladies at TM&M Co.'s office this afternoon and later dined with the Earles at Mrs. Prestons. J. P. Clum back at the P.O. Could have had it if here.

Monday, February 23, 1885: Took things easy, saw the boys and went the rounds and dined at Mrs. Berry's where were Mrs. Havland, wife of my traveling companion, and Mrs. Earle. Music later. At P.O. I ran against Maurice who had come in from Huachuca in response to telegram. Long confab later about business and then a game of billiards, first one in a long time for me.

Tuesday, February 24, 1885: M and I had talk today with Tom Corrigan about the Trinidad mines, the latest Sonora excitement. Immense thing, so said. Womble at head. We'll sound him. Frank Earle fixed my gold I brought up and I have a pretty bar now of $2^9/_{10}$ oz. which is the admiration of all. Must rustle now and see what I can do.

Wednesday, February 25, 1885: Rain let up today; cold night though. I dine at Clark's now and this evening we had great fun at cribbage. Mrs. C and I against Col and Maurice. First though a little whist at Vickers'. Long letter and quite satisfactory one from Bidwell last night. Must prepare report on property.

Thursday, February 26, 1885: At last this journal is up and I am happy. Scraps all copied. Don't want another such job. Very pleasant day. My gold bar growing. Called at Mrs. Goodfellow's tonight with Maurice.

Friday, February 27, 1885: Commenced a report on our gold property today to send Bidwell. Worked at it hard. Called with Maurice this evening on Miss Fish at McFarland's, the Chiricahua fair one, and later at [Samuel] Shaw's, not being any one there, thence to Herring's where somebody is always bound to be.

Saturday, February 28, 1885: Hard work today from nine a.m. all day. M copies it and I got the report off by night's mail and it is said to be very complete and thorough and I think it is. It contained proposition also to give one half for $10,000, $2700 for selve, $3500 to buy the mill, $1500 to move and such and balance a fund for development, etc. Called at TM&M Co.'s house tonight with M and spent pleasant evening with Mrs. Cheyney, Miss Neal, Miss Keith, and M in high spirits; I'm tired.

Sunday, March 1, 1885: Wrote Bagnall and Milton today. Attended church a.m. and p.m, in evening at Presbyterian. Standing room only to hear Rev. Wills, post chaplain, lecture on love. A very humorous preacher; rather much levity. Mrs. Stevens at dinner. While at dinner Frank L arrived from Nacosari with dogs and baggage and, of course, there was a great time a while. Dogs glad to get back. Four now at house.

Monday, March 2, 1885: A letter from a stranger in Kansas, through Bidwell, came last night offering to put up money for our gold mine if as represented. So it all looks like business. Upon opening door of cabin last night there was a terrible scratching and running around, and a cat jumped past me out of doors. How in the world it ever got in there I don't know, as there was no possible entrance. Strange thing. Spent pleasant evening at Shaw's. Col had a time this p.m. Two men jumped on him and he pulled his revolver. I ran up and Bob Hatch and hostilities ceased.

Tuesday, March 3, 1885: Beautiful weather now. Map of property prepared today by Howe and mailed tonight. Have now done all in my power and must await results. It won't be very long. Col had another little racket this evening on way home. Appetizers. Some discouraging whist tonight. Took Con Cutler home this noon and called him at 2:30 according to promise. Got a ten out of him. He was painting the town red this afternoon and to night was carousing at a terrible rate.

Wednesday, March 4, 1885: New administration goes in today. Spent pleasant evening at [Robert] Eccleston's by invitation, where a goodly company of friends were gathered together; old man's birthday, 55th. Doesn't look it. Came from Benson for occasion. Met the latest school marme, Miss Powell. Played cards with her. Music and pretty fair time.

Thursday, March 5, 1885: Am expecting now to go to Santa Cruz to find Capt Tronquilino Cuen, who wants money for wood cut and used by others. Am to have Tom Moore's horse for certain consideration. Wish the confounded mill business was over; it is my nemesis. Will take in the Huachucas as well. Dined at Reppy's tonight and spent evening.

Friday, March 6, 1885: A house racket today. Col wanted M and me to guard certain premises so we did. Everything all O.K.; no blood. I dined at Clark's now. Maurice and Mrs. C quite insisted upon my taking all of my meals there but that of course I wouldn't do. They're very kind. Called on Mrs. Stevens this evening with M; very pleasant call.

Saturday, March 7, 1885: Same old thing today. Town very dead with no visible present hopes of resurrection. Pumps may bring it around.* Called at Herring's tonight and later at Shaw's, where M was, much fun, music etc. Great time with Don Augustin Pesqueira tonight. He wouldn't let me leave him till after midnight and then I had to force myself away. His plandits of me to others were rather embarrassing sometimes.

Sunday, March 8, 1885: Another racket with burros last night. Awakened me out of a sound sleep with the confounded bell. I went out with my bowie, corralled the bell burro, took off his bell and cut his hobbles. Guess he won't bother soon again. Church this a.m. Walked to TM&M Co.'s place with Miss Keith and Miss Neal. At Berry's and Earle's tonight.

Monday, March 9, 1885: Cloudy still. Nacosari heavy weights still on hand. Cutler a hard game. Nothing doing, simply awaiting events. Called at Cheyney's tonight, Goodall and Walker there; latter quite humorous.

Tuesday, March 10, 1885: Rain in afternoon, hard. Horse came in this afternoon so I must pull out day after tomorrow. Must await action by Bob Matheson, claims that $2000 or so was stolen from mill by McKee or McGee, a partner. Barker also implicated. Rather mixed business. Not necessary for me to go to mill but to the line.

Wednesday, March 11, 1885: Pleasanter today. [Lon] Richards came last night and the gang leave tomorrow for Nacosari. Can't get anything more from Cutler. He's played out credit and all. Translated for Pesqueira today at Revenue Collector's office, helping his friend Ensinas of Magdalena. Subpoenaed in Matheson case today. Quite a gala today. Wizard oil Concert troupe dog fights and Nellie Boyd band. Did best I could for mill interests with Barker and Scott. They declare good intentions.

Thursday, March 12, 1885: All the gang left today for Nacosari—Zulick, Connolly, Brodhead, Dawson (I think his name) Pesqueira, Con Cutler, Richards, Nightingale, Barney, McDonald and brother. Three different lots. Now we'll see what we will see. I don't take much stock though in the future. Took home Miss Goodrich. Believe I called late at Shaw's.

Friday, March 13, 1885: Maurice in bed this a.m. when I called for him to go to Custom House and I left very much disgusted with him. He said last night he could go "anytime after eight a.m." I went to expense and trouble on his account chiefly. He's entirely too trifling and this isn't the first instance of it. Cares nothing about keeping engagements and isn't willing to repay favors. Am afraid our business relations must cease unless he acts differently. Nice fellow socially but not a bit of business about him. I have dome much for him and his in ways he knows not of. Doesn't make me feel kindly and the desperate wind in my teeth all day seemed to aggrevate my feelings.

*The *Tombstone Epitaph* of December 7, 1884, summed up the feeling in the mining camp. "Our prosperity depended upon pumps, for the ore is below the water sure. The pumps are a fixed fact, and the prosperity of Tombstone ditto." When the contract was let for the Grand Central pumps, businessmen were jubilant, "their faces . . . wreathed with smiles, they now feel that they have not lived in Tombstone in vain."

Saturday, March 14, 1885: Meeting young Cuen just inside the Mexican line yesterday, short distance past the monuments, I learned sufficient to prevent going further about the mill wood racket and headed horse towards Ash Canyon, arriving there in good season at [A. H.] Emanuel's. Found there Mrs. Ellsworth, Miss Birdie and Miss Mary Farish. Emanuel full of fun. This a.m. early all except Mrs. E took a walk before breakfast. Girls escorted me to gate horseback on men's saddles. Arrived in Tombstone in good season and met Gelli with the long list of letters and packages we wrote since middle of Dec. Some words with M, didn't say all I thought of.

Sunday, March 15, 1885: At church this a.m. as usual. Quite a number there. Escorted home Miss Keith. In afternoon called on ladies with Mrs. Earle, Mrs. Berry and Annette. Called on Mrs. Goodfellow.

Monday, March 16, 1885: Struck a new lead today with Collins. Gold proposition near San Pedro river, big thing probably. M went to Ash Canyon today and I gave him Emanuel's name. Vick invited me to go to his ranch today, White and Vickers, Chiricahua's.* Got ready quickly and we started in wagon about three p.m. Late start for 45 mile ride. Went through South Pass and were lost in dark. Camped about midnight. Cold, only one small robe. Wanted to take blankets, but Vick said no.

Tuesday, March 17, 1885: Vick had a wrestle with one of the mules this a.m. and was thrown and scratched. Nothing serious. Reached cottonwoods in little while and ranch house at 8:30 in time for breakfast. Fine place and magnificent range of about 20 miles square; probably 6000 head of stock, two steam wells and all improvements necessary to a first class range. Grass pretty short—crow foot, white, and all varieties of grama grasses. Mrs. [Anna Maxwell] White very pleasant indeed and a sweet singer. Music and whist tonight, and this afternoon a ride over the range and quail hunt. Crowds of small game.

Wednesday, March 18, 1885: Rain last night, stockmen's hearts therefore gladdened. Made early start and went to S.W. well. Steam machinery all in order. Cost heavily at two wells. Met Childs here. Much fun at Vick for losing road and getting scratched. Rain today, light. Reached home about 5:30 and I dined at Vickers and spent evening. Mrs. V a mighty nice little lady, also Mrs. White. Old Arrastra Johnson tried to talk me to death yesterday at corral.** Quite original. Prospecting here 20 years ago and still at it. He had the McComas buckboard, showing a big bullet hole, and one

*This is a little confusing. El Dorado was White and Vickers ranch headquarters. Situated on the east side of the Sulphur Spring Valley where Turkey Creek enters the valley from the Chiricahua Mountains, this ranch was established in 1877 by Theodore, Thomas, and Jarrett White. Friends and relative soon joined the enterprise: James G. Maxwell, Robert Woolf, J. H. McClure, James Pursley, and Walter Upward. In December 1883 Thomas and Jarrett passed their interests in the business to John V. Vickers.

**James S. Johnson derived his nickname from construction of a battery of four arrastras at Dos Cabezas to grind and amalgamate gold ore. All four batteries were driven by a sixteen horsepower steam engine, the power transmitted through a series of belts attached to spur wheels.

of Lieut. [John A.] Rucker's mules on which he was drowned [on July 11, 1878] while the other mule had killed his man. Buckboard killed three—bad outfit.

Thursday, March 19, 1885: Rainy at intervals. Am on to several new things. Saw Crocker of Cleveland last night. Not a very satisfactory talk though about the Ruby. Howe told me I had left my Winchester outside of cabin upon leaving and he had taken it home for me. Careless trick. I determined to take the Remington, long range, for antelope and forgot other. Game very scarce. Maurice back. Dined there tonight. Called a while at Herring's and then went to Judge Peel's and staid the night with him. Laid down about one a.m. Judge not very restless.

Friday, March 20, 1885: Helped in preparations for the first Library Association entertainment and it was a great success everywhere, I was door keeper and took in $59. Admission 50 cents. Some kids made a disturbance outside and I had to send for an officer. Grabbed one of them. Mrs. Cheyney sang beautifully. Mrs. Capt Seamans, deceased, originated enterprise and I was with her but left for Sonora and couldn't assist. Staid with Judge Peel tonight.

Saturday, March 21, 1885: Had a pleasant evening at Cheyney's. Progressive euchre the evening. Quite a party. Maurice won first prize.

Sunday, March 22, 1885: Judge [Peel] about today. Church this a.m. Quite a good house. Dined at Herring's. Spent balance of evening at Earl's.

Monday, March 23, 1885: No word yet from Davenport. Several other propositions on hand. Spent a pleasant evening at Mrs. Berry's. Progressive euchre again. Grim for the Cheyneys, Misses Keith and Neil.

Tuesday, March 24, 1885: Began Spanish regularly today with the Mexican Consul Don Joaquin Diaz Prieto. He teaches me Spanish one day and I him English the next. I have advantage though as he hardly speaks English; understands only a few words. I taught him English today.

Wednesday, March 25, 1885: Called at Mrs. Berry's tonight, pleasant time.

Thursday, March 26, 1885: Gala day; ball match this afternoon attracted the whole town pretty nearly. Huachuca soldier boys played the Tombstone boys and beat them, score 18 to 25. Many ladies out, Cheyneys, Blinns, etc. Lots of fun. Maurice ran a foot race with a rancher named Bradley at close, 100 yards, declared a tie. Race will probably be run again. Whist at Post Office about 11 or 12. J. P. Clum and J. Fonga played Tom Sorin and me. Called at Shaw's tonight.

Friday, March 27, 1885: Went to the GAR post ball tonight. Shook my foot a while and talked considerably. Some Spanish ladies present. First dance since last spring. Consul wants me to act for him during his expected absence of several weeks. Am afraid my Spanish is not suffficent.

Saturday, March 28, 1885: Grand weather. Up rather late this a.m. Not fit for anything today. This kind of life won't do. Must have a change.

Sunday, March 29, 1885: Church this a.m. Attended funeral of Mrs. [C.

E.] Frederick today. Received at last, tonight, an answer to my Davenport matter which argues well for the future. Attended Presbyterian Church tonight. J and C and I sat together. Rev. Wills, post chaplain, acted the mountebank well. In order to make truth attractive, he said, it must be attractive, and accordingly read a pile of sickly stuff, jokes antiquated, etc. Too bad to court such sacrilege.

Monday, March 30, 1885: Replied to Davenport today. Rather looks like business. Called with Consul tonight at Aztec House and saw Mrs. Olds, Chase, King and Miss Russell. Mrs. O very pretty. Fine head, speaks Spanish well; music, piano and guitar.

Tuesday, March 31, 1885: Strallus seems to have gotten ahead in her Brooklyn school project as a circular came tonight. Looks and reads well. All are hating me; am getting disgusted. Dined at McFawn's this evening where was also Collins. Called this evening at Mrs. Stevens, cribbage and euchre with her; very pleasant lady.

Wednesday, April 1, 1885: Frank Walker arrived from "Lunnon." Leavenworth up from below, also Huneke, Frank suspected as a dynamiter in London and shadowed, good joke. Leavenworth at my cabin, busted and disgusted. Telegraphed for funds to leave country on. Has got enough; four or five years of it.

Thursday, April 2, 1885: Am feeling around all of the time, but don't see any money. Time tonight to hear from Bidwell again. Went to a social gathering of A.O.L.W. tonight. Rather uncomfortable, good thing though.

Friday, April 3, 1885: About all are up from Nacosari now, only two left there, T.F. and S. Earle's safe cracked last night, $185 taken and bag of coins belonging to Frank, value $200.* Neat job. Genl Rollins, Frank Walker, Maurice, Col. and I discussed mining project today and this evening at Calico, Cal. Hope there's something in it. I want to leave here. Am disgusted. Maurice and Bradley have come to terms and the race for 100 yds comes off April 25. Is bad business for me to go to California now.

Saturday, April 4, 1885: Frank Walker left this a.m. Was to meet Milton tonight but Mrs. Berry, Earle and Frank went down. I drove around and collected flowers for Easter tomorrow. Had undertaker's wagon, consequently considerable fun was poked at me. Acquainted Vick with [Sam] Brannan and Pesqueira. Land in view. Found Milton at barbershop. Looked well. Saw Gathrell when I left and staid around until he went off, fearing trouble between he and Clapp. After I left though he went for him but friends interferred. Threatened shooting, etc. Dined at Berry's, all nervous. After visiting Herrings I persuaded M to walk up town, first arming myself. We met G and he looked around quick, I doing same but he didn't want anything. Was ready for him. Too much bluster, but he's cranky too.

*The burglary occurred at the Cochise Hardware & Trading Company. According to the *Southwest Stockman* of April 4, 1885, the robbers got not only a little money, but considerable county warrants which they will find it difficult to realize."

Sunday, April 5, 1885: Easter Sunday and glorious day. Full church, $43 collected. Major read service and Hawkins did the music. Went about with Milton this afternoon calling as he leaves tomorrow. Talked of leaving this a.m. on account of threats, but I dissuaded him and told him I would stay with him which I did, going to church armed and remaining so all day.

Monday, April 6, 1885: Drove Milton down with the blacks of Bramer's. They're a holy terror around cars. Nice buggy. Met G coming out of corral. M had much to tell me going down. He knows what high NY life is. Some billiards in Benson and called on Eccleston. Left all O.K. Miss E Fonk on returning train. Brought her up. I was nearly left at one station where car I was in was switched off and I had to jump and run. Fine old system on the Sonora RR. Won't even tell passengers. Took Mrs. Clark on short ride upon return and dined there later. Maurice at Huachuca.

Tuesday, April 7, 1885: Nothing new and still waiting. I keep busy all of the time. A big disgust is commencing to grow upon me.

Wednesday, April 8, 1885: Spend several hours a day with Consul. I translate English into Spanish for him. Maurice and Genl Rollins were to go to Calico, California, today or tomorrow but passes haven't yet come. A probable chance for all of us there if reports are correct.

Thursday, April 9, 1885: Rather out of sorts. Dined at Berry's and took Mrs. B and Annette to theatre later, Judge having tickets and unable to go. "Toodles" and "Turn Em Out"—Mitchell excellent, good house, amateur company. Letter from Bidwell tonight finally and very unsatisfactory.

Friday, April 10, 1885: Well, perhaps another world may bring me better luck. I'm certainly out of it in this. Have been through a fire, been banged about, narrow escapes from Indians and bullets, never home, have toiled long at hardest kind of labor, and starved and bore all sorts of hardships, and it seems thus far, all for nothing. This kind of thing has got to stop. My disgust had grown extensively. I'm down to bed rock once again with chances against me. Guess its about time to quit. Would like money for father and sisters more than self but no, it seems it must not be. Party at Goodrich's tonight. Took Miss Shaw by invitation.

Saturday, April 11, 1885: [J. H.] Bostwick has signed all necessary papers and the Nacosari people are happy. He may die yet though. Is very low—struck Gage and Huneke this a.m. Must do something and that very quick. Mrs. Steins took me riding this p.m., spent part of evening with her.

Sunday, April 12, 1885: Church this a.m. The Major read. Mr. Bostwick died about midnight last night. Some scandalous transactions attended his closing hours. It was too bad. Genl Rollins, Mrs. Steins and I dined at Mrs. Clark's. Heard Rev. Adams at M.E. Church in the evening.

Monday, April 13, 1885: The friends of Bostwick here, went down to meet his wife at Benson today. I procured after some trouble a certificate of death from the Dr., a fraud named [W. W.] Fetterman. Ellsworth arrested by the nigger in the watch business; an outrage. I offered to run the nigger out of town with three or four others. Great time at Aztec tonight. Consul, etc.

Tuesday, April 14, 1885: Called on Mrs. Goodfellow tonight and met a Dr. Brun of the post and Mr. [C. M.] Bruce, a cattleman. Expected somewhat to go to San Francisco today with Bostwick's body. Was ready at 8:30 but the dinero was wanting so I didn't go.

Wednesday, April 15, 1885: Still furious today. Hope to see the T.T. [transferred] to Dick Rule in a day or two. Great time hunting Cutler. Mrs. Steins kindly gave me bottle of Magrief Cologne today. Some whist at Herring's tonight. Maurice a very fine player. Has made a study of the game.

Thursday, April 16, 1885: Havland got off this a.m. and Sam Brannan [Sam, Jr., educated at Freiberg, Germany] and others. Mrs. H also. All for Nacosari or bust. Will be bust I know it sure. Nothing good can come out of Mexico until it changes hands. It's a gouge game right and left and a bankrupt country. Plenty of good land and mines, but nothing under the Mexican flag. Consul Prieto and I spent evening at Aztec House. Shaved off whiskers today and sandpapered head. Not recognized hardly by some.

Friday, April 17, 1885: Helped fix Library Hall for entertainment. Took Mrs. Clark. Pleasant evening, dancing and lemonade; cleared $25.60.

Saturday, April 18, 1885: Sad accident today. Sandy Bob's housekeeper was burned to death this afternoon. Clothes took fire at store where she was destroying some old letters. Poor thing suffered from three till eight p.m. Spent evening at Shaw's; Dick sick.

Sunday, April 19, 1885: Church as usual this a.m. Cold streak is upon us, unpleasant. Genl Rollins at Clark's to dinner. M and I went home with Mrs. Stevens and plagued her a while about her sister's letter.

Monday, April 20, 1885: Cold, unpleasantly so. Sold Heneke Mexican silver today and have $4 now. All money I've got in the world. Serves me right. Called at Goodrich's tonight and Miss G and I practiced several duets together. Discovered we were reported engaged. Fine old town. I've been there three times in my life. I believe, possibly four.

Tuesday, April 21, 1885: Blinn offered me charge of swimming bath house this summer if he takes hold, as he probably will. Will go for any and everything now. Hope Cal business will carry me out of this before many months.

Wednesday, April 22, 1885: Maurice's foot race off tonight. Bradley paid him the $100 forfeit. No cause assigned for failure to come to term. I took Mrs. Herring to Miss Hart's and M came later. Some instructive whist according to Cavendish. A great study this game. Maurice will now go to California as soon as possible. [H. M.] Ellsworth, W[ells] F[argo] & Co agent, stricken with paralysis in Tucson this evening; not serious, I guess.

Thursday, April 23, 1885: Very sad news. Poor Ellsworth died about six this a.m., ill 11½ hours. Offered my services and did what I could for the poor girls. Mrs. E and Farishes went to Tucson this a.m. Spent this evening at Mrs. Berry's, Goodriches there. Music and talk.

Friday, April 24, 1885: Maurice hoping to get off every day now. Genl Rollins the only one keeping him. A "Mum" social tonight at Mining Exchange hall. Methodists didn't go. Too poor. Major and I had our usual casino tonight.

Saturday, April 25, 1885: Went to the track today with Maurice and saw the race between Shoestring and Broken Leg, alias Cochise; dead heat. A scrub race later. Rode home with a Lieut. Richards and Mr. Vandever of Fort Huachuca—Raced. Reached town on a dead run, good span. Nothing on hand tonight. Consul Prieto left for Nogales today and left me in charge of house.

Sunday, April 26, 1885: Church as usual. Walked home with Mrs. Stevens and paid her quite a visit. Dined at Berry's and called on friends, among them Mrs. Vickers. Her friend just from England whose husband bought an interest recently in White and Vickers ranch, Mrs. Upwood,* had a truly western experience on the cars. A gentleman she was conversing with at the time being shot by a party who was polite enough to say "Excuse me" first.

Monday, April 27, 1885: Maurice not off yet. Odd Fellows ball tonight was quite a success. Great crowd there. Ladies up from Charleston. Danced with Mrs. C frequently and adjourned with them at media noche to refresh. Kept it up until three or later.

Tuesday, April 28, 1885: Liborio Vasquez in town, in fact not many left. Mexicans and Yaquis at it and Col. Torres wounded. While Capt. K (Amalio) [Emilio] is reported killed. Spent evening at Earles.

Wednesday, April 29, 1885: Maurice and Genl Rollins at last got off this a.m. Will be gone two to three weeks probably. Loaned Matheson $4 today to collect of Bill Farish. He was broke and so was I but I borrowed for him as I see something ahead now. Liborio Vasquez dined with me today and I took him home.

Thursday, April 30, 1885: Rather busy today, the Tombstone Public Library opened tonight with myself as Librarian. A very good opening. Started by Mrs. Capt Seamans. Hours at present from 6 to 9 p.m. Funeral of Mrs. Meagher, a gambler's wife, this p.m. Was asked to be pall bearer and officiated. Sad.

Friday, May 1, 1885: Weather milder. Wish I could get out of this. Had the hardest experience of my trying life today but conquered myself thanks to my maker and I hope I have done some good to a woman of strong charac-

*This was the first of several unpleasant experiences suffered by Mrs. Upwood, wife of Walter Upward, an Englishman who had a share in the Chiricahua Cattle Company (White & Vickers). When Geronimo and his renegades left the reservation in May of 1885 and raided the Sulphur Spring Valley, she packed her bags and returned to England. Never reunited with her husband, Walter eventually filed for divorce.

ter and attractions [Mrs. Stevens]. We're a miserable lot of mortals. I try to live for good and may God help me. We're all so weak. I take no credit to myself in this matter because I know I should sin apart from God. I am not one to make first advances either. Oh what a struggle with fierce passions. A long walk today. Library only fairly attended tonight.

Saturday, May 2, 1885: Procured some books today. Have adopted a system of my own for checking books and time. Helped by Vick. Didn't sleep much last night. Wish I could always remain in the right frame of mind. Was interviewed by a certain husband today as to my non attendance at dance last night to which I had been specially invited. Some cards tonight and Carrenza at said hubby's house.

Sunday, May 3, 1885: Church as usual this a.m. Library open tonight. Dined at Blinns, pleasant time. Called at Cheyney's and around this afternoon. Walked home with Mrs. Stevens and staid a while. Left coat to be fixed.

Monday, May 4, 1885: Nothing new. Library open as usual. Not very largely patronized as yet. Pleasant time at Aztec House this evening. Some casino and good time generally. Mrs. and Mr. Old, Miss George Russell and I. Were beaten badly, Mrs. O and I. Was hoping to take Frank Hatch's place in the bank for several weeks, but my intimacy with Clapp and others at bank prevented. So much for friendship, but that's all right.

Tuesday, May 5, 1885: Was to have another experience today but fortunately it did not come off. I wish with all my heart that I was out of this country. Still another pleasant evening, interspersed with dancing.

Wednesday, May 6, 1885: Perhaps I am too good natured at times but I want to do right. Howe relieved me tonight and Dennis McCarthy and I drove to Charleston and attended the grand party given by the Cheyneys. Great time. Lots there, from the Fort too. Good music. The brass buttons catch the girls. Good time. Home and bed by three a.m.

Thursday, May 7, 1885: Cloudy; climate changing. Didn't arise until very late. Probably missed a chance as I was referred to as a suitable party to take charge of the city's money and pay warrants during City Treasurer's illness. Had a ticket to C of Eden show tonight and took it in. More fun with baldheads than at anything else. Crowded house, poor show.

Friday, May 8, 1885: Several rackets on hand now; one to take charge of accounts and collections of the boss newspaper, the *Record*, to see if there is any money in it or not and the other the swimming baths. Blinn and I examined the baths today and estimated things. Library doing fairly well. Will be pretty busy with all of these things but can't be made too busy. Quite a talk with Miss GR at Library. Was somewhat surprised at some-things I heard. Woman is a strange creature and I have lately had a strange adventure. Spent evening after nine at Mrs. Stevens. Cribbage. Dined with Capt Seamans this evening.

Saturday, May 9, 1885: Getting warm. Am learning pretty Spanish song, the Morning Glories. Capt Seamans and I sent letters today relative to ranch business. Letter from Maurice tonight looks encouraging for a future emigration to Cal. Hopes to bond six mines. Likes country well. Late this evening at Consul's practicing little music. Mrs. Berry and A went to Huachuca today, Miller's Canyon. Sam Brannan in again. Boys all pretty well busted. Trying hard to sell mill.

Sunday, May 10, 1885: Warming up. Church this a.m. Costello and wife two more victims to the death epidemic buried together today. Dined at Clark's as usual. Had library open as usual this evening. At Mrs. Stevens this evening by invitation.

Monday, May 11, 1885: Letter from Maurice. Has bonded six mines, he and Rollins. Hope it all may result in my leaving country.

Tuesday, May 12, 1885: Everything very stale, flat in money and unprofitable. Tom Farish and Sweeney arrived today. Both outfits. No more Sonora for them. Am learning pretty Spanish song from Consul, "Compamillos." No attendance at library tonight. Swimming bath business off for present, also the newspaper racket I guess. Took Mrs. S a package tonight. Pleasant evening.

Wednesday, May 13, 1885: Pleasanter, no wind. Am making my time count at Consul's. No money, but study and practice. All of this won't last much longer. At Consul's tonight practicing la musica.

Thursday, May 14, 1885: Nothing new. Same old thing. Received letter from O tonight. Boxing match today. Got in a knock down on Bob.

Friday, May 15, 1885: A possible chance to make something out of the swimming baths. Was given an order today for the books and accounts of the Tombstone Daily Record-Epitaph, but they were refused me. Some fun ahead. A pleasant evening at Major Earle's; their 19th marriage anniversary. Some friends present.

Saturday, May 16, 1885: Maurice arrived this evening with Genl Rollins and we had a long talk at the library. He's pleased and the prospects seem good in Southern Cal for us so I hope ere long to pull up stakes and skin out. Grand boxing match this afternoon. I got a knock down on JPC. Great time. Took account of stock at Bath House for Blinn today from Mitchell and guess we'll open on the first. Pleasant evening at Mrs. Stevens. Took my gallery along.

Sunday, May 17, 1885: Church this a.m. Saw friends this afternoon and dined at Herring's. Judge a little left on his dinner. Library open as usual.

Monday, May 18, 1885: Court opened today, new Judge, [W. F.] Fitzgerald, presiding. Was nailed as a grand juror and appeared at two p.m. After the preliminaries I was ordered by the Judge to arise and be sworn as foreman of the Grand Jury. Was very greatly surprised as there were others more experienced and much older than I, but as there was nothing else to do, I was sworn in. Was told that I was considered an unpartial and fair man. We retired to B of S now and organized with McFawn. Rev D as clerk.

Tuesday, May 19, 1885: Got to work today in Grand Jury and worked hard. Did well too. I get along better than expected. Twenty-three jurors, a quorum is 17 and necessary to convict 12. At Mrs. S this evening. Another Indian outbreak. Reservation broken loose as might be expected and 500 Apaches said to be out.* They're in good trim now.

Wednesday, May 20, 1885: At it hard today. Made partial report. Bad Indian news. Rumors though. Some folks at Nacosari reported killed. Am out just in time then. W. Farish got away for Ash Canyon with family this evening. Ice cream party—Maurice, and I and Nichols. Later I went to Goodrich's; cards and music. Took Miss Shaw home.

Thursday, May 21, 1885: Getting warm. Another good day's work. Made partial report to the Court this a.m. I had hard work to hold them together this afternoon after four p.m. One poor fellow in jail three months and 21 days on false charge, we settled. Pleasant evening at Prescott's, music.

Friday, May 22, 1885: A hard day's work. Announced my committees today so they could work tomorrow if they desired. Great time this afternoon, but we finally got straightened out. Rather remarkable letter tonight. Grand Jury adjoined by order of Court till Monday. Glad of it. Spent evening at Mrs. S. Took book and skins from Tobasco.

Saturday, May 23, 1885: Pleasant weather. Lazed around today. No Grand Jury business by order of the court. Called at Cheyney's tonight. They were up and a friend, Mrs. Quigley. Stanton gave us some banjo music and we had quite a time on the porch.

Sunday, May 24, 1885: Rev. Mr. [J. H.] Young, new rector, arrived last night and preached today. Held communion service as well. Liked him very well. Quite a good attendance. Library open tonight as usual. Church this evening too. At Mrs. S.

Monday, May 25, 1885: At it again today. Grand Jury business not very easy work for the foreman and I don't want any more of it. I earn $3 per day and so does Rev. McFawn, the clerk. The sensation of the day, the M and L matter, on order for the day. Now we're in for it. I sent for Judge Fitzgerald this afternoon to come to the Grand Jury room and advise on several points of law. He came down from the bench and served us. First time Capt Seamans says he ever saw it done. Am getting to be quite a lawyer—good thing for me.

Tuesday, May 26, 1885: Quite a pleasant time at Judge [A. O.] Wallace's

---

*Fed up with what they considered the whiteman's double standard, and tanked on *tizwin*, 124 Chiricahua Apaches headed by Geronimo and Nachez, son of Cochise, jumped the San Carlos Reservation on May 15, 1885. Traveling south along the Arizona and New Mexico line at a rate of seventy-five miles a day, the Indians stole livestock and killed whoever happened to be in their way until they reached Stein's Pass. The Apaches then turned west, crossed San Simon Valley and disappeared into the Chiricahua Mountains. Emerging from the other side of the mountains, they attacked Riggs' ranch in Pinery Canyon, wounded a woman, and then headed for White's El Dorado Ranch.

this evening. Great time at boys and girls. Rather too much dissipation after hard day's work. Went down to the baths with Blinn today to figure on putting them in condition. Tonight we had the church social at Mining Exchange hall. Quite a success. I took Mrs. Stevens. Judge Fitzgerald was there; Judge quite friendly. Made him acquainted. Had to wind up affairs.

Wednesday, May 27, 1885: Still on the M and L case, 3rd day. Very mixy; made a ruling. Hard work. Warning at me. Too much of a thing day and night. Rock from Calico came at last today and will be tested tomorrow probably. Hope we'll soon know something about the California business.

Thursday, May 28, 1885: Still at it; hard work. Meade arrived tonight. In consequence of likely important events very soon Mrs. S treated to ice cream tonight. Mrs. Woodman, Maurice and I on hand. Didn't feel very well this evening; ate something probably that didn't agree with me. All adjourned to Mrs. S. Stebbins called while we were there.

Friday, May 29, 1885: The Judge is first rate and talks to the point. A tedious day. Adjourned this afternoon till 10 a.m. Monday. Dined at Clark's. Beautiful moonlight night. A four in hand went to Charleston dam tonight. Mrs. S, one of party Dr. G drove. Called at Earl's and Goodriches tonight and Sam to say adios for the moment. At Seamans met Meade and Stebbins and M had quite a good time. M told me considerable about his Washington ex[periences], president, etc.

Saturday, May 30, 1885: Decoration Day; lazed heavily. Cal samples show up well, so possibly we may go there. Maurice always speaks as though my going was settled, so I suppose it is. Indians reported tonight in Dragoons. Went down town about midnight with Capt. Howe, but upon seeing the youth who brought the news, young Garrett, I disbelieved him, he's such an infernal little liar, and went home. About 20 went out. Too much of the mob anyhow for me.

Sunday, May 31, 1885: Church this a.m. as usual. This is two weeks old now and I don't remember things. The valiants [the Tombstone Rangers] returned home today, chased part of their own party. No Indians. One of the party accidentally killed as a result of the Garrett boy's lying.

Monday, June 1, 1885: My Court opened again as usual at 10 a.m. Hope we can adjourn by Wednesday. My good friend, Mrs. Stevens, obtained her divorce today and is a free woman. She had a hard, hard time of it doing her short marital experience.

Tuesday, June 2, 1885: Judge Fitzgerald called us into Court today and gave us a special charge with reference to bribery and corruption in the Davis murder case and a civil case. We were charged to go through the entire list of trial jurors, some 30 or more. So we've a job now. M and Lurgan case finally disposed of.

Wednesday, June 3, 1885: Hard at it today going through the jurors. Some bad business. Jury, or some in D case, tough ones. Sad commentary on human nature these results. Such monumental lying is terrible. Am learning a great deal these days. Fine experience for me. Human nature is indeed weak and vacillating.

Thursday, June 4, 1885: Examinations still going on. We have no district attorney except at very rare intervals and it's hard work. I have an immense amount of swearing and questioning to do. Am a son of a lawyer and perhaps come naturally to my liking for questioning and cross questioning.

Friday, June 5, 1885: Nearing the end. Committees got in some work today. We must finish tomorrow. Believe I dined at Clark's today.

Saturday, June 6, 1885: Committees all in by this evening. Short ride with Mrs. S this evening. First dined with her and then went to Maurice's house with her. Well, we were unable to obtain conclusive enough evidence to justify connection before trial jury in the corruption cases. The Judge came in to us this afternoon at my request when I submitted matters to him. He could only advise, of course, as to law. I was requested to make very strong report and had all ready this a.m. Grand Jury applauded me. I went [at] it as strong as I knew how. Reported at 8:30. I had to read all reports besides my own in court. Quite a job, about 20 reports on County and City matters. Judge complimented me, etc, and we each other.

Sunday, June 7, 1885: Church as usual. Communion Sunday. Mrs. S requested me to sit with her and we took communion together. The first time for her in Tombstone. Quite a talk later. Am very glad my jury task is over. Think I got though in good style. All reports printed this a.m. Mine is called a moral lecture by Meade. Quite a tilt with Mrs. Berry this evening. She knows positively, she says, that the first big fire was in May, while I know better, having good reason to remember that it was on the 22 of June. She was quite incensed that I should think so. Chicken dinner for me. Candy here.

Monday, June 8, 1885: Well, today began business in another way. Vickers received word about noon that a band of 75 hostile Indians were on his ranch and he gathered a few of his friends and started, fearing safety of White and those at the house. A party there, Mrs. Reppy and Mrs. Ward. We started about two p.m. My animal, the "Lang" horse, bucked and acted the fool at the start. Horses were pushed, 50 miles nearly if not quite, to make. I wouldn't push my animal so hard until heat of sun was past. Young Doc William Pendleton (Indian hater in paper) and I in rear some distance. Struck Cottonwoods after dark and the I.W.O.P. having complete knowledge of country insisted on our taking a trail I thought to be wrong and so discerned after going five to ten miles and getting amongst some Indians in all probability from the signals. Our man skipped, Doc's horse fell and caught his leg in stirrups. I jumped from my horse and caught his. Might have been bad business.

Tuesday, June 9, 1885: Doc and I retraced steps to Cottonwoods, where was an old corral and house. Couldn't enter house but turned horses loose in corral and laid down, keeping eyes and ears quite open. Some strange sounds during the couple hours we laid down. Deeming it very prudent we arose an hour before daybreak and I cut trails until I found the one I remembered when with Vickers several months before. We followed this to the ranch and found things all O.K. Arrived about sunrise. Had a hard night of it. Didn't know what to expect but we have done some good work, I think. All reports very true at the ranch. After breakfast a while we all took up line of march for [W. N.] Fife's and found him all O.K. Straggling Apaches reported. We took the fresh trail and followed a while some miles. Found carcasses of two heifers of W & V from which meat had been cut but a while before, in all probability about a dozen and I think the same lot who seemed to be about us last night when we were going in direction of Swisshelms on wrong trail. We picked up one of their hide horse shoes. Not enough men to follow trail any distance. White's people were up a canyon Sunday p.m. when a vaquero notified them of Indians and they harnessed horses and came in on the dead run, having to go a mile in plain view of Indians. [See page 267 for additional details] Top of house well fortified, loop holes, etc. Started for town again after lunch.

Wednesday, June 10, 1885: Had a very hard ride last night and afternoon. Scared one party badly. Thought we were Indians and after running a while proposed to give and take medicine. Several experiences yesterday. Mrs. R and Mrs. W with party of escort returned via Soldiers Hole—Vick, Charlie, Doc and I returned via South Pass and Dragoons to cut any possible trails and ascertain the situation. Everything quiet and nothing new. Got back at 10 p.m. after a very hard and tedious trip. I rode over 100 miles, had no sleep, muscles were soft and we were a used up community when town was reached and relished the good oysters and steak Vick treated us to. Town excited. Bill Daniels reported killed near Bisbee.* Men got together this a.m. and left for Bisbee. Great excitement. Daniels I tried to find just before I left for Vick's ranch, but didn't find him. He'd reported a hot trail. We were in a hurry to discover the situation of White and family. They were not attacked fortunately. Mrs. W. Cavil, others excited. Bill Farish wanted me to go to Ash Canyon in the Huachucas with him and others and about one p.m. we started, seven of us well armed, in a two seated wagon and reached ranch all O.K. Indians probably badly scattered now and much more dangerous.

Thursday, June 11, 1885: Everything all O.K. last night. Ranch here rather exposed and we're all careful. Frank Earle, Tilden, Thad Empy, Stuttering Jack, Frank Labrocci, WF and I think we can stand them off in good style if

---

*This is the same William A. Daniels, who as a deputy sheriff pursued and captured Dan Dowd. While acting in the capacity of a mounted collector of customs near Forrest's ranch six miles from Bisbee, he and several other men were surprised by Apaches on the evening of June 9, 1885. Wounded in the thigh by an arrow, Daniels would have escaped had not a bullet killed his horse. The fall broke Billy's neck.

they come. Lazed around today. Mrs. Farish, Miss Mary, Lill, Will and Emanuel, with chinaman, constitute our company. Tonight several of us went down to wire fence and were surprised to find a large signal fire burning at base of our mountain a few miles ahead. Frank L, Harry S and I rode around to the telephone in Miller's canyon this afternoon and I called for, and talked with Genl Rollins, who said we could not yet get soldiers here as wanted. Said he'd come if necessary. Told him no.

Friday, June 12, 1885: Emanuel and I went to Fort Huachuca today. He drove his fine team. I was guide. Distance about 18 miles. Were heavily armed. No signs. Pleasant two hours at hotel. Apaches split; some reported coming our direction. Some soldiers killed. Citizens haven't found them as I thought. Met Mrs. Springer and had quite a chat; also Bennett and several friends. Dr. Brun, post surgeon, as well. Very clever fellow. Wished to know particulars of McSwegan case. Couldn't of course tell much. Through the glass several bodies of men could be seen in valley this a.m., all evidently in great haste. Whether Indians or not we couldn't determine. We communicated facts to commander at post, E did and Genl Crook was telegraphed then.

Saturday, June 13, 1885: Returned all O.K. before dark. Frank went over yesterday afternoon with HS and telephoned his father. Nothing particularly new. Indians most anywhere and were reported leaving reservation every day, emboldened by the success of their fellows. Today Indians are reported in Ramsey's Canyon. Did my best to get word to Sherman over the mountain and presume he's all advised and others. Had a singular pain at base of spinal column today. We're all having a good time. Don't want trouble but guess we'll give a warm reception if necessary.

Sunday, June 14, 1885: We had a scare last night. FL came up hurriedly and reported a fire just outside fence. Lights were turned down, guns grabbed and several scouted. Finally discovered, after both sides had been covered by rifles, that three parties shortly before with us had camped instead of prosecuting an intended trip to Ramsey's Canyon. Large signal fires south and east of us last night. Have a disagreeable pain at end of spine bone caused I don't know how. Probably result of very hard trip; bruised. Went mule back to Miller's Canyon tonight and learned through telephone that Apaches had all probably crossed the line. Things quieting down. Guess we'll go in tomorrow or next day. Big fires tonight in Manzanas or Galiuros.

Monday, June 15, 1885: Beautiful day. Feeling pretty good these days. Fine weather and a generally good time. WF and wife went to telephone this a.m., he to determine on movements. Farish returned with conformation of my advices yesterday and determined that we should return to town. Three of us started for the four horses. I found them. We had to wait for Stuttering Jack some time. Finally the goodbyes were said and we all started for town, arriving shortly after dark. Called on Mrs. S and first on

Nightingale about a little piece of business for her. She was as charming as ever. I like her immensely well. She's so clever and goodhearted.

Tuesday, June 16, 1885: Got around today; saw everybody. No scalps, but we got as many of the Indians as they did of us. Was much provoked because Maurice did not care to hunt me any. I doubt him now. He's not the man I thought, I'm afraid. At Mrs. S this evening a while to give her a tree or rather bunch of flowers from Mescal plant. Al Jones crowd arrived today. Went as far as Bacuachi. Called at Clark's. No Maurice there. Hunted about town; no good. When close to a possible good thing, "shaking" is the the order with some.

Wednesday, June 17, 1885: Warm now. Good report of late G.J. My report well liked. Maurice Clark left this a.m. for Calico, said he wanted me to come. I went to the house and saw him off. Wrote letters today. One to old man Redfern; another to Florence and one to Rich, S.F. At Mrs. Berry's a while this evening. She acknowledges her defeat on the fire date and I go to chicken dinner there on Sunday next. At Aztec House a while and I ended at usual place. Old man Adam there, also Meade. Considerable fun.

Thursday, June 18, 1885: Fine weather. Balance of Indian hunters in last night. Things quiet at present but will hear from them ere long. Don José María Torres in town. [G. Gordon] Adam started for Washington today to represent Cochise County in relation to calling particular attention to our Indian troubles. We want the San Carlos reservation removed. It must be done to insure safety. Adam knows LaMar well and that's about all his recommendation. Don't go anything on him. My letter to R may do good as he's a strong friend of Hendrick's.

Friday, June 19, 1885: Am doing what I can towards increasing the revenues of the church, raising subscriptions and collections. Buzzed Walker quite a while this afternoon at his office. Reminiscences. More fresh trails reported, so there may be some more fun yet. Was to take Mrs. S to call on Mrs. Clark tonight, but we didn't go. Joshy time at House. Hardest place to keep away from and get away from I ever knew. I don't care to keep away nor get away either and that's what's the matter.

Saturday, June 20, 1885: Couldn't sleep much last night. A certain fair one on my mind too much. What an old fool I am anyhow, but then the world is full of my kind and kicking won't do much good now I'm afraid. More church collecting and soliciting today. Poor Frank Hatch, City Treasurer, passed in his check today about one p.m., typhoid. Evening at usual place. A spat today with Mrs. B. I spoke rather plainly and quite to the point and don't believe I'll hear anything more on the subject of my good friend Mrs. S. Called on Mrs. C with Mrs. S tonight.

Sunday, June 21, 1885: Walked home with Mrs. Stevens from church and remained a while. Dined at Berry's in payment of her wager that the first big fire, when I was nearly made an angel of, occurred in May and not in June; June 22nd was the date. Church in evening after this date. New minister, Mr. Young, not liked very well. Seems to be a sponger and woman-izer. Major [probably William H.] Bayless returned from Kansas tonight.

Monday, June 22, 1885: First big fire was four years ago today, I have some of the marks. At Clark's a while this evening. Took two dispatches. Sixteen years ago today dear Mother went to Heaven.

Tuesday, June 23, 1885: At Mrs. S this a.m. a while and about two p.m. we drove down to Fairbank for Mrs. C and Miss Daisy. Mrs. C went to Benson this a.m. to meet her daughter. [Daisy had been attending Ellis Seminary in Los Angeles.] A jolly good time with Mrs. Stevens. Shot full of fun and so sensible. I like her very much. Miss D much larger than when I last saw her over a year ago. A muchy muchness there. I nearly broke Mrs. S up returning. Lots of fun. "Scattered" tonight. Advised so to do.

Wednesday, June 24, 1885: Vickers and family, except Lillian, went to California today and I went down in stage this a.m. and drove back the carriage with Lill. Rain caught us. Rain every day now. Great time in stage with Mrs. Peck and Tevis; latter full of yarns. At Mrs. Clark's a while this evening and Mrs. S balance of time. Worked hard today on the school trustee business selecting candidates and proposing same to prominent men. There'll be a hard fight.

Thursday, June 25, 1885: Some opposition to Vickers but I'm going to run him and CS Clark, and [T. F.] Hudson, druggist, and names will appear to-morrow. It must bring out good men on opposition. Idea is to retain Miss Herring. Believe I "scattered" tonight. Lon Sweeney and I walked to Bassett today and examined shaft. Quite a pull. Nearly eight miles. Short ride on Vick's Buckskin this evening. Called around generally.

Friday, June 26, 1885: The school racket was started this a.m. and suddenly great interest was manifested, H and C very diffident. Didn't even see about tickets. About 11 p.m. tonight ordered some on my own responsibil-ity. Can't expect to do much if they won't work. Dined at Clark's tonight. Maurice wants me to go to Calico. Can't see what I should go for. Am bet-ter off here for the present. Want to see what the pumps will do for the camp. Funds getting low. Trying hard to sell. At First and F streets tonight fellow tried to kill officer Holmes today. Would have done a good job they say.

Saturday, June 27, 1885: Busy and lively times today. Same candidates in field. I had my straight tickets ready. I very soon saw though that Willis and McFawn would carry the day and mixed. Had a lot of McF, W and Vickers tickets struck off and made something by it. Sherman hurt Vickers very much. I was alone, no mercy nor carriages. Vick though was highest of the left candidates. W, McF pledged themselves to me to sup-port Miss Herring, also B[agg], but I doubt him. So Miss H is all O.K. I was working hard for her. Vote stood McF 288, B 236, Willis 220, Vickers 132, Clark 94, Hudson 84, Howe 84, Morris 1; 383 ballots cast. Watched the count, sandwiches and beer. Tried Buck tonight. Mrs. S nervous. We're going to reservoir, late talk.

Sunday, June 28, 1885: A bed late. No church until evening. Time changed. I'm going crazy I guess. Head full of one subject continually. Impossible to shake it off. Rain started in about four p.m. Pleasant ride with Mrs. S this afternoon about five in her rig and later dined with her. Church at 7:30. Quite considerable attention attracted. The dear tender sensibilities of some of the City's elite are apparently touched and moved. Dominos, Stebbins, Meade, Walker and I at W's office tonight a while.

Monday, June 29, 1885: Well, waiting for something to turn up. Hope it'll come soon. Invitation today on a 4th of July picnic. Boston Mill; Mrs. Goodfellow. Another's suggestion. Horseback ride arranged for tomorrow evening.

Tuesday, June 30, 1885: Had our horseback ride this evening as far as the state of Maine. Returned lower road. Back by eight p.m.

Wednesday, July 1, 1885: Mrs. S sick today. Too much work yesterday and exercise. Did what I could. All right this evening.

Thursday, July 2, 1885: No rain past couple days. Warm. Hope to hear something before long. Usual place this evening.

Friday, July 3, 1885: Went down for Vickers and family. Tried to take saddle horse too but combination wouldn't work. Found them all O.K. Returned on the stage. Vick and family all well and had a pleasant trip. Didn't retire until rather late, considering time to arise tomorrow.

Saturday, July 4, 1885: The glorious Fourth. Arose at 4:30 and was at Mrs. Goodfellow's for coffee shortly after five a.m. Stebbins on hand. Hadn't turned in. Hard work to arouse Walker. Hose turned on him in bed, bomb discharged in front of room and pack of firecrackers in adjoining room. Finally got off at eight a.m. Mrs. Stevens, Mrs. Leach and Edith, Meade and I in one wagon. Stebbins, Walker, Mrs. Goodfellow and Miss Leach in another and Leach, Batterman and wife and Bob Kenny in another. Hard time persuading Mrs. G to go. She was persuaded finally. Some kicking and jumping. Pleasant time. Quite a spread. Champagne, sherbert, etc. Boston mill pleasanter than I thought, although 100 in shade. Returned at 7:30. A few fireworks tonight.

Sunday, July 5, 1885: Stopped a while last evening at Mrs. G's porch where were Miss Leach and Bob K. Guitar music in order and I had to furnish it. About 10:30 went to the GAR reunion, thence to the Calico ball a while, only looking on. Later there was a cutting scrape and also a shooting racket I was told, so things were quite lively. Churched this a.m. Not many on hand, rather hot. Went around amongst friends this evening. I feel very mean these days. Everything is so unsettled with me. Future is bleak. Am broke and my best feelings are troubled on another matter.

Monday, July 6, 1885: Very warm. Invited to go down the San Pedro with Doc Hudson on a week's trip but don't feel at all in the humor for it. Hope my unpleasant feelings will not last much longer. I seem to have a rather hard row to hoe in this world, but then cannot tell about others who may be worse off. I pity them if they are. Sleep is the panacea for all ills and I'd like to sleep a while, am tired. Want and must have a change. This existence won't do. Jury today. At Mrs. S tonight. Racket on home business today 5%; half for me.

Tuesday, July 7, 1885: Sold Tom Gregory my saddle, spurs, blankets, rifle, scabbard and whole outfit today for $50. Cheap. Easy payments too. Spent evening at Herrings. Mrs, Miss and Mr. Leach there. Cards.

Wednesday, July 8, 1885: Cloudy, little rain. Go to Huachuca with Vick and family tomorrow for few days. Godfrey also. Wrote letters and fixed things. Went to Old Guard today. Looks very finely indeed. Wants a mill badly. Alexander went with me. May strike ranching together. He has means and I have experience. Am willing to do the square thing. Won't take his change for all of my experience.

Thursday, July 9, 1885: Got away at last about 10 a.m. I drove the two horse wagon with Susie Mayer for passenger. Had all the camp equipage and supplies. Took the lead beyond Charleston and showed the other carriages the way. Arrived at destination, the reservoir, about 5:30, 30 miles, two hours in advance of the others as my two horses could travel the road better than their one apiece, it being a double team road. Made camp and put Mrs. Vickers and family into Mrs. Berry's tent standing there. G said I should be recommended to Crook if he wanted to get anywhere as I'd get there, road or no road.

Friday, July 10, 1885: Confounded horses made a racket last night. I damaged one, didn't know he was tied, however. Fine air. Terrible appetizer. Having some mail for the Farishes, I hoofed it over the mountains four miles or so to Ash Canyon and spent the day. Saw all hands and the Mitchells and ate with all—never refuse a meal these days. Nichols and oldest daughter and Mrs. E there. Hard tramp returning. Didn't strike right trail and had tough time descending.

Saturday, July 11, 1885: Took things very quiet today. Didn't go anywhere nor do anything. Mrs. Moore, Miss Owlsby, Miss Gerty Howe and Charlie Read all camped at reservoir. Kimball, keeper of reservoir, nice fellow and quite accommodating. Fine place up here in Maple Canyon or Miller's Canyon. All hands enjoying themselves and adding health.

Sunday, July 12, 1885: Took a long walk, going up canyon two miles to [Ed] Stump's place; pretty good climb. Magnificent views; nice cabin. Found Mr. and Mrs. [J. W.] Stump, Ed and Mr. St. Clair on hand. Pushed on to summit about a mile further and had a magnificent view of the whole country and a hundred miles or more into Mexico, seeing Bacuachi peaks and I thought also Nacosari Mountains. Dined at Stump's and examined their mine and [Dyer] cannon ball mill, about ready to run. Didn't take any stock in either. Ascended to the Nellie James and got specimens returning.

Monday, July 13, 1885: Arose early and had deuce of a tramp after horses, going from shortly after five till between eight and nine. Hot. Hottest part of day seems to be from about seven till nine or ten a.m. Mercury not higher than 88 thus far, 100 and more in town. Camped near Rainy's a while while Vick and Godfrey shot some wild pigeons. Don't like them very well—plentiful, but no rifle game. Sad accident at Charleston about time we got there. Mrs. [E. T.] Garlock burned to death. Reached Tombstone a little before a heavy thunderstorm and lightning struck Durkee's. Mrs. S next. Supped at Vick's. Quite a talk with Mrs. V. Strange world.

Tuesday, July 14, 1885: Skirmished around today. Miss Kittie Goodfellow here. Saw her this afternoon. What will Mrs. Clapp say. Things so so. Nearly time for pumps to start up. [William Kidder] Meade U.S. Marshal for Arizona. Congratulated him today. If [I was] a good Democrat instead of Republican perhaps I'd stand a show for deputy. Called around generally tonight; scattered.

Wednesday, July 15, 1885: Pleasant most of day. Will fix up Doc's accounts tomorrow. Dined at Clark's tonight. Walter Locker on hand. Hope to work ranch scheme with him. At usual place this evening.

Thursday, July 16, 1885: Collected today for account of church—all matters have been turned over to me. Lon Sweeny, wife and child, left today for Denver, Col., and at Mrs. Stevens invitation, Mrs. Sweeny rode down with Mrs. S in her cart while I went down on the stage and returned with her. Mrs. S did the whole thing. Mighty goodhearted. Dine at TM&M Co. house tonight with Williams who is much interested in some mining chances I told him of. Mary waited on table. Quite a Clapp dinner.

Friday, July 17, 1885: Well, Casey Clum [younger brother of John Clum] and Miss Mamie Herring have agreed and I congratulated Casey. Meade left today to qualify. I had a hard night. No sleep, all a mistake. Drove to Merrimac today with Mrs. S, she not feeling well. Finished collecting today. Pleasant weather. Great experience tonight until two a.m. with a sick friend. The die is probably cast.

Saturday, July 18, 1885: Not up very early. Did all I could for my sick friend today—better. Smith's lodging house destroyed by fire tonight about one o'clock. Was awakened by the alarm and thought it must be close to, if not Mrs. S's house. Went there like a streak. Mrs. G much alarmed. Staid with Mrs. S until all danger was past. Home about daybreak.

Sunday, July 19, 1885: Quiet day. Dined at Clark's. [J. H.] White of Contention there. Break in GC pumps will delay matters three or four weeks. Too bad. Took Mrs. S to church this evening. Am looking young less and less.

Monday, July 20, 1885: Up this a.m. at daybreak, four a.m., and searched a long time for a pin Mrs. S thought she had lost last night but which she subsequently found on herself. Helped Miss [Kittie] Goodfellow on Doc's books today. My friend quite untamed tonight.

Tuesday, July 21, 1885: Some correspondence commencing to bear fruit. Letter from Dave[nport] last night commenting upon the scheme of opening up business with Mexico. Nothing new these days.

Wednesday, July 22, 1885: Same old story today, things stale. I see much of my good Mrs. S. Like her more and more. She is certainly a character and a strong one too. At Goodfellow's tonight.

Thursday, July 23, 1885: The sad news of General Grant's death this a.m. at 8:08 at Nat McGreger, reached this place about 10 or 11 a.m. and the city was put in mourning. I helped Vick with his crape. Hoping to hear something from judge, silent every day now about ranch scheme.

Friday, July 24, 1885: Some more Indian killings reported in the Cananeas—about tomorrow news will come from Huachucas probably. I wrote father a strong letter last night. First he has ever received from me on such a matter. I want his advice and need it. Pleasant ride with Mrs. S today. She took me beyond Merrimac. We visited old Macquire. She's too venturesome.

Saturday, July 25, 1885: Had a very enjoyable time indeed. As expected, Indians reported in Huachucas, stock stolen and killings. Went out with Napa Nick and Frank E to the ranch, Ash Canyon, Huachucas. H[oward] H[erring] horseback and Judge M[itchell] later. [F. L.] Moore went for his folks at Miller's. We left about six p.m. at Courtneys and was looking for boys from Tombstone to help him. Facts were not known. Indians took his stock only mile from C's and killed fell mare's colt. Kept sharp look out. Reached canyon little after 10 p.m., all up. Retired late.

Sunday, July 26, 1885: Lazed well today and read some. Practiced with revolver a while with Judge Mitchell. I don't approve of this kind of thing generally, but the Judge and I tried our pistols to try ourselves, and then in a quiet way. Things seeming to be quiet and no one afraid; we all returned tonight. I drove M's team in with Etta H[erring], Lily Farish and Ella Ellsworth. Very enjoyable ride till past Lewis Springs, where wind arose and never blew harder, I think. Regular gale. Home in four hours.

Monday, July 27, 1885: Rainy and cloudy. Good sleep. Things quiet in town and no interest taken in late Indian racket. Excitement too much before probably. Am going to King's Hot Springs Wednesday with Judge Stilwell and wife and Meade perhaps. It's going to be the swellest thing ever given in Arizona tis said. Hooker, the Cattle King, gives the entertainment. Military will mingle and band be in constant attendance. Hope Indians won't bother. I skipped around lively today. Called at Clark's tonight with Mrs. S. Col had neuralgia again.

Tuesday, July 28, 1885: Pleasant ride with Mrs. S this a.m. in the two wheeled contrivance with "Bones" as propeller. Got things in readiness today for an early start tomorrow morning. Rather venturesome trip, particularly for Mrs. Stilwell and she goes against the earnest protestations of friends, as the Apaches are still prowling about, but guess we can stand them off if they come around. Called at Goodfellow's tonight with Mrs. Stevens. Cake later.

Wednesday, July 29, 1885: Well, we got started at 5:30 this a.m. on our 50 or 60 mile ride to Kings Hot Springs, lately bought by H. C. Hooker and where the big entertainment is taking place.* Johnny Fonga went along with us. We were well armed, five rifles, pistols, etc. At P[ackard] & T[weed]'s ranch, 17 miles out, they were hunting 12 horses just missed and probably taken by the Indians, so that wasn't encouraging news for us. At Billy Furrs [Fourr] we ate something. He had his castle or fort in the rocks all ready for occupancy in case the Indians attacked him. At Dragoon Summit were some few soldiers and others were in the Dragoons close to us after Apaches, chasing them. Next halt was at Russelville where we refreshed horses and selves. Got off road beyond Johnson which was literally a deserted village, not a soul in sight and we brought up at Point of Mountain where Dibble was killed. Found we must be wrong and retraced. Finally got right direction and struck a ranch house. Indians routed here, all armed and soldiers after them in the mountains. We had just left. Had a bad thunder storm about this time, fearful crashes. At last got to destination about dark after a long and hard drive and much watchfulness.

Thursday, July 30, 1885: Here very warmly welcomed by Mr. and Mrs Hooker and their son-in-law, Mr. [M. W.] Stewart and wife, and later made acquaintance of Col. [William Rufus] Shafter, wife and daughter, commander or Col. rather, of the 1st Infantry stationed at Fort Grant, who is here with his band and a detail, their friend Mr. McKittricks of N.Y., leading tenor at St. Thomas, N.Y. At Mrs. Lieut Barrie (nee Bester) [this would be Ellie Bestor Barry], Miss Nugent, niece of Hooker, Lieut. Barrie [Thomas Henry Barry], Mr. [John W.] Norton, Stewart's partner at Willcox, 15 of us,, all told. Had Mr. Stewart's tent and were very comfortable last night. Pretty spot, some half dozen warm springs; two bath houses. Water very hot, 120 degrees and more. Had bath this a.m. Lawn tennis this a.m. The Col. is a mighty nice man. Miss Shafter has cousin in SF I've met. Miss S pretty and pleasant. Fine singer. Also Miss Nugent. Exceedingly pleasant company. No danger of Indians here as there is a detachment of soldiers, and there too, the Apaches have never been in here, seeming to be superstitious about the springs. About 30 camped on or near the road we took several days ago. We probably travelled 15 to 20 miles out of our way. Were fortunate, I thought we'd have to camp and we were not prepared for it. Some magnificent band music tonight and the Col. took me to see one of the coronets, a very handsome one and the boxes and wagons he had made for instruments. This band is said to be the finest in the army. Music in tent this evening. McK has a grand tenor. I twanged a guitar and got off several Spanish pieces and we had good time.

---

*Kings Hot Springs is located in the Galiuro Mountains, thirty miles west of Willcox and eight miles east of Cascabel. According to the Tucson *Weekly Citizen* of July 27, 1885, Henry C. Hooker purchased the Hot Springs ranch and 160 adjoining acres for $1,050 from the administrator of Dr. King's estate. For a while it was known as San Pedro Hot Springs, then Gatewood's Hot Springs; today it is called Hooker's Hot Springs.

Col and I quite agree on Indian matters to my surprise. Sensible old gentleman.

Friday, July 31, 1885: Johnny and I sleep well in our tent. Quite a departure this a.m. Judge S went horseback with Mr. Hooker to his ranch, the Sierra Bonita.* Col. Shafter and Lieut. Barrie [Barry] took the ambulance and six mules to Ft. Grant, 50 miles distant, and Messrs. Stewart and Norton went to Willcox, all to return by Monday. Weather warm with rain storm tonight. Croquet and cards today, tonight too. Jolly good times these. What a change for me from the hum drum of Tombstone and its staleness to these new surroundings. In the evenings we listen to the finest music in the U.S. Army. All of [us] arrayed in our best in front of the tents, and in the hills about us are the hostile Apaches. What strange inconsistencies there are in life and contrasts. Away out here in the wildest spot on the continent amidst savage surroundings we enjoy what the largest cities seldom afford, fine music and dinners and clothes and the great congeniality constitute this Arizona's boss picnic.

Saturday, August 1, 1885: This a.m. a horseback ride was indulged in by three or four couples of us, I having Miss Shafter, the Col.'s daughter, for companion. We were attended by a mounted guard, rifles in hand, and had a pleasant ride. Several of the 10th Cavalry, Colonel, accompanied us. The Col has but one company of the 1st at Fort G and five of the 10th Cavalry. I tried the grey, one we drove, and he bucked badly, but didn't unseat me. Finally exchanged for a cavalry horse. Wrote two long letters today, one to Alexander about this place and another to Strallus. Whist today and cards tonight. Magnificent sky tonight and more fine band music. Grand effect, combination of glorious skies, scenery, music, thunder and lightning. Later big storm magnificent sight. Beats any stage effect possible. Wish I could describe what we all enjoyed so.

Sunday, August 2, 1885: Wrote this up this a.m. Most of others played croquet. Army life is a promoter of too great liberality in some things to say the least. Mrs. Lieut. Barry and I discussed mutual friends this a.m. in the Redferns, she living opposite them in Washington and knew them all well, particularly Louis. Also Miss Annie Almy is her oldest friend. Truly this is a very small world. How strangely people meet. Well, the days are

*Situated at the northwest extremity of the Sulphur Spring Valley eight miles south of Camp Grant, the Sierra Bonita Ranch was the oldest cattle enterprise in the area. It was the creation of New Englander Henry Clay Hooker who came to Arizona from California in 1866. In partnership with Hugh L. Hinds, Hooker furnished beef to the entire military department of Arizona, and several posts with hay and grain. The partnership of Hinds and Hooker was dissolved in 1871. A year later Hooker became half owner in the two year contract of W. B. Hooper & Co. for furnishing the army with beef, a contract that called for 30,000 beeves, averaging 800 pounds each. It was after fulfilling one of his beef contracts in 1872 that Hooker became aware of the spring which would become the operational headquarters of the Sierra Bonita. There he constructed an adobe hacienda eighty-feet square. A large windmill was erected, an irrigation system put in, corrals and stables built. Hooker homesteaded, preempted and purchased additional land and water rights until he had an uncontested hold over 625 square miles of rolling valley and tablelands.

going, but the time is being improved. The owner formerly of these springs, Dr. King, was killed here [about August 28, 1884] and in the old adobe facing were found two skeletons after his death. This locality used to be resort of desperadoes, rustlers, etc. They're pretty well killed off now.

Monday, August 3, 1885: All hands back now. Some croquet this a.m. A fine hot bath and sweat this afternoon. Tried it this morning early too but didn't sweat enough. Great times. Horseback ride after band music tonight. I rode with Mrs. Stewart. An immense rattlesnake jumped and scared the horses and I shot it. Eggnog later, Mrs. Shafter chief concocter.

Tuesday, August 4, 1885: Lots of fine drinkables sent out from Willcox and some ice on hand. Well, we leave all of this tomorrow. Croquet today. Horseback this evening as usual, I with Mrs. Stewart. An immense rattler jumped at and frightened horses and I shot and scared folks at house. Cards in tent this evening. Very hot, thermometer about 100. Had a great old sweat and bath this afternoon. Going deferred till day after tomorrow.

Wednesday, August 5, 1885: Reading aloud, etc. Horseback this evening. I was to go with Mrs. S riding McK's animal, but we got twisted up and I rode most of way with Mrs. S who was to ride with her brother. Fixed things at Lawrence's and got myself disliked perhaps, but did only what was right. Was surprised to find Lawrence out here. Knew him some years ago in Tombstone. He and King of [Hot] Springs at outs. K[ing] shot at him 14 times [him]self and hired assassins. Hit twice. Got in his work. Hard country. Miss S told me the true status of affairs returning. Great times. Champagne tonight and music; pleasant times almost gone. McK and Col S went to Benson today to return tomorrow.

Thursday, August 6, 1885: We got off about 8:30 amid much wailing and mashing of teeth. Had an awful jolly time and was glad of the chance to forget myself a while. Mrs. Hooker a very charming woman, so quiet and ladylike. All, a most delightful company. Met Fisher short distance out, who wanted me to return with him. Made several stops for lunch and supper and after a very pleasant ride, arrived in town a few minutes after nine o'clock after one of the most delightful little experiences one could possibly have. No danger of Indians returning.

Friday, August 7, 1885: Got around today and saw folks and was not long in finding the one I wanted most to see. Nothing much new. Ninth Cavalry scout going. Water handled without any trouble.

Saturday, August 8, 1885: The Marshal of the day awoke me early wanting me for an aid in the Grant funeral obsequies, saying I was put on the list originally and replaced by Cap Taylor when I went away and now T is sick. So I served. Had charge of the school children in the procession. Was quite gay with scarf and batan and mounted. I didn't remain to hear the services but joined Mrs. S, and together we visited the GB and Merrimac, at latter place she received a severe fall but was not hurt much. She got out of the way, very lively of "Bones." Tonight usual thing.

Sunday, August 9, 1885: Passed day quietly. Dined at Herring's. Took Mrs. S to church, although Stebbins was to do that. He got around a little later than he should have. Judge Stilwell and wife leave tomorrow a.m. for the Cananeas. They are goers.

Monday, August 10, 1885: Went over the hills today with Dave Hutchison. Examined the Tom Thumb, Black Top and Bassett. The BT didn't look inviting and in fact, looked quite dangerous, but we made it and got samples. I returned via the GB; ore streak gone there. They're trying to find it again by following the manganese in which the rich stuff was. At the usual place tonight. Received at last a very satisfactory letter from father on a near and dear matter. No it was tomorrow night, not tonight.

Tuesday, August 11, 1885: Rain nearly every day. Was to go for Judge Hoover and wife to Fairbank today, Miss Daisy and I, but missed team. Had very large toe nail removed today for the second time. Four years ago I underwent the same operation. Got the Hoovers a place to stop in, Eccleston's. Mrs. S made me present of a handsome scarf pin tonight.

Wednesday, August 12, 1885: Suggested to White and others some matters today in their business firms and had a talk with White [probably Theodore F. White] about trying to take part of his interest. I have some cattle business in mine and mean to have some if I can. Quite a confab with Walker tonight. Very clever fellow.

Thursday, August 13, 1885: Rain as usual at times. Am getting desperate. Can't stand strain much longer. Talk with Vick today on cattle racket. He'll help all he can. Believe it was today that I walked out in country and repair road for Mrs. S and returned via Merrimac.

Friday, August 14, 1885: Nothing new. Letter from Judge [Charles] Silent tonight, I think it was, about Arivaca Grant.

Saturday, August 15, 1885: Springer kindly told me of a chance at [Samuel] Katzenstein's, but I care very little to go there. Must stick it out here a while longer. Drove Walker to Boston mill today and had pleasant time there. Ice cream, mescal, etc. Returned with several fair ones and Mrs. S and I had great feast tonight. Took Miss K Goodfellow [on] short ride, returning early.

Sunday, August 16, 1885: Wrote letters today and at 4:30 went for Mrs. S to go with her to Clark's to dinner, it being Miss Daisy's 15th birthday. Presented her with pretty card. Judge Hoover and wife and Major Rouse were also present. Later took Mrs. S to church.

Monday, August 17, 1885: Collected for church and also helped [H. A.] Tweed with his stock of goods. Checking against Hull of S.F. T is buying out B[othin], so I have business for the present. Much fun. Steb wanted me to wear pair of gay pants, offering to present them. Declined.

Tuesday, August 18, 1885: Taking stock today. Rather tedious and strenuous work. Trying night work too. Steb breaks a fellow up—he's a great case. Evenings spoiled now.

Wednesday, August 19, 1885: Same old thing tonight until almost midnight. I enjoy the change immensely from idleness to activity.

Thursday, August 20, 1885: Finished the dry goods which lets Steb out. Tomorrow hardware with Pack[ard].

Friday, August 21, 1885: Tackled hardware to day; [B. A.] Packard for Tweed. A let up tonight and I called at Clark's and Stilwell's. Col is free man. Has closed out all townsite and mining business here and goes to Washington to prosecute Cotton claim ere long. At Stilwell's met Mr. and Mrs. [Charles] Benham and enjoyed the evening very much. They had fine news at Cananeas, mine and C. Very heavy rains tonight.

Saturday, August 22, 1885: Hardware today and I am to work tonight. Have worked half of the time nights this week or more. Got good pair of undressed leather shoes and pair pants from store at cost.

Sunday, August 23, 1885: Had to work till noon today. Called some this afternoon. Took Mrs. S, as usual, to church this evening. Great times at races.

Monday, August 24, 1885: At it again today and until 12 o'clock tonight. It's a tremendous job and they're in a hurry to finish. Joaquin unable to reach Arispe on account of the Apaches, so the mill racket is again bust in the head. Champagne late to help things along. I'm going at the Bassett when I get through store.

Tuesday, August 25, 1885: A busier day today. Hope we'll finish the hardware by Thursday night. Don't like this figuring through till 12 o'clock at night. Tomorrow I turn 35 and don't feel very proud about it either. Worked till 11 tonight. Beautiful moonlight nights.

Wednesday, August 26, 1885: Am 35 today and don't feel very proud over it either. No work tonight for a change. Mrs. and Miss Daisy kindly presented me with a birthday cake this evening. Did a little calling tonight.

Thursday, August 27, 1885: One of these unpleasant experiences caused through a grave misunderstanding occurred today. I was pained. I must be more careful in the future. Worked tonight as usual till late. Later, things all O.K. again.

Friday, August 28, 1885: Still hard at it, working about all night. Clock struck three before we quit. Old Judge Fetter was up, great Judge, and dined at Clark's this evening and took Miss Daisy down to Schieffelin Hall. Library concert; home talent, thought pretty good; good house.

Saturday, August 29, 1885: Again all day and until one o'clock tonight when the confounded hardware stock was virtually finished.

Sunday, August 30, 1885: Pleasant day though hot. No church, Young in Bisbee. Am afraid Young won't do. He'll have to go. Had to put in part of the day today, taking figures on bolts. Would not work tonight. Some good news at last. Looks like commencing of better times. Don José María Torres and Liborio Vasquez in town. Am asked to go to New Mexico on a racket that may pay to make examination and perhaps take hold of some mines for Davenport parties.

Monday, August 31, 1885: Commenced groceries today, Taylor helping. Worked tonight as usual. Some little fun late. Bill Ives, and I against Paul and Taylor at billiards. Must have some fun even though we take it late.

Tuesday, September 1, 1885: Major Earle spoke to me about a possible chance at Nogales with Blinn so will see him. I don't believe I'll be gone long. Liborio got away today and Don José María Torres. Lent Liborio $5 and C. Watts $1. All busted and hungry. Am busted myself but must chip in. Worked as usual tonight.

Wednesday, September 2, 1885: Finished taking stock this morning and now comes the figuring and a job it will be. Saw Blinn today about Nogales and I can have the place if I want it but must first hear from Davenport.

Thursday, September 3, 1885: Still grinding along. Figuring up now and there's a pile of work to do. Have 125 pages to put in one large book and 25 in another smaller. Took dinner at Clark's tonight.

Friday, September 4, 1885: Figuring all day and last night. A daisy lot of work. My good friend, Mrs. Stevens, had a very narrow escape while driving Mrs. Adams this afternoon. The cart upset not far from the Merrimac House and but for the good behavior of "Bones," one of the best animals in the country, it is horrible to think what might have happened. They were very fortunate indeed to escape with a few bruises. Mrs. S was very plucky.

Saturday, September 5, 1885: And still I'm at it but almost finished today. Blinn is now pressing me to go to Nogales and I've written to Davenport, Iowa, to telegraph me at once whether I'm wanted to go to New Mexico or not. Don't want to miss anything nor do I want to leave somebody. No work tonight. I called at Goodfellow's this evening, meeting Leaches, Mr. Bryce and all. Quite tired.

Sunday, September 6, 1885: Church this a.m. and communion but I couldn't take it from the present minister. I don't believe in him. We must have a change. Better off without anyone. Rested well today.

Monday, September 7, 1885: Some finishing touches this a.m. Amount about $45,000. Busy for Hull balance of day. Poor Mrs. S down again tonight. She was crunched other day badly but is not one of the complaining kind. Discussed spiritualism with Walker and Mark Smith tonight and earlier at Herring's; also giving synopsis of the *Sun Maid,* a new book by Miss Grant and powerful one. I see why it was given me to read, I think.

Tuesday, September 8, 1885: Morning beautiful and clear now. Huachuca Water Clark left this a.m. for the East and last night I had quite a talk with him about the mill and Hohstadt's mine. Am to forward a description.

Wednesday, September 9, 1885: Quite an excitement today over the discovery of an attempt to blow up the Clarks. A can with considerable Giant powder, fuse attached, candle, etc. Fortunately had gone out. Fortunate, very fortunate. A bitter feeling exists over probable supremacy now of mining title over townsite. May be damage yet. Telegram from Iowa. Nothing definite. Don't want to go to Nogales.

Thursday, September 10, 1885: Collecting on church matters again. Stebbins, Earle, Mitchell, and I met tonight and decided that the Domine must go. I spoke very plainly indeed and I didn't like it. I don't do any more collecting for him. Don't take any stock in him. Quite a time at Aztec tonight. Mrs. Adam moved there and Mrs. S and I called. Shot at pet bird this a.m. from cabin door and had business a while.

Friday, September 11, 1885: A bad shooting racket in Bisbee. A Mexican shot five men and was lynched. Napa Nick gave me a description. Was dealing at time; two men on one side, one on the other and one in front of him hit.* Managed with Fisher today to work Bassett. Am to get $^1/_3$. Good arrangement; will pay owners 20% as agreed, royalty. I will get $26^2/_3$ clear.

Saturday, September 12, 1885: Still in doubt on Iowa matters. Nothing new. Yellow fever from below. Church collections pretty hard.

Sunday, September 13, 1885: Pleasant today. Church as usual this a.m. Went up on the hill this afternoon, little Edith Goodfellow and I, and called at Leaches, staying to dinner. Miss Kittie G was there. We had a pleasant time and in evening Mrs. L, Miss KG and I went down in the cage 15 feet below the 700 ft level [of Grand Central Mine], where the great work is being done. The water poured in like a river. Fine sight. Edith and I walked rapidly home and I finished evening as usual with Mrs. S.

Monday, September 14, 1885: This a.m. I accompanied Mrs. S at her invitation to Fairbank. Meade went off to Tucson and we saw him off. He is now U.S. Marshal for Arizona. Mrs. S much worried on account of some party evidently shadowing the house. I got sight of party tonight and tried heading him off but he got away. Employed Jennings as guard tonight.

Tuesday, September 15, 1885: Well, there doesn't seem to be anything in the Iowa racket at present and I told Blinn I would go with him to Nogales on Thursday. Jennings on hand again tonight and he scared the party so badly that I hardly believe he will show up any more. Poor madame is very nervous. Wish I could catch the blankety, blank, blank.

Wednesday, September 16, 1885: Squared up with Tweed today and charged him only $6 per day because he had to stand it all alone: $120 for services. Took Mrs. S home from Clark's tonight and had Aleck Lamniore employed tonight as guard, Jennings having to go to Turquoise. On hand

*According to the *Weekly Citizen* of September 19, 1885, this incident occurred over a faro game, when one player, a miner, objected to a Mexican resting an elbow on his shoulder. A scuffle ensued and the Mexican was hit over the head with a chair, and ejected from the saloon. He returned about four o'clock the next morning with a rifle and opened fire upon people gathered about the gaming table, wounding Dave Hickey, James Kehoe, George Sales, Jack Welch, and Jack Gardiner. The gunman then went to Pierce's saloon and fired several shots through its glass doors. Located at his room, irate miners hauled the Mexican up the canyon and hung him.

myself until rather late these evenings. Squared up with Maurice today and it comes in good time, as he is hard up in Calico.

Thursday, September 17, 1885: Yellow fever reported at Nogales; three or four deaths. Don't care to run any risks but will go down and see probably tomorrow. Was exceedingly surprised to see Stanley this evening. He came in on stage direct from Cleveland. We dined together and had much to talk about. WP looks if anything better than ever. Is on his way to California on important mining business and ran in here to see about Ruby matters.

Friday, September 18, 1885: Won't get off now for a few days. Arbitration matters detain Mr. Blinn. Considerable discussion over Ruby matters today, Stanley, Bayless and myself. Matter referred to Col. Herring. I say to abandon for time being at least if we're going to gamble on prospects of the Camp.

Saturday, September 19, 1885: Today Stanley and I had a team and went over the hills visiting our mining interests and discovering that the Little Giant ledge does not touch the Ruby ground. Got considerable information from a party named Cook about matters and things. Expect now to get off on Monday for Nogales. Ended at the Grand Central and Leach took us to the bottom where the water passes in like a river.

Sunday, September 20, 1885: Church as usual today. Dined at Blinns. We don't get off tomorrow. Leave Thursday.

Monday, September 21, 1885: Nothing new. Confabs with Stilwell and Herring the order of the day. This afternoon Mr. Stanley and I had a long conference with Mr. Blinn, and in the morning one with Vick about a gold mining proposition in Cal, and both gentlemen were favorably impressed. I shall blow up the matter hard. I must get back to Cal. This thing here is played out. Fine today. Cabin burned, also a woman. She died tonight.

Tuesday, September 22, 1885: Am quite resolved to return to Cal if this matter near Placerville is consummated or an arrangement can be made for me to take hold with Stanley in the Independence and buy his $^4/_{100}$. Oh, for $1000.

Wednesday, September 23, 1885: Am afraid no pool can be formed here but I hope to manage it elsewhere. Grand moonlight nights, moon full. Mrs. Stevens and I had a delightful horseback ride tonight, and pleasant course later. We don't go tomorrow. Blinn still detained. At Mrs. Clark's this afternoon. Am trying to help her in a matter of business.

Thursday, September 24, 1885: Weather very warm. Con Cutler died yesterday or the day before at Hermosillo of yellow fever. Goodbye old son. You were your own worst enemy. Here was a character truly sometimes flush and often broke.* He's ahead of me $20 now, but that's all right.

*According to his obituaries in the Tombstone *Daily Record-Epitaph*, September 24, 1885, and the Tucson *Weekly Star* of the same date, Con Cutler died on Monday, September 21, 1885. He was fifty-five years old. He left a wife and an eighteen year old daughter, both residing in Martinez, California.

Others are doubtless ahead of him. He took me into Nacosari and brought me out. I thank him for my exit and our debts are squared.

Friday, September 25, 1885: Sad experience today. Heard of a fellow named Keller, plasterer, who seemed to be alone and dying. I went for Doctor Willis, got a wagon and carted the poor fellow to hospital, where [he] died in a little while. Had money and some well to-do relatives in Cal. Beautiful nights now. Mr. Blinn seems to have postponed his Nogales indefinitely, owing to presence of yellow fever there. Mrs. B very nervous. Called at Goodfellow's and Herring's. Some spanking at former place.

Saturday, September 26, 1885: Indians news again; 60 said to be captured and 20 killed in Cananeas. May have to go to Ash Canyon this afternoon if Emanuel can't return, as there might be trouble. Charley Watts sick and I'll look after him for Steb unless I go to the mountains.

Sunday, September, 27, 1885: In in a bad condition of mind; need and must have a change. Well, Emanuel couldn't leave owing to telegram from Zulick so I mounted Packard's horse and after several ineffectual attempts, owing to contrariness of horse, got away. Reached ranch, 30 miles, shortly after dark. All well. Church this a.m. as usual.

Monday, September 28, 1885: Returned to town today on another animal wishing to see Stanley again before he left for California. Had to work my passage on the old plug. Had final talk and shall go the Cal scheme all I can. Spent evening as usual. Nothing in Huachuca Indian matter. I'll return today to get Emanuel's return to ranch unless I have to go to Nogales.

Tuesday, September 29, 1885: Finished business and got off again this afternoon for the mountains. Gave Stanley letter to [T. E.] Cox [State Geologist of Indiana] on this mining business. I rather feel that with S this thing will go in some shape. I've done well by him before and hope the luck will stick. Found Col [C. Meyer] Zulick and two English experts named Markam and Davies, also two Denver gents, Col Beaumont and Mr. Wurtzbaugh, at the ranch all ready for the morrows trip to Nacosari, though nervous about Indians. Col Z quite familiar and seems to be very please to see me. Mrs. F[arish] had a huge family tonight.

Wednesday, September 30, 1885: The gents named, with Emanuel and Brigham for drivers, got away this a.m. and took my rifle with them, I lending it to Col B. E was crazy, wanted all the rifles on the place, a foolish idea on his part. He didn't get them. The Englishmen were badly frightened about Indians. Well, household is settled again.

Thursday, October 1, 1885: Lazed must thoroughly today. Read *Wreck of the Grosseur*, great sea yarn. Laziest kind of an existence possible, this here. Time is passing rapidly. Wonder where I'll be and what doing by Xmas. Hard rain today; came down very solid indeed a while.

Friday, October 2, 1885: I wished to see Stump's cannon ball mill working today, and accordingly went to Miller's Canyon and the two young ladies with me, horseback, Miss Willie Snead, Miss Roberts, daughter of Jas. Layson Williamson. At the telephone I learned the startling news that more Apaches had left the reservation and were then in the Dragoons and heading our way, dealing death and destruction right and left. Major B also told me that four men had been sent to our assistence from Tombstone and were then enroute. Bad news. While going up trail to the mill met the Squaw of the Mountains, Mrs. S, riding straddle. She was surprised. So was I at the apparition. Rescued a pie and returned and reached ranch all O.K with girls. Went up canyon to Robert's cabin with Will Snead and broke in to get coffee.

Saturday, October 3, 1885: Well, the crowd came last night about dark, Genl Adam sending them, being badly frightened—Bob Gray, McFawn, F. Earle and H. Herring were the party. They reported bad state of things all over the country. How I did kick myself for allowing Emanuel to take my rifle. Nothing but six shooter. Once more the savage is upon us and we don't know what to expect. I went over to the telephone today to learn further Indian news, but couldn't connect with office. Finally got Mr. Gage at the reservoir on hill who knew nothing and arranged for me to have news at 10:30 tomorrow. Long wait of three hours or more, folks uneasy.

Sunday, October 4, 1885: Once more I went to the canyon this a.m. at 10:30 and learned that there was nothing alarming enough to warrant further stay of posse, so they returned to town this afternoon. Frank E remained to go in with me tomorrow. Read some poetical selections this evening for benefit of children and old folk too. Last night we moved Mrs. Mitchell, four children, Chinaman, etc., to the Farish house for better protection in case of trouble. Houses several hundred feet apart.

Monday, October 5, 1885: I went in[to] town today, Frank and I, after first ascertaining through telephone that Indians were quiet. Very pleasant ride across country not taking road. Found considerable excitement and the governor (Tritle) on hand. Meetings afternoon and evening. Gov sympathized with Crook and was sat upon at meeting. After stating that Crook had all soldiers needed, he wanted people to put mounted couriers in the field to warn settlers, etc., etc. Most absurd proposition. Same old story. Soldiers camping on hot trails, Indian scouts misleading, etc. Stopped and saw Mrs. Earle and Miss Miller on arrival fresh from East. Genl Adam and Bob Gray trailed me to Mrs. Stevens tonight and we held a council of war. They thought Farishes and Mitchells should move into town immediately. I deferred, stating that they, the Apaches, would not operate in the open country and would not bother us. Had never passed close to us and that the rodeos [roundups], now in progress, would keep them off anyway; the open country having many stockmen and cowboys just now all very busy.

Tuesday, October 6, 1885: I had a moment with Governor Tritle this a.m. but he couldn't tell me as much as I knew about the Indian racket. Had some hot words with some folks this a.m. who said our folk were not deserving of sympathy if they would not leave the mountains and come to town. I suggested that the sympathy was not wanted and we could take care of ourselves. I then put matters as I saw them with my knowledge of Indian trails, doings in past, country, etc., representing the hardship attending removal of nearly 20 women and children and took responsibility upon myself of keeping them all where they are. Finally all concurred with me. Am to receive daily word at telegraph during present excitement. Same old thing and people scared to death. Nogales matter suspended. Got rifle and lit out at two p.m., arriving at seven with letters, candy, etc.

Wednesday, October 7, 1885: According to agreement I was at the telephone at noon in Miller Canyon, five miles distant, but neither Genl A, Mr. Mark Smith were there and I was hot. Waited 2^1/$_2$ hours when I got Judge Mitchell, who arrived last night and stated he would be out in the evening. Good news. I sent some impolite messages to Adam and Smith, and felt better. The Judge arrived about 7:30 with a fighting man, Shaw. Had much today including direct news from father where he saw in N.Y. a terribly big house. Two married ladies, three young ladies and two girls, six boys. Regular pandemonium most of the time until mothers are nearly distracted. Hard work to keep children close to the house. They don't seem to realize danger from Indians.

Thursday, October 8, 1885: The Judge moved back today to his old quarters. Dined with him tonight; some fresh meat, a luxury. Dick Reynolds went in town today driving Judge's team. Am thinking of writing to Chicago *Tribune* a long letter on Indian matters. Received invitation some time ago to do so, they remembering my long interview when in Chicago 2^1/$_2$ years ago.

Friday, October 9, 1885: Went to telephone at noon today and learned that there was no Indian news, things being quiet. The Judge then went to town, leaving his Indian fighter to guard his household. I had a little scare just after leaving the canyon. Half a dozen dark skinned beings rode out from under some trees, but proved to be Mexicans. I, however, went forward and discovered it was all O.K. Am to go to canyon at 11 a.m. tomorrow to get the news from the Judge.

Saturday, October 10, 1885: Was at telephone at 11 a.m. and Judge said that Indians were in the Swisshelms and Sonora, so probably have abandoned these parts. Had a time getting Pack's [Packard] horse started. He's cranky. Lots of fun teasing the girls, some cards tonight with them. Dick Reynolds came out last night and brought me a letter from father. He can't do anything for me on gold racket in California.

Sunday, October 11, 1885: Spent today writing a letter to the Chicago *Tribune* on Indian affairs and state of things arising from Genl Crook's failure to accomplish anything. Got a pretty strong letter together and hope it may do some good. Judge M came out this evening. No fresh Indian news.

Monday, October 12, 1885: Copied my letter to Chicago *Tribune* today and have it in good shape. Will send it right along now. Gov Tritle has resigned, good news. Too bad Col Zulick is not here. Hope it won't make any difference in his chances for the vacancy. Had an excitement at last. Miss Willie frightened the horses in front of house and they dashed off with wagon. Caught the wildest one by the head and hung on until I stopped them and saved them and wagon all O.K. Looked like bad business though at one time. I made some huge leaps. Fresh meat again, quite a luxury. Dick and girls brought up quarter from the San Pedro.

Tuesday, October 13, 1885: Judge Mitchell took ("Huachuca bill") Miss Willie Snead into town today and I started ahead on "Pack." At Lewis Springs found a poor steer doubled up in a mud hole. Got the men at ranch and good rope and pulled it out. Judge caught up to me here and had to work his passage into town. I helped him a little. Shot off revolver close to horses' heads, twisted ears, etc., but they played out and had to be left at First Chance and stage taken to town. I struck across country to Bassett and found a 10 ft hole and two men on hand. Some ore, but things not looking as well as I expected. Brought in two bird's nests. Indians in Sulphur Spring Valley and cattlemen afraid to round up. Met Mrs. S and Mrs. Adam driving and gave them a scare—was such a hard looking case.

Wednesday, October 14, 1885: Had a lot of running around today to do, seeing folks, etc. A little grouthy last night but better tonight. Can't stand this thing very long. Matters though are probably coming to a head.

Thursday, October 15, 1885: Drove out to Nightingale's this afternoon and poor old Cutler's team and buckboard had quite a load. Mrs. S has bought Maurice's old house. Trouble about taxes yet. Brought out Nightingale's dog. Didn't reach ranch until after dark some time. Good moon though and light and pleasant. An uproarious welcome to Georgiana. Letters and candy and great time. Col Zulick sent for by M & M. Donovan went.

Friday, October 16, 1885: Well, quiet reigns supreme out here. Read all day and evening. About midnight Emanuel came rolling into camp having arrived in town that afternoon, all hands in fact from Nacosari and Zulick is governor of Arizona. Commission awaiting him in Tombstone. Think he'll make a good one.

Saturday, October 17, 1885: Went into town with Emanuel. He drove Cap and Billy in in three hours or little more. He's hard on horseflesh. Congratulated Gov. Zulick. Went over to West End with Vick shortly after arrival to see a Burleigh drill work. Quite interesting.* A great time in town this evening. Speeches, banquet, etc. Arizona's first Democratic governor.

*Burleigh Machine Drill was a pneumatic drill designed by Charles Burleigh at the Putnam Machine Works in Fitchburg, Massachusetts. Following the Civil War it was proven at the Hoosac Tunnel through the Green Mountain range of Massachusetts, and put to use in California mines and on the Comstock in the 1870s by Burleigh's West Coast representatives Parke and Lacy of San Francisco. It seems inconceivable that this device was not in use at Tombstone prior to 1885.

Tombstone quite forward; Gov., Marshal, and probably U.S. District Attorney from the City. Quite a harrah. Lots of powder burned.

Sunday, October 18, 1885: Church this morning, full house. Turned over possible job at Banning of day or two to Joe Taylor for $^1/_4$ commission and left town horseback and driving in front of me the two horses which Mitchell had such a time with. Had a little work to get them out of town, but then made them pay for their recent bad business by putting them all though in about four hours. Looks as though I was going to be dragged into the Tweed-Britain law suit. Affidavit probably wanted.

Monday, October 19, 1885: Slept 10 hours last night, very tired. Must now go and lay for a mountain lion which appeared yesterday about this time and scared the Chinamen. Want his skin and head. Waited an hour or more for his Lionship but he didn't appear. Beautiful moonlight nights. Studied D. E. Tornos today. Emanuel came out late tonight, about midnight.

Tuesday, October 20, 1885: Spent today studying D E Tornos. Helped get up Mitchell's stove this a.m. The stove pipe came down on me once. No damage done though. Study and read all of the time now.

Wednesday, October 21, 1885: Emanuel and I drove in today starting at 8:45 and arriving at 12:45. I came in to stay this time, hoping for good news from Stanley. A letter awaited me but was far from satisfactory. The property gone I was working for. Another promised. Just my luck. Things quiet at Bassett for present. Called on Mrs. S this evening.

Thursday, October 22, 1885: Nothing new in town. Things very quiet indeed. Made some ranch purchases today. Called on Mrs. Adam tonight, also Goodfellows. Don't know what to do now except to wait on Stanley.

Friday, October 23, 1885: Fine weather these days. Was jumped for the U.S. Grand Jury in Tucson last evening and don't like it worth a cent. Meade let me go in the first of this jury racket knowing my means were limited, but at last I'm pulled. Wouldn't care if even expenses were paid. After a long rest of six months or more I took my guitar home today from Mrs. S. Don't want to forget my little music. This evening marks a sad experience for me. I don't undertstand the aggressiveness of her. I thought a friend if nothing more. Spent quite a time with Cap Seamans tonight who is just back. Later with Stebbins till midnight.

Saturday, October 24, 1885: Well, I suppose that tomorrow morning we all have to leave for Tucson. W. Gird will go and we drive down in his team. We should at least get mileage both ways. A suspension of Judges has been made and we who are summoned are in a quandary. The Democrats are going red hot for Arizona now. Spent this evening at Major Earle's and Judge Berry's; Goodriches, Miss Shaw and Earles at Berry's later; music.

Sunday, October 25, 1885: Well, this a.m. we got off, I going to Fairbank with Gird in his carriage. Detained at Benson until nearly four o'clock. Finally decided on taking rooms at Cosmopolitan, the other places being faulty. Frank Lord I understand to be the clerk at the C but we discovered him to be the Nacosari FL instead of our Tombstone Frank.

Monday, October 26, 1885: We all assembled at the Court House to answer roll call, but were delayed till two p.m. when the Judge, as Meade advised, discharged us all; then there was a skirmishing for pay and we got our coin, $13.30 each, $2 per day for three days and mileage one way at 10 cents or 5 cents each way. Under pay regarding expenses. Lunched with Scott and dined with Jim Eccleston, first taking a ride with him behind his fast horse. Fine country.

Tuesday, October 27, 1885: After dining with E last evening I went to the San Xavier to see Governor Zulick who greeted me cordially and I accompanied him and Meade and Walker, foreman of the U.S. Grand Jury and Pomeroy to a church to hear a Genl Wilson on the Sandwich Islands. Walker put up a job on the Gov., and he was compelled to address the large audience, getting nicely out of a scrape but vowing vengeance on W after he knew the true business. After the lecture we all went to the club. Saw the boys off this a.m. Dined with Ed Hudson and a number of pleasant gentlemen at the bachelor headquarters. Judge of County Court Gregg, City Attorney Franklin, Judge Anderson and Lieut Foreman of the Army. Pleasant talk and then went to Pomeroy's at Mr. P's invitation to meet the Gov. and other gentlemen. Gov. had to leave town. Meade and Walker present. Miss P as pleasant as ever and Judge Campbell as lively as ever.

Wednesday, October 28, 1885: Had pleasant evening last evening and we had a jolly time, the good punch helping things along. Mrs. Pomeroy lively and agreeable. Called this afternoon on Mrs. Judge Stilwell and her sister, Miss Bean, whom I had met in Cal. some years back. Spent the evening by invitation at Judge Haynes where I met his wife, her sister, Mr. and Mrs. Black and young Mr. Hayne. Music, cards and refreshments and a good time generally. Am afraid I am not in the most proper house in Tucson from what M tells me and my own experiences. Was all right though when I was here last. Arizona is a pretty tough country.

Thursday, October 29, 1885: Spent several hours this a.m. in Judge Gregg's office learning Pima County affairs and comparing with Cochise; also discussed the various law points involved in some important issues. A great kick is going on about Judge Fitzgerald's suspension and it is very prodigiously discussed. He declines to hold court pending his successor's arrival and seems quite determined and rather bitter. It seems to me that he is right, but it is a badly mixed state of affairs and causes much pecuniary loss and great inconvenience. M is now awaiting a telegram which may settle matters. Spent this evening calling. Went to Gray's, Eccleston's and Foyes and Eudes at club, beating E Hudson one point at billiards.

Friday, October 30, 1885: Nothing decided this a.m., so I took train and left for home. Train three hours late but made connection all O.K. Mrs. Aleck Robertson was on the cars with baby and I rode in pullman with her to Benson. Made acquiantance of a very pleasant gentleman, a Mr. Hood of Boston, who knew Tweed well and acquainted me with his father, who was on the train, Judge Tweed. terribly dusty stage ride. Quite a chat with Mr. [Fred W.] Smith of the Associated Press in S.F., who came up in interest of the *Star*. Cool.

Saturday, October 31, 1885: Quite a talk with Benham today of the Cananeas, also his supt, Williams, and arranged for Fred Castle and myself to tackle his books on Monday, which seems to be in a bad mess. Well, I saw Mrs. Stevens this evening at Post Office and saw her home. Seemed surprised to see me. Women are strange people. Halloween. Spent evening at Herring's. School Trustee entertainment, number present. Smith of the Press I took to the jail tonight and about some. Pretty busy tonight.

Sunday, November 1, 1885: Lang in church this a.m. helping out Mrs. Hawkins. Things getting down. Mrs. S had to go out. Mrs. Gage present with a Miss Ames, a rather pretty young lady. Young will have to go I think without any doubt, sooner the better. At Walker's this evening.

Monday, November 2, 1885: Fred Castle and I commenced work this a.m. on Mr. Benham's books and find a rather badly mixed state of things. Head a little off tonight in consequence. Went around some tonight. Am doubtful about the friendship of one party.

Tuesday, November 3, 1885: More work today and it looks as though the job would last several week at least. At Herring's tonight a while and met a Mrs. Shurtleff whom I saw home.

Wednesday, November 4, 1885: Hard at it today again. New postmaster, [C. S.] Clark. Takes terribly long time to distribute. Rather under the weather last night and today. Invited on the hill to Leach's this evening but didn't feel able to go. Made some calls tonight.

Thursday, November 5, 1885: At it hard today. Looks as though the job would last another week. At Herring's tonight and accompanied Howard and his love and her sister, a Mrs. Shurtleff of Napa, a pleasant lady.

Friday, November 6, 1885: Another day's tussel. Rather complicated mess. B, no man for detail. Well, I may have done wrong but was certainly much relieved by a statement I made to Mrs. A tonight. I cannot stand the strain much longer and must get away. Nothing but hard lives since coming to Arizona. They say "it's a long lane." Wonder if it was ever longer for any one else. Perhaps I deserve it all. God in heaven only knows and I shall always trust in him, but this last is almost too much for human nature after what I have tried to do too. Social tonight [for] aid of library, pleasant.

Saturday, November 7, 1885: Still at it, getting things down slowly. Played whist last evening in Goodfellow's room after the dance while the Leaches waited for the liege. Whist tonight at V's and a great time afterwards. A lively skirmish over and for lemon pie. The madame and I got the pie and licked Howard and girl in pantry. They hide out, chase, dodging, etc. Great time. I must be very careful again.

Sunday, November 8, 1885: Helped in choir again this a.m. Dined at Major Earle's. Splendid turkey dinner. Walk and talk with Huneke in afternoon. I like him exceedingly. Not feeling good today. Called on a few friends this afternoon.

Monday, November 9, 1885: At books as usual again today. Nothing new.

Tuesday, November 10, 1885: Same old racket today. Williams and Castle get at each other in fine style.

Wednesday, November 11, 1885: Getting along well. Called around.

Thursday, Noevmebr 12, 1885: And still our fight goes on. Looks as though the accounts were not crooked.

Friday, November 13, 1885: Another day's labor. Mrs. Benham seems devotedly attached to her liege. She left today I think it was for Fairbank to go to Cananeas with "Charlie."

Saturday, November 14, 1885: Again today. The business is coming soon to an end. At Mrs. Stevens this evening. Pleasant evening. Later at another Mrs. S and got away with a whole mince pie.

Sunday, November 15, 1885: I've a fine stomach, wasn't fazed a bit by the mince pie racket of last night. Must have off a little. Too much of a muchness. Sang in choir this a.m. and took up collection. Heard Rev. Wills tonight, considerably circussy. Mexican Consul [Prieto] had long confidential talk today with me on a delicate subject, saying I was his friend.

Monday, November 16, 1885: Court opened today with the new Judge Barnes on deck. County Court constitutionality discussed. Will probably go to Supreme Court of the U.S. Bouquet this evening to madame. Called upon Mrs. McNeil tonight and at Blinn's where was Mrs. Adam. Pleasant.

Tuesday, November 17, 1885: At work as usual today. This afternoon got note from Miss Goodfellow that she would go on hill to Leach's if agreeable. So about 4:30 we walked up there while Mrs. and Miss Leach and baby drove. Dined there and played whist. Pleasant time. Pleasant walk home by moonlight. Quite a confab on way up. Always troubles, hard world. A late session with Stebbins who goes to S.F. tomorrow. We are going to work up a Sunday school boom.

Wednesday, November 18, 1885: No work today. Had conference with Paredes of Fairbank this afternoon about mill. Was just starting for Fairbanks and horse was at the office door. Looks as though there was a possible chance now for final disposition of mill. I hope and pray so. Sent Miss Clapp Dr. [John] Turner's circular today. Pleasant horseback ride this afternoon.

Thursday, November 19, 1885: The old Bassett is not looking well. Am afraid she's going back on me. Think I spent evening at Nichols, that is, part of it. Went to Cheyney's this evening with Mrs. Earle, her sister and Frank. Met a Miss Birdston of Atchison. All just arrived. Methodist social tonight.

Friday, November 20, 1885: Went over and into the Old Guard today with Geo Williams to try and make a deal. Must do something. Went over part of the mine. Think he likes it. Make calls every evening as my shanty is too cold and cheerless for anything but sleeping.

Saturday, November 21, 1885: Made another trip to the Old Guard today and finished examination with Williams. Put him at 30 cents and I am to have commission from him and one from Vick's side as well. Hope to make a stake here. Mexican Consul J. Diaz Prieto goes to S.F. tomorrow to try to get his wife and child. I hope he can. Divorce is deplorable. Taught euchre tonight. Must stop it.

Sunday, November 22, 1885: Beautiful weather. Churched as usual, about 25 present. Called to see if Mrs. S was sick as she was not at church. In evening heard the new Methodist minister [G. L.] Pearson and liked him. Full house. Called at Clark's and Adam's. Am in charge of Mexican consulate now. Prieto left this a.m., also Capt. Seamans. Poor Casey got left.

Monday, November 23, 1885: Brought Williams and Vick together today on the Old Guard racket and the outlook is promising. Am trying for stock of H. Hope to make a turn there too. Got rid of Reddy's paints this p.m., gave them to several lady visitors. Second time my shanty has been hound[ed] by the opposite sex.

Tuesday, November 24, 1885: Nothing new. I have strange experiences at times. Another tonight. I came out ahead of myself and hope some good has been done. It's hard to do right at times (???).

Wednesday, November 25, 1885: Benham back and Fred and I put in part or all of today on accounts, don't remember which. At Mrs. Clark's a while tonight and Mrs. Stevens. I believe Doctor and I had a horseback ride this afternoon. Went out to the "Gordon" and saw Charley Watts.

Thursday, November 26, 1885: Thanksgiving Day. Worked on accounts till 1:30. Four invitations to dine. Ate my turkey at Mrs. Goodfellow's where also was Walker. Whist, jolly time till midnight. Was requested to meet Bishop Dunlop at the stage this evening. Did so and escorted him to the Cheyneys. Told him a few things and left others for himself to discover touching four.

Friday, November 27, 1885: At work on accounts today. Vice President Hendricks died yesterday, I think it was, so we'll probably have a Republican vice president, and I hope Edmunds will be the choice. Would be strange now if Cleveland should go.

Saturday, November 28, 1885: Some more work today. Horsebacked this afternoon. Met Bishop and Rector at Girard mill and took them over it, then galloped ahead and notified Leaches to be in readiness for their call. Taught Mrs. Cheyney euchre this evening. Letter from Miss M. Redfern, Louis just sailed for Paris. Will soon be a full fledged artist. Tells me to sell for $2000. Cries of murder tonight and Judge Berry and I were on hand. Drunken row.

Sunday, November 29, 1885: Fine day. Bishop Dunlop preached a.m. and p.m. Fine discourse, "All scripture is given, etc." Walked at noon a while with the Bishop and tonight escorted him to Cheyney's carrying his surplus for him. While visiting at Consulate this afternoon, Walker drove up with Mrs. and Miss G and Edith and we all drove to the Grand Central mill and paid Dr. Goodfellow a visit. Pleasant ride though dusty at times.

Monday, November 30, 1885: At work on books again today. Seems we'd never get through. Tomorrow will finish, probably. Mrs. Stevens sick. Troubled with severe headaches. Indian excitement again. Two persons reported killed in the Dragoons. Col Herring out and Howard worried. Was looking for it. Some more hard riding possible and risk. Finished work on books today. Benham owes us for 18 days at @ $10, $180. Called at Goodfellows tonight. Not feeling at all good.

Tuesday, December 1, 1885: Some more Indian news. Sheriff [Ben M.] Crawford of Graham County killed and two men. [A false report.] Terrible state of affairs. Will take the field again if necessary. Hold myself in readiness. Fire this afternoon next to Clark's. Got around there lively. Nash's bakery burned. Four deaths last night, and amongst them that of Mrs. Brederick who yelled murder the other night. Good thing for her children she's dead. Subscribed towards necessary expenses.

Wednesday, December 2, 1885: Nothing new today except Indian news. The devils seem be having their own way again about things. Just as usual though. Not feeling good, am almost at bed rock again. Benham doesn't come in time and its bad business for me.

Thursday, December 3, 1885: Vick, Dr. McGenard and Hanna and I took carriage this a.m. at Vick's invitation and went to Bisbee. Arrived in time for Vick and Hanna to do considerable accident insurance business during afternoon and evening. Doc and I took in the town. Didn't know I knew so many. Lots of bustle, but town is close together. Visited Heyne and examined his Copper Prince smelter. Whist tonight. Good bed but no sleep for me. Too much excitement outside and rustling about.

Friday, December 4, 1885: Vick and Hanna did up the town right well. Met Dr. Andrews and Lieut. [M. J.] Jenkins and Doc and I drove down to camp outside of Bisbee about a mile at the point. From top of large hill, the scouts with glasses could cover Sulphur Spring Valley pretty well. Only five Apache scouts at post. Capt Woods [A. E. Wood] in command. Met all but Floyd. Expect we spotted a hostile yesterday from up in rocks. Left about four p.m. and reached town a little before nine p.m., pretty tired.

Saturday, December 5, 1885: Fine weather. Joe and Hanna left for Los Angeles this a.m. Vick and madame went to Benson with them. Prieto arrived today and relieved me of the consulate. Divorce will have to come. Felt off today. Benham left yesterday a.m. for Colorado to be gone several weeks. No money. The madame though told me all about it. Had two ladies at consulate today. Called on Mrs. Stevens and at Herrings tonight. Six handed euchre.

Sunday, December 6, 1885: Thin congregation this a.m. Helped out in the choir. No one but Mrs. Hawkins and myself. Called on friends this afternoon. But six at church tonight. Bishop rather woke up Young. He seems to be quite universally disliked both here and in Bisbee. Will leave next week. Will be glad when he's gone. Don't think him a sincere man. Spent evening after church talking with Miss Goodfellow; old times, religion.

Monday, December 7, 1885: A rather disagreeable day on account of the dust. Sent a letter to Jesus Aguirre today, prefecto of Arispe, about mill business. A terrible town for gossip. Never saw anything like it.

Tuesday, December 8, 1885: Cold day. Little ice this a.m. as late as 11 o'clock. More gossip. Went up on hill to Leach's this afternoon. Saw Mrs. and Miss L and staid to dinner. Royal old time at L, away with Gage and Durkee. Great fun on subject of Herbert. Called on Mrs. Stevens this evening. Very pleasant evening.

Wednesday, December 9, 1885: Cash very low. Several dollars left yet. Too bad for Xmas. Must have my gold bar split and send sisters and Sam pieces. No money sure. Business for a Mexican today in having his taxes reduced. Am also employed to go off on a secret mission tomorrow. Made arrangements today. Am to inspect stock at Palominas as to whether or not there is sufficient for attachment; including a Bisbee matter.

Thursday, December 10, 1885: Well, I had a good horse, "Benny," and got off this a.m. While resting at Crystal Springs Duvell and wife, who had passed up the road, came back reporting strange and suspicious maneuvres on the plains towards San Jose Mountains. I accompanied them to Ochoaville and found that everything was O.K. Mrs. D alarmed and wanted me to go to Custom House with them but my horse favored one foot and I was afraid. Well, I did my questioning and got information desired through old man Peterson. Have to go to Bisbee now. Stock enough. O'Gorman on his way to see after J. Gird who accidentally shot himself at Cananeas other day.

Friday, December 11, 1885: Awfully cold night. Large bucket of water froze solid. C. B. Ayres , driver of stage from Cananea to Charleston, stopped over night. Had talk about mill matters. Well maneuvered for a good start to Bisbee. Very lively, not to say dangerous ride between the Mule and San Jose Mountains. Indian fire or presumably one with fresh moccasin track across river near smelter. Didn't care much about proceeding but did so and ten miles farther found fresh signs in the road. On the que vive constantly. Reached canyon all O.K. and met probably smugglers (Mexicans) emerging. Exchanged Apache news. Reached Capt. Wood's camp in a little while. Bad cold. Bisbee a little later. Cold.

Saturday, December 12, 1885: Didn't sleep any last night, terrible cold in head; a tough time of it. Fixed business with Preston this a.m. and got off shortly after nine a.m. Tired going back. Reached Tombstone about 3:30 and reported at once so that immediate action could be taken which was done. Quite a successful trip though risky. At Mrs. S a while and then went home. Mrs. Earle kindly gave me a mixture for my cough which helped it.

Sunday, December 13, 1885: Churched as usual. Called on friends this afternoon. At Clark's met Mrs. S. Bade Miss Birdie adios at Cheyney's. Spent balance of evening at Goodfellows. Cold weather for this country.

Monday, December 14, 1885: Was successful before supervisors this a.m. in my Mexican case. Am to start in taking stock for Blinn tomorrow at the Cochise Hardware Store. A two week job, so I seem to get a lift always when I get away down. Capt. Seamans back for a day or two. Helped him some this a.m. in the clerk's office. Collected for the Rector this afternoon. Quite successful. He goes this week and I'm not sorry. At Mrs. S tonight.

Tuesday, December 15, 1885: Started in today taking stock for Cochise Hardware Co. Pleasant kind of work. Korner in town. Other attachments are out. I was not too far ahead. Quite a little walk with Mrs. Benham and Mrs. Hines tonight. Called and found them just going out. Meade arrived tonight and Mrs. Stevens goes Friday a.m. She took "Bones" to Sandy Bob's ranch today and at midnight he had returned the 27 miles to town.

Wednesday, December 16, 1885: At work as usual today. Job likely to last several weeks. At Mrs. Stevens tonight. Am very sorry to see her go. I wish she understood me better. It's an unfortunate world in many respects. One cannot talk as they wish, owing to so many circumstances. Spent the evening pleasantly at Mrs. S. Meade was there.

Thursday, December 17, 1885: Hard at it again today. Frank Earle after much trouble granulated some of my Sonora gold and I sent two pretty specimens by Wells Fargo to sisters today for them to have breast pins made from them. Know they'll appreciate them. After five trips found Mrs. S, M and Stebbins at former's house and spent evening. Stebbins as usual cross grained on church matters and Young affair. Better talk less and do more.

Friday, December 18, 1885: Well, Mrs. Stevens got off this a.m., driving to Benson with Meade and taking the 500 lb. trunk along. Saw her off about 8:30 or 8:45. Thus endeth the first lesson. In a rather poor state of mind. I shall act only and at all times for the best and in the right, God helping me no matter what my passions may try to dictate. Shower must have caught her and they had an open wagon. Called this evening.

Saturday, December 19, 1885: At work as usual today. Sent a pretty card to Lakewood today or rather, got and mailed it. Nothing new. Called this evening as I do every evening. Very cheerless house mine, and cold. Called at Leach's on the hill tonight I think it was.

Sunday, December 20, 1885: Major Earle read the service this a.m. I took hold of the Sunday school today and shall stay with it now. Think we can build up quite a school, 18 children and four teachers. At Mrs. Clark's this evening. She told me considerable and something too about Mrs. S. Spent balance of evening as usual at Goodfellow's. Frank Earle there. Saw Mrs. Benham this afternoon and Mrs. Shuntleff.

Monday, December 21, 1885: At it again today. Easy time though. Pump rod broken in Grand Central and now another stoppage of several months. Won't be much left of the town I'm afraid by that time. At Mrs. Blinn's a while this evening, where was Mrs. Adam. Gave latter several silk scarfs for crazy quilt. Our Rector Young left this a.m. and we're all thankful. I was the only one who saw him off.

Tuesday, December 22, 1885: Beautiful weather. Job lasting still. Good for week possibly. Quite a talk with Van Lien today of Sonora. Knows Sheldons and Lees of Bloomfield. Sent cards today to Mrs. Clapp and Miss Daisy C. Sent Sam a pin by Express tonight of my gold. Quite a pretty one. Gold dropped in water and mounted.

Wednesday, December 23, 1885: At it again today. Dined at Clark's today and sent off her package to Miss Daisy tonight. Minstrel show tonight at Schieffelin Hall, and although I expected to help decorate didn't see why I shouldn't accept Vick's kind invitation to go which I did—a rather stupid affair though. Nick Stanton has showed up at last. Wants me to go to Cal with him and if he gets money I wrote for tonight I may go.

Thursday, December 24, 1885: One day more will finish stock taking. At Goodfellow's this evening and took Mrs. G around to Sol Israel's [Union News Depot] to exchange Xmas card. Stebbins on hand with pictures of his old home, exterior and interior. Helped this a.m. an hour at decorating church. Contention shut down; bad thing. Camp will now be idle till spring. Wonder what will be left of it then.

Friday, December 25, 1885: Xmas Day and a rather quiet one. Engine and Hose races this p.m., also coupling contest. Race now by latter and the other by the former. Lots of fun. Hose broke loose and wet the boys. Nearly caught me. Got some tobacco from Sam, handkerchiefs and memo book from Strallus. Turkeyed at Clark's, nice dinner. Spent evening at Herring's. Great time. Whist till midnight. Refreshments, Mrs. H and I badly beat Miss H and Mr. Ferry.

Saturday, December 26, 1885: Completed stock taking today and about Tuesday will conclude the figuring I suppose and let me out. Spent evening at Judge Stilwell's. Fine pumpkin and mince pie.

Sunday, December 27, 1885: Fine music this a.m., Mrs. Prescott and Mrs. Cheyney. Eighteen at Sunday school. Did my part. Hard rains this afternoon. Nick wants me to go to Cal and I want to go. At Earle's this evening. At Blinn's a while. Mrs. A there, Genl Adam away.

Monday, December 28, 1885: Put in a good day's work in Recorder's office and writing out location notices. Nick will relocate the "American Boy" and I must look out for the "Tom Thumb." Sunday school children met at Mrs. Cheyney's this afternoon at two o'clock, remaining till four. Xmas tree and suitable presents, helped. Very disagreeable day. Called at N's this evening. Later watched Steb, Walker and others at poker.

Tuesday, December 29, 1885: Cold yet and cloudy, snow on mountains.

Tramped over the hills today. Out most of day, tracing up our TT matters. Cup of coffee at Dan's cabin. Long talk with the boys. Spent evening at Herring's. Whist, Mr. Ferry and Miss H, Mrs. H and I; just beaten.

Wednesday, December 30, 1885: At work again at hardware store today putting in figures and figuring. At Goodfellow's this evening, cards.

Thursday, December 31, 1885: Fixed Nick Stanton out today with notices to relocate American Boy for Stanley, Amesty for Mrs. F, Nick and me and "Minnie" for Nick and Ward. Loaned him my six shooter and knife. Hard at work all day figuring; put in night at it too at the store and finished footing the Cochise hardware stock at 1:10 a.m. Great din and great times at street at midnight. No charge for hot scotch. Stopped few minutes at Firemans Ball and had to dance one dance, one waltz. Couldn't get out of it. Adios año viejo. Bien venido el futuro. Anything for a change.

James E. Brophy before the headquarters of the Chiricahua Cattle Company. This picture was taken in spring of 1885, shortly after Geronimo emptied the ranch corral. Note cavalrymen at right. (Photo courtesy Arizona Historical Society)

1886

Friday, January 1, 1886: Here it is 16 days after the first as I had to send to S.F. for this diary. Intended making a number of calls but weather was too unpleasant. Finished evening at Goodfellow's where were a number. I relocated the "Tom Thumb" this a.m., "Pentagonal" now. Well, I wonder what this new year will do for me. It seems to open up well and I feel as though I was going to do well. Time will tell.

Saturday, January 2, 1886: Weather still bad. Mr. Blinn wanted me to attend Sheriff's sale at Ochoaville on Monday to protect his interest and take charge of goods if bought. I consented though it may be a risky job for me as I started the racket and the line is a lonely and wild place. Two other men wouldn't go. I'm in for anything. Figured on inventory tonight and estimated $1040. I think Mrs. Herring and I played whist this evening against Miss H and Mr. Ferry.

Sunday, January 3, 1886: A cold snap is upon us. I do not remember seeing so much snow and experiencing such cold weather. Mercury went down to 15 to 20 degrees below freezing point. Church this a.m. I do all I can for the Sunday school. It is gaining. Arranged matters with Blinn today for the Ochoaville business. At different friends this evening.

Monday, January 4, 1886: Well, with Nick Stanton for company I started for Ochoaville about 8:30 to attend sale and got there about the time Sheriff Hatch did, 12:30. Katzenstein of Charleston* the only other bidder and he wouldn't do better than $725. I bid $800 and took the stock, locking up store. Sent word to town for wagon by Sheriff. Later sold some goods after first talking friendly to Korner and Peterson. Thought there might be trouble with them and their friends as I first spotted things. Nick and I were ready though for anything. Sold K&P a lot of stuff this afternoon. Did big business. Cold tonight, went out about two a.m. to see horses.

Tuesday, January 5, 1886: This point on the San Pedro River is the coldest I know of in Arizona. It's a terror. Indians around last night, killed a cow of Gray's off four or five miles and another was found later on their range.

---

*This was Samuel Katzenstein, "Dealer in Dry Goods, Groceries, Hardware and Provisions." In early 1882 he was managing the store of L. Zeckendorf & Company at Charleston, and that year purchased the company's interest in the business. From 1885 to 1888 he served as Charleston's postmaster.

Did good business today. Kept quite busy. K&P put up coin in great style. Had about $200 tonight. Bashford, Noonan and Jack camped with us tonight on way down to B's camp below Bacuachi. Cigars, drinks and Nick's recent Indian experiences kept things lively tonight and the cold off some.

Wednesday, January 6, 1886: Morning opened finely. No wagons at hand [this] a.m. and I decided to visit Ash Canyon, seven miles distant, and take the girls some candy. Nobody would go with me. Indians are bad but then it's an open country and a fellow could run his horses and was about starting when the eight mule team hove in sight across the plains and sun came up. Then we all pitched in, and in about four hours I think it was, had goods on the two wagons and the business traveling to town. Quick work. I lifted perhaps too much. Didn't know what might take place if I stopped any longer consequently hurried all I could. Nick and I got off in our buggy shortly after but had to return for sugar.

Thursday, January 7, 1886: Left wagon in corral at Hereford last evening about dark all O.K. and then put our team of whites through. Got dinner at Hemset's after dark. Florence, the eldest girl, is running things now and has the care of five children, age one to 10 years. It's a sad case. Indians came up to their wire fence other night. An intensely disagreeable ride to town. Rifles over laps for Indians or "bad men" wanting my money. Cold as Greenland. Moustache froze stiff. Away from river much warmer. Warmed up with hot scotches in town. A time with Nick. Got myself together today and will have my hands full of business now.

Friday, January 8, 1886: Wagons arrived last night and unloaded at store over Fountain on Allen St. Missed but little. Shaped things around some today. Expect to close out to the merchants. Am rather sore and stiff from lifting and working so hard at Ochoaville. Cold weather still.

Saturday, January 9, 1886: Well, had a daisy of a time of it today. Mrs. Adam wanted a few things which I let her have. She told some other ladies and the result was that I was mobbed very shortly. Had my hands, head, and eyes full and went it strong. Was kept going until dark.

Sunday, January 10, 1886: Not so cold. Major Earle reads service and reads well. Quite a good attendance. Sunday school growing, 22 or 23 today. Afraid somebody might try to steal some goods by back entrance. All O.K. so far. Visited Mrs. Shurtleff tonight, Goodfellows also.

Monday, January 11, 1886: Ball opened for me today in style. Things lively, outlook favorable the way things are going. Jews kicking. License man I'm afraid will show up. Some whist tonight at Herring's.

Tuesday, January 12, 1886: Cloudy still and some rain. Goods going like hot cakes. Am selling at S.F. wholesale prices and less. Am doing well. Daw caught me for license, sweetened him with two cups syrup. Reppy's birthday party or social this evening. I was requested to make presentation speech to accompany some trifling gifts given in fun. Had great sport; a number present and jolly good time for all. Dan O'Connor and I exchanged knowledge of Spanish and guitar evenings now.

Wednesday, January 13, 1886: Ben Titus, G.M. of Arizona Masons now, helps me out. Ben's a pretty good fellow. Goods pretty well cleaned out. The bid of $725 is well covered; my $800 judgement is all O.K. and I'm feeling better. At Herring's tonight. More whist tonight. Took Miss Hart there. Were beaten. Not feeling good. Rain still.

Thursday, January 14, 1886: Very unusual thing this cold weather. Made collections today and yesterday afternoon. Have worked hard and the stock is gone. Will take in $975. Pleasant evening at Herring's—company in honor of Mrs. Shurtleff who goes home to Cal Saturday. Great time. Dancing, singing, supping. Wrote to Bisbee today for French Joe.

Friday, January 15, 1886: I told Mrs. Shurtleff last evening that I would telegraph her husband today that Indians, etc., would prevent her departure. She bet mince pie that I wouldn't. I did. "Indians, storms and friends may prevent departure." Closed out everything today, only had scales left. I'm ahead and am satisfied and so I figured closer than I thought. At Mrs. S's tonight. Later at Dan's and later yet tried him at billiards. Met a number of ladies by appointment at skating rink, about time, and had some fun. Got along on skates very well.

Saturday, January 16, 1886: Well, another friend gone. Mrs. S went to Cal this a.m. and I was very sorry to see her go. She's a fine looking, sweet, bright woman, and I like her. All the desirable ladies seem to have husband attachments. Don't suppose I'll ever be married. At last this thing is written up and I am thankful. Cover only morocco but couldn't do any better. No eastern mail in six days. Terrible storms and cold east. Glad I'm here at present. Rain tonight and this afternoon. Music and Spanish at Dan's tonight.

Sunday, January 17, 1886: A rather unpleasant day. Not many at church. Major read as usual. Good Sunday school attendance. Had the mince pie today sent over by Mrs. S in payment of bet. Miss Bayless, Tom Buckalew and I had a feast. Adams and I dined together at Clark's. Goodfellows and Earles tonight, also later saw Steb, Meade and Walker. Well's pardon discussed. Other cussing. Eastern mail tonight, first in a week. Nice long letter from Miss Annie Lake Townsend tonight, first one in two years.

Monday, January 18, 1886: Still cloudy and disagreeable weather. Storm not broken yet. Cleaned guns today and prepared for another circus— Micaberish now. Frederick in today and I made one more effort on behalf of the gold mine and the stamp mill in Sonora. Will see what comes of that. At rink a while this a.m. Herring's tonight and Mrs. H and I beat at whist. Rather bad luck lately with Ferry and Miss H.

Tuesday, January 19, 1886: Well, things very quiet about town and the country generally. Not even any Indian rackets of late close by. At Genl Adam's tonight. The Genl going to San Diego on an inspection tour. Thinks of locating there.

Wednesday, January 20, 1886: Well, the back bone of the cloudy and rainy spell of weather which has been upon us the past ten days seems to be broken at last, leaving us a very delightful day indeed. This climate certainly can not be surpassed in the world. Italy cannot hold a candle to our fine days and they are the rule during winter. It's a grand sanitarium all of S.E. Arizona. At Goodfellow's this evening till very late. Rink carnival, looked about ten minutes.

Thursday, January 21, 1886: Still another beautiful day. All will be fine though now probably for a while to come. Road washed out and bridges down between Yuma and Los Angeles so no western mail. Blinn's side tracked, also the Tombstone boomers, White, Parson's Co., who are to infuse new life into the camp tis said.* Was asked to be sec[retary] of the Prompter today by Judge Berry for awhile to make transfers. At Goodfellow's this evening till late, Walker, Bob Kenny, Frank and Mrs. and Miss Leach. Walk with Miss L this a.m., visited Mexican shanty.

Friday, January 22, 1886: Rev. Mr. [Thomas W.] Haskins arrived last night and I met him at Earle's, dining last evening. A good style of man, one of considerable force too, am very glad. Our poor church has had some rough deals of late. Skunks make air thick at church so today Childs made a trap and Major set it. Must do something by Sunday. Spent evening at Goodrich's where were also Hudson and wife, Judge Street and family, Miss Ellison and White and wife, all met accidently. Quite a happening at Adam's a while.

Saturday, January 23, 1886: Am discussing San Diego. Adam goes there on a tour of inspection and Ferry wants me to go and take a look. Had I funds I would. Seems to me a very likely place and being by the sea adds an additional charm for me. At Dan's a while with the Consul this evening. Later at Herring's. Choir rehearsal this afternoon. Had a big contract on hand in removing skunk from under church; put on overalls and crawled length of church underneath, having to slide at times on stomach. Skunk dead. Could almost cut the air with a knife. Something had to be done and I did it. Was glad to find a dead skunk, but don't want any more.

Sunday, January 24, 1886: Mr. Haskins made a decidedly favorable impression this a.m. and preached a very forcible sermon extempore. He's a man every inch of him. Nothing of the bum about him. He talked very nicely to the Sunday school children later, only 19 today. No bad odors today. I was warmly thanked for removing the cause. Visited the Elias a while this evening and practiced Spanish. A pretty señorita with them who has bought Clapp's piano and has it at the San Pedro Custom House. At Goodfellow's in evening; also Blinn's, just returned from Cal.

Monday, January 25, 1886: Settled with Blinn today on Ochoaville business and got $130, my price. He was exceedingly well pleased with what I

*J. H. White and W. C. Parsons were among the earliest developers of mines in the Tombstone District, having interests in the Contention, Toughnut, and Sulphuret mines. Researchers often confuse mining man J. H. White with Theodore White, the cattleman and county supervisor. The fact that Theodore White had mining claims at Tombstone and J. H. White had ranching interests adds to the confusion.

had done which was gratifying. Had quite a talk about San Diego. He thinks very favorably indeed of the place and may go there to locate himself. Was elected secretary of Prompter G&S Mining Co. the 21st and took my seat today. Put in a hard half day's work. Spent evening on hill at Leach's; good time. Don't like Siberian blood hounds much though.

Tuesday, January 26, 1886: At work with Ferry today helping to straighten out matters, hard day's work. This evening I spent at Dan's on music and Spanish. Sent to Sumner [Vickers] today to N.Y. for cigars.

Wednesday, January 27, 1886: Most perfect climate to be found. Looked after some of my own personal matters today. Talking up San Diego still.

Thursday, January 28, 1886: Another meeting today of Prompter folks at two o'clock. Gradually bringing things to a focus. Lively work for me. Arranged to go to the Huachucas tomorrow. First rehearsal of the play *Esmeralda* this evening to be given by St. Paul's Guild. I'm in for it. At Mrs. White's later. Quite a nice time there, cards and music. Took home Miss Goodrich and Miss Shaw.

Friday, January 29, 1886: Well, Fisher, his party, La Fay and I got off about 10 a.m. Had a terribly bronco caballo in the team, one that kicked and raised the devil in general, so at Ground Hog we exchanged for the whim horse and made Miller Canyon just before dark. No more short cuts for me. I've said that before though. Got horse and rode to Ash Canyon to see Farishes. Very dark. Made me stay all night. Better than sleeping out doors. Emanuel anxious for us to see property of his at Montezuma. Quite a talk and smoke and exchange of news. Packard at ranch tonight.

Saturday, January 30, 1886: Up at daybreak and back to other canyon. Grand morning. Too exquisite for anything in mountains. We with Hollenstein climbed the mountain to the Nellie James mine over the snow and had a tough climb. A new kind of business for me, climbing over snow, crusted and slippery, several feet deep. La Fay wanted a shovel slide badly. Sampled mine well and returned to dinner at Hollenstein's. Hitched up and went to Ash Canyon and thence with Emanuel to Montezuma Canyon about a mile from line of Mexico to see the old "Mexican mine," now the "Chicago." Sampled it well. Boys seem to like it rather better than the other. About eight miles from Ash Canyon. Pleasant ride back to Ash Canyon where we staid the night. Telephoned in to F's people or otherwise they'd think some Indians had killed us.

Sunday, January 31, 1886: Started about 9 or 10 a.m. and had fine ride in. Stopped at Lewis Springs a while and buzzed the old man. He's about to build, looks as though. Sorry not to be back for Sunday school and rehearsal last night. Church tonight. Haskins a very fine preacher and able man. Called at Clark's and Goodfellow's.

Monday, February 1, 1886: Hard day's work on Prompter business. Meeting this evening; no quorum, adjourned till tomorrow evening. At Herring's a while, cards, etc. Farishes all came in tonight.

Tuesday, February 2, 1886: Some more work on Prompter matters, considerable to write up. Assays beyond expectation in lead and silver. Things look well. Hope I can make a raise out of this and get out of the country. Rehearsal of *Esmeralda* tonight. I have two parts. Prompter meeting detained me till too late for service at rehearsal, 35 cents assess on P stock.

Wednesday, February 3, 1886: More writing today on Prompter minutes. Tight rope performance in street, quite good. At Judge Stilwell's tonight. Forgot about parish meeting, too bad.

Thursday, February 4, 1886: Another half day on minutes, Prompter business about up. Bayless takes my place. Guitar fixed, practice with W. Gird quite often. Major played me on Prompter stock with Fisher. Will look out for him another time. Was asked by John P. Clum to stand as Godfather for his child next Sunday at its baptism. The madame's request; complied. Just six years ago today since I left Cal; guess I better return.

Friday, February 5, 1886: Know my two parts now fairly well of Drew and Marquis in *Esmeralda*. At Goodfellow's last night and bested them. Sumner Vickers arrived tonight with JV so spent evening with him. We attended Taxpayers meeting together. Action decided upon. Election the 10th. Must defeat the apparent steal of $8500, more than twice amount necessary. Wrote up Mrs. Berry's accounts this afternoon, making ledger from cash book so that she can make her report for the year. Dined there.

Saturday, February 6, 1886: Windy and dusty sometimes. Practice guitar music with W. Gird about every day awhile. At work another half day on Prompter business and now have it concluded. Rehearsal tonight at Schieffelin Hall for the first time. Miss Goodfellow and I seemed to be the only ones who had memorized their parts. Choir rehearsal this afternoon.

Sunday, February 7, 1886: Communion this morning. First time for me in quite a while as I could not feel right in taking it from Young. Mr. Haskins is a thoroughly good man as well as able. Poor Dr. [H. M.] Mathews died yesterday and was buried today, 61 years of age. Funeral at two p.m. Sunday school service at three p.m. Preaching to children once a month now; good thing. Before the service several children were baptized and I was Godfather to Mrs. Clum's little one, Caroline Kingsland Clum. She is two years old and a bright little thing. "What's that papa," she kept repeating, pointing to the bowl. Told her mother I knew she was a girl from that. Evening service, Farish's later.

Monday, February 8, 1886: Caught for jury duty this a.m. Made Bob Hatch stand the Major up too. A letter from Frederick at Sinoquipe, Sonora, received last night stated that Geo Capeland who was camped just below him on way down near Chinapi was killed during the night by Apaches or Mexicans. They didn't know which. Rough, but the usual thing. Might as well go that way as any other I suppose. Rehearsal tonight and I got Sumner Vickers to assist Mrs. Austin. Good thing.

Tuesday, February 9, 1886: Great times expected tomorrow. Am made clerk of the Citizens Committee of Taxpayers but probably cannot serve as I'm wanted by the Copper Queen and Arizona Prince Mining companies to look after the jury and officer in charge. They couldn't agree on another man for night work so I camped at Court House tonight and laid by the door. Looked after things. The paper tonight says "Geo W. Parsons Dude—no children—tax his—Yankee Doodledo."

Wednesday, February 10, 1886: Election day; cast my vote this a.m. Left Court Room on assembling of Court. Nothing suspicious yet. Must try to get in old man Childs for tonight. Interesting case. Slept fairly well on the floor right at the court room door last night. Looked after things today and tonight, finally got attorneys on both sides to allow Childs to take my place when not able to be on hand. Rehearsal tonight. All growling. Spent balance of evening at Goodfellow's. Childs relieved me tonight.

Thursday, February 11, 1886: Vote 210 no tax to 61. Good. A rather uninteresting day in court. Some ladies on hand this afternoon. Am kept quite busy looking after jurors. On hand tonight all night. Good sleep. A suspicious rustling once during evening; woman in the case.

Friday, February 12, 1886: Better sleep on the floor last night at entrance to court room. Rehearsal tonight at Schieffelin Hall and I attended, being relieved by Childs tonight. Spent balance of evening at Goodfellow's; singing and [having a] good time.

Saturday, February 13, 1886: On hand at nine a.m. Relieved Childs. Tedious business looking after this jury. A most excellent crowd, far above average jury. Nothing suspicious yet. Took some of fellows to rooms tonight for things, etc. Barbered about nine p.m. in court room.

Sunday, February 14, 1886: Slept fairly well. A slow day. Read and reclined. Walked and ate. Well, this may be called a soft racket but I'd rather work; head work. Read Joakin Miller's "49er" story.

Monday, February 15, 1886: District Court met at 10 a.m. Barnes presiding, adjourned to chambers in time for us at one p.m. Went home and had bath and change and felt much refreshed. Harvey Solan and I took the jury off on a walk this a.m., going to the two grave yards. Rehearsals every night but I can't afford to lose any more $5 bills. Case resumed at one p.m.

Tuesday, February 16, 1886: Lawyers at it hard and heavy. Judges Mitchell and [John] Haynes for Copper Queen and [James] Robinson, Ben Goodrich and Mark Smith for Copper Prince. Hard fighting. Am kept quite busy looking after the jury and doing their errands when in court. On hand tonight as usual.

Wednesday, February 17, 1886: Very fair meals. Lawyers summed up today and at 4:30 the Judge charged the jury. Dress rehearsal tonight and I got a chance to go through my parts. Judge called and he instructed again about 10:30 p.m. At midnight I knew a verdict had been reached. Great noise and carryings on till two a.m.

Thursday, February 18, 1886: I called the Judge about nine a.m. and later the attorneys. Verdict unsatisfactory to both sides though favoring the Queen. Quite in accordance with instructions. District Court met immediately after and the squaw [named Na-dis-ah] was tried for grand larceny [horse stealing]. Prepared this afternoon for the play tonight. A tremendous house, finest Tombstone ever saw. Shortly after eight I opened the ball in my character of Geo Drew. Shaved to goatee between acts and was ready for Marquis character on time. All did grandly. A dance later and good time, cleared $155.50 at 50 cents entrance.

Friday, February 19, 1886: Compliments in order all around; paper quite flattering. I seem to have satisfied my friends. A really elegant affair and possibly the best amateur performance, certainly one of the best ever given on the coast. Our talent here is quite remarkable. Left town horseback about two p.m. on Deputy Sheriff business. Found my parties near Fairbank and then went to Benson, arriving shortly after eight p.m. Dispatched business there and routed up a Chinaman for grub. Watched sheet and pillow case party a while at school house. One hubby was dragged home by spouse for dancing too much with another.

Saturday, February 20, 1886: About 25 miles back. At St. David, the Mormon settlement, I was hot being unable to get beer or water at the store and got a little on my ear. Was pretty tough in appearance and manner I suppose and wasn't answered back. Am a gentile and what a birthright. At Herring's a while tonight and Adam's. Judge Mitchell complimentary. Someone thought possible jury was tampered with. He said, "Oh no, we had Parsons."

Sunday, February 21, 1886: Church morning and evening, Sunday school too, also choir business—keeps a fellow going Sundays with everything. Called on Mrs. Beau de Zart with Sumner Vickers this afternoon, Miss Ellison there. She displayed the true instincts of the School Marme. At Goodfellow's tonight. Mr. Bruce there and had quite a tale of European ex- periences to relate.

Monday, February 22, 1886: Washington's birthday. Quite showery and heavy drops they were too. Nothing done to celebrate the day. *Esmeralda* is probably to be played at Ft. Huachuca as the officers are very desirous to have us come there and extend a cordial invitation. Looks as though we'll go. Called at Clark's and Blinn's tonight. Met Mr. and Mrs. Harper of El Paso at Blinn's. H his agent. Adames later.

Tuesday, February 23, 1886: Took up the Minister collection busness today. Am supposed to be the only one who can rustle the coin out of the faithful. It's hard work but a good cause. I mean to always do my part. Bought 2000 shares of Old Guard mining stock today, price only five cents; no more cheap stock out. Called at Goodfellow's tonight with Sumner Vickers, Mr. Heany of San Pedro there. Billiards later.

Wednesday, February 24, 1886: Working again on minister salary business, got in some more money. Pulled on the jury today. A premium put on crime. Two shooters discharged by two juries. I don't care, man or woman should suffer the penalty of the law. Bruce was shot at and have had a duel if aggressor wasn't a woman. May look for bad times again now. Taxpayers and Trustee meeting tonight. I was called as secretary, but clerk of Board is that capt; harmony. Whist in office tonight with Sumner.

Thursday, February 25, 1886: Caught on jury today for tomorrow. Busy times these days for lawyers. Town quite lively again. The *Esmeralda* business seems to be off for Ft. Huachuca. Several individuals desirous of making trouble have sown seeds of discord and the result is not very flattering to them from my standpoint. Called at Leaches tonight with Sumner. A black night and we had trouble in keeping road and avoid tumbling into some shaft. Mr. Heany there. Not a very pleasant evening there for me and won't go there soon again. Had to have lanterns returning.

Friday, February 26, 1886: Quite a spell of weather, usual late winter rains. Having an unqualified opinion in the vitirol case, I was let go this a.m. Miss Goodfellow and I rode horseback to Charleston, or mill rather, this afternoon to notify Mrs. Beau de Zart that the play was off, she having consented to take Miss G's part of *Esmeralda* at Huachuca. Met them two miles out and went to house and passed pleasant time, returning to Tombstone after supper. Fine ride, bracing air, no dust and best of all, a very pleasant and agreeable partner in Miss G. Spent evening at Herring's. Met Tinker of Chicago. Quite a chat and smoke later with him in his room.

Saturday, February 27, 1886. Still busy times at court. Collected some more for the minister fund and have done about all I can for the present. Practiced some today with Prieto and W. Gird, Spanish and guitar. Called this evening with Miss Adam and Mrs. Blinn on Miss Fish at the San Jose House, kept now by Mrs. McFarland, Miss F's aunt. Miss F engaged to Mr. Ipstein. She played on guitar and sang for us.

Sunday, February 28, 1886: Church a.m. and p.m. and Sunday school as usual. Thin attendance. At Clark's and Goodfellow's this evening.

Monday, March 1, 1886. On jury still, no work today. Mr. Tinker of Chicago, connected with Prompter, left today. Quite an artist. Revised my work on Prompter business with Ferry today, who kicked at my charge, but then he has a good reputation as a kicker. Spent evening at Reppy's.

Tuesday, March 2, 1886: Jury yet. Had an opinion this a.m. and couldn't serve in the Colym-Fitz-Mans case. At Goodfellow's this evening to get Capt. Floyd's letter. Pleasant evening. Doctor Brun in a while.

Wednesday, March 3, 1886: Jury discharged. Only six days coming to me, only $2 a day in scrip. That's better than nothing. Musicked this afternoon pretty well. All collecting done possible now. At Blinn's a while this evening. Bean bag throwing into a slanting box with hole in top afforded us considerable fun. Herring's later, lots of talk.

Thursday, March 4, 1886: Tooth filled yesterday; all now in fine order. Hard afternoon's work at music. Heard something about muscle, pistols, etc., last evening with direct reference to me. Am in for anything. Have good muscle and nerve and am good shot; go at old son whoever you are. Sam's birthday I believe, 22 I think and getting along. Spent evening at Eccleston's, his birthday.

Friday, March 5, 1886: Eclipse partial of sun today, about one quarter. Great thing occurred. Mrs. Head played smart in selecting store for hiding place for $230, a band and gold watch, when she went to dress rehearsal last evening for *Andy Blake* and this a.m. started the fire and burned up the whole business. A regular woman trick. Studied music some more today and wrote Maurice. Entertainment for cemetery fund tonight. *Andy Blake* by Gregory crowd, Clum very good. Also Prescott in the farce, Betsy Baker later. Sumner and I went, he returning just in time this evening from hunting. Godfrey blew off piece of finger.

Saturday, March 6, 1886: Things getting stale again. Am writing parties at San Diego. Indians at it again. This time they killed poor Jim Moses and W. Burin. Terrible. Don José Mesa up. Fares away down on account of the great railroad war between the transcontinental lines, $12.50 to Kansas City from San Francisco and about $50 to N.Y. from S.F. Wish I had some coin now. I'll go home a while. At Herring's this evening. Helped Sunday school children sing this afternoon, rehearsal.

Sunday, March 7, 1887: Have a fair tenor for the choir now and a good quartet so my services not being wanted, I retired to body of church. No evening service on account of children's service and baptism at three p..m. I stood as Godfather for Judge [Webster] Street's boy of 14, Lawrence. A bright boy and a little wild. Responsibilities increasing. Took Miss Goodfellow to hear Rev. Adams this evening at Methodist Church. He's a good talker though lengthy, sermon an hour long.

Monday, March 8, 1886: Well, nothing doing now but practicing on guitar and studying the flats and sharps. Good time to practice up. Wish W G[ird] was a little more thorough. He's a great goodhearted fellow though. Helped the Methodist ladies this afternoon dress the theatre stage for their entertainment tomorrow night. Spent evening at Goodfellow's with Sumner and later billiards till quite late.

Tuesday, March 9, 1886: Sumner left this a.m. and I was sorry to see him go. He's a very clever, smart fellow. Helped Methodist ladies again today. Their entertainment this evening was a complete success and I'm very glad of it. Good house and performance. The duet between Mrs. White and Prescott was grand, Mrs. Austin's recitation was also very fine. A little vulgarism at or near close during lantern scene by Adams.

Wednesday, March 10, 1886: A decidedly bad day; wind and dust very bad. Ash Wednesday services at 10:30 a.m., also prayers at four p.m. The Rector wishes me to read at services in afternoon until his return. This afternoon though I had to preside at drawing of a prize for benefit of the Public Library. Little Edith G blindfolded, drew numbers and I called them. At Herring's this evening. Quite an array of grass widows. Husbands absent at Tucson Supreme Court.

Thursday, March 11, 1886: Snow fell last night. Things quite white this a.m. Another talk about the poor mill. This time with Mr. Freeman who has money. The Indians are the drawback. If the Apaches were only corralled I might do something. Good read at Vizina office tonight. Read the Lenten service this afternoon at church by request of Rector Haskins. A walk with Miss Goodfellow whom I met at B's. We called at Goodriches.

Friday, March 12, 1886: Went out to Bassett today horseback. Got pick at Gound Hog and worked hard and long to find something new but without avail. At Mrs. Berry's this evening. Quite a chat with her and Miss Miller and quite a good time.

Saturday, March 13, 1886: Very fine again. Wrote Stanley today in acknowledgement of check. Also wrote Mrs. Hewes of Tustin City. Want San Diego points. Read services at church this afternoon, four o'clock service. Rather bad times below, Apaches thick.

Sunday, March 14, 1886: Church and Sunday school as usual. Rector in Bisbee. Earle read service. New man at Presbyterian Church tonight, Davis, so heard but didn't like him. Goodfellows this evening. Johnny Hohstadt is said to have killed an Indian at mill or corner of corral about last Sunday, $200 and gold watch on the rascal. Bully for Johnny.

Monday, March 15, 1886: Usual routine today. I don't waste any time but it isn't profitable. Letters from home at last. Wrote Milton tonight on San Diego. I must make a break mill or no mill. Can't stand this much longer. Judge Street's and Herring's tonight. Read service as usual at four p.m.

Tuesday, March 16, 1886: Same old course of things. Three men reported killed at the Lillian this afternoon a mile from town for a change; probably nothing in it. Blinn's tonight, bean bag thing.

Wednesday, March 17, 1886: Employ my time at Spanish and guitar practice. Keep pretty busy but there's no money in it. Geronimo said to be willing to surrender, in fact to have surrendered. Doubt it very much. Called on Mrs. Adam this evening. She goes East with Judge Mitchell as escort tomorrow a.m. Sorry to see her go.

Thursday, March 18, 1886: Fearful day, wind and dust horrible. Saw Mrs. Adam and Judge M off this a.m. Some old proceedings through day. Am studying with guitar quite persistently at present. Quite [an anti-] Chinese meeting at S[chieffelin] Hall, much talk. Lacks support of bus[iness] people, the movement. Same causes don't exist here as in S.F. Presbyterian social this evening. I assisted Rev. Davis's inauguration.

Friday, March 19, 1886: Terrible news this a.m. Mrs. A and Judge M's train was five hours late and they took a drive, were run away with, thrown out, bones broken, special train brought them back to Fairbanks and they arrived in town about 10 a.m. I got Doctor G for them. Sorry looking specimens and the Eastern trip spoiled. They're fortunate in escaping as they did. Mrs. A was not here to be killed in that way. Practiced, etc. Had talk with Governor [C. Meyer] Zulick who said he wanted to see me before he went away. Perhaps he's got business for me. Must strike him tomorrow. At Goodfellow's tonight wth Frank Earle.

Saturday, March 20, 1886: Tax of $2000 school racket today. Want to go to [G. W.] Lang's ranch to see Geronimo but can't find any one yet. [C. S.] Fly left today to take views. Guess there's something in the surrender business. Invalids progressing. The 2000 voted, ten to one, so I was right and Herrings very wrong.

Sunday, March 21, 1886: Services morning and evening with Sunday school. Thin attendance all day, discouraging. At Clark's a while this evening. Wrote to Sam and Mrs. Townsend tonight.

Monday, March 22, 1886: Had quite a chat with the governor tonight who wanted information about some extradition business. At Mrs. Adam's awhile. She and Judge getting along finely. At Herring's tonight.

Tuesday, March 23, 1886: Governor left this a.m., saw him off, also Judge Mitchell and Miss Elsie Ferry and Mrs. Herring, last two going to San Diego. At Goodfellow's tonight. Leaches there, supper, etc. Didn't remain Figured with Howe today on the contract for surveying hill between this and Prince Co. Called on minister this evening, pleasant call.

Wednesday, March 24, 1886: Another letter about mill, this time to P. Ostermann of Rogers Bros., Benson. Practiced as usual with guitar. Made church collections, minister salary. Read the Lenten service this afternoon. Cigars arrived today and pistol from Sumner.

Thursday, March 25, 1886: Same old thing. Called at Blinn's tonight, also at Herring's. The Leaches were at the latter house, pleasant evening.

Friday, March 26, 1886: At Goodrich's this evening. Ran against Capt. [A. E.] Wood of 4th Cavalry tonight. Dropped H's watch accidentally. Jewel broken, just my luck. Practiced as usual.

Saturday, March 27, 1886: Windy and dusty. Prepared request and obtained names today to Rev. & Mrs. Haskins asking services to young men. A nice letter from Mrs. Annie Lake Townsend on Indian matters, offering help in making known the state of things. I must get up another article. She's a good friend. Spent pleasant evening at Hart's, some whist.

Sunday, March 28, 1886: Good attendance this a.m. I woke them up a little yesterday. Very unpleasant evening so only the very few faithful on hand. Dined at Berry's. Col. Clark down again, sciatica. Mrs. Adam doing well.

Monday, March 29, 1886: Mr. Theo White invited me to go to ranch with him today as Geronimo is expected in and would pass through his place. I went with him. Between 40 and 45 miles to ranch through South Pass. Arrived about sundown. Genl Crook was at ranch in the a.m. returning to Fort Bowie, 22 miles distant, from interview with Geronimo at San Bernardino about 75 miles south at the line. Indians were made drunk by C. Tribolet and nearly spoiled the whole thing. He sold mescal across the line about 400 yards to the hostiles.* He should meet his God quickly. Crook

*There's confusion here as to who is C. Tribolet. The Great Register of Cochise County for 1884 lists five Tribolet brothers: Abraham, Albert, Sigfried, Robert, and Godfrey—all were involved in the legal sale of beef and booze. It is Robert who is usually linked with plying Apaches

told Geronimo he had lied. Old rascal shook all over. Chihuahua, Nana, Natches and others on hand. Crook and his aids Capts [C. S.] Roberts and [J. G.] Bourke say he has surrendered.

Tuesday, March 30, 1886: Drove [to] other part of range today with Mr. White, visiting the Roberts and Meyers places and the White Water range. Returned in early afternoon and found Geronimo's wife, daughter and little son awaiting their liege, Crook having promised Geronimo he would send his family to meet him, but their trip was in vain as a courier arrived with news that the hostiles had gone off again. Tribolet should be killed. I didn't think he was quite so bad. Young Geronimo is a very bright and lively child of six years, never tiring. When captured last year he would trot along on foot 25 miles a day from choice, never tiring. Daughter about 18. They strained their eyes to the far south to no avail. I bought a necklace of Mrs. G and bracelet of daughter. She was wearing all beads.

Wednesday, March 31, 1886: Geronimo's family were returned to Ft. Bowie today as the hostiles were off again. We thought last night the old cuss might try to recover them, so took my revolver to bed. The family tried walking off to no avail. A detachment of colored Cavalry is stationed here. We all thought the old lady would kick or make a break upon seeing she was to return, but no. Mr. White as president of stock association [Tombstone Livestock Association] notified numbers of ranchers of time of roundup, etc., I went with him—first to Riggs, thence Fitches, Servoss, Gottleins and to Dos Cabezas. The town certainly gone in. Some good milk and butter at Gottleins. Drove over mountains until a Mr. Attenburg was found and then drove to Sulphur Spring ranch and passed the night.

Thursday, April 1, 1886: The old Butterfield overland stage station here, remains of house.* Present ranch house a fine one too. Lots of water and a

with liquor, blowing Crook's career in Arizona. John G. Bourke labeled him a "wretch," and a foe to human society." Charles Lummis called him an "unsavory character," a notorious . . . fence for rustlers." Pretty hard accusations, and hard to prove. Although Robert managed a mescal ranch south of John Slaughter's San Bernardino ranch, he may not have been solely responsible for the decampment of Apaches at Cañon de los Embudos. It was his older brother, Godfrey, who had contracts to supply beef and horses to twenty-four military companies in the field, and at the time of the critical negotiation between Crook and Geronimo a Tribolet wagon was tailing Crook's column, dispensing booze to officers and enlisted men alike. If Tribolet dispensed liquor to the Indians on March 30, 1886, than the army bore some responsibility as well. Now, back to Parsons' referral to a C. Tribolet. He could be referring to Godfrey, who very well may have been called "Charley" by fellow Tombstoners. The Tucson *Weekly Citizen* of May 7, 1887, states that "Charley Tribolet of Tombstone will take a trip to Europe this summer." This is none other than Godfrey who left for Europe to avoid repercussions from the alleged plying of Indians with mescal.

*The Sulphur Spring station, located in a treeless expanse of prairie between two springs, belonged to Missourian Nicholas Rodgers. It was one of many relay stations along the Butterfield Overland Mail Route in 1857-58. It was abandoned from 1861 to 1872. That year the small adobe structure became headquarters of the Chiricahua Apache Agency. Its location, however, proved distasteful to Apaches and the structure reverted back to Nicholas Rodgers, who again turned it into a way station for travelers. On April 7, 1876, Rodgers and a hired hand named Spence were killed by a drunken Apache. The land and one of its nearby spring were later claimed by Robert Woolf and Robert C. Pursley, both of whom became shareholders in the Chiricahua Cattle Company in spring of 1885.

dozen or more dead cattle from miring, slightly tinged with sulphur. Ducks here. Fourteen head of animals run off last year one night when Si Bryant was sleeping by corral too.* Indians did it well. Grass short, cattle little weak. [Walter T.] Fife and Sam Coleman in charge. A blood and thunder book to read by a cowboy in which Coleman is mentioned, capture of the kid, etc. Quite exciting and truthful C said. After breakfast this a.m. drove to West and S.W. wells and thence home completing a hundred miles or more about encircling range—a big enterprise. May do something with White on Cachute range in Sonora.

Found Indians, a few had surrendered and passed ranch this morning when we arrived, so I went horseback to old man [Brannick] Riggs, 14 miles distant, to see them and found the encampment in charge of Lieut. [S. L.] Faison, whom I knew but who seemed to be very nervous, to say the least, about the 11 bucks and 39 women and children who had surrendered and were in his charge on way to Ft. Bowie, nine miles distant. He was afraid to take me about as Indians still retained arms and were very suspicious. Saw Chihuahua, Dutchy and some others and the white captive child.** Also another wife of Geronimo and Cochise's grand daughter, a saucy young one. Left about time they lit their camp fires and had great time reaching home over the hills. A Mr. Peake travelling for Bancroft on hand. Twenty scouts with captives, 22 bucks out with Geronimo and 15 or 18 women; Chihuahua, Nana and the Alcatraz prisoner on hand—old people, women and children leaving, balance in good fighting trim.

Friday, April 2, 1886: Geronimo said to have left in direction of Dragoons, so we may see something of himself or his marks today when crossing mountains. Got off about 10 o'clock and reached town about five. Was jumped by Prescott and [Harry Ellington] Brook and an account of my Indian experience wired to S.F. *Chronicle.*

Saturday, April 3, 1886: Quite an account in morning's *Epitaph.* Brook says my name is all over the coast this a.m. Must now get up an article against Crook and his Indian policy. At G's tonight, Leaches and Dr. Brun there. Also found Mrs. Adam at Mitchell's improving. Attended anti-Chinese meeting tonight at Schieffelin Hall and heard some fellows make

*In early October 1885 Geronimo and his Apaches struck El Dorado Ranch. Contrary to what Parsons says about Apaches not raiding during the night, they emptied the ranch's corral of horses while Si Bryant slept in one corner of the enclosure. They then crossed Sulphur Spring Valley and attacked Mike Noonan's place, leaving its owner dead in the doorway, a bullet in the back of his head. See *Weekly Star,* October 8, 1885.

**The white child was 10-year-old Jimmy McKinn. His father was Irish, his mother Mexican. In September 1885 Geronimo raided his parents' ranch on the Mimbres River east of Silver City, New Mexico, killed his brother and carried Jimmy into captivity. Despite hardships, the Apaches treated Jimmy well, speaking to him in Spanish and calling him Santiago. Upon his release, Jimmy was met by his father in Deming, and returned to the family ranch. He later moved to Phoenix and operated a blacksmith shop there until his death in the 1950s. For additional details see Marc Simmons, "The Captivity of Jimmy McKinn," *New Mexico Magazine,* May 1983, pp. 49-50.

asses of themselves. [S. C.] Bagg at their head. I'm anti-Chinese, but in a practical way. Boycotting doesn't go with me and there is no reason for an anti-Chinese movement here.*

Sunday, April 4, 1886: Tooth filled last month troubled me so I had Ryder take out his filling this a.m., painful. Fair attendance at church this a.m. and tonight we had quite a crowd to hear the first of the series of lectures entitled Manhood. I wrote a notice which appeared in this a.m.'s paper and we got a pretty good crowd out for this godless place, about 80 or more. A good lecture. At Earle's later and went home with the minister and had quite a talk. Wrote sister and Mrs. Townsend an account of Indian trip. This evening S.F. *Chronicle* arrived with my long interview on Indian business in it.

[Editor's note: George Parsons contributed segments to three stories that appeared in the San Francisco *Chronicle*. The first, published on April 2, was a long article covering Geronimo's surrender. The first two paragraphs are attributable to Parsons. It is included in its entirety because of historical value.

Tombstone, April 1—The universal sentiment in this section regarding the escape of Geronimo and his band is one of the most intense disgust with General Crook. The press of the Territory almost without exception had been very severe in denunciation of the General's policy during the past six months. Their indignation now knows no bound. The Epitaph says: "Our dispatch regarding the escape of Geronimo charges that it was due to the selling of whisky to the Indians by a white man. Even supposing this to be true, it is in no way relieves General Crook from the responsibility for this most unfortunate affair. Why, when the Indians surrendered, did he allow them to retain their arms? Why did he not place them in irons? If he had not a sufficient force with him to overpower them, then why did he not take more troops along? He had almost half the United States army within call. These Indians are not at war with the United States. They are simply bloody murderers. When the Sheriff goes to arrest a criminal does he say to him, "Mr. Smith, will you have the kindness to let me know what time will best suit your convenience to come in and be hanged? You will of course retain your arms." No, he disarms and mancles his prisoner. The same course should have been pursued by General Crook. This action of his is, however, in strict accordance with his treatment of these desperadoes up to the present time. He has now, we trust, reached the end of his tether. Let some man be put in his place who

*In its heyday Tombstone boasted an Asian colony of 400 to 500 individuals. As in San Francisco and elsewhere in the West, they iked out an existence doing laundry, working as servants and cooks, and growing vegetables. When hard times engulfed the community an anti-Chinese movement was launched. Spearheaded by the Tombstone Republican Central Committee, the movement's basis seems to have been resentment over Asians "not spending their earnings in the city." Tucson *Weekly Star*, October 7, 1886.

believes that the life of a white American citizen is of at least as much value as that of a brutal red-handed Indian fiend.

Charles Tribolet, the person accused of being the cause of the escape of the hostiles by selling whisky to them and working on their feelings, is one of several brothers of that name who were among the earliest settlers of Tombstone and have been engaged in many enterprises here, chiefly in the saloon and brewing line. Charles was formerly a partner with the present proprietor in the ownership of the principal hotel here. For some time past he has been located just across the line from San Bernardino, where he had a sutler's store, trading with the troops in the field. He also had a Government meat contract.

Colonel Herring, a lawyer of this city, returned today from Fort Bowie, where he had an interview with General Crook. The following is Crook's version of the circumstances attending the departure of Geronimo: Geronimo alone came in to talk with Crook the first day, and wanted to go back in the reservation. The second day Natchez and Chihuahua came in and offered surrender unconditionally. Geronimo then said if they came in he did not want to stay in the mountains alone, and would come, too. What has been called a surrender was, Crook claims, no surrender, but only the agreement to surrender at Fort Bowie. They were not prisoners and were not guarded, the terms of surrender not requiring a guard. If Crook had gone there with a larger force he says he would not have seen them, and he knows through an interpreter that the Indians in the hills had orders to fire as soon as any attempt was made to disarm these hostiles. This is claimed to be the first time on record where the Indians have not kept their word when they have formally promised to come in.

Crook was further induced to believe the surrender bona fide because Geronimo asked him to send his wife, who was a prisoner to Bowie. This Crook did, but while she was on the way he heard of the departure of the renegade.

Geronimo came about twenty miles from the starting point to within a short distance of the line, when he left, taking with him twenty-one bucks and thirteen squaws as already reported. In the conference Geronimo gave as the chief reason for leaving the reservation his belief that Micky Free, the noted Chihuahua scout, Chatto and Lieutenant Davis were putting up a job on him to have him arrested and sent to Alcatraz, where Kaontena [Kaahteney] had been sent.

Crook says the public can have no conception of the difficulties of capturing the Indians. They go unheard of distances without water, eat food that a white man would starve on, scatter when attacked, and are equally well armed as the United States troops. Ten hostiles who were with Geronimo in the conference had each two belts of cartridges. Crook claims to have very strong reasons to believe that the hostiles are supplied with ammunition by Mexican merchants in the town of Sierra Madres.

It has been discovered that during the late raid the hostiles had been as far south as Durango, five hundred miles from the frontier.

A large party, including Governor Zulick and Judge Barnes, which went to Bowie at the special invitation of General Crook to interview Geronimo have returned to Tucson much disappointed at not having a chance to see the noted renegade. The people of this section congratulate themselves at having at least secured an authentic photograph of Geronimo, and hope after another ten months to get his scalp.

C. M. Strauss, ex-Mayor of Tucson, arrived here this evening from Mud Springs. Mr. Strauss was, with the exception of the photographer and his assistant, the only civilian present at the interview between General Crook and the hostiles. The following graphic and circumstantial account of that event has been obtained from him:

They camped on Wednesday evening at Smuggler's Springs, about thirteen miles from the place of conference. Kattenal here came to General Crook and said: "You are as big a General as Geronimo; why not he come meet you, instead of you him?" Crook replied he was not going to Geronimo and did not care if Geronimo came to him, but if Kattenal wanted to send for him he would have to do it on his own responsibility.

On Thursday morning, the 25th, they started early through some of the roughest country the informant ever saw, although the officers familiar with the country assured him that this was a perfect tableland compared with the country where the Indians have their haunts. In one place all had to dismount from their horses and scramble down, leading the animals. The party consisted of Crook, Captain Roberts, the aide-de-camp; a son of Roberts, 9 years old; Captain John S. Burke [Bourke] ex-Mayor Strauss, C. S. Fly, the photographer; Mr. Chase, his assistant; four interpreters, four bucks, two squaws and one papoose. A pack train followed an hour later by a different trail.

On the trip Strauss with the bucks became separated from the rest of the party, and suddenly found the four bucks increased to ten or fifteen villainous looking specimens of painted humanity, among them one whom he afterwards found to be Geronimo. Shortly after they came on the temporary camp of Maus, Crook and the others. This was in the canyon de Los Embudos.

A conference took place at the bottom of the canyon, the hostiles being in an elevated position commanding the camp and surrounding country. In the afternoon Geronimo came over with Natchez, Nana and three warriors to Crook and squatted on the ground alongside of him, with Strauss at his side.

After waiting a few minutes Crook said: "Geronimo, you sent for me and I came. If you have anything to say I am ready to listen to you." Thereupon Geronimo commenced to reply and talked about an hour. Many things were repeated a dozen times; for instance, the cause for leaving the reservation, which Geronimo claimed he was induced to go by much bad talk about him and an order said to have been given by Crook for his and Chatto's arrest. He repeated this several times. He said he was contented with life at San Carlos and wanted to go back, never to break out any more.

During this talk Crook was silent, and presently said: "You liar, your promised the same when I took you in the Sierra Madres. Nobody can lie to me more than once."

Geronimo again talked of the cause of leaving and Crook asked if that was a good cause for killing innocent people. Geronimo made no reply and then shifted the talk to the two chiefs Alchese and Kattenal. They were loud in their expressions of great pleasure at meeting their chiefs, whom they thought they would never see again. Crook again replied that he was a liar. He had asked Geronimo a year ago if he wanted to bring Kattenal back from Alcatraz and he told the General no. Kattenal is now better off than if he came back.

Geronimo said he was an old man and had but one life to live. It was immaterial to him when or how he lived it. The General thereupon told him he had not come there to negotiate or do anything except to receive an unconditional surrender. If he accepted those terms Maus and the scouts would bring him to Bowie, where he would receive him and he could remain for the present.

This, evidently, was not what Geronimo wanted, and he thereupon said he would talk the matter over with his people that night and meet in the morning to have a further talk with the General. During the above conversation Chihuahua, with the bucks, squaws and scouts, rode up and shook hands with the General.

The second day's conference (Friday) was short and practically a repetition. A postponement was then had until Saturday. At this pow-wow all the chiefs were present, including Nana. Chihuahua first opened the talk, saying: "I surrender to the great General who rules the sun by day and the moon by night. I give myself up boldly to the General, to do with me as he thinks fit, but pray of him to act as a master would who has a little dog to which he feels kindly disposed and treats well." He then said he would like to have his family with him. He believed Crook was a great and good man, and anything he promised he believed would come true. He offered his hand, which Crook took, saying, "Ee juh," meaning "It is good."

Natchez next took a seat and indorsed the remarks of Chihuahua. Next came Geronimo and made the same statement, but he repeated that he had been abused and lied about by the newspaper people. He wound up by saying he wanted an expression from Crook, who simply replied that he must in future pay no attention to what anybody says and must keep to the contracts and there would be no trouble.

The General then asked the chiefs if the surrender included all the people, to which they answered in the affirmative. There was then hand shaking between the hostiles and whites, between the whites themselves and between the hostiles. The General then informed them that if they got ready early in the morning Lieutenant Maus and scouts would conduct them to Bowie. They asked the privilege of being somewhat slow on the road, as their stock was very poor. The General said there was no objection, and that he was going ahead to Bowie and would be there long before they reached that place. Geronimo said he wanted to have another talk with the General after they reached Bowie, and would tell him about valuable mines they discovered in Mexico, and all about other matters—all of which was agreed upon.

Editor's Note: The *Chronicle's* April 3 story, reproduced below, refers directly to Parsons.

Tombstone, April 2.—The following additional facts have been obtained from ex-Mayor Strauss in regard to what took place after the so-called "surrender" of the hostiles to Crook: On the evening of Saturday after the conference Geronimo, who was in bad repute with the rest of the hostiles, realizing that his chances for life were slim, evidently determined to escape, provided he could get assistance in the undertaking. This was attempted, but he was unsuccessful in getting any of the other hostiles to share his views. He thereupon procured a quantity of mescal and made Natchez and several bucks drunk, the result being a row among themselves, which ended in the shooting of one of the squaws, who probably will lose one or both of her legs.

Geronimo then went to the San Bernardino rancho with six or seven bucks, and obtaining a further supply of mescal, they all became drunk. Taking advantage of this, Geronimo, who has more brains than all the other chiefs together, worked upon their feelings so that Natchez and his followers consented to accompany him. Chief Keltena, who had come with Crook, left camp with these hostiles Tuesday morning, and was gone several hours attempting to persuade them to return. After the failure of his attempt he returned to camp and notified Dr. Davis early Tuesday morning. This was the first known of the departure of Geronimo and Natchez. Lieutenant Maus at once followed with seventy-five scouts and one pack train, at the same time sending a dispatch to Captain Allen Smith at Silver Creek and another to Captain Thompson at Guadalajara. Captain Thompson, in company with Lieutenant Wilder and sixty men, at once left camp and followed the trail. Up to this time they have not been heard from.

After the conference between Crook and the hostiles, on the same afternoon, Mr. Strauss, by permission of General Crook, had an interview with Geronimo, who, in reply to an inquiry from Strauss, said that during his entire raids he never saw or heard of any Mexican troops except at the killing of Captain Crawford.

IT WAS A SURRENDER

Geo. W. Parsons, in company with T. F. White, a leading stockman of this county, came in this evening from White & Vickers ranch, at the east end of Sulphur Spring valley, at the base of the Chiricahua Mountains. They arrived there Monday evening last and found about half a dozen colored troops stationed as a base of supplies. On Tuesday morning General Crook, Roberts and Bourke arrived at the ranch from San Bernardino ranch. Crook and all those with him stated positively that a surrender had taken place. They also spoke in bitter terms of Tribolet, who had sold whisky to the hostiles. Crook and party left shortly after Geronimo's wife and daughter, about eighteen, and a child arrived from Bowie, having been sent from there by Crook to meet Geronimo. They waited there till next morning. Meanwhile a courier had arrived from Lieutenant Maus at San Bernardino, with the news that the hostiles had decamped. Word was brought from Bowie to return Geronimo's family, and they went back reluctantly, after first attempting to escape.

Yesterday (Thursday) afternoon a large number of scouts and hostiles passed the ranch on the way to Bowie. They occupied two hours in straggling past a given point. The hostiles were armed and were not prisoners, although supposed to be under the escort of the scouts. They camped at a point thirteen miles north of the ranch. Mr. Parsons visited the camp just before sundown. Lieutenant Faison was in command. He had twenty scouts with him, the number of hostiles being fifty, including eleven bucks, the remainder being women and children. Chihuahua, Katenal and the Chief of the Warm Spring Indians were among the party. The scouts and hostiles mixed together in the most friendly manner. Except for the blue coats of the scouts they could not distinguish them from the hostiles. Lieutenant Faison appeared to be very nervous and apprehensive, not without cause, as if the hostiles had take it into their head to go off, it would have been a very difficult matter to prevent them. The Lieutenant asked Mr. Parsons not to look at the hostiles too closely. Among the squaws was another of Geronimo's wives and a granddaughter of Cochise. They expected to reach Fort Bowie by noon today, that place being only nine miles distant from the place where they camped by the trail.

Editor's Note: Parsons' long article on Crook, referred to in his April 5th entry, appeared in the San Francisco *Chronicle* on April 20, 1886. It is reproduced below.

A VOICE FROM ARIZONA
Arraignment of the Imbecile Treatment of the Apaches

Tombstone, April 6, 1886—Southwestern Arizona for a long time has patiently and quietly borne her load of troubles imposed by the mistaken Indian policy of General Crook and the disinclination of the General Government to make an honest effort toward bettering our condition, until patience has ceased to be a virtue with the last fiasco—Geronimo's surrender; and it may not be out of place to review the past somewhat, and then to leave the reader to judge whether or note the people of Cochise county have just cause for complaint.

In April, 1877, Geronimo, a leading spirit of the Chiricahua Apaches, after a bloody raid was arrested by the Indian police under John P. Clum—the best Indian agent the San Carlos Reservation has ever seen—was released, without trial or punishment, by the authorities to whom he had been transferred by Agent Clum, and four or five months later again started and raided one and a half years, after which pleasure trip he surrendered as prisoner of war, to be once more turned loose, in order to prepare for his next campaign, this time operating mostly in Old Mexico, and so successfully as to be able to dictate terms to General Crook in the Sierra Madre nearly three years ago, when the "Gray Fox" was caught by the wily Geronimo, and all of his old women and superannuated bucks turned over to Crook, after which the gang of cut-throats raided the country to their hearts' content, until too tightly pressed by the Mexican forces, when they recrossed the line with their stolen stock and passed immediately under the patronage and protection of the United States army, which even went so far as to retain the stolen stock for the direct benefit of the hostiles themselves, against the earnest protests of rightful owners—men able to prove their property, but who were obliged to stand aside and see their own stock sold for account of the assassins and robbers, often having insult added to injury—might making right.

It seems hardly possible that this chief should be again turned loose, but such is the fact, and he then made preparations so openly for another raid that there could be no possible excuse for those in power not to arrest, disarm and imprison himself and followers, but the fact remains that this was not done, and those same authorities so derelict in their duty are certainly morally responsible for every death since 1877. Since 1881 certainly 300 persons have been killed and still the death harvest is gathering. What record can the army show during all of this time? General Crook says "killing the Indians could not bring the dead to life." Let him be judged by that remark. When an officer of the army in bygone days chanced to be killed by Indians the army would display much feeling and spasmodic energy, but now, when a poor settler is the victim, it cries, "Another interloper gone! Served him right!" and our people are considered in the light of outlaws or desperadoes in their efforts to do what belongs to the Government to do for them—they being the ones who supply the funds to a great extent to carry on the Government and enable the army to do the society act.

But to return. October 1, 1885, Geronimo outgeneraled Crook a second time in our neighboring mountains by misleading his soldiers and throwing them upon wrong trails through the agency of his pet Apache scouts, to say nothing of his little visit to the reservation just before this time when he recovered his women and regained the mountains without any trouble. Crook's pet idea has been to fight Apache with Apache, which accounts in a great degree for his inability to accomplish anything, and he seems to place implicit confidence in his scouts. The policy of late years has been to place about twenty-five San Carlos Reservation Indians at each of the several army posts for use as scouts, keep them a few months until they are thoroughly familiar with our methods and practices, meanwhile having abundant time and opportunity to steal and cache guns and ammunition, and then to replace these Indians by others. This certainly is all wrong, as these scouts are often hostiles later on, helped in the matter by the Government itself. As fighting men they are a failure, as it is against nature itself to suppose that these Indians do not possess instinct, to say the least, and will try to destroy their own blood. There are some exceptions, which only prove the rule. Many instances have occurred of assistance rendered by the scouts to their friends and brothers, the hostiles, notably in the case of Chatto, the murderer of the McComas family, and leader of the scouts who, on the Gila river, twice assisted the hostiles to escape when he was compelled by his commanding officer to tightly press them. Again, in an engagement with Loco, the Lieutenant in command of the scouts was obliged to jump in amongst them, revolver in hand, and threaten the first scout with instant death who should endeavor to join Loco, who was holding out inducements to them across a ravine during the engagement.

Again, in the writer's experience, the command was called out one night at Fort Huachuca to guard the Indian scouts, who had heard a report of an outbreak at the reservation, and were uneasy, to say the least. A former chief of all the scouts in the field, a frontiersman, and many of the army officers themselves, declare that their Indian scouts have misled them, throwing them off the trail repeatedly, and that they communicate with the hostiles, aiding and abetting them. What more can be expected, when the scouts of today are often the hostiles of tomorrow, and vice versa? It is the settled conviction of some at least of the army officers that these Indians should not be used as fighting men, and but a very few of the most reliable and trustworthy as trailers only, and in no other capacity. Why does not General Crook employ the hereditary enemies of the Apaches as scouts and fighting men, as he formerly did? The Papagos and Pimas have plenty of old scores to settle. Why should he not allow hot trails to be followed—once in particular, when telegraphed to in the words, "Shall I follow?" Why did he persist in declaring that but thirty-five Indians were out last spring and summer, when a count of but one party gave twice that number? And why was it that he allowed three days to elapse before notifying the settlers of the outbreak last May? Something is certainly wrong when hot trails are camped on and hostiles allowed within a few hundred yards of the scouts camping place with impunity.

The Governor of this Territory last summer visited Tombstone and asked our long-suffering people to go down into their depleted pockets to keep thirty couriers in the field to notify settlers of the presence of the hostiles, in the face of his friend Crook's assertion that he had more men than he knew what to do with—a rather remarkable proceeding, and the Governor probably was so convinced before he left town. Why has Geronimo repeatedly been turned loose, why permitted to retain arms year after year, and why was he permitted to leave the reservation, having openly and grossly insulted the commanding officer? There are doubtless uglier facts than questions if the truth could be known. Our Indian ring is still alive, may the present Administration throttle it. No rights of any Indian have been tampered with, no irksome regulations imposed and no troubles existed about rations, neither were any encroachments made by white men upon their lands.

Away with all sentimentalism in this matter and let us have plain justice. We know that many good army men would have helped us if not handicapped by Crook or the powers that be, and why he has not been removed after such universal condemnation of his policy remains a mystery. The army has hitherto proved a broken reed. Worse than that, it has indirectly caused many deaths and misfortunes because it has been looked to as our natural protector and deceived us all. Lies flourished abroad as to military achievements in the field have resounded to the discredit of the army and our material damage. Better, far better, would it have been for us in the past could we have been left more to our own resources. With a bounty offered by the Government for scalps and the sinews of war furnished our hardy frontiersmen, who understand this Indian warfare, many valuable lives would have been saved, property preserved and a great pecuniary saving ensued to the Government.

Then we say, in conclusion, remove the Indians from the reservation, so that the Chiricahua, Swisshelm, Dragoon, Huachuca and Mule mountains in Arizona and the Sierra Madre range in Old Mexico shall know them no more; indemnify our people for losses sustained and Mexico also for depredations committed by our Indians upon her soil, and an era of prosperity will dawn and this country, so long held in the background by these adverse causes, will advance rapidly to the front. We already feel cheered by the report that General Miles is to succeed General Crook and trust that our milliennium is at hand.   G. W. P.]

Monday, April 5, 1886: Good pictures of Geronimo and his cutthroats by Fly. He showed me some this a.m. He'll make money. Wish now I'd got a horse and gone with him. Might have collected some curios and made money. Meade served me with summons for 12th at Tucson as U.S. Grand Juror but Genl Adam may want me so must get off. Worked today on my Crook article. At Adam's and Herring's tonight. Jeffrey Lewis in town—Lent and can't go.

Tuesday, April 6, 1886: Worked hard all day and mailed to Mrs. Townsend article on Genl Crook, his Indian policy, etc., together with a fine photo of

Geronimo and Natchez, or more properly Natchee. Letter endorsed by Clum, Vickers and White. Suppose the *Chronicle* will publish it. Brook of *Epitaph* offered to telegraph it to the *Chronicle*. Too long for that though, I think. Report came tonight that Benham had been shot dead by a Mexican hostler at Hermosillo, Sonora.* Though late, I notified Fred Castle and Judge Stilwell. Am glad our $180 is gone now. Must be terrible shook to madame. At Earle's and Adam's this evening.

Wednesday, April 7, 1886: Fearfully windy and dusty. Guess I've got to go to Tucson, Meade seems obdurate. Am having bad time with a tooth. Shall shortly attend to some government business in connection with the Genl. At Clark's last evening and had a great time. Old Col nearly gone in I'm afraid. Has doctor every evening now. Quite wild tonight. Maurice should be with him. Mrs. C carries a big load. I'm sorry. At Clark's tonight, also at Goodfellow's, where were also Walker and Henney.

Thursday, April 8, 1886: Got some fine photos this a.m. from Fly. He favored me greatly in price and gave me some of his experience. Capt. Bourke told him he was a d-d fool for going into the camp and that he'd never come out. One interpreter was not afraid and went with him. Wish I'd gotten a horse and gone along. At Clark's as usual. At prayers every afternoon at four o'clock.

Friday, April 9, 1886: Tooth bothering still. Don't see that anything was accomplished today. Sent to Strallus and sister a photo of Geronimo.

Saturday, April 10, 1886: Sr. Don Augustin Pesqueira in town today and had an interview with White, he and I. At Clark's as usual to see what I could do this evening. At Blinn's a while and got some Spanish exercise books, M system from Miss G. Quite a talk with Mrs. Prescott. Talked confirmation. She has been confirmed in the Catholic faith but cannot go the confessional; doesn't believe in it.

Sunday, April 11, 1886: Got off this a.m. on the opposition hack or wagon, 25 cents each. Was with Mrs. Benham much of the time who was on her way to S.F. with her husband's body. Her mind dwelt continuously upon the subject of the shooting and what might have been done at Hermosillo had she only looked around.* Did all I could for her, helping Price, her escort. Very, very sad. Train late. Good to see strange faces. Congregational, 10 people, no other meeting except Methodists.

Monday, April 12, 1886: Met at 10 a.m. we Grand Jurors. Some opposition to my sitting. I knew too much for case. Tuttle appointed foreman in afternoon. We met at two p.m. and organized then. Tracy, clerk. I was afraid of being appointed to some position and guess my kicking helped on foremanship, and as the Tombstone boys were conferring evidently with a purpose, I got ahead by nominating a clerk. Did considerable business this

*According to the Tucson *Weekly Star* of April 15, 1886, Charles Benham was shot and killed by Fred Sweet during an altercation over the care of Benham's horse.

afternoon. Good District Attorney, Rouse. Called at Judge Haynes this evening. Had quite a Fly or Fay experience tonight.

Tuesday, April 13, 1886: Got to work in good shape today and did considerable business. Carried all of my points even to a re-reconsideration. Working hard and harmoniously. At Eccleston's tonight. Saw Mrs. E and Walter Harvey. Old Hudson house; what wonderful changes in two years. Old town quite sleepy. Railroads agitating them somewhat.

Wednesday, April 14, 1886: Talked with Rayfield about cap[ture] of Hawkins. No so much work today but progressed satisfactorily. Am lecturing considerable G.J. law. Had quite a walk with Frank Wolcott this afternoon late, going to Warner's mill and on the hill back in search of cacti Sanhana, Sentinel Cactus. He got two and a Mexican boy to bring them in. Called at Col Beans this evening, seeing all hands. Miss B very pleasant, knew her in Cal seven years ago.

Thursday, April 15, 1886: Fair day's work. Hope we'll get off Saturday a.m. Went to train today and sent word to Major by Renough to retain mail. Looked after Mrs. Benham's trunks seeing they had been neglected. Bailey of Bailey's Wells and I dined together; great talk, full and confidential like P yesterday. Called at supper Miss Pomeroy this evening, who sent message to Miss G about Doctor and and major commanders. Later called upon Miss Fay. Sheriff [Bob] Paul took a few of us through the jail this a.m. He told us of some desparate deeds by captured smugglers.

Friday, April 16, 1886: Looks as though we will not get off tomorrow, more business piling up. Had to adjourn from 10 a.m. till four p.m. Down to only one more than a quorum. Had talk with District Attorney Rouse on some matters, amongst others that of timber. I am working for him and the government and we've done some good work so far. Bishop Dunlop arrived last night from the East and put up at Miss Fry's. Tucson a dreadfully tiresome place and very quiet. Met the Bishop this evening walking with Miss. Pomeroy. Spent evening at Judge Haynes, Mrs. H, Mrs. Stiles, Mrs. Hill and Miss Henney played euchre against Judge, Mr. H and me.

Saturday, April 17, 1886: Examined two Indian scouts this a.m. and wound up business making final report about 11 a.m. Twelve indictments in all. Train delayed so we caught it, we Tombstone fellows, and reached home about sundown. Col. Clark's house took fire this a.m. and was partly destroyed. Warmly welcomed back by friends. Went the rounds. Clarks at Berry's.

Sunday, April 18, 1886: Church and Sunday school as usual. At lecture this evening, large attendance. The cause has provoked opposition from Father Doyle, the Roman Catholic Priest, and Haskins is doing him up in the newspaper controversy. They're hard people to get out to church here. At Earle's a while and then at Goodfellow's. Later had talk with Stebbins.

Monday, April 19, 1886: Made preparations for trip to mountains for account of U.S. Will soon get off on my mission. Spent evening at Leach's on the hill where was also Howard L. Quite a time. Cool evenings. Church at 10 a.m. I'm the only male at Lenten services.

Tuesday, April 20, 1886: Church again this a.m. Helped Mrs. Clark make her estimate of loss on furniture this a.m. Col. went out, driving a short distance for first time. He's improving. They're having a tough deal, much sympathy for her. At Major Earle's tonight where were Judge and Miss Hibbard of Chicago. Invited to meet them. Both very pleasant, agreeable and quite sociable. So nice to see strange faces and such refined ones too.

Wednesday, April 21, 1886: Expected to leave town today but didn't get off. Keep pretty busy all of the time now but no money in it. At Adam's and Herring's tonight. Have an uncomfortable neck. Cold I suppose.

Thursday, April 22, 1886: Didn't get off today. T. S. in town. Did considerable business for the Judge of the First Instance of Arispe today. Helping him at Judge Herrings, also agreed to give him use of mill till June 1st, he to repair without cost and to sell for $2000.

Friday, April 23, 1886: Good Friday, at church as usual. Had a great time this a.m. with a bucking horse. He bucked very badly and it was quite a circus for Fremont St., but I staid with him and didn't quit until he fell and then I was afraid he'd roll on me and got off. Am tired of bucking horses and don't want any more. Vick said, "you staid with him." I told him that's what I intended doing but I might not have been able to do so very long. Started for Tom Sorin's and met him on wagon near Middle Pass. Gave him horse to go ahead and get grub ready and drove with Morris. Two Indians caused us uneasiness in the canyon. Guess they were all right, but one cannot always tell. They were well mounted and well armed.

Saturday, April 24, 1886: Confirmation service tonight, Miss Ellison, Willie Ashley, Sam Mitchell confirmees. Got all information I could for my particular business and was ready to go this a.m. Tried returning a new way through mountains but horse didn't seem to be accustomed to mountains so I returned. Tom and I later climbed a mountain in front of camp from which we could look into Cochise Stronghold beneath us and at same time have a very extended view of the whole country, a truly fine view. Tom is very energetic and deserves great praise. Returned about four p.m. The *Epitaph* had notice of my handling Crook and his Indian policy in S.F. *Chronicle* without gloss.

Sunday, April 25, 1886: Easter Sunday and a busy day for me. Church beautifully decorated, quantities of Calla Lilies. All fortunately arrived in time. Church should be photographed. Every seat occupied, communion, probably 30 communicants. Fine sermon by Bishop Dunlop on the usual topic of the resurrection. Very interesting. Lunched at Berry's with Bishop, Rector and Earles, also of course, Miss Miller. Interesting children's service at three p.m. Distributed Easter eggs and flowers.

Monday, April 26, 1886: Quite busy today collecting for church. I find lots to do all the time but not much money in it. I like to be busy though and to do good when I can. Nearly a fire in Major Earle's tonight. Took guitar to Mrs. Adam's tonight and sang her some songs Spanish, etc. Quite a merry time. Stebbins, Meade and Judge Benson there later. Sent off some papers today with article on Crook and his Indian policy.

Tuesday, April 27, 1886: Gave Judge Berry letter this a.m. to Don Augustin Pesqueira at Hermosillo, the Judge and Mrs. Berry going there today. Walked out to Gentle Belle mine today with party I am leasing to and measured depth of shaft, 37 feet. Wrote Pesqueira. Business meeting at church. P's actions disgraceful. Was appointed by Bishop Dunlop one of the trustees on committee of church. Spent balance of evening with Walker. He's a good man.

Wednesday, April 28, 1886: Will not go tomorrow, Indians coming this way. Want to see in what direction they are going. Wrote letters and did something for Mrs. C. Shaved off whiskers. Very busy all the time. Wrote off lease for Furman for G.B. mine. Pink Tea tonight at Cheyney's. Tableaus, singing, etc. Quite a crowd. A new young lady, Miss Fortney, from Ft. Huachuca. Quite a gay time. Got in our $40 clear for rectory fund.

Thursday, April 29, 1886: Signed papers in G.B. matter. Wrote Huneke. Am fixing matters for my departure for Chiricahuas tomorrow. Don't like the Indian business but can't afford to wait on them. Went the rounds this evening, Earles, Blinns, Herrings, etc. Saw the Bishop off for Nogales. Great excitement there. Indians very bad, Miles to the front.

Friday, April 30, 1886: Pack[ard] reported killed, arrived all O.K. Told me to be careful. Indian news bad and I was advised not to leave town, but I hated to give up after deciding to go and accordingly left about 11:30. Pump broken other side of pass and couldn't water my horse. Had to push on after pushing mail under door for Root, man in charge for Hudson, and ride to Cottonwoods before finding water. Horse stood it well, 35 miles. Bartlett, man in charge, knew me at Nacosari. Was the party going with Moulton in the Sierra Madres. Quite a chat. Seem to know and be known everywhere now. Reached ranch in 7½ hours from town, 42 miles by South Pass. Good horse. Hearty welcome by White and Upwood.

Saturday, May 1, 1886: Out on range today with [James E.] Brophy hunting horses. Saw a living curiosity, a burro with fore legs bent in so that they crossed while the hoofs were probably eight inches long, grown that long because unused, the animal having to walk on sides of his hoofs because of angles in legs. Indians nearing. They are badly scattered. Liable to be most anywhere. Got and booked some useful information today to matter in hand. Genl [Nelson A.] Miles has begun signal service [heliograph]. First station established here about 500 feet east of house. Communication established with Ellen's [Helen's] Dome, one mile from Fort Bowie, nearly 20 miles distant.

Sunday, May 2, 1886: Apaches drawing closer, may have seen few. Passed day quietly. Examined signalling business. Simple, nothing but ordinary looking glass necessary. Sun is caught and reflected to Helen's Dome and a screen is worked in front of the flash on the dot and dash plan, Morse's alphabet being used, the improved Morse. Whilst I waited a message was received of Indians raiding to south of us and orders were sent by Major [Eugene B.] Beaumont to send 30 men after them with orders to follow, half command to remain and others to take their animals as relays. Looks like business on Miles part. Geronimo beat Crook with signal fires but Miles plan works well, as in this instance he saved four or five precious hours.* Wish we could give the Indians a rattle. Top of house is all fortified and loopholed. White went to Sulphur [Spring ranch] about two p.m.

Monday, May 3, 1886: Left about nine a.m. and returned about five p.m. Saddled up and traversed Morse Canyon today. "Coyote" Smith lives at mouth of canyon. Fresh moccasin tracks seen by the boys yesterday about mile from house near Rock Creek, in front of White's. Old lady told me about a handsome saddle blanket found in an Indian cave alongside an Indian's body. Boy was hunting Indian caves yesterday when presence of Indians manifested itself. Capt. [Theodore A.] Baldwin notified. Visited Dan Freeman, [E. O.] Hornbeck, Mexican Rafael Duarte and [Fred] McGowan, who was shot in his garden last October by Indians. He showed me and told me all. I notified all of presence of Indians and kept sharp lookout. Stopped a while with Capt. B of 10th Cavalry, H Co., stationed to one side of canyon, who sent message by me to signal officer. Accomplished my business purposes in good shape.

Tuesday, May 4, 1886: Upward and I rode to [William M.] Downing's saw mill today in Pine Canyon. Had crack at antelope perhaps 300 yards off, but didn't get it, though made a couple of good running shots. A long ride up canyon. D high up; had quite a sight. I was quite successful in main mission. Met Elwood there. I strike people all over country in most unaccessible places who knew me even though I may not know them. Quite remarkable. Good mill capable of 15,000 ft, also very fine lumber indeed. Some trees 17 feet around and 150 feet high, 3000 ft in some. Pretty good for Arizona. Near Fife's a Mexican was hung to limb of tree who killed Mrs. F last Oct. Opposite tree a shallow grave was dug but coyotes got away with body. Held U's horses while he tried to dig up skull which we wanted. Ascertained another fellow had it. One bone only on surface; clean. Returned via Apache trail commanding grand view of

*Brigadier General Nelson Miles was the first to attribute the surrender of Geronimo to the use of the heliograph. Paul Wellman echoed Miles' assertion that the signaling device was the decisive factor in bringing the Apache wars to a close. Beginning in the 1950s historians claimed it was no more than an expensive toy. Recent evidence adds credence to Parsons' observation. According to Bruno J. Rolak, "The defensive screen which Crook established at the border water holes and trails proved ineffective. . . . Miles' efficient communications system, employing the telegraph, the heliograph, and couriers . . ., served to reduce Geronimo's advantage. The line of flashing mirrors made the difference." Consult the latter's article, "General Miles' Mirrors. The Heliograph in the Geronimo Campaign of 1886," *The Journal of Arizona History*, Vol. 16, No. 2, Summer 1975, pp. 145-160.

Theodore Frelinghuysen White, founder of the Chiricahua Cattle Company and a stalwart of Cochise County industry, was born at Upper Dublin, Pennsylvania, on August 13, 1844, one of five children of James White and Lydia Jarrett. Educated as a mining engineer at Tremont Seminary and Polytechnic Institute, Philadelphia, he first worked at Austin, Nevada. Between 1871-76 he was chief engineer for the Surveyor General's Office and subsequently served as deputy mineral surveyor of public lands for Arizona and Texas. Retiring from the Arizona cattle trade, he became manager of Gird's ranch at Chino and later looked after L. W. Blinn's Lumber Company interests in southern California. He also made a reputation as a West coast road builder and developed the first oil macadam techniques which earned him the title of "Father of good roads in the West." He retired to Hollywood, California, and died in a drowning accident on January 27, 1914.

James G. Maxwell and Anna Matilda, parents of Anna (Annie) Maxwell, were originally from Chambersburg, Pennsylvania. In 1850 James moved to California and established a store at San Francisco. His wife followed two years later and Anna was born on February 10, 1854. She was educated in Santa Rosa and at the San Diego Academy for Young Ladies. She met Theodore White in San Diego, where he was working as a topographer for the Texas and Pacific Railroad, and they were married on April 14, 1874. As George Parsons alludes, Anna Maxwell White was musically talented. She could play the accordian at age three, and when she turned ten years old her father gave her a Steinway piano which he brought around the horn by sailing vessel to San Francisco. Her talent and humor made her a gracious hostess and the White homes in the Sulphur Spring Valley and at Tombstone were centers of political and social activities, especially after Theodore was elected a Cochise county supervisor in November 1882. Anna outlived her husband, dying at San Gabriel, California, on April 13, 1948. (These wedding photos and biographical data courtesy of Nancy White Orshefsky)

country. Gone all day till eight p.m. Horse cast shoe. Two graves of persons killed by Apaches opposite of trail.

Wednesday, May 5, 1886: Reports by signal officer of engagement with Apaches near Calabasas by part of 10th Cavalry "coons," and two soldiers killed. Apaches reported heading this way. Top of house is well fortified, good adobe wall with loop holes. Would relish a rattle with them. Want a scalp badly. Had to have horse shod, believed today. Quite tenderfooted. A soldier did it for me. Bad business for me just now to have a tenderfooted horse. Lieut. [Wilber E.] Wilder of G Co., 4th Cavalry, with us tonight. Pleasant fellow. This evening he, Upward and I tried to find a fresh Apache trail several miles above house reported by the "coons." Cattle probably destroyed it.

Tuesday, May 6, 1886: Great fun in watching boys tailing calves; great rough and tumble. Mr. White did most of branding and branded 262 calves, also 202 in a.m. Roundup reached the Cottonwoods last night so Upward and I rode down this a.m., and meeting some of the boys, helped to drive in the cattle. Great work. After dinner the "cutting out" of cows and calves for branding took place on the plains and after that the stray herd was formed, cowboys riding in and cutting out their brands. The three bunches were close herded, of course, all of the time. Great sport for the cowboys, cutting out and roping. One obstinate stray had to be be knocked down. One fellow, a Mexican, threw her by running horse along side, seizing tail and darting ahead, then ropes by tail and horns, dragged her half a mile or so. Common trick though one cowboy had a fight with his bronco, they tumbled over a lassoed cow. Excited woolly cowboys; there were 40 or 50 others. Branding then took place and such a scene. It seemed like Hell let loose with the plunging horses, roped calves, smoking flesh, blood, etc.; and the din of 1000 crazy animals.

Friday, May 7, 1886: Strong guard for herd last night on account of Indians. Slept amongst the boys on ground. Lively scenes all of the time, one grizzled cowboy thought I was from Colorado and was glad to see me. Quite insisted that I must be one of the Schultz boys. Up at daybreak, breakfast and all scattered. Next task was to bring in cattle from the base of some hills north of the Southwest well. Rounded them up and joined them with the main herd. Quite a bunch, something over a thousand, perhaps two. Ran them out on the plains a mile or so and then the cutting out took place. I was placed as aid to our cow and calf herd. Great times. Some terribly obstreperous cows and calves. The little devils were crazy at times and would run as fast as the horses and keep it up too. I wouldn't have believed it. The cook had water in a wagon near my herd and while fooling with a six shooter accidentally shot himself. I didn't share much sympathy for him. Flesh wound. Was sent to hospital. Drove cows and calves five miles to the cottonwood corral and had hard time getting them there, particularly the calves who hadn't ever seen a gulch before. Probably were afraid to cross. Had to be roped and dragged. Mr. White out of luck. His horse bucked him off and another was kicked and had leg broken necessitating shooting. Branding when I left; nearly 200 to brand. Returned to home ranch in afternoon pretty tired. Terribly hard, dusty and dirty work.

Saturday, May 8, 1886: Roundup will be here today probably. Lieut. [A. M.] Fuller arrived last night to establish more heliograph stations. Cook, Neil and some others, packers also. One quite musical and tried organ. Steward at Rucker. A guitar was found and I entertained the boys some. Seemed to please them immensely. Couriers have been doubled, it being considered too dangerous traveling for one. Went out with Lieut. Fuller, Upward and I to establish another sun telegraph station. Tried a bald hill few miles from house but couldn't get Helen's Dome at Bowie. Flash from Ft. Huachuca, 70 miles distant, very plain. Fuller had appointment to signal about that time, but they didn't seem to find us very well. I left about noon for Ross and Shearer's saw mill and had a hard time getting there in trying to cut across mountains. Not pleasant when Indians might take you in. Hard climb. Finally got there and did my business, reaching home about dark. Roundup on hand. Things lively tonight.

Sunday, May 9, 1886: 300 calves branded by ten a.m., about 75 an hour. Quick work for four operations; cutting, tarring, branding, etc. I went down to Cottonwoods this a.m. for carbolic acid which was forgotten. Helped drive up some cattle and also caught a cowboy's horse which fell and threw him, hurting him temporarily. A smoke this afternoon in direction of West Well, 13 miles west, caused apprehension. After dark the fire was very plain. Men sent down. May be work of Indians, though they don't do much firing. Another fire towards Ft. Bowie. Upward returned in afternoon. They established station at a point evidently recently used by Apaches as point of observation from many signs.

Monday, May 10, 1886: More branding this a.m. Probably 1500 branded. Whole branding will probably reach 2300 or 2500. I must now pull my freight for Rucker, finish up there and get back to town. Bad news. It was West Well on fire last night. U went this a.m. I wanted to go but time is now limited. U returned before I left and reported all gone and suspicious tracks, Indians probably, so White sent some cowboys trailers to the scene with instructions to follow the trail up. Reached Rucker in three hours from here and found all hands well and glad to see me. A Mr. Beal there too. Is post trader. Four companies of 4th Cavalry there and 62 Apache scouts. Quite a lively camp. I reported to Lieut. [Fred] Wheeler fact of business as requested by Lieut. Fuller. Didn't like the man. This evening some guitar music by Miss Trixie [Emma Fish] and Lieut. Huber and Smith and Dr. Fisher were over. The Dr. very pleasant.

Tuesday, May 11, 1886: Did my business here quickly today. Nothing in trip probably. A Miss [Laura] Hunsaker, formerly of San Diego, at house this a.m. Quite a pleasant and pretty girl, also a little sister, Edith, and young brother [James L. Hunsaker]. I knew the lawyer brother [W. J.

Hunsaker] some years ago in Tombstone. Looked at Indian scouts camp today, they evidently didn't like it. Watched a great gambling game of their's with a small hoop and two long poles. A hard crowd—they all ought to be planted. Quite lively times about the store which is really a saloon. Lots of money in it.

Wednesday, May 12, 1886: Learned a new cavalry guitar song from Miss Trixie Fish this a.m., took a walk with packer O'Neil through the Indian camp looking at some beads and stones and got an Apache boy to write me his name. Some thing very new and strange for an Apache. Yuma, Mohave and Tonto Apaches in the crowd. He wrote me his name, probably that of his benefactor, with a 45-70 gov't. cartridge, having no pencil and called himself Oliver Eaton, educated at Hampton, Va, a Mohave Apache. Left after lunch with number of commissions and hearty invitation to make long visit. Mighty clever people. Reached ranch all O.K. Branding just concluded, 2500. It was the West Well burning, loss probably $1000.

Thursday, May 13, 1886: Started for home this a.m. via West Well. Lonely ride. Quite a scene of destruction at well; cause unknown, probably not Indians. Reached town about four or shortly after. All glad to see me and relieved. It seems that I was thought by some to have been taken in by the Apaches. Quite tired tonight. Made 250 miles horseback in my two week trip, perhaps more. At friends a while this evening. Had to give paper an account which was telegraphed to S.F. Called on Mrs. McFarland tonight to deliver messages and package from and for Mrs. Gray of Rucker.

Friday, May 14, 1886: Just in time to see Huneke, who left this a.m. with Sam Brannan [Jr.] for Sonora. Returns in two weeks. Prepared statement today for Genl. Quite busy all day. Major and Mrs. Earle's China wedding day tomorrow; was held this evening at Town Verein Hall and prolonged until the 15th. Didn't close till two a.m. Present Ambegina glass decanters, or some such name. A great success, the entertainment this evening in every way, 110 present. Fine floor, good music, delicate ice cream, pretty girls, etc. The success of the past years but good Mrs. Earle never fails in anything and certainly not in entertaining her many friends.

Saturday, May 15, 1886: General Adam left for Los Angeles this a.m. Tom S in town; dined him. Had a close and confidental talk with him. He is worried, certain parties seem suspicious. I shall go ahead though with my duties and if anyone wants any rough business they can have it. I'm rather handy with a six shooter myself and I ain't scared much. At Mrs. Adam's this evening. Indians very bad still. Seem to have located near Nogales, probably awaiting reinforcements from reservation.

Sunday May 16, 1886: Major Earle sick today so I took charge a.m. and p.m. Sunday school changed to 10 a.m. Didn't work well. Fine sermon tonight, closing one, of course, of lectures. Collections $22. At Walker's after church where was Bruce. Quite a talk. Some exciting Indian news. Fighting reported and seven soldiers reported killed and others badly licked. Served them right the way they acted, coming through a box canyon.

Monday, May 17, 1886: Attended to some business today for Don Augustin Pesqueira of Hermosillo. Wrote Col. Shafter of 1st Infantry, and sent statement to San Carlos trying [to] recover Pesqueira's stock stolen by Apaches and now on reservation. My article in S.F. paper seems to have attracted great attention amongst Mexicans. *Las Novedades* in New York and *Chronista* of Los Angeles reproduced letter in Spanish commenting very highly, so I am solid with Mexico. Pocket struck in "Gentle Belle." On Herring's porch a while this evening.

Tuesday, May 18, 1886: Helped Mrs. Mitchell and Mrs. Earle and others prepare for lawn party this evening at former's residence. Worked this evening running in folks and helping. Brought Miss Birdie Herring around. The pale moon didn't show up until sometime after announcement of festivities. Col Clark left for Washington this a.m., am very glad he was able to get off. Apaches ran off some horses from [Apollinar] Bauer at Antelope [Springs] last night, 12 miles east, 25 soldiers camped there too.

Wednesday, May 19, 1886; Apaches in the Dragoons this a.m. shot a fellow at Granite Springs 12 miles from town, and killed one of the Lutley boys not far from Sorin's. I'm back from my wanderings just in time. Had some photos taken today a la Mexicano. Wore my fancy Mexican hat to perpetuate it and a serape loaned me by Walker. At Berry's where [I] met Miss [Rachel] Young, sister of Mrs. [Robert] Eccleston. Later at Goodfellow's where we had some guitar music. Walker and I singing.

Thursday, May 20, 1886: Indians bad still. I haven't lost any, but will go when necessary and try to be first one. Experience has taught me a thing or two. Dr. R [E. P. Ryder] pretty near the JJ's [jimjams or delirium tremens]. Nice letter from Col. Shafter about stock probably at Ft. Apache. More reported killed. Seven within 27 miles of town. Genl Miles seems in earnest, but why doesn't he place more men in the field. Clum and I framed a telegram tonight to the president. I withheld it until tomorrow. Terrible state of things. Spent evening with Rev. Mr. Haskins.

Friday, May 21, 1886: Got off a letter tonight telegraphic prepared by Rev. Haskins with points by me, to N.Y. *Post* giving statement of the terrible condition of things in our county. I got necessary signatures for indorsements. Opened up church at four p.m. for burial of Lutley, killed by Apaches yesterday [actually May 19] on Middle Pass road summit where I was lolling recently and waiting alone.* Exact place. Good attendance. Major Earle indisposed. Helped some at store tomorrow. Methodist ice cream festival tonight. Took Miss Goodfellow with Miss McNeal, we all had good time.

Saturday, May 22, 1886: Called on Mrs. Stewart of Willcox this evening. At store at odd times today for the Major. Opened up church this afternoon for burial of Geo. Buford's child. Had to hold casket alone several

*Fred Lutley, one of four brothers from Somerset, England, was killed May 19 at his wood camp near Dragoon Summit while chopping wood which he sold in Tombstone. His body was found beside the tree he was working on.

times. Great excitement in town this a.m. Mexican came in about 10 a.m. and reported three men killed at or near Sycamore Springs, eight miles from town. Bob Hatch, Brad Roberts and a few others went to place and found all false. Scouts instead of hostiles. They deserve killing anyhow on general principles. Some of us were talking about going out tonight and taking mountains afoot on a still hunt for scalps. Indians skipped again. Called for Mrs. Adam and Mrs. Street at Goodrich's tonight.

Sunday, May 23, 1886: Sunday school at 10 a.m. Full attendance, about 40. Church in morning and afternoon. Had to officiate as last Sunday. Have hands full with Sunday school and officiating otherwise, opening and closing church, seating, collecting, etc. Rev. Pearson, Methodist, very sick indeed, life despairing of. Large fires at base of Dragoons, mesa all afire. Bad for the feed. Magnificent sight nights. Fire this p.m. Mr. S's house slightly damaged. Wrote five letters today, Bagnall and others.

Monday, May 24, 1886: Lieut. Fuller arrived last evening, just having placed station at Antelope Springs. More excitement today. Apaches said to have raided Tres Alamos. Telegrams sent to Benson, 10 miles distant, for help. At Prieto's a while this afternoon. At Taxpayers meeting this evening and joined, although one of the charter men and with it from the first on school business. Have been away though and unable to follow everything up and besides am probably smallest taxpayer of all. Spent evening with Lieut. Fuller and friends. Another strike in Old Guard-Contention stope, said to be a fine one. Hope it is.

Tuesday, May 25, 1886: Major Earle still indisposed. Helped this p.m. at Sunday school entertainment given by Walker, NB, who is greatly interested in children. Worked hard, the ladies at ice cream, etc. Great time by Walker, Meade and Mitchell at Aztec. All hands renewed their youth. After [ice] cream and good things there was a magic lantern display. Little Charley Stilwell and Edith G friends, amusing. All kinds of games and good time for big and little.

Wednesday, May 26, 1886: Got my photos of self in Mexican sombrero and serape today. Quite good. Main object, to preserve my fine silver bullion hat. Quite a la Mexicano. At store today, quite continually, Blinn thinking it better. Sent off photo today. At Eccleston's tonight. Took home Mrs. Pito. Singing, etc. Miss Young, Mrs. E's sister, pleasant. Another fire tonight making four in four consecutive days. About 11 p.m. the Grand Central hoist caught fire and illuminated the whole country.

Thursday, May 27, 1886: Everybody feeling very blue today over last night's fire. Blinn away down, thinks it's a two year set back. Very bad business. No pumping now nor work on the hill, stoppage of everything and a terrible black eye to the town. Looks as though the Devil is surely foreclosing his mortgage.* Major little better. At Blinn's a while tonight.

*This is not Parsons' phrase. The *Daily Epitaph-Record* of May 23, 1886, states that A. H. Stebbins says "the Devil has a mortgage on this country. He seems to be trying to foreclose it now." The statement, however, was accurate. Burning of Grand Central hoist was a major ca-

Friday, May 28, 1886: General Adam arrived tonight. Major on hand to-day, all day. Collected for church today and was quite successful. Bade Mrs. Blinn goodbye tonight. Must send note to father to call upon her at the 5th Ave. hotel. Mrs. A's trip delayed. Mrs. Stevens said to be returning next month. Poor move it seems to me. Am kept busy running around evenings for my neighbors. A meeting was held this evening called by Mr. Haskins to discussed advisability of establishing high grade school.

Saturday, May 29, 1886: Another fire alarm tonight. Lamp exploded, Breen and Hams. Great excitement this a.m. Charlie Leach and three oth-ers caught in the [Grand Central] mine and two overpowered by gas and foul air, L & Taylor. I joined [Henry A.] Tweed and others and drove up in hot haste. They were on the 200 [level] and after much delay and consider-able excitement, fainting, etc., by the women, Leach and Taylor reached surface, the latter in rather bad condition. A close call.* Walker than upset Mrs. Goodfellow's cart and I finally drove it home for her. Men all better tonight. Wrote Stanley about lease today I think it was. Called on Mrs. Prescott tonight. Guitar music and pleasant time. Mrs. Bagg there. Great time tonight, Judge Benson arrived, another husband off.

Sunday, May 30, 1886: Sunday school and church as usual. A Mr. Lank-ton, commercial traveler, took class today. At breakfast Walker joined me and acquainted me with his friend Van Sickler, or [Sick]lien, from New York. Fair congregation today, but rather small Sunday school attendance. Stebbins miffed at me tonight but I would not apologize, not considering myself in the wrong, nor was one due, so S's friend said. Miss Miller sick and Mr. Haskins blue. Went around and braced him up. After talking him to sleep went home. Fire this afternoon near Durkee's, big excitements within eight days, seven fires and nearly some deaths.

Monday, May 31, 1886: Decoration Day and well celebrated it was for a small town like this. Helped get flowers this a.m. A general turn out of all orders and societies, the GAR leading. On Goodfellow's porch some of the time. A full attendance this evening at Schieffelin Hall and Col. Herring was particularly good and happy in his oration. An interesting program. Escorted home Mrs. Clark and Mrs. B.

Tuesday, June 1, 1886: Need rain badly and although quite cloudy at times we cannot expect [it] in less than two to three weeks. Expect to go to the Huachucas tomorrow. Still another fire, this time at Grand [Central] Mill, TM&M Co. about noon. Controlled before much damage was done. De-struction of that would just about have finished things. Huneke, Judge Harlow and wife and Van Lien arrived today from Nacosari. Hard trip for Mrs. H. Visiting friends this evening.

lamity. It destroyed the pumping capacity of that mine, and while pumps at the Contention Mine were large enough to hold the flow of water in check until the Grand Central restored their pumps, the companies bickered over costs and refused to cooperate. And the water rose.

*According to the Tucson *Weekly Star*, June 3, 1886, foreman Charles Leach, shift boss William Bishop, boss carpenter Lon Anderson, and assayer Walter Taylor were overcome by foul air in the Grand Central's Garrison stope.

Wednesday, June 2, 1886: Prepared to go to mountains again today. Orders countermanded though tonight. Just as well perhaps, as Indians were too close again for comfort, reported in Dragoons and Mules. Huneke and I cleaned house this afternoon preparatory to his reception in la casa. Found a terrible lot of truck, accumulation of years, flour, coffee, frijoles, pinole and camp outfit. Fixed up bunk. Letter from Maurice unsatisfactory. At Adam's till late and then awhile at Walker's watching Mitchell and Meade play chess. Left off provisions at Mrs. Newman's door.

Thursday, June 3, 1886: First few drops of rain fell today initating season. Ascension Day, church and communion this a.m., attended both. The church is truly a great help. I know it and wish the whole world might realize it more. If true to ourselves there is no denying its great power and efficacy. Why cannot people be as rational about this matter as about the other affairs of life, which though great, are of far less import. Too many of us, as Mr. Haskins said this a.m., are willing to accept the incredulous in other matters and deny the truthful. No Huachuca today. Indians reported near and I may go out. Sent Geronimo's wife's beads to sisters yesterday. Spent evening at Goodfellow's. Miss G told me some rather startling news about my gov. business. Singular how things get out. Am reported to be infatuated, in love too. Lots of idle tongues as well as hands now.

Friday, June 4, 1886: Huneke came in last night very late. Row at hotel, etc. Wish we could get off to Cal together. First really decided rain fell this afternoon but didn't last long enough to do any good. Will come now though pretty soon. Season very early this year, rainy season. More Indian news. Several reported killed at my old mill site, Tanner Canyon, Huachucas. Huachuca trip delayed, just as well, on account of Indians. At Herring's tonight.

Saturday, June 5, 1886: [E. B.] Gage and [J. H.] White are both here now so we'll soon see if they mean business. W. C. Davis's brother killed by Indians below Walter Haney's. Fires in Dragoons and Whetstones, Indian fires probably. Whist this evening at office. Fixed up balance of house this afternoon. First time it has been renovated since I moved in I think. Must now get at papers and letters. Have just got a scrapbook to paste in my public experiences, all I can find.

Sunday, June 6, 1886: Sunday school as usual this a.m., communion. Fair number out this a.m. considering and good number tonight. Mr. Haskins too unwell to lecture tonight. I wanted Huneke with whom I have had some talk on religious matters and who cannot see things as I see them to call on Mr. Haskins this evening which he did and we had a long and instructive talk. I presented H's doubts and others I considered stronger, got Mr. Haskin's views, presenting my own, and we had an interesting talk until midnight, taking home several books I am interested in. Shall do all I can for him [Huneke] and all others sincere on vital questions.

Monday, June 7, 1886: Got Mr. Haskins some medicine last night which had done him good when I called this a.m. Charlie Frederick's child died last night, making loss of wife and three children within a year. Too much for him and he went on a big drunk it is said. More Indian killings, this time between Harshaw and Huachucas and on road between Benson [and] here. Genl Miles says it isn't safe to go out of town. Even road to Fairbank not entirely safe, regular stage road. Spent evening at Goodfellow's.

Tuesday, June 8, 1886: Funeral of Frederick's child this afternoon, attended. Quite a gathering of sympathizing friends. Mrs. Clark feeling good this afternoon over receipt of telegram from Colonel at Washington announcing fact of bill having passed Senate and more than likely to pass House. Congratulated and am very glad for her sake especially she has had to endure so much and has stood up so bravely under it all. At Mrs. McNeil's this evening, she goes to California tomorrow.

Wednesday, June 9, 1886: Maurice has taken charge of the Belmont hotel, old Ellis villa, at Los Angeles. He had to do something and I am glad he has taken hold and buckled right down. Am glad for his sake. Huneke got off this a.m. for Lake Valley, taking Maurice's letter about the mine. Hopes to sell out when I expect we'll go to California. Things now seem to be working Californiaward for me. Arranged my scrapbook today at Mrs. Earle's. Am very sorry to have lost much of my personal material. Dined at Berry's this evening and had quite a talk with Mrs. Clark, whom I see every evening as I carry her mail to her. Another telegram today from Col announces positiveness of his bill passing the House. Quite a talk with [C. S.] Fly and wife on old times.

Thursday, June 10, 1886: Quite amusing in Court this a.m. General Wardwell, the war horse, trying to reclaim property from Mrs. Cooley, nee Tempest, given her on condition of marriage. Some funny scenes and passages. Have submitted report to Supervisors and says we'll start Monday to check recent survey of [Pima-Cochise] County boundary lines. Indians very bad and Mrs. [H. G.] H[owe] has declared positively H shall not go, but he will manage it some way. Will be five of us probably and I guess we can stand the Apaches off. Possibly Miles may give us an escort, he probably will as he says country is full of Indians and very unsafe. Expect we'll run against some.

Friday, June 11, 1886: Making preparations to get off Monday. Si Bryant, Frank Ely, a reliable Mexican, Howe and I constitute party. If we can't stand the Apaches off I don't know any outfit that can. B and E terribly good men for an Indian racket. Better than three or four times the number of soldiers; in fact, we don't want any escort, certainly not of such fellows as generally make up the file. Called at Goodrich's tonight and later attended drill of Knight of Pythias by invitation of Clum, commanding. Evolutions very fair considering. Dance, etc., didn't participate.

Saturday, June 12, 1886: Judge Barnes and wife receiving considerable attention. Got things together today, etc. Boys having lots of fun at me about an unfortunate legging purchase. Will go well fixed for a rough, rough time and climb Rincons and Whetstones, said to be the worst mountains on trip. Our starting point, a ranch on San Pedro, has just been jumped by Indians, also another just above, so we'll have lively times may be. At Goodfellow's this evening. Later at Walker's. Long talk with Vansickler about country, mining, etc. Pleasant fellow. Visited the Gentle Belle and Old Guard this afternoon on a mule I think of riding on trip.

Sunday, June 13, 1886: Church and Sunday school as usual this a.m. Mrs. Smith house burned down and no roof over her head. Will take out a $2000 accidental insurance policy through Vickers tomorrow which will give me $10 per week in case of accident and $2000 to heirs if Indians kill me or other accident. I wish ¼ to go to Sam and ¾ to sister and Strallus evenly. A risky and spicy trip, and I guess my last before I leave Territory, and I don't want to quit broke, dead or alive. I'm called and supposed to be deputy U.S. Marshal.

Monday, June 14, 1886: Made final preparations for getting away today. Spent evening at Herring's, where were Judge Barnes and wife. Judge quite jolly. Was called on for guitar song and responded. Small fire at Nigger Sam's tonight.

Tuesday, June 15, 1886: Howe and I each took $2000 accidental insurance today for one year. Howe and I with Frank Ely and Antonio Rodriguez with two pack mules well loaded, carrying probably 200 lbs. each left at 8:30 a.m. Quite a crowd to see us off. I took back street. Si Bryant is to join us tonight, completing our force of five good men; five men and seven animals. We are thought to have considerable temerity in face of present Indian troubles.* Lunched at St. David, Beck's. The Mormons treated us well. H and I left others here and went to Benson for promised military escort. Found four dismounted men awaiting us. We were hot and told them to go back to Tucson. We'll put her through without any assistance and will be better off. Wrote Huneke and after stop of two hours pulled out for Tres Alamos, nine miles distant. A few Indians seen near Benson, so H and I kept sharp lookout. Reached the dobe house called Tres Alamos about dark. Boys had camp made. Found here Mrs. Tony Baker, nee Collins. Strange world. Soldiers camped here.

Wednesday, June 16, 1886: Started about 7:30. About 20 miles to Dr. Pooles. Met him on road with one soldier. Soldiers stationed at several ranches en route on river. Met Granger near White's [Thomas White, Theodore's brother]. Rested and lunched at Poole's, then went on to Zoyas ranch, eight miles beyond and camped. Fight here other day and Indians worsted. Indians are said to be very bad here by the Mexicans and Americans, who have had several rattles with them lately and see them most ev-

*Civil engineer and Cochise County surveyor H. G. Howe was commissioned to check the accuracy of initial survey of the line between Pima and Cochise counties done by George Roskruge. Howe and his colleagues found the earlier survey correct.

ery day. Some Mexicans were chased in yesterday or today, three miles and shots exchanged. Mexicans and all say that we have a dangerous job on hand as we have to go right through the places in mountains where they are supposed to be living. An Apache came down to river today with gun and canteen. They are very bold and impudent; guess we'll have all [the] Indians we want. Sounds very encouraging all of this. Very scary I guess these fellows. Dogs made terrible racket tonight. Little sleep. Si caught up with us today about 10 a.m. on whoop.

Thursday, June 17, 1886: Very hot. Indians killed some 14 horses in this section lately. Howe pulled out this a.m. with Si and Tony for end of the line or commencement rather, to start the due south line to Mexican border and see if the Inn. posts were in line. Point about three miles distant, near Redfield Canyon or in it. Very poor horse, will have a good rest today and he needs it. Good bath in San Pedro river this afternoon. Water didn't quite cover me lying down, but had a good wash, meantime keeping lookout for Indians. School teacher named Conrad on hand today. Mosquitoes bad tonight, unusual experience for me. Good supper with jerky and onions. Thirteen Indians reported on hill tops yesterday a.m. Men came in about six after hot day's work. Are very hard on horse and mule flesh.

Friday, June 18, 1886: Howe has made a big error. We separated this a.m. Howe sent Frank and me with pack animals to meet him at certain point on map known as Paiges near Vails in Happy Valley between Rincon and Granite mountains. We were to cross mountains through Turkey Creek Canyon, a few miles up the river. Not a particularly pleasing undertaking in face of so many reports about Indians being in there, in fact, living in there, so on entering canyon we took out rifles and held ourselves in readiness for trouble, having agreed on a plan in case of ambush or fight on more even ground. Kept sharp lookout. Thought we struck moccasin tracks but they proved to be bear tracks later on, at least we took them for such. Rested at 11:30, having found a little grass for our animals and not knowing when we might find anymore. Slow headway, very hard traveling indeed, rough and dangerous in places. Had to shove my horse through one place from behind, tearing off some of his hide. The pack mules were contrary, packs slipping from time to time and we had a devil of a time generally. Cattle near head of canyon, branded V. No signs of habitation though and we had to camp after dark. Nothing for stock to eat and we had to tie them to trees near us and let them eat the bark. Lit small fire and got some supper and then arranged packs as breastworks in case of attack by Indians and turned in head to head, I booted and spurred. Terrible crash at midnight caused by my horse falling over dry tree which scared a big bear prowling near us and he went off up canyon like the old boy was after him, more scared than we were.

Saturday, June 19, 1886: No Indians yet nor signs. On trail at six a.m. without eating anything, so anxious to get somewhere and traveled main canyon until unable to proceed further. Then retraced over the rough

rocky canyon bottom to camping place and struck out over the hills westerly on top of high ridge. Saw a wickiup in distance in rincon [of] foothills
and finally reached it to find it abandoned. Some good water but little
feed. Resolved to cut back to canyon, and if not trailed up soon, to return
to Zoyas, our starting point on river. Very bad piece of business. Left note
at house in case Howe went there. When just about to put the diamond
hitch on one of the packs there was a shout and jumping around and we
saw Tony, and to say that we were all glad to meet but very faintly expressed it. Howe discovered in Happy Valley that we could not get
through and sent Tony to trail us up and he performed a remarkable piece
of trailing, having followed us progressively over confused marchings and
countermarchings through a labyrinth of cattle and other trails, out of
canyon and over mountains, he thinking at times what if I am trailing up
Apaches, until at last he found us and we lost no time in striking a south-
erly course, happening onto good trails. A pleasant thing after our rough
breakneck traveling. Finally reached the H[arvey-]Vail ranch [the Empire
ranch] and were allowed to turn animals into an old barley field where
they got good pickings for first time in 24 hours. Rested awhile and then
pushed on for ranch where Howe and Si were supposed to be. Found ranch
abandoned. Some dove notes were unnatural to Tony so we kept sharp
lookout for Indians. Went out of valley between Rincon and Granite
mountains, about dark and being unable to find Coronado or Tores ranch,
camped on mesa, hobbling stock and turning it loose. Tremendous granite
formation. Raw bacon this a.m., no time to cook in.

Sunday, June 20, 1886: Terrible nuisance packing two animals, demanded
hitches, etc. Frank's mare broke hobbles but Tony finally tracked her up.
Tony beats the world on trailing. Heard voices and soon on a rise saw
some men and pack animals, part of a party of 40 soldiers who were on a
hot Indian trail thought to be made last night. The Apaches probably
passed close to us, but fortunately did not strike any of our stock. Boys
hunted water and I kept camp. Frank found it and returned for a second
lot of animals upon his second trip, but a very little time intervening,
found at the water tracks of three horses, rawhide shod, and moccasin
tracks of two Indians, also marks in the soft dirt where one Apache had
been down on his knees. Frank got back as quickly as possible. Indians on
both sides of us it seems, as Lieut. Johnson went into the Rincons with 40
men on fresh trail as we came out. Near Mescal Siding at Turntable we at
last came up with Howe and Si, and of course, there was a grand powpow.
They had a hungry time of it. Were at Tores ranch to west of us a ways
last night where the people were all under arms on account of the Apaches
and the 40 soldiers were on hand this a.m. When the east bound overland
train from Cal came along we stopped it, and Ed Suman being on board, I
got a lot of papers and big hunk of ice, a rare treat to us way out on the
desert. We were the observed of all observers and were a tough looking
crowd I guess. Had a great time under the turntable eating and drinking

and finally pulled out across the hot plains to Kennian's [Kinnea's] ranch in Whetstones Mountains which was deserted as others. Bad place for Indians. Good bath with sharp lookouts; ants too numerous.

Monday, June 21, 1886: Went with Howe and Si this a.m. to find a line monument which didn't take long. Square gal[vanized] iron post between ranges 17 and 18, well planted and marked. Pima and Cochise counties shook hands here. Broke camp later about eight a.m. and had a rough, hard climb over a backbone of one of the Whetstones. A hard pull for men and animals. One of the pack mules turned a double somersault alighting on its feet all O.K., but with pack badly disarranged. Rough descent, plenty of soldier and Indian signs. Lots of Apache tracks and we were very careful, particularly in canyons. Reached Mud Springs after a 12 mile pull, where Greenbaum was recently killed. Nobody there, deserted. Apaches had also killed G's burro and dog and the stench was very bad. A pile of stones mark the spot where G was buried and was probably killed while all around are scattered cooking utensils and mining implements. A bloody shirt in one place. No horse. Found an Indian litter, small olla, probably left by the Apaches and packed it along as a momento of the trip. No drinking water here. Animals made out with the mud and water. Hot ride from here to Bear Springs about eight miles, where we camped pretty well played out. Little water. Wasn't too glad to drink out of cattle tracks. Gritty and dungy but it was water. Apache tracks here. Ants again. Small black ants seem sweet enough but the big red one we cannot go. Boots on tonight. Signals agreed on in case of Apaches as we had to separate tonight to get good feed for horses.

Tuesday, June 22, 1886: Anniversay of big fire and my hurt. Better luck this a.m. Survey force all O.K. thus far. Good roads now. Passed out of the mountains through pass between Whetstones and Mustangs into the valley of the Barbacomari river. Crossed some fresh Apache tracks in the pass. Crossed railroad west of Huachuca siding about a mile and watered at [Moore K.] Lurty's ranch. The Barbacomari river entirely dry where we crossed near siding. Six miles to [Victor H.] Igo's ranch from Lurty's over good trail and we reached it in good time. This ranch is beautifully located at northwest end of Huachucas. Fine outlook, fine water, good shade and all of the conveniences of a No. 1 camping place. We have now left the Indian infested territory. Traveled quite steadily from 6:30 till 1:15. Igo is a character. Great butter at Lurty's, they thought it a very risky piece of business crossing through the Indian country as we did and seemed surprised at our temerity. But 15 miles now to the Mexican border, that is on a straight course. Will complete business tomorrow and reach home on Friday. Longest surface of water I've seen in Arizona here. Had novelty of [fishing]. We caught mess for breakfast. Fresh eggs tonight. Too slick of a time. Splendid camping place, caught a turtle.

Wednesday, June 23, 1886: Splendid weather all of the time. Hot though, especially in some of the canyons where there isn't a breath of air. Came down west side of Huachucas today, passing Evans' camp, Parker and Judson's where we got some radishes and finally camped at Wrights, three or four miles from the line. After dinner Howe, with transit on his shoulder, Si and I all mounted, struck out for the line via Campini's and after crossing his canyon rode out onto the high table or mesa land. Saw the last wooden mile stake in the distance on our left and then separated to find the last gal[vanized] iron post marking the boundary line of the U.S. and Mexico and Cochise and Pima counties. I was nearest and first to it though not seeing it first. We crossed some distance into Mexico before finally discovering it. Howe was just in time to get his observation, it being then about 6:10, and pronounced the survey correct. Thus ended the examination.

Some parties are surprised to find themselves in a different country from what they thought. I took a westerly direction from this post to find the Emory monument, about 1700 ft distant, and finally found a scattered lot of stones with a mescal pole inclining at an angle which Howe said later was the monument, but I doubt it. Lost sight of others and didn't reach Campini's without trouble. Looked as though I might have to camp alone for the night at one time. C favored me with what mescal I wanted although Howe and Si were refused as mescal business on the border is a ticklish thing and only those well known are favored. Reached camp some time after dark. Horse wouldn't hold trail well. All hands were called and we discussed sharks, alligators and turtles, Florida, not being believed until we rolled over in blankets and were soon obliged [to tell] stories of sea and land.

Thursday, June 24, 1886: Good feed for animals here, best in fact since leaving San Pedro river. Too much mescal for Frank. Hard time finding horses this a.m. as two strayed off. Si took my plug and Tony his. Can take things easier now, 45 miles to town and we can make it in two easy stages. Men and animals need the rest. Considerable hard traveling with little feed for animals at times. Country very bare, rain badly needed. Best grass yet here. Crossed Huachucas today and camped mouth [of] Tanner's Canyon. I went up to old mill site and ruminated, four years since removal. Got some vegetables from soldiers at canyon.

Friday, June 25, 1886: Got started in good time. I led party across country to Charleston, where we beered up and got news. Made good time. On road beyond met Curry and his cowboy friends returning from coroner's inquest over body of Mexican killed by Choate in self defence in Huachucas. Choate one of party. Curry told me the circumstances. Reached town in good shape and were warmly welcomed. Ours seemed to be considered a very risky trip and I supposed it was. Received congratulations of friends and finally got dust washed off and boiled shirt on. Got around some tonight.

Saturday, June 26, 1886: Mrs. Clark gone, went yesterday a.m. to Los Angeles, leaving house in my care. Unable to sleep much last night. Too close after open air and too soft bed. Nothing much today, everything quiet dead. Did considerable for Prieto today, Mexican Consul, trying to regulate a difference between himself and another Mexican. Was finally successful. Quite a number gone including Mrs. Adam. School trustee election today and Bagg finally squelched. Wolcott, Coffman and Geo Cheyney elected, good men. Good for Taxpayers Association.

Sunday, June 27, 1886: Sunday school and church as usual. Mr. Haskins last Sunday for some weeks as he goes home on business to Jubilee, Illinois. Service this evening as usual. Rev. Adams on hand tonight. Went home with Mr. Haskins, wrote note to father and then tied up his [Haskins] trunk for him. Also read his *Post* articles and criticised them.

Monday, June 28, 1886: Flies bad, hot. Saw Mr. Haskins off this a.m. Dr. Willis drove him to Fairbanks. I nailed up back door and windows. Took a few traps over to Clark's house this evening and will sleep there according to promise. At Goodfellow's this evening; on porch. Quite a discussion with Doc on Nacosari. He's not very gentlemanly at times; too positive.

Tuesday, June 29, 1886: Very hot. I don't dislike the warm weather though. Quite a clearing out of the fair sex, about 20. Very few left. Our trip quite well discussed and thought perilous undertaking. Did some church collecting today. Spent evening at Herring's. Quite a talk with Miss H on education. Finished copying my pencil account of trip into this today. Quite a job.

Wednesday, June 30, 1886: More church collecting today, but it goes very slowly. Well, we're all going along in a lazy kind of way. Nothing doing in town, though they talk of rebuilding GC shaft as it isn't hurt below the 300. At Mrs. Prescott's a while at her invitation and exchanging guitar news. Escorted Miss Goodfellow home from Berry's, staid a while and then returned awhile with guitar and we all, Earle and all had good sing.

Thursday, July 1, 1886: Hot, 108; no rain, faint signs. Country and cattle very bad off. Must have rain quickly. Report of burning of mill reached me today. Nothing in it. Party named Campbell of St. David talking about buying part of it. A cow is nightly raiding gardens. I chased it from Clark's twice last night and will do something more next time. Commenced long letter to sister today relating trip. Called at Stilwell's this evening and had pleasant time. Quite a talk later with Campbell, an insurance man who has lived at Elizabeth, New Jersey. Mrs. Stevens came tonight.

Friday, July 2, 1886: Finished letter to sister today and mailed it. Called on Mrs. Stevens tonight and found her well and looking well, having gained 18 lbs.; trip did her good. She had quite an accumulation of news.

Saturday, July 3, 1886: Thermometer from 106 to 108 these days, but heat is not unbearable. Old town seems to be going down more yet. Hope I can soon get out and away. Waiting for Huneke. Hope he'll soon turn up. I want to go to southern California. At Mrs. Theo [Anna] White's tonight and saw her and Mrs. Reppy. Pleasant call. Saw Vanlien later, he goes to Nacosari tomorrow.

Sunday, July 4, 1886: Sunday school and church as usual this a.m. Major Earle read service. Few in attendance and a small Sunday school. Usual noises for the 4th. Poor Bill Bickerton is taken in by the Apaches near Cumpas. So they go, terrible. At Goodfellow's a while this evening.

Monday, July 5, 1886: Celebration of the 4th took place today, very quiet one it was too, as we are all busted. No rain in country and no water in reservoir. Fire crackers prohibited, or their prohibition called for as there is no water in case of fire. First time the Huachuca reservoir in Miller Canyon has gone dry. Quite a day for me helping Consul in another matter. He has lots of troubles. At Mrs. S few moments, then to Earle's where we [ice] creamed and I brought along guitar. Fireman's ball.

Tuesday, July 6, 1886: After a terrible amount of sputtering and blowing, regular sand storms, a little rain fell today which is the first fall of the season, as the rainy season may be supposed to have commenced now; terribly needed. Don't know what poor cattle are doing to live. No feed, browsing only as a rule. Called at Cheyney's tonight and had pleasant call. Mr. C, sr., goes East tomorrow a.m.

Wednesday, July 7, 1886: Doc Goodfellow this afternoon cut out my big toe nail again for the third time, right foot, and this time dug out and scraped away underneath killing the matrix. Toe etherized and not very painful operation. Hobbled somewhat awhile and went home early so as to rest and unshoe toe. Read a long time tonight, a work on infidelity, also *Innocents Attuned*.

Thursday, July 8, 1886: Down town quite late. Toe better. Rain threatened in abundance, hope it'll come. Letter from Strallus last night. Mrs. Townsend, nee Anne Lake, visited her. Strallus pronounces our friend and her school mate a woman of genius, which is intellect in its highest source, also as distinguished, and she's quite right and very correct. Called at Second and Fremont tonight. Huneke and McDonald came in today at last. Ran against Geronimo and had hard time for grub and water.

Friday, July 9, 1886: Glad to see Huneke back. He had a rough trip. McD left for St. Louis this a.m. Toe getting on all O.K. Practicing "La Paloma." At Goodfellow's this evening. Letter from Mrs. Townsend this a.m. as usual light and interesting. She quite insists on my writing a book of frontier adventures. Have plenty material in my journals and experiences but am afraid it might not pay. She's been visiting Strallus.

Saturday, July 10, 1886: A few drops of rain. We're talking Australia, H and I. Judge Benson left for Santa Monica, Cap. Hayne for East and Leach and Goodfellow for California. Quite an exodus. Wrote Geo Woodward today in reply to a letter received last night. Wants to sell cattle and rent ranch. Have another racket on hand with Consul Prieto now, a matter of land colony near San Diego. Must raise something ere long.

Sunday, July 11, 1886: Sunday school and church as usual this a.m. Arose late for breakfast, so lunched at Earle's. Believe I was at Goodfellow's a while this evening.

Monday, July 12, 1886: Am acting as deputy clerk of Board of Supervisors while Vickers is away at Bisbee adjusting loses by recent fire.* Things gradually going down. Bottom must be nearly reached.

Tuesday, July 13, 1886: Supervisors acting as Board of Equalization now. Adjourned today till 19th. About eight p.m. Mr. White and Mrs. White, Mrs. Berry and I started for Sulphur Springs ranch. Good morning and pleasant ride. After getting through South Pass and the mountains the ladies felt better. Stopped at [T. F.] Hudson's and watered and reached ranch, away out on the plains on the old Apache reservation made by Genl [Oliver O.] Howard between one and two o'clock a.m. Mrs. W is going to California and desired to visit home ranch [El Dorado] to get some things and pack up others, and Mrs. B after much persuasion went. Trip made in night time on account of Indians. Ladies rather nervous going through mountains but were brave. I go as escort as well as company.

Wednesday, July 14, 1886: Mosquitoes bad last night and tonight. Lounged about today. Had a good bath in the sulphur water, slightly tinged. Cattle doing fairly well considering. The looked for wagons arrived tonight.

Thursday, July 15, 1886: Mr. White did some surveying today for water and I helped some. Got away about five p.m. for the home ranch about 20 miles distant. When within a few hundred yards of the cottonwood adobe it being just dusk and right hour for Indians, bang, bang, bang went several rifles ahead of us and the ladies thought their time had come. I got out with rifle and recruited Mrs. B, calling out to keep well in bushes and discovered that some one was shooting skunks at adobe. I nosed the trouble before hallowing. Good supper at headquarters home ranch and good bed.

Friday, July 16, 1886: Mr. and Mrs. White hard at work today packing. Played Mrs. W's fine guitar and passed the time rather lazily. A couple of Apaches scouts camped at ranch last night enroute to Geronimo's camp, they claiming to know where he is. Idea is to sound the old cutthroat. [Tom] Horn, who was with [Emmet] Crawford when killed and who was wounded, also along. Heliograph stations work well. Music tonight on the organ by Mrs. W. We're having a jolly time. Fine turkey dinner tonight.

Saturday, July 17, 1886: After further packing we got started at 10:45 and returned via Meyer's place, Brophy's and Soldiers Hole. At Soldiers Hole stopped to see Mrs. Tasker. Miss Pauline Owlsley a very pretty girl. Much fun on road over "Spruce gum and Buttermilk." I claimed to be taking points too. Miss B has a very hearty laugh and she and Mrs. White just

*This would be the fire of February 16, 1885, which inflicted a property loss of $100,000. J. V. Vickers was a representative of the New York Life Insurance Company, as well as Travelers Insurance Company. He also wrote fire insurance policies.

turned themselves loose, as the saying goes, laughing to their heart's content. Reached town about eight p.m. I supped at White's and later housed at cabin for night. Huneke on hand. No Indians.

Sunday, July 18, 1886: Saw Consul Prieto off this a.m. for Los Angeles. He quite declare that he shall get me a good position with a new colony started in Lower California near San Diego by a Mr. Fuller. One of our horses, a large bay, died last night. The black seems to have the wind of a locomotive and probably killed him by being hitched to him. We made the 49 miles in $7^1/_2$ hours, probably too much for the bay. Sunday school and church as usual, 25 out this a.m. At Mrs. S tonight, Earles in p.m. H and I talked christianity till one a.m. at C house tonight. Am sorry he cannot think as I do. Shall do everything I can.

Monday, July 19, 1886: Everything remarkably quiet. What with the shutting down all over, drought, etc., I'm afraid for us all. We're gone for about two years. Wish I could pull out. Paper from Mrs. Clapp today with statement of drowning of poor Osgood Bradley. Recognized only by clothes and ring. He had reached Australia all right but his steamer, the *Lee Moon*, was lost with nearly all on board enroute from Melbourne. Don José María Torres and four Mexicans killed between Lampas and Tepachi by Apaches, though possibly by revolutionists, as he is a rural prefect and the one in power. I thought considerably of him. Two friends in one day. Life is short and strange. Called on Mrs. Stevens tonight.

Tuesday, July 20, 1886: Couldn't find anyone at mine, so guess they're all skipped. I'm only one square. A young cyclone struck us Sunday afternoon leveling English's house and partially unroofing Court House. Yesterday I discovered that the house on the Gentile Belle mine, $1^1/_2$ miles from town, was gone and today I drove over with Fisher and found that the wind had lifted and overturned the building, wrecking it completely. F offered me $10, and if nothing better comes, I must take it in preference to losing everything. Tried Bradley on it and may do something with him. At Herring's a while and later Earle's where quite a number was gathered. Annette arrived tonight.

Wednesday, July 21, 1886: Nothing doing; nothing new; hard times are coming. Reading tonight, *Scribners*, first reading in some time. Hope I will locate soon where I won't go to rust this way, where surroundings will be more conducive to reading.

Thursday, July 22, 1886: Same old thing. Sold Gentle Belle house to Fisher for $10. Better than nothing. House would soon be dragged away, this is, the wreck. At White's this evening, where were also the Reppy's. Some music. At Berry's first. Some hats from Mrs. Berry.

Friday, July 23, 1886: Same old run of things. Fine ore struck in Old Guard-combination shaft. Col. Clark passed through to Los Angeles to night and sent a darkey boy of 16 to me direct from Washington to clean up, etc. Great darkie. At Mrs. S tonight where was also Stebbins.

Saturday, July 24, 1886: O.G. stock improving. Am afraid TM&M Co. will close down next month owing to low price of silver, 95 [cents per ounce], and that will fix this camp. A great clearing out for Cal. An exodus to Kingston, NM, too. I'm quite sure this camp will boom again and so predict, but it will be two or three years hence. Indians, drought, depreciation of silver, etc., have brought us down. We'll rise again some day.

Sunday, July 25, 1886: Sunday school and church as usual; 21 at church. Destroyed about 50 of my letters today. I lived our old times a while today. What sadness and what changes there are in the world. I opened a ten year old package, sealed by myself with forcible instructions. It was hard to tear up some letters recalling pleasant moments, but of course, all had to go. At the two S's and Earle's tonight.

Monday, July 26, 1886: Mrs. Earle and Miss Miller left this a.m. for S.F. via Yosemite. Major had to go to Benson to give them advantage of GAR rates. Goodfellow's this evening I believe.

Tuesday, July 27, 1886: Busily engaged destroying old letters these days. Have a heavy task. All of N[athalie]'s letters. Dislike to do this but cannot pack them about any longer. At Herring's tonight. First good shower fell today. Huneke telegraphed on Crable business tonight, $125 in it for me if successful.

Wednesday, July 28, 1886: At White's tonight with Mrs. Berry to say adios. Saw Cheyney home. Letter from Col Clark. Coming this week; got house ready. People getting away at a lively rate. War cloud in sky; Cutting trouble at El Paso.* Nothing in it. Still at work on letters. At last letter from home with cuttings wanted for scrapbook. They're after me too to publish a book.

Thursday, July 29, 1886: Moved back to house, or cabin rather, today as Col may come tonight. Mrs. Clum and Mr. and Mrs. Blinn arrived last night. At it destroying letters again today and dined at Berry's. Took Miss Goodfellow some. Called on Mrs. Blinn tonight. Alice [Strallus] missed her at 5th Ave. She was in all of the time. At Goodfellow's later. Quite a talk about oil country. Miss G unwell.

Friday, July 30, 1886: Hard at it today destroying letters; see the end now. At Mrs. Stevens this evening, walked up to Sol Israel's with her. Cribbage, etc. Unpleasant episode at Goodfellow's on porch, where I went with a book and found Walker and Genl Adam there.

---

*Parsons is not referring to knife play, but to the arrest and imprisonment by Chihuahuan authorities of A. K. Cutting, owner of *El Centinela*, an El Paso newspaper. It all started when Cutting denounced Emigdio Medina as a fraud in the latter's efforts to raise subscriptions for a rival newspaper published across the border. Outraged, Medina filed a complaint of defamation in a Mexican court. When Cutting crossed the border he was charged with slander, arrested, and thrown into prison. He was sentenced to a year imprisonment at hard labor and fined $600. Unable to pay the fine, Cutting's confinement was lengthened by 100 days. Thereupon the U.S. State Department stepped in and sought his freedom; the contest becoming so serious that at one point war with Mexico was threatened.

Saturday, July 31, 1886: Great time with watermelons today. Got two for one out of the dealer, much fun. Hard at [it] again today destroying and separating letters. Am reaching the end. Some good fortune today. Got away with Marsh on shirt trade and H received check for $650, so if matters go through I net $120 on a matter I didn't think there was anything in. Called on Miss Herring tonight, all well.

Sunday, August 1, 1886: Sunday school this a.m. Had my hands full, Miss Miller being away and Redstreet who was to help, sick. Opened and closed, led singing, took attendance, distributed papers, and taught large class. Lively work. Finished looking over old letters today. A week's work. Have reduced bulk wonderfully. All of NHR's letters destroyed, nearly or about 75 I think. Judge Mitchell read service and I took up coll[ection]. Called on Mrs. J. P. Clum tonight. Little Caro [Caroline Clum] well.

Monday, August 2, 1886: Magnificent storm today, first of season. Well, I worked faithfully today on the A. S. Crable matter and consummated the matter after much trouble, netting a $120. A pretty good thing and easily made. I do have a little luck once in a while. Sorted letters this p.m. and have the big job about concluded. Am feeling pretty good tonight; so nice to feel that way sometimes. Pleasant evening at Mrs. S.

Tuesday, August 3, 1886: Apaches showing up again on the lower San Pedro. As I predicted the TM&M Co. shut down on the 15th. Silver has dropped too low for them, 91$^1/_4$. Too bad. Things are bad enough now, but by Sept. 1st looks as though grass would begin to grow in streets.* Folks feeling blue. Guess we'll have to get out—California ho. Kingston I don't believe in. At Mrs. S tonight.

Wednesday, August 4, 1886: Nothing new. Cutting business seems to hang fire. We're ready to jump in here and lick Mexico at moments notice. Want something badly to stir up our blood. Spent evening at Judge Street's. Saw Mrs. Rood today and reduced church cleaning from $10 to $6 per month. Rain nearly all night and a good, soft one.

Thursday, August 5, 1886: Have slight cold. Bad weather for colds. Vickers goes to California tomorrow and wants me to go too, and I thought about it seriously as the cost would be greatly reduced but Judges Berry and Stilwell think war inevitable and advised me to hold on and take a hand in things when issue is forced. Guess I'll wait a while. May be a dollar or so here yet too. At Berry's tonight. Took the Misses Herring home. A cheery letter from Mrs. Clapp tonight all about GAR.

Friday, August 6, 1886: Sun these days till afternoon when clouds gather and give us some rain. Well, matters with Mexico seem mixed. A few days ought to settle them. Some very rediculous performances by el juen Mexicano. No mail east or west tonight; second time in a week or ten

*George W. Cheyney, superintendent of the Tombstone Mining & Milling Company, ordered the shutdown, throwing 200 men out of work.

days, washouts. At Mrs. S this evening. At request was to bring down mail.

Saturday, August 7, 1886: Wrote Stanley and a Mr. Skinner today. Nothing new. Guess there's nothing in Cutting affair. Must go to California.

Sunday, August 8, 1886: V[ickers] off to Cal this a.m. via Phoenix. Possibly may meet him at L.A. Sunday school and service as usual. Had my hands full, but Redstreet assisted at Sunday school. Wrote Mr. Haskins this afternoon. Miss Goodfellow and I walked down to Berry's this evening. Had another warm discussion, Earps, etc. What constituted the true cowboy. [Too bad Parsons was not moved to elaborate on this topic.]

Monday, August 9, 1886: I find plenty to do but no money in it. Acted as clerk of Board of Supervisors this afternoon. The levy made, 3.90 I think for year. Don José María Elias with wife and nice, Señorita Rosita, are in town, arriving from Custom House last night, and I spent a very delightful evening with them. Much fun in the fair one and myself trying to get the old gent to speak English. He would go for her. None of them speak it.

Tuesday, August 10, 1886: Same old thing today. The General is packing up to leave. Whole families it seems will not be sorry. I haven't anything against him. Have, in fact, made something out of him. Mrs. Benham arrived from San Francisco last night. Miss Goodfellow and I went to Stebbins to see her, but she was at Eccleston's. I called there later and had quite a chat.

Wednesday, August 11, 1886: Nights though are magnificent. Lots of yarns today. Can get anything you want up on the street. [Capt. Henry W.] Lawton captured and not captive.* Indians in Bisbee canyon. Ben W[illiams] after them. Soldiers out from Huachuca, etc. Fire last night at Stage station on Fairbank road. Mrs. Blom burnt out. A few of us drove down there today. Shots during fire, bad blood.

Thursday, August 12, 1886: At Mrs. Stevens last evening where was also Stebbins. Had considerable fun with the hose, etc. Later played billiards with Stebbins and repaired to his office where we talked until one a.m. Adam, of course, figured conspicuously. Hard at it fixing my scrapbook; ought to have started one years ago. At Herring's this evening.

Friday, August 13, 1886: Put in my time as advantageously as possible. At scrapbook again today. Got coat from General today. So it seems that the Kansas parties have gotten the better of Crables here, paying us the $650 for a property worth $3500 or more. We may be able to get something more out of it yet. At Blinn's this evening. Reppys not home.

*According to the *Arizona Weekly Star* of August 12, 1886, the quiet of Tombstone was shattered the day before when a courier brought news that Captain Henry Lawton's command had been captured and disarmed by Mexican troops in Sonora. When the intelligence was confirmed, troops from Forts Bowie, Huachuca, and other points were ordered to "push forward to the relief of Lawton, and to cut their way through at all hazards.

Saturday, August 14, 1886: Finished scrapbook today. Helped general on matters. Wish the war would come, if it's coming, can't wait forever. Think I was at Goodfellow's this evening.

Sunday, August 15, 1886: Sunday school as usual. Did the best I could. Judge Mitchell read service. Fair number out, considering. Wrote home. They are very charry there with their letters. At Mrs. S this eve where were also Stebbins and Meade. Adjourned later, we three to Judge Mitchell's. Judge and Steb are going for office now; considerable fun.

Monday, August 16, 1886: Acted as clerk again today of Board of Supervisors. At Herring's tonight. Cutting business seems to subside somewhat. Some more bad Apache business below. Kirk and party attacked. All killed and wounded but him [in] Santa Rosa Cañon. Guess I'll withhold and not go down yet a while anyhow. Bad, bad business, three killed and two wounded. When will the end be. McMahan wounded, J K was lucky.

Tuesday, August 17, 1886: At work on dup[licate] assessment roll book today for Board of Supervisors, footing up the tax. Saw Nick, M's old horse, today. Seems to be recovering. Mary Ryan married tonight. Stebbins told me today in case he was elected County Treasurer he would like me in the office with him if possible. No pledges made. Judge Mitchell will soon come out as delegate. Hope he'll get it. Casino tonight with Major. Scrapping match at Maison Doree tonight. The Genl and Walker, great times. Curtains down.

Wednesday, August 18, 1886: Completed footing today $108,000 and over. Have another job for tomorrow. Indian excitement today. Heliograph station at Bisbee reported Indians. Dispatch sent to Huachuca, its destination. Soldier showed me the dispatch and I announced myself as ready for the field if necessary. Help asked but dispatch was for post Huachuca, so suppose they complied. Spent evening at Goodfellow's, and at 10 p.m. attended Col Herring's champagne supper at Maison Doree as guest. Meade, Stebbins, Mitchell and Walker on hand. Great times.

Thursday, August 19, 1886: Another day's job comparing rolls. Some changes now make assessment roll close to $112,000 ($111,931.96). I found some defects. Reported to chairman, Board of Supervisors, today and am through. Expect I saved county several hundred dollars. Nothing particularly new on Indian business, some reported around. Rich in cheeks. At Mrs. Benham's a while. Later at Mrs. Stevens, Stebbins also there. A blowy night, no rain. Casino with Mrs. S.

Friday, August 20, 1886: Long talk with Mr. Blinn this a.m. at store. This evening I took Mrs. Benham to call on Mrs. Stilwell, pleasant evening. Joe Pascholy and bride, nee Miss Hayes, arrived this a.m. and tonight Joe turned himself loose at his hotel and we all had a good time in the parlor and outside. Liquid refreshments and cigars were plentiful and music enlivened us all. I sang *Prospector*. Later some of us gave them a chivari [sic] in great style, waking up the whole town and old Judge Peel got on his muscle. Dog upset him, etc. Lots of fun. We fixed hose so that it wouldn't work. Joe had it ready. Later they ran in a cold deck on the old Judge.

Saturday, August 21, 1886: San Francisco pilgrims slowly returning. County Treasurer [A. J.] Ritter scared at false report. Statement in paper of my footings for Board of Supervisors settled matters. At Herring's this evening. Later worried major at casino and got cigars. Very close games.

Sunday, August 22, 1886: Sunday school and church as usual. Have hands full Sunday mornings. Earles arrived on stage this evening, also McDonald. At Mrs. S a while and later at Berry's, where Earles were gathered telling their experiences. Quite a time. Later went to Springer's and had talk with McDonald. S later.

Monday, August 23, 1886: Flies exceedingly bad. Nothing but talk today. Took McDonald to Earle's this afternoon. Mrs. Blinn there and Mrs. Clum. Quite a time. Well, I want to go to California now badly. At Goodfellow's tonight. Casino with Mrs. G.

Tuesday, August 24, 1886: Huneke awoke me this a.m., coming early to house and saying he was off for N.Y. Rather startling news. Goes to St. Louis with McDonald. Wouldn't take anything along. Springer asked me to help him as his books were behind. I went in and got them up. H may return in three or four weeks. Sudden notion. Gave him letter to father. Well, I'm in for a job now, I suppose. Must get some thing more ahead and clear out. Mrs. S is right.

Wednesday, August 25, 1886: The Major (E) full of Los Angeles and San Diego and guess we'll have to migrate. Marvelous stories of fortunes made with limited means, alluring certainly. At work in bank today too. Springer and I agreed today that I would do the work at the low rate of $15 per week, having time for any business of my own and privilege to go away to Cal at any time. Cheap, but work is over three hours daily, I think. Called at Blinn's tonight, first at Earle's.

Thursday, August 26, 1886: Pretty steadily worked today in bank. When I can land in L.A. with $250 clear I think I shall go and that ought to be some time next month. Thirty-six years old today. Must never make a break again. Am in full flush of manhood and think that in civilization I can make myself felt. Have close that here and can and will do it elsewhere and where chances won't be so against me. Sad news tonight. Long letters from Milton about an appopletic stroke Mrs. Davis has had and which will probably cause her death. Communicated the sad tidings to Earles, Berrys and Heney. Letter from Huneke tonight—must meet him in California in a few weeks.

Friday, August 27, 1886: Bank work is quite an agreeable and pleasant change. Called at Fremont and 2nd tonight, Hall, Insurance man from San Francisco, is with us. Pleasant and nice looking fellow.

Saturday, August 28, 1886: Quite a lively day's work, bank books wouldn't balance for some time and at two o'clock went to Court House, got Supervisors together and had session till nearly five p.m. Got my bill allowed of $16.50 for services. At Goodfellow's this evening I believe.

Sunday, August 29, 1886: Sunday school and church as usual this a.m. Major read the services. Wrote some this afternoon to Mrs. Annie Lake T and Strallus too, I believe. This evening called upon Mrs. S a while.

Monday, August 30, 1886: Well, I'm let out. [L. M.] Jacobs sent [Albert] Springer word that times were too caulky to have help, that he must do his own work. Springer told me though of another possible job. Primaries today and considerable excitement at elections for delegates to convention on the 13th. I was present at Court House to see fair play for J. Montgomery, candidate for Sheriff at his request. Am afraid there is a majority of delegates elected adverse to him. At Herring's a while tonight. Numerous rumors about old Geronimo. I had the most reliable information though for the second time.

Tuesday, August 31, 1886: Had an offer this a.m. through Springer to go to Fairbank for Katzenstein at about $125, but declined as I am determined now to go to Cal and am going, although it is quite possible that the Geronimo business is nearing an end from what General [G. A.] Forsythe told me this afternoon. Had quite a long talk with the General whom I like very much. Sent word to S.F. *Call* tonight through Brook of *Epitaph* that I would go to the front for them if wired and report the Indian Apache business. Wrote Huneke enclosing letter from Sudulmeyer and Scott of Arkansas City on Crable matter. Bade Cheyneys and Mrs. Goodfellow adios, one goes to Kansas and other to California tomorrow a.m.

Wednesday, September 1, 1886: Diphtheria bad, three deaths in a day of little ones. Yesterday I went with Major who read burial service over a little one on Allen St. near 9th, Washbourne, while I made responses. Good game of whist last night. Well, the end of this month must see me in Cal. We shall see. Practiced guitar, read Spanish and wrote Mrs. Redfern this afternoon. Saw Mrs. Stevens this evening and later cards at office.

Thursday, September 2, 1886: Flies fearful. Wrote out some revenue papers for Andrew Yerger this a.m., Ramsey Canyon. Mrs. Davis is dead, died the night of the day Clapp last wrote me; am sorry for them all. At Herring's this evening. Miss H and Mrs. H were together in sweet companionship. No company for them this time.

Friday, September 3, 1886: Rushed around yesterday and made a little off indigent witness. Terribly hard scratching now. Nothing doing. Am too late to report on the Geronimo business now I'm afraid. Whist at office tonight. In fact quite often in evenings.

Saturday, September 4, 1886: Cool weather too, quite. Put in my time quite steadily—music, and Spanish. Nothing else to do. Getting monotonous. Old Geronimo probably corralled this time, though I don't count it sure until he is disarmed and fixed so that he cannot get away.

Sunday, September 5, 1886: Sunday school and service as usual. Mr. Haskins coming back soon to stay by the camp. Returns on missionary fund $50 per month and goes to Phoenix, Tucson, etc., scattering. Wrote home enclosing Grandma's letter written to me 35 years ago and Bagnall's kind letter, both of which I prize very much. At Goodfellow's a while this evening where were Mrs. Stevens, Stebbins and Walker.

Monday, September 6, 1886: Cummings reports mill jumped by petty Mexican officials. Am trying hard to find a horse for tomorrow's trip to Sonora. Must get off if possible as Don José María Elias and family and the new custom collector now in town will go then. I can pass over the line all O.K. Can't find a horse or mule in town yet, stables or elsewhere. Great time at hotel tonight. Called on Elias outfit. Mr. and Mrs. Prescott also there. Music, dancing, Sandilla, etc. Watermelon weighed 90 lbs.

Tuesday, September 7, 1886: J V[ickers] returned tonight well and hearty. Well, [Barton J.] McGrew I met this a.m. who told me he had a fine horse at his ranch which he would rent me at $1.50 per day, cheaper than the livery here, and as I had never been to his ranch at the Whetstones I prepared to start at one p.m. Waited around till between seven and eight p.m. when we finally started and when within 10 miles of ranch, 27 miles distant, discovered that a blanket and coat, his, as he then supposed, had dropped overboard. Returned few miles not finding it. I insisted on going all the way back and we found them just where I thought and said, on last hill. Returned to within four or five miles of town. Then pulled out again and reached ranch between one and two a.m. Narrow escape from an upset once. Bad mud hole.

Wednesday, September 8, 1886: A rather pretty ranch location. Felt rather broken up for a long ride so didn't start today. The Pitos here. Mac Pito and I went for a deer hunt today. Shortly after separating at base of mountains a terrible rain and hail storm caught us. Have been in many storms but this took the cake. A small scrub oak partly protected me from the fury of the storm which was a quite unprecedented one in that the hail stones grew to be cakes of ice which pelted me most unmercifully. Couldn't get away although I changed trees once. One cake hit me in the forehead hurting considerably. A whole hour this pelting continued until things began to look serious. Finally the hail stopped and we joined each other on a common trail and reached home through the rain. Cards this evening.

Thursday, September 9, 1886: Of course the horse had to be hunted this a.m. and it was 11 o'clock before I was in the saddle. Horse was hurt some in hind foot by rope when caught, but Mac said that he was all O.K., although I told him of my long trip. A ride I'll remember, nearly if not quite 60 miles to Custom House. Horse an easy trotter. After leaving Charleston where I lunched twice and where now are eight men, a deserted village and once so populous, I was caught in a hard rain storm and horse wandered off road during storm. Knew country well and cut across to Crystal Springs, arriving about dark. Deserted, sad memories here. Pushed on. At Hereford old John brought me a drink. Didn't like to dismount I was so broken up. At Ochoaville found Dougherty camped. Dismounted and rested a while. Badly shaken and very sore. Very hard time rest of way. Arrived at 11:30 and could hardly stand. Looked after horse and got bed; no sleep or very little.

Friday, September 10, 1886: Good care taken of horse. Having a Mexican brand he was passed all O.K. An American horse though, I believe. Very sore this a.m. Well, didn't feel obliged to be constantly on the qui vive for Indians. Quite a change. Struck Sonora river about four, met Jeff Bickerton a little later with Mexican on way to Arizona with ore. Found Hohstadts at Masons. Pushed on to mill after dropping gun and blanket and arrived before sundown. Found 50 or more Mexicans camped at it and thought surely enough it was jumped, but they proved to be Jeff's outfit from Campus with ore on burros. Knew some of them. Found mill in much better shape than expected. Grease preserved [it] from rust. Indians only took tent, at times they roughed up old man H.

Saturday, September 11, 1886: Stopped a while last evening at Bill Miller's on return trip from mill, where I staid ³/₄ of an hour, and staid quite awhile at Bill's where were Johnnie Rankin and an American farming near Bacuachi. Quite a chat with the boys and I found how the land lay. Staked horse out last night. Quite a crowd at Bonerang's old place. Two Masons, Dick H and cousin John, and rest of family. This a.m. had a long talk with Johnnie Hohstadt and offered him a ¹/₂₀ interest in mill if he would act as agent and look after it. He accepted and I gave him a paper simply and only appointing him an agent with the elder Mason as witness to signature. Made two copies and brought away one. Reached the Custom House in good season. Very satisfactory arrangement for me about the mill. I am very well pleased with all I've done so far.

Sunday, September 12, 1886: Don José María Elias presented me with a fine bottle of mescal. A bad beginning makes a good ending they say. I am much pleased at all I've been able to do. People in Sonora feeling happy over Geronimo's capture. I had quite a reception at the Mexican Custom House last night. Elias and Señorita Rosita, another young lady and several older ones, Señor Carrillo, the collector, and several assistants. Quite a time. Music, etc, some fine mescal tambien. They made me sing *La Paloma* and *Las Companillas*. Guitar not a good one. Rode on wagon with Max Marks at whose place I put up, to or near Clanton's today and rode in horseback from there via Bassett mine, scaring a fellow in brush off of road by shooting revolver. He put spurs and lit out.

Monday, September 13, 1886: Had quite a reception. No McGrew so attended to horse last night and he was all O.K., but this a.m. he was very stiff in his fettick just where hurt previous to my departure and McGrew was hot until I told him all I did, where I went and care taken of his horse. I rode 175 miles in four days, big riding, but he knew I was going too, and bragged heavily about his horses. Republican convention met today which was reason I wanted to be here. Great times. Hatch finally nominated after a long struggle. Am afraid Stebbins will be left, of course, I will then be too. Called at Mrs. Stevens. Convention in session until 11 p.m.

Tuesday, September 14, 1886: Convention at it again today. Steb was left as expected, so my deputyship vanishes. Was hoping for that and to be clerk of Board of Supervisors. Cal only place for me now. Did some work for Col. Clark today in CountyTreasurer's office. Convention made some poor nominations. Am glad Stilwell was nominated. Think he'll get there. A pleasant gathering at Major Earle's tonight in honor of Gages.

Wednesday, September 15, 1886: At work for Col. Clark today on assessment lot business. Looking out for horse too as McGrew and JV went out to the Whetstones today. Called at Herring's tonight. First at Goodfellow's but didn't see Miss G, probably through Chinaman's stupidity.

Thursday, September 16, 1886: Democratic Convention today. A strong ticket nominated but the Irish are very mad and fun may be expected as they were badly left. Great excitement. Douglass shot and killed Luistnum this afternoon early. Talk of lynching tonight particularly so as people are aggravated by acquittal of the murderer [A. H.] Davis at Tucson. Well, I must get out and away now. Called on Mrs. Benham this evening.

Friday, September 17, 1886: In court today, County Court for Col. Clark testifying as to value of Pasqual Nigro's property. Col. Herring tried beautifully to down me unsuccessfully. Called on Mrs. Stevens tonight. Vickers wishes me to remain until Major Bayless returns from Kansas where he goes next week to marry a daughter, so I suppose that it will be 1st to middle of Oct. now before I can get off. Major Earle may go with me, also Vickers. Blow out at Blinn's. I am now rather old for young folks and young for old folks and get left.

Saturday, September 18, 1886: Marked all of my clothes this a.m. Nothing new today. Major E is through on the 1st. Guess there will be a party of us leaving for Cal next month. Pleasant call upon Miss Goodfellow this evening. Whist later. Ben Cook and I cleaned on Major and Professor.

Sunday, September 19, 1886: Sunday school and church services as usual, 26 scholars. Wrote Miss Bessie, Sam, Maurice and Huneke this afternoon. Dined at Judge Berry's and Mrs. Stilwell this evening. Little Caro [Caroline Clum], my god daughter, is a pretty bright little thing and we're great friends.

Monday, September 20, 1886: [M. M.] Sherman has showed up and is off again. Great arguments today on recent decision of U.S. Supreme Court respecting townsite and mining claims. Fields delivering, that where nature of land is known, if mineral, it is exempt from townsites, preemption or homesteading. Meeting this evening at Herring's to discuss propriety of church entestancy.

Tuesday, September 21, 1886: Up earlier than usual. [William H.] Bayless left this a.m. for Highland, Kansas, to marry off his daughter and to be gone three weeks probably.* Mrs. Vickers and entire family also left for Freeport, Ill. Major looks after them as far as Kansas City. *Epitaph* a little premature this a.m. about my going. Mrs. Stevens sick with scarlet fever. At Mrs. Herring's this evening. Miss Sarah and I were ahead at whist. I have to camp at office so as to protect it as much as possible, three safes.

Wednesday, September 22, 1886: Had a pretty rough night of it last night at office. Mosquitoes very bad. A party of nearly 20 left this a.m. early for Ft. Huachuca returning tomorrow via Tanner's Canyon. Possibly I can combine forces with Tweed, Stebbins will see, $2000 isn't to be sneezed at although I want to leave badly and my friends are giving no sendoffs. *Democrat* was particularly pleasant. Mrs. S better. Called tonight.

Thursday, September 23, 1886: Mosquitoes very bad last night, no sleep scarcely. Collecting very poor, town going, bad showing. Party returned this evening from Huachuca. At Charleston they had a runaway and Annette ran good chance of being killed. Little injury fortunately. Annette plucky. At Goodfellow's tonight. Quite a time after a rat which was finally killed, thought supposedly dead before. Seemed to play possum. Cribbage with Miss G, Doc looked interesting in pajamas and plug hat going for the rat.

Friday, September 24, 1886: Am quite busy looking after renters. Coin very scarce. Hard work to collect any. Have people well in hand now. Called on Mrs. Benham tonight. Quite a talk with her. She goes East very shortly. Precious little sleep nights, mosquitoes are fearful.

Saturday, September 25, 1886: Another dose of mosquitoes; get probably three hours sleep a night now, consequently don't feel very brilliant in the mornings. Wrote up all minutes of Board of Supervisors this afternoon. Qute a job. Go to Earle's tonight. Pleasant time, progressive euchre. Took the Herrings; called at Blinn's first.

Sunday, September 26, 1886: Little sleep, mesquitoes very bad. Sunday school and church as usual. This afternoon wrote letters, Mrs. Bartlett, Milton and Schlaet. Called upon Mrs. Stevens tonight. Also at Blinn's to say adios as they start for California tomorrow.

Monday, September 27, 1886: Coin getting scarcer every day; got in some today. Had Ben Titus's netting last night and had a sleep. None in town, netting. Bought Gil Blas today, fairly cheap copy in Spanish. Blinns got off today for Cal. called at Reppy's tonight and found Mrs. Berry and Annette there, both of whom I took home later.

*A self-proclaimed Parsons' Boswell states that George Parsons "did not know William H. Bayless." Here is proof that Parsons did indeed know William H. Bayless, who attended the marriage of his daughter Cora to Ed Vinsonhaler in Highland, Kansas. This expert should read what he claims to have transcribed, as well as consult the Bayless family papers at the Arizona Historical Society and the article by Dawn Moore Santiago, "Charles H. Bayless: Educator, Cattleman, Businessman, and Banker," *The Journal of Arizona History*, Vol. 35, No. 3, Autumn 1994, pp. 367-300.

Tuesday, September 28, 1886: Like pulling hen's teeth to get any money out of people these times. Collecting bad. Met Lieut. [Harry C.] Benson at Earle's tonight. Met him on the Mexican border for first time several weeks ago fresh from the Geronimo chase. Camp at office every evening.

Wednesday, September 29, 1886: Earthquake predicted by Wiggins didn't show up today. Still at it collecting. Old Granville Johnson, the jest of the town, disturbs me every a.m. early. The dog Poindexer, is aboard once more and the slaughter is quite gratifying to me. I like a good dog but these casses are detestable. Will Gird got away this a.m. for Sonora with a mule well loaded; goes directly to La Bota. Some cards this evening with Mrs. Stevens. Doesn't seem to be well of late. Mrs. Clark arrived this evening and I called, looks well. Mrs. Bartlett and Mrs. Goodfellow at Hotel Belmont.

Thursday, September 30, 1886: Well nothing new. Trying to collect as usual. Hard work. White arrived from Oakland tonight. Called on Miss Goodfellow this evening. Quite a talk. We don't agree very well on views of life and Christ's life. Quite a banking business today. Made some Mexican silver business and a profit.

Friday, October 1, 1886: Vickers and White drove to ranch today and I had my hands full today, it being the first of month. [M. M.] Sherman and Carroll also started for Sonora. S has bought out C below Nacosari, the San Rafael ranch, and has a good thing. Wish I could do likewise. Perhaps I can, who knows? At Herring's a while this evening after business all over. Restreet and Cheyney there. Bill and Major are let out of the CH&T Co—corporation thanklessness.

Saturday, October 2, 1886: Runaway this a.m. past office. Horse attached to a hand truck. I ran out pen in one hand and a check in other and held horse by head after he fell a moment later until he was cut loose. Was sorry for the poor brute. Criminal carelessness on part of a Chinaman. At office all evening.

Sunday, October 3, 1886: Cloudy in a.m. and rainy in p.m. and hard rain till late into night. JV and White returned late this evening wet and hungry. Sunday school and church as usual this a.m. Thin attendance at both. Spent evening at office reading. Let Mrs. Berry test some good old mescal this a.m. which I had to see what it is like.

Monday, October 4, 1886: Office somewhat like a hunter's cabin with the bear, lion, and coyote scalps sent in for rewards by Board of Supervisors, $25 lion, $10 bear and $25 coyote. Smell not pleasant, particularly with regard to a bear scalp received through mail last night. Had to throw it under the safe. Pretty loud. Called on Mrs. Stevens this evening. At Mrs. Clark's this evening a while.

Tuesday, October 5, 1886: At it today collecting as usual. Long letter from father tonight speaking of Rector Haskins visit and his desire for me to become connected with the Copper Queen which is to start up ere long upon an enlarged scale. They expect to do something as well for the moral welfare of Bisbee. Cards at office every evening.

Wednesday, October 6, 1886: Same old thing every day. Milt Queener, Nacosari blacksmith, in town and talking about buying mill. Two years since I've seen him. Old Moulton is at or near Hermosillo. Went to Berry's with White this evening, later to Earle's. Annette distinguished herself by accidentally discharging rifle in house and frightening everyone. Second recent exploit of her's, runaway and this. Fine whist at office.

Thursday, October 7, 1886: Coin very scarce; hard work to collect it. At it hard today. Called on Miss Goodfellow this evening. Doc G has more cheek than any man in town. He packed off my guitar to Huachuca today.

Friday, October 8, 1886: A party on hand for tonight and I am supposed to pack a number there. A very successful affair all around, goodly number, fine floor, good music, excellent supper and everything fine. The Bs did well. I took Mrs. Pito as her husband couldn't go and saw Mrs. Street home. Up till very late, between two and three sometime.

Saturday, October 9, 1886: Out in the hills this a.m. with Howe helping in the Old Guard survey. On the ground and carrying chain at nine a.m. Pretty warm. The Old Guard is to be patented at last. Calves a little sore from last night's dancing. Some lively getting around today. Board of Supervisors adjourned tonight until Nov. 10th.

Sunday, October 10, 1886: Sunday school as usual, but church unusual, as reading the service and carrying it though devolved upon me. I got through with it though in good shape and was complimented upon my reading. Wrote Mrs. Kip today and this evening heard Rev. Adams at Methodist Church try to explain the faith and works matter of James and Peter. Guess its all right.

Monday, October 11, 1886: Weather cooling these days. Lively getting about today. Nothing new. At Herring's this evening where were Mrs. Cheyney and Sullivan. Boys and girls euchre and we were badly left. Miss Mamie [Herring] to be married to Casey Clum the 20th it is said.

Tuesday, October 12, 1886: JV preparing today for a Sonora trip with Charlie Smith and S Cheyney, to be gone 10 days to two weeks, thus leaving me alone again.

Wednesday, October 13, 1886: JV got away this a.m. with Sam Cheyney and Charlie Smith for the Sonora river and Carroll's now Sherman's ranch, ostensibly to see the country, hunting trip, etc. Really to see some ranch property I put them on to. Wish I could improve some of my opportunities. All alone again. At Miss Goodfellow's this evening.

Thursday, October 14, 1886: Three exercises today, fellow who thought identification unnecessary for payment of check, Riley who thought I should draw warrant on County in JV's absence, and a dame who thought me disagreeable because I detained her till I got the coin. Great time this evening at the Occidental reliving Cap. Lawton's capture of old Geronimo. Stand erected and Cap. L, Cap. [Leonard] Wood and Lieut. R had all something to say and said it in few words and to the point. Herring and Robinson expatiated at length, also Stilwell. I liked Cap. Lawton's face and his plain "Thank you Sir" when I shock his hand and spoke a word. He's a fine specimen of vigorous manhood.

Friday, October 15, 1886: Today I looked up a job for myself with Board of Supervisors after my time is out here, viz: preparing for administering property of county passed to Supervisors by County Treasurer. Made preliminary arrangements.

Saturday, October 16, 1886: More preliminarying today with Col. Herring. Seems as though it was a terrible job and no clear understanding of its requirements. Got down to cases though I think now. Mr. Haskins arrived tonight and I was very glad to see him. Looks well. After closing office went down to Earle's and saw him, etc. Accompanied him home.

Sunday, October 17, 1886: Sunday school and church as usual. On hand a good congregation, about 50. Mr. Haskins was good as usual. He returns as missionary with extended jurisdiction reaching to Phoenix and Tucson, if not further. Mr. Haskins at office some time this afternoon. Prescott in and we all had quite a talk. This evening called on Mrs. Stevens, Stebbins on hand. Church people are very blighty and fainthearted.

Monday, October 18, 1886: Pleasant so far as temperature is concerned, but very windy and dusty. Farrell in town, politics probably. Sent Miss Mamie a pretty little book finely covered, *London Lyrics*, by Locker. Old parchment style and much admired by her when I called this evening to pay my respects. Spent very pleasant evening, our last before her marriage on Wednesday to which I am invited and am almost the only "young" outsider.

Tuesday, October 19, 1886: Some lively getting around today. Finally got paper O.K. for Territory property sale. Called upon Mrs. Reppy this evening and had a very pleasant call.

Wednesday, October 20, 1886: The great event transpired today. At seven a.m. at Herring's home Miss Mamie and Casey were joined in wedlock by Rev. Haskins. It was an early hour but all guests were on hand except Judge and Mrs. M who were two minutes late. Quite a number were on hand. No young folks except Frank E and Annette. Flowers abundant. The sun shone in at its splender upon the two as they knelt in the SE corner of the room. Rice and old shoes followed the carriage a distance. Fine wedding breakfast. Later at office Mr. Haskins and I had a long and confidential talk about my going to Bisbee in capacity of moral maker, etc. I don't know what else to call it and mean no disrespect. W. E. Dodge* wishes someone there to look after the men's morals and I am wanted to go there.

*This is Presbyterian William E. Dodge, who with Anson G. Phelps, formed Phelps, Dodge & Company which involved itself in general mercantile trade, lumber, the manufacture of cop-

I want to do all the good I can and want money too, so don't know about this, but Mr. H proposes to write Dodge about me. Two men killed today, one in Bisbee; Giant powder. At Earle's and Haskins tonight.

Thursday, October 21, 1886: Enough rain to settle dust. Coin very scarce in town. Skirmishing today. Believe I called on Mrs. S this evening. No signs of JV or Bayless yet. Worked on deed today.

Friday, October 22, 1886: Got in some coin today and can meet drafts all O.K. now I think. A pleasant evening at Mrs. Eccleston's who had a progressive euchre party for the young folks and I was included and asked to take Miss Sarah Herring, which I did. Worked on deeds today.

Saturday, October 23, 1886: Great times today; paid Major Davis quite a draft and had circus with the old man. Great Republican day. Bean on hand tonight with lesser lights and spoke an hour and a half lacking a few minutes, telling a plausible story. My vote goes for Mark though this time. Bean himself says that it makes no difference whether Demo or Rep goes as delegate. Worked later to get near the end of the Treasurer's deed business.

Sunday, October 24, 1886: Sunday school and church as usual. Mrs. Mitchell being unable to come longer, I now take over class of boys in connection with my other duties. Communion for the first time in a good while. At Berry's and Earle's a while. Took Miss Etta [Henrietta] Herring to church tonight; first evening service of season; thinly attended. Later at Miss Goodfellow's where was also Mrs. Stevens; bought daisies in high spirits and quite giddy. Called also on Clark's.

Monday, October 25, 1886: Busy; finished finally the interminable deeds and have them now ready for publication. Spent this evening at Springer's till quite late. Casino, Russian, beer, etc. Quite a time.

Tuesday, October 26, 1886: Hard at it today on tally lists for election, very tedious work. Worked tonight on the lists till late. Am having my hands full now with Vickers' business and these private rackets, these two, the deeds and tallys. With everything I ought to do very well this month.

Wednesday, October 27, 1886: JV, Sam C and Charlie finally arrived this a.m. from Sonora. Had gone to Oposura and into the mountains about. Hard work tonight on tally list. Completed altogether 44 by or before midnight; 40 names of candidates have to be written between 50 and 60 times besides the certificate on back of each which is quite extensive.

Thursday, October 28, 1886: Jeff Bickerton back from S.F. Gave him an order for M and my quicksilver if he could find it. He thought it was in Cumpas. After all business was ended I worked again tonight till late on

per and brass ware, and eventually copper mining in Arizona. In 1881 they purchased the Atlanta claim in the Mule Mountains. Acquisition of the adjacent Cave and Copper Prince claims formed the basis of the great Copper Queen Mine.

the tally lists and finally completed them and felt pretty good over the completion as it was a very unpleasant job.

Friday, October 29, 1886: At my old work after collecting today, copying minutes into the Board of Supervisors' minute book. Nothing entered since my last entries. In fact, I seem to have run most of the business since 29th of last July. Dined at Herring's this evening. Present only the young ladies and Miss Annette. A nice dinner, singing, candy racked in which I got the most of it and a good time. Lots of fun.

Saturday, October 30, 1886: Business for Springer and Mrs. Jacobs this a.m. Finally invited Mrs. J, Colgrove cabin. Had some other business for her with Major Earle which I consummated this evening and then went to Schieffelin Hall and heard the tail end of Mark's speech. Good one. Blinn good but too long. Democrats away ahead this year. Much better men than Republicans and they'll get my vote. Ben Goodrich waxed hostile against Stilwell tonight, in fact, was needlessly very warm.

Sunday, October 31, 1886: Sunday school and church this a.m. as usual. It is good to have preaching again, small attendance. At service tonight and I took Miss Birdie Herring. Am getting the family there one by one by slow degree. Major arrived this evening so my service is ended for J V Vickers and I took home my traps tonight and slept in my own house. Called on Miss Goodfellow a while.

Monday, November 1, 1886: Everybody all excited. Election tomorrow; great rushings around, etc. Republicans had mass meeting tonight when Stilwell replied to Ben Goodrich in a gentlemanly manner. Not as much enthusiasm. Huneke and McDonald at last turned up tonight, all well and hearty. Am to be clerk of 1st ward tomorrow for city. At Mrs. Stevens to-night but a very little while and guess it will be sometime before I'm there again.

Tuesday, November 2, 1886: The County and City election opened briskly this a.m. and continued pretty lively all day. Was at my post on time and knowing so many was instrumental in keeping out some illegal votes. Spanish helped me some too, as Mexicans now thick in our ward. We stopped all funny business early in the day and consequently were not much bothered. Out of 40 candidates I voted only five or six Republicans and most of us having the County's good at heart voted the same way. We had 161 voters in our ward. Finished at 7:30 or 8. Indications are that Democratic ticket is largely ahead.

Wednesday, November 3, 1886: Boys still counting today into the night. Bracewell has got it and I am glad. He is our next delegate to Congress. Good enough. He's at the top now. Mr. Blinn is all O.K. also. Stilwell is left for which I am sorry, also Hatch for Sheriff. [John] Slaughter is ahead. Quite lively today. No bad business though, today nor yesterday. Well, things are squared now. Two years ago the Democrats stood in with the Republicans for the best men and this time the positions are reversed.

Thursday, November 4, 1886: Nothing new. Huneke seems to have lost money in wheat; is going below with McDonald and the chances are that he will be in Mexico another year; so I'll have to move without him. One bad piece of news. This evening I called at the hotel on the Elias and Señorita Rosita. El Señor Juez Pujol was there. Quite a chat with McDonald and Huneke.

Friday, November 5, 186: Well, Mr. Haskins has heard from Mr. Wm Dodge of NY City about me and he seems to be favorably impressed, especially so as Mrs. Willie Kip is at his house and of course is talking me up as she and I are the best of friends. He wants me at Bisbee and if Mr. D will pay enough, I'll go. Am to invite him tomorrow. Wedding passed off in good shape. I was usher. Geo. A. Metcalf and Bessie Tolman were married at church at 8 p.m. Home of Eccleston later and after that I went to Herring's where Sam Cheyney, R and S were and we had a great time till very late.

Saturday, November 6, 1886: Talked with Beau de Zart today about Sonora and my properties there and he wants to make a trip and see what there is in the gold mine and mill. Dined at Berry's and had a fine dinner and lots of fun. The Herring girls there and I took them home later. This evening committee on the farce met at Mrs. Mitchell's and I was cast for one of the two male characters, but as I'm going away cannot, of course, act. Went for at Willis.

Sunday, November 7, 1886: Sunday school and church as usual a.m. and p.m. A Mr. Bliss of Chicago at church today, a very pleasant gentlemen, attorney for Field Lieter & Co., Chicago. At Goodfellow's this evening to see Miss G, wish her a pleasant trip to Ft. Huachuca, where she goes on Tuesday.

Monday, November 8, 1886: Went over the business today with Beau de Zart and party arranged to go to Nacosari and Sonora river in a day or two. Got on to a school warrant today in which there may be $25. At Major E's a while, Mr. Bliss there. I wrote Mr. Wm. E. Dodge tonight at 11 Cliff St., N.Y. City, on a matter of interest between Mr. Haskins, Mr. Dodge and myself respecting doings at Bisbee. Also wrote Mrs. Clapp.

Tuesday, November 9, 1886: Not able to get away today. No mules. Spent afternoon in getting estimates for repairing the new rectory. At Major's this evening a while and had quite a talk with Mr. Bliss again, who is a very pleasant gentlemen. Is here I expect on the Gage business. Spent balance of evening at Herring's.

Wednesday, November 10, 1886: No mules yet. Hoping to get off tomorrow morning. Beau de Zart's this evening, pleasant time. Took Miss Miller around; progressive euchre. I was a blanket coat, had considerable fun   won
over it. I took the chief gentleman's prize. Some fun at the hotel later.

Thursday, November 11, 1886: A few cents only in the warrant business. called with Miss Miller on Mrs. Beau de Zart this evening. Prospects not very favorable for getting off. Drove down to Charleston this afternoon with Geo. Cheyney to try to find some mules. Walked up ditch, got muddled and mad and nothing in it.

Friday, November 12, 1886: Nothing new. Will now wait until Monday to see about a mule team of Carr's. Called this evening on Mrs. Pito and we had some good music. First, however, there was a meeting of church trustees at Major Earle's and I reported on passage or victory, having gotten an estimate of necessary repairs. Geo. Cheyney, Staunton, Major E and I present.

Saturday, November 13, 1886: The Riggs murder trial occupied general attention today and I was interested spectator the most of it. Baldridge wants to lease the Black Top.

Sunday, November 14, 1886: Sunday school and church as usual a.m. and p.m. Sunday school attendance very slim; things getting worse, very little doing. Dined at Blinn's today; Mrs. B and Meade. This evening persuaded Mrs. Clum to go to church as she hadn't heard Haskins, and John P. staid at home with the baby.

Monday, November 15, 1886: Riggs jury discharged this a.m., no agreement: nine acquittal, one manslaughter, and two conviction.* Wrote Stanley on Black Top matter tonight. At Board of Supervisors today contending for rebate of tax on Corella house, as it is church property. The attorney sided with me. Got my bill through too all right.

Tuesday, November 16, 1886: A cold snap is upon us, very cold. Water froze in my room tonight and I half froze. Rustled around on warrants today and made a very little. Took constable to house today to estimate and he is cheaper. Rectory I mean. Rehearsal of wax works tonight at Schieffelin Hall. Am wanted for the door. Took home the Herrings. Mrs. Street was in and we had tea and talk and a great time. Pomeroy of Tucson on hand, so looked after him tonight.

Wednesday, November 17, 1886: Had to crawl into my blanket coat tonight. Very cold and disagreeable. A good warrant transaction today. A musical evening at Pitos. Mrs. Prescott sang well. Took around guitar.

Thursday, November 18, 1886: Went out to Prieto's ranch today and did what I could. Guess I'll have to turn it over to J.V. Congratulated Mrs. Bartlett upon the birth of her daughter. Born the 2nd I think. Rehearsal tonight "Frank Wilde" and "Wax Works," very good. Letter from father last night. He's working up a mining scheme with possibilities of trip to England for me.

---

*Barney Kemp Riggs, a nephew of rancher Brannick Riggs, shot and killed Richmond L. Hudson on September 29, 1886, near Dos Cabezas. He was sentenced to life imprisonment on December 31, 1886. Instrumental in saving the life of prison superintendent Thomas Gates, he was pardoned by Governor C. Meyer Zulick on December 21, 1887, on the condition that Riggs "leave the territory forthwith, and never return thereto."

Friday, November 19, 1886: Up late. Haskins back. Miss G goes direct to California from Huachuca probably. Harvey Johnson told me this a.m. in Co. Hospital that I was a successful man. He meant that for purity and character. It's pleasant to hear. Well, the event came off tonight and was a great success financially as well as otherwise. I acted as money and ticket taker at door and took in $44 and 120 tickets. More to hear from. Will clear probably $75, expenses $31.

Saturday, November 20, 1886: Helped gather up and take home the things at the theatre, Schieffelin Hall, this a.m. I have quite decided to discontinue visiting a while Mrs. S for very good reasons. I appeared before Board of Supervisors this afternoon and finally now my point exemption of tax of the Corella property near the rectory. Paid my taxes today. County $4. Saved $26.11 on rectory by dint of considerable work. At Peto's this evening. Mrs. Prescott sang sweetly. Mrs. Bagg a good talker. Prescotts leave in a day or two for Santa Barbara.

Sunday, November 21, 1886: One of the dirtiest, windiest and altogether most disagreeable days on record. Sunday school and church as usual. Very few at church tonight. Hardly a corporal's guard and only 13 at Sunday school in a.m. Too bad a day. Cold too.

Monday, November 22, 1886: Disagreeable still. Cloudy and cold. Took Ulmer to rectory today to estimate. Two invitations Thanksgiving Day. Will go to Earle's; Berry other. Mrs. Cheyney's birthday. Took over there this evening Mrs. Berry, Mrs. Earle, Miss Miller and Annette.

Tuesday, November 23, 1886: Geo. Cheyney offered me a chance this a.m. to go over to Oro Blanco for the TM&M Co. and superintend and look after some work on a mine of their's. Accepted; can't wait on Beau de Zart to exclusion of profitable business. Will take several weeks or more. Will go Friday or Monday. Caught on jury tonight by Bob himself. Called on Mrs. S and Mrs. McNeil this evening. Mrs. McN just back.

Wednesday, November 24, 1886: Bright and cold today. Too strong an opinion in the Douglass murder trial, so didn't sit; dismissed. Corralled a lot of jury certificates, 16, mine making 17, picked them up at 8:50. Lively and hard work.

Thursday, November 25, 1886: Attended services at 10 a.m. at our church. The Methodists invited with us and Rev. Pearson assisted in the chancel, a sight I was very glad indeed to witness. He made a few slips owing to remissiveness. Mr. Haskins made a very fine address indeed. Dined at Earle's where were also Rector Haskins and Mr. and Mrs. Metcalf. A very pleasant dinner party. In the evening the matrons' party took place which was a decided success everyway. I had to bring the music though, part of it being "very tired." Chief musician, got things started finally. Old fashioned dances.

Friday, November 26, 1886: Cleared away the debris this a.m. and had quite a job. Court met again today. Not much to be made these days.

Called upon Mrs. Clum this evening at Mrs. Castle's, Clark's a while I think. Will have to leave for Arivaca Sunday a.m. I think, as stage seems to run only once a week. John H., C and Dan O'Connor are in San Bernardino where they seem to be doing well in stamp [mill] business. Called on Mrs. Blinn this evening.

Saturday, November 27, 1886: Got myself together today and made arrangements to go tomorrow. Geo C thought I should take 2:50 so got it conveniently changed. Got in some more orders for warrants. Am turning my little capital over as well as I know how. Upward in town, fine fellow. At Herring's a while this evening. Douglass jury finally agreed tonight to murder in 1st degree without death penalty. Statute allows this; D escapes strict justice.

Sunday, November 28, 1886: Left on stage this a.m. [Henry Clay] Hooker, the cattle king, and I having the top seats. Quite pleasant chat with Hooker over my visit to his hot springs and the good times there and people, Shafter, Van Fleet, nee Nugent, etc. On SP met Col. and Mrs. Rouse, U.S. Dist. Atty. and had pleasant time. Genl Adam met me at Tucson and wanted me to go home with him but I preferred the Cosmopolitan. After a wash, spent several hours with him in Col. Wardell's room, where called later B Hereford, Saterwhite and others. Dined with General, attended service at the Methodist Church, rather secular performance.

Monday, November 29, 1886: Started shortly after seven a.m. Buggy and one horse, 68 miles to Arivaca, where arrived about five p.m., making four changes. South 40 miles and west 28. Barboquivari peak to right and about equidistant from Tucson. Passed San Xavier del Bac church on left. Hadn't seen it since Clapp and I walked out there seven years ago nearly. Arivaca an old camp, quite deserted now. On road we passed the famous Sierra [Cerro] Colo[rado] mine and deserted camp, where Col. [Charles Debrille] Poston figured prominently years ago,* also the San Xavier furnace and machinery.** Bad business. Quite an adobe hotel.

Tuesday, November 30, 1886: Indians were very bad even here. Employed Tom Collins and Gus Hacker. Went into the hills with them today, they going for tools and I to see the mines, formation, etc. Went down the Nigritor, belongs to Collins, and found a strong ledge and good one I believe. Arranged to go to the "Montana," my objective point tomorrow.

*In 1856 Charles Poston, Samuel Peter Heintzelman, and Herman Ehrenberg formed the Sonora Exploring and Mining Company. Although headquartered at Tubac, the company acquired the 17,000 acre site known as the Arivaca Grant, which included both prime ranching and mineral land. It was upon this tract that the company's geologists Frederick Brunckow and Charles Schuchard discovered on the southeast side of a large reddish hill (Cerro Colorado) a rich deposit of silver ore that developed into the Heintzelman Mine.

**The San Xavier furnace, three miles north of San Xavier del Bac, was in operation at this time. It was a thirty-ton water-jacket smelter built in San Francisco, which processed copper carbonate from the San Xavier or Pima Mining District. Louis Williams, of Copper Queen fame, was an investor in the enterprise.

Have to operate from here. Oro Blanco, no one with lodgings. Passed another of Poston's camps where thousands had been squandered. Mexican dog took piece out of trouser's leg this p.m. Longed for my six shooter.

Wednesday, December 1, 1886: Got started early and made Oro Blanco O.K., passing Arizona Con mine on left. To OB seven miles. Road not so good here on, fair to Kirkpatrick's. Saw and talked with K, an old resident, good reputation. At bottom of hill stopped and hoofed it in search of Montana. A Mr. McClanahan [J. B. McClenahan] helped me out and I got all monuments and selected place for work on hill top. Blue capping and well stained, about center of claim. Good day's work. Some time after dark before I reached Arivaca and hotel. Seems as though I was doing double assessment on Montana. Wrote Geo. Cheyney in full tonight for tomorrow's stage.

Thursday, December 2, 1886: Somewhat sore today after exertions yesterday. Had a long hunt over hills after stakes yesterday. Got them all with McC's help who is executor of Gratticap's estate. An obliging man. Can't say any more. Met himself and daughter horseback while going for points to Kirkpatrick. Montana a good property, deserves a plant on the ground, smelting proposition, big lead percentage. Loafed heavily today and rested up. Couldn't sleep much last night so sore. Letter from Genl Adam last night, got it this a.m. [Noah W.] Bernard, formerly of Huachuca, runs store here. Read and rested. An American, an Irishman, a Mexican, and a Chinaman had scrap tonight over game of cards while I read at second table.

Friday, December 3, 1886: Took the caballo blanco and rode down to the two mills this a.m. First about a mile [from] town, a dry crusher, 20 stamps; other one, wet crusher, of 10 stamps, another mile beyond and where 80 tons of Montana ore were awaiting treatment. Sampled ore, pulp and tailings, got all points I could, and after return and dinner wrote Geo. Cheyney in full; make a difference of $5000. This going to bed at 8:30 instead of 11:30 doesn't agree with me and the bed is too soft. I don't sleep worth a cent.

Saturday, December 4, 1886: Well, I mounted the caballo blanco this a.m. and in due season reached the Montana, where I found men doing fair work. Rock very hard, blasting much. Some good ore uncovered which I ordered trimmed and left on the hanging wall. Staid too late not arriving till after dark. Returned a new road via ranch of a nice fellow, one Tompkin, across from the "Alaska." Had access to some of Mr. Gratticap's accounts and found that best working percentage at mill was 72%. The 27 tons gave $36 profit. Selected ore. Labor 27% per ton, hauling 11; mill 220. Seems strange that the Idaho is neglected; Alta a mystery. Finished *Secret Despatch* tonight. Russian story with Scottish heros, exciting at times.

Sunday, December 5, 1886: Terribly and oppressively quiet in my exile today. Wrote long letter to sisters and read Nelson on Infidelity, a very strong work, very powerful and I should think all convincing. Will have a copy and a number when I can afford it for distribution amongst certain friends. Will wear my eyes out. Haven't read so in years. Suppose I'll be off for California shortly after return to Tombstone from what Stanley writes. Three white men here and two women. A regular Mexican pueblo.

Monday, December 6, 1886: Must await stage before going out again. May have to stop "Montana" work. It ought to be. Is double assessment. Some mistake. Idaho, a fine claim, is evidently forgotten. Wrote Cheyney about it today, also wrote Col. Clark and Major about mail. Stage in tonight. Nothing from Geo. Cheyney. Note from Genl Adam. The Mexicans had a baile or dance at hotel tonight and had a great time. A new feature to me was the breaking of cascorenes or eggs over the head of a favored partner. Two old dames had them for sale. They are decorated and filled with fine particles of fancy paper. Secured one. Couldn't sleep for the racket. About one a.m. the bucks getting too drunk and noisy. Carmille [Camille Roullier, host of the Arivaca hotel] sent all home.

Tuesday, December 7, 1886: Went out to the mine today carrying five lbs. powder and seven lbs. of meat, besides caps and cigars. Went out in three hours. At Oro Blanco, while resting, discovered horse's sheath bloody. Nothing external. Probably water bad. Hard country on animals, especially mules they say. Water very bad. They boil it for use at the hotel. Otherwise I would have to drink beer or wine. Found McClenahan at mine and with him examined tunnel and cross cuts; 300 to 400 ft of tunnel. Much work done. Ledge left, not followed correctly. Made notes for report. Quite thorough examination. Boys doing well at my shaft. Down eight or nine feet; some good ore. Returned via Idaho and looked at it. Got some rock. Returned over hills, new way. Struck good trail, shorter route by mile or two. A couple of drunks in next room kept me awake tonight. Casino with Camille.

Wednesday, December 8, 1886: Wrote out my report on Montana today. Nice breakfast for a change. Snipe and duck killed by Camille yesterday. If Charley wouldn't pull plasters from his body to showed me and discuss his bodily infirmities my appetite might be better. A good lot of mail in tonight. Letter from Cheyney and telegram. Geo. says I know as much as he and to go ahead although it looks strange. Wrote him about "Idaho" tonight and enclosed my report on the tunnel which is full. Letter from Stanley tonight to effect that I could get $250 to go to California to examine and report on MEC's property. Wrote accepting conditionally and also wrote Col. Clark for M's address.

Thursday, December 9, 1886: Went out to Montana by trail several miles nearer, and near mine met Bartlett, or Hank or Yank as he is called, a case. Quite a chat with him. Boys about as deep as they can profitably work so told them to square up; good showing. Kept on to McClenahan's, about four miles further south and only a couple of miles from the Mexican line. Finally found him in the mountains and he took me all over his gold district which I wished to examine. Seem to be three main lodes here and he has control of about all the locations: the old "Oro Blanco" with extensions St. Louis amd Genevive, the Hardscrabble and Cleveland, the Oro Blanco is famed; much old work done, and Lexington seems to be the best. Mexicans driven away by Americans. Arrastras covered the little flat at one time; $300 from 300 lbs. or a cargo of ore produced. Got samples. Mrs. McC and daughter pleasant. Talked Indians tonight. They had bad time of it. Indians were bad, only 20 miles to Calabasas. This is old Oro Blanco.*

Friday, December 10, 1886: Rained in night last night and I didn't sleep much in my little cabin adjoining house. Rather open. This a.m. we caught horses and visited the Warsaw and Esperanza mines and mills, Esperanza machinery though gone. Fortunes uselessly, wickedly and recklessly wasted here. Very rough, broken country. McClenahan was member of the ill-fated Crabb party, who were executed at Corborca below here perhaps a hundred miles, but after putting up his $40, didn't get away. Says Pesqueira played traitor after having written a contract with Crabb. Treachery rank. McC said he'd have shot Pesqueira on sight. Returned to Montana and got samples from my shaft of some fine ore and directed work on opposite side of ledge, 75 ft distant, to be continued. Shaft looks well and I am pleased. Sampled the tunnel, up raise and chamber and brought quite a lot of samples to Arivaca, leaving More's overcoat at Oro Blano. Brought some gold rock samples too. Nothing in mail tonight.

Saturday, December 11, 1886: This a.m. after breakfast I started a foot with old Joe Robinson to see Wallace's properties several miles north, the old Cal lead now relocated and called Black Bear, and two extensions called Cumberland and Age of Science. Some old workings here too and a little rich rock. Several cross locations and a gold lead. Got samples. Liked the looks of the group for prospects. Water is the great enemy here, you can't go any depth without meeting it. Met a Mr. [A. W.] Unthank at mines whom I saw last night at store. Is an engineer of extended experience in South America, Japan and elsewhere, but near crazy about his prospect. Drops a certainty for a vast uncertainty. Met Mrs. [Amy Price] Bernard at store too last night.

Sunday, December 12, 1886: Talked all forenoon with Bernard at his store, discussing Clum, Stiles and others. Got considerable news. Was shown today and given some samples of rock from the Black Bird, Patrick Powell. Wrote letters today, Mrs. Kip, Geo. Jackson, sister and Major Bayless. Read some Spanish and Nelson on Infidelity. Am much pleased with this work.

*Old Oro Blanco came into existence in the early 1870s when a party of Tucson prospectors located a two to three foot wide gold-bearing vein. Running for 300 feet, the outcrop yielded from $60 to $300 a ton, creating a "first class poor man's mine." The camp blossomed to about forty miners, who processed their ore with twenty-two arrastras. See Tucson *Weekly Citizen*, December 27, 1873, for additional details.

Monday, December 13, 1886: This a.m. I rode with Joe Robertson to see his mine, nine miles distant, near the Sierra [Cerro] Color[ado]. Passed the Dos Gringos, Mentor and Imperial, close together. Nothing much there. At the Blue Bird, R's property, found best showing yet, everything ship shape too; good looking ledge and no water. Went from here to the old Sierra Colorado mine, the scene of Poston's early mining exploits, where stands the wrecks of many holdings. Lord and Williams got a start here 25 or 30 years ago.* Fort and this were connected by road via Arivaca, and an escort of soldiers had to accompany the Supt. everywhere. Met Miller and Ryan chloriding the Root mine close to the Colorado camp. Made a fine line shot at coyote, 500 or 600 ft distant with six shooter. Returned just before dark. Another presence of extravagance.

Tuesday, December 14, 1886: Well, by telegram from Cheyney last night I am elected to spend Xmas in ths God forsaken part of the world. Must grin and bear it as business is business. Am to do assessment on the Idaho now. Went out to Montana this a.m. Didn't find things particularly encouraging at new hole although indications are fair. Will move men on Friday to Idaho and get two more and hurry up the work. Examined Idaho ground thoroughly for monuments and had a tough, rough climb of it over the broken hills and peaks and rough ground. Secured satisfactory evidence of ground though monuments are not marked. On return met Tomkins. He knew me by reputation in Tombstone as a Sunday school man. Was glad to find a man a little interested anyhow in such things. Engaged him for work at Montana and gave him a note to McClenahan. Carried out horseback 17 lbs of meat to the boys.

Wednesday, December 15, 1886: Got off a burro load of provisions and 10 lbs of Giant powder to men at Montana this a.m. Will go out early Friday a.m. and start men on Idaho. Camille Rouillier goes to Tucson tomorrow,. proposes big Xmas dinner. Wrote this up and a letter to Cheyney for $100. Terribly tiresome evenings. Mail in tonight with letter from Adam in Spanish. Has a large gold property he wants me to see and examine, expenses paid.

Thursday, December 16, 1886: Camille got off this a.m. for Tucson. He's a great Frenchman. From Mr. Middleson I learned today that about 25 tons

*Parsons is right here. The mercantile and banking firm of Lord and Williams did get their start at Cerro Colorado. Charles H. Lord, a physician from Boonville, New York, was transferred to Tubac following the Civil War to administer to the needs of army personnel. While there he was offered the position of medical officer to the Arizona Mining Company. Not being able to serve two masters, Lord resigned as contract physician to the army and in August 1865 became superintendent of the mining company. At Cerro Colorado, Lord came in contact with another New Yorker, Wheeler Washington Williams, who managed the mining company's store at Arivaca. When mining faltered, the two men took the store's stock and opened the first wholesale and retail mercantile company in Tucson. The firm grew quickly, engaging in transportation, lumbering in the Santa Ritas, freighting, and then branched into banking, becoming a U.S. depository in 1869. The company failed in fall of 1881.

of ore are on dump and will not be worked. Will not pay them over $4 per ton. Cannot pay expenses. Excellent concentrating proposition, nothing less than 15% lead up to 40. Will average 18 to 25% lead. Row today of words between Williams and McClenahan. Can't even get up a fight here, disgusting. Joe Jefferson could have slept 40 years or more here.

Friday, December 17, 1886: Got off early. Stopped work on Montana and have a fine showing at 2nd shaft. Discouraging at first but men kept at it by my orders and struck good wall and six inches solid mineral. Better than in shaft #1. Am fortunate. Moved men to Idaho and started two tunnels. Gus and Griff Jenkins below shaft and McClenahan and Tomkin over hill to north at old cut. Cullen had to leave on important business. Was sorry as he's a good miner, best in outfit. Started in on mineral almost immediately on tunnel below shaft. Expect to strike it good on the Idaho.* Will finish the Monday after Xmas and take stage for Tucson next day. Won't be sorry to get away. Wrote Cheyney about good luck tonight.

Saturday, December 18, 1886: Read Gil Blas today and killed time as well as I knew how. Considerable antagonism between the McCafferty mill men and miners here. Unfair treatment allegedly [by] latter. Am reading Geo. Rumbaugh's *Mistake*. Pretty fair yarn.

Sunday, December 19, 1886: Propose to write Mr. Haskins, Alston Hayne, Father, Sam and Geo. Jackson today, enclosing a fiver to Sam for Xmas. I wrote the above letters and also others to Mary Whitwell, Joseph Redfern and Mrs. James Smith, father of my dead friend, the Judge, for a photo. Think my correspondece is all up now. Dreadfully boring here. Am practicing reading Spanish. Great book, Nelson on Infidelity. Much interested in it.

Monday, December 20, 1886: Worried the day through somehow till stage time and then there was but one letter for me. Going to bed at 8:30 and 9 don't agree with me. Bad place for malaria here. All a big bottom country and the fever bad at times. Dislike drinking water. Tulles and long grass once abounded but cattle have destroyed it all.

Tuesday, December 21, 1886: Got out to Idaho and found the two faces of tunnels looking well. Had Unthank's compass and located my NW end monuments of which I was not positive before. Claim originally set off by degrees. Some hard work climbing but I found remains of monuments. I was after 32 degree west of N, variation here 13 degrees. Examined Idaho shaft and workings. Found shaft on 40 degree incline about 80 feet to wa-

*It should be mentioned at this point that the Montana and Idaho claims became important mines. They passed into the possession of Louis Zeckendorf, who patented the properties in 1907. A settlement called Montana Camp sprouted at the workings, and on May 1, 1910, a post office was opened, and the community was renamed Ruby, in honor of Mrs. J. S. Andrews, wife of the first postmaster. In 1916 the Montana was leased by Goldfield Consolidated, which extracted $265,000 in gold, silver, and lead in three years. In 1926 the Montana was optioned by Eagle-Picher Company which erected a 400-ton flotation mill. In the years prior to World War II the company extracted $7,000,000 in metals.

ter. Said by McC to be 110 ft. deep. 50 ft. down is a 45 ft. drift S.W. with 25 ft. winze about end of drift. Everything seems to be in ore. Was much surprised. Big thing, looks better grade than Montana. Some hard climbing. Gus with me and we sampled shaft at water level, drift near entrance and in face and bottom of winze. Good galena in both new works.

Wednesday, December 22, 1886: Cullen had to go to Tucson tomorrow so sent him to Phillps at Oro Blanco to make affidavit of work. Wrote out my other affidavit and receipts afterwards and expect balance of funds tonight with which to settle in full on Monday. The $100 arrived tonight by Camille. Paid off Terry Cullen. Terry and I went out into the hills today to the north. Visited Unthank's mine and examined the 400 or 500 ft. tunnel and some of other workings. Must be nearly 1000 ft. of work done. Some rich kidneys. Then saw where Genl Pesqueira camped when driven out of Mexico. Not far from there is the Gold Mint which T.C. claims and proposes to locate me in on it the 1st., 30 or 40 ft of work done. Good looking vein. Brought away a good sample. Pesqueira camped here shortly before the Crabb trouble, probably in 1857. At the Sasabe Custom House is now the party [J. C. Hernandez] who executed the Crabb party. Also saw Conde's mine.

Thursday, December 23, 1886: Letters from Maurice and sister last night. M in charge of a large hotel at Santa Monica, to open the 1st. Wants me to visit him. Writes encouragingly about the gold mine. Party named Shetterbrand has a large gold property near Kirkpatrick's I must try and see, the "Forsaken" mine. Went to see Patsy Power's "Blackbird" this a.m. near the McCaffrey mill. Merely prospects. He and Wallace are two wild Irishmen. W wants $25,000 for his prospects and has come down from $50,000 he says. No developments by either. Sounded Mr. Forman at the mill house on Montana rock. Says it's an excellent concentrating proposition. Will average 20% lead, from $10 to $40. Has battery and pan and settler, samples of 275 tons taken evey $1/2$ hour. Returning I met him on road, stuck. He's moving to Nogales, expects to start assay office. Thinks rock will average over 16%.

Friday, December 24, 1886: Went out to mine today. Got directions to "Forsaken" and finally found it away up on top of a mountain, SE of the "Old Stiff." A big ledge and lots of rock. Flat though. A hard climb. Had a warm invitation by Tomkin who is working on the Idaho for me to take Xmas dinner at his ranch but declined as Camille is expecting me and then too it would be terribly tedious to me in many respects. Am expected though to be present at Xmas tree and SS festival, five or six children at Oro Blanco in evening so will attend that as a S school man. Young T greeted me on return from mine. Asked after Mr. Haskins and talked S school. Seems a bright pleasant fellow. Letter from Rev. Mr. Haskins and Miss Miller tonight. Latter very newsy, also roll of *Epitaphs* which were highly welcomed. Stage late too, much Xmas boxes.

Saturday, December 25, 1886: Perfect weather a month now. Partly compensates for lack of other things. Charlie, Chinaman and cook, got off this a.m. drunk and Camille had to look after the Xmas turkey and goose. He, Joe R and Gus, one of my men, and I comprise the party at dinner. In p.m. I went to Tomkin's ranch and there had a piece of mince pie and some egg nog and we then walked over to Oro Blanco school house, $1^1/_2$ miles distant, where a Xmas tree festival was to be held. Quite a house full. After the opening exercises I was called on for an address and spoke a few words. A Mrs. Searls had gathered the children together and formed a Sunday school class. I said how gratified I was to see this away out here and I held up the Good Book as best adapted for guidance of all, etc. A dog followed me from town and insisted upon sticking close to me all of the time and when the Santa Claus came jumping and shifting my way, the dog went for him and spoke his mind freely. He was a big one too.

Sunday, December 26, 1886: The old horse took me off of trail last night. Got back though shortly after ten, the big dog at my horses head. Wrote probably my last letter from this place today to Strallus. Finished Nelson on Infidelity and must have a copy. It's a wonderful book. Well, my stay, thank goodness, is about over. Tomorrow will finish up things.

Monday, December 27, 1886: This a.m. settled first with Camille and then went out to settle with men, taking Phillips from Oro Blanco; Gus missing and I was hot. Thought dead, I thought dead drunk. Paid the others, got papers settled and returned to hotel about dark. Brought samples of course. Well, am all ready now for town. Joe R got his parties to agree to take $2000 for Black Bird. Unthank on hand till late.

Tuesday, December 28, 1886: Up at daybreak. Mail from Oro Blanco late. At last minute a young surveyor appeared saying his mother was dying, so he had to be taken into the small buggy, making three. Pretty hard yarn I guess as he began to whistle "Sweet Violet" shortly after starting. I left Arivaca in a very bad humor. Stopped at San Xavier church on road back, but than dame wanted a dollar from me and being no sucker and having seen church before, I didn't bite. Took some brick for Miss R, Cosmopolitan. Retired early. Genl Adam came later and I had to dress and go to Furgeson's office to see some gold rock and hear a long description from F.

Wednesday, December 29, 1886: Too close to dining room and hotel being full, I changed to the Russ House. Looked at records today on Alta business. Saw considerable of the General. We dined together at Cosmopolitan. Pretty busy day. Called on Mrs. Bean and daughter and Pomeroy. Found P sick. Also saw Judge Haynes and Stiles. Wrote Terry Cullen and also Phillips for copies of papers.

Thursday, December 30, 1886: Started for home. Train on time. Met Gage and Meade at Benson just in from Steins Pass, the new excitement. Had to fight some for seat on top of stage, but got there. All very glad to see me. Had a hearty welcome.

Friday, December 31, 1886: Dragged samples over to the TM&M Co's office this a.m. Made report to Mr. Cheyney in person, the father, and it was received in a very gratifying manner to me. Some papers misplaced or lost. Can be easily duplicated though. Great times tonight letting out the the old and in the New Year. At Fireman's ball a while looking on. Adios old year. I hope the new will find me differently circumstanced. I hope on and hope ever and believe my day will yet come.

Photographer C. S. Fly took this picture of Santiago McKinn, the captive white boy, in Geronimo's camp. According to observers, McKinn was "absolutely Indianized" and did not want to return to his New Mexican family.

(Westernlore collection)

1887

Saturday, January 1, 1887: Arose late. Commenced calling early and made about 25. Pleasant times. Blinns leave mañana. The day not well observed. Hart's the only place where the custom was duly observed.

Sunday, January 2, 1887: Church and Sunday school as usual. Sunday school attendance slim. At evening service fair attendance. After service Rev. Mr. Haskins and I had an interview with Meade, the Marshal, on a matter of interest to community.

Monday, January 3, 1887: JV came to house this a.m. before I arose and made me an offer to go to San Diego. Was obliged to decline it later as Mr. Cheyney agreed to pay my expenses to see and report upon a mining proposition in southern Cal. Was finely treated by him in my Arivaca and Oro Blanco business. Wrote Stanley I had accepted another offer. So I shall soon see California now. My county warrants loomed up unfortunately, but I don't care now.

Tuesday, January 4, 1887: Started this a.m. with Walter Upward for Chiricahuas and arrived all O.K. about four p.m. Made good time. A little cool some of the time. Some guitar music in evening and arranged for hunt tomorrow.

Wednesday, January 5, 1887: Got off in fair time and made for Rock Creek on our bear hunt with buckboard and team. Found company of soldiers camped in the canyon from Fort Bowie on a hunting expedition too, so we were out of luck as of course they had scoured the country. We went away up into the mountains as far as we could get and had a variety of bumpings, etc. In fact, we were quite reckless and didn't care whether school kept or not, but managed to stay with the buckboard and not be thrown out, though the chances were pretty even sometimes. Camped away up in mountains and I started out and climbed one mountain for signs. Thought I had a bear once. No signs. Reached camp about dark.

Thursday, January 6, 1887: Water froze in creek this a.m. and I half froze last night. Had three pairs of blankets apiece though. I selected the hunting ground this a.m. and WU and I tried it. Some tough hoofing. The Cavalry tracks though were too thick and but two deer were seen and they by Upward, who shot one but he got away. No bear signs. Too much against us so we got back to ranch in time for dinner. Some more rackets. The broncos were unruly in woods, so the others got out and pushed while I held lines. Pretty soon away they went through the woods. I steered them all O.K., passing between large trees and going over small trees and coming to a bank went off in fine style and landed all O.K., although boys thought I was gone. Pretty wild and enjoyable ride. Gave soldiers meat. Sang for the cowboys at ranch tonight.

Friday, January 7, 1887: Well, too cold for camping and hunting so Walter and I returned to town today bringing along a saddle horse which was quite unmanageable at times. Finally got through all O.K. Well, I never knew it to fail that something bad didn't happen or something quite remarkable occur during my absence from town, but when I learned that Mrs. Clark was at point of death from injuries sustained from an attempt to kill her and the Col. by dynamite in the wood for stove, I felt as though there was something mysterious over my life. The dastardly attempt was made Tuesday afternoon and children sent for as her life was despaired of. Maurice showed the wreck in kitchen. It's a wonder she wasn't killed outright. At Cheyney's tonight.

Saturday, January 8, 1887: Looked after some matters this a.m. Argued before Board of Supervisors matter of wrongs done of us by the former board. Mark thought as I did and he and board thought and argued case should be submitted to Judge Barnes of District Court. Mark offered to represent us. Mrs. Clark somewhat easier this a.m. Mrs. Clark easier today. A strange happening today. I went to Mrs. B with Mrs. S, object to see Miss Daisy of course. I hope bygones are bygones. Called on Mrs. Pito this evening and later was stuck for oyster supper, Upward, Major and I. Good oysters at 11 p.m.

Sunday, January 9, 1887: Miss Miller is taking care of Mrs. Clark so I took charge of the Sunday school and did as well as able. Lay services again, Major read and I collected. The Dr. Boren, of such wonderful mind, is probably a rascal, seems though. Hope there are not many like him. No evening service. Dined at Berry's where the Clarks are and spent part of evening at Herring's. The Col. is very enthusiastic indeed about his Swisshelm prospects. Hope he won't be left, but am afraid he will be.

Monday, January 10, 1887: Mrs. Clark the same. Tenney, the grand rascal, denies the act in a statement. He's a monumental liar I believe. Tonight I'll know my fate. Well, Mr. Cheyney agreed this evening to give me $100 with which to examine the Cal mining project and also a land scheme. He spoke very kindly to me and I think I have a good friend in him. I admire him as a consistent Christian gentleman.

Tuesday, January 11, 1887: Well, the idea is to get off on Thursday a.m. Maurice and I to go together as his mother is sufficiently improved. Began my preparations today and have a lot to do after my seven years residence. Big lot of odds and ends I'll have to leave. Mr. C paid me the money tonight and I gave receipt for object intended. Am sleeping with Col. Clark at rectory these nights, he's so nervous; very little sleep though for me. Dancing school tonight. Lots of fun, Mrs. Earle my girl.

Wednesday, January 12, 1887: Cannot get off tomorrow but must try to make it the day following. Crowds to do. Got things pretty well together today. Called at Cheyney's tonight with Mrs. Berry and Mrs. Earle and bade them farewell. The straggling Indians at it again below.

Thursday, January 13, 1887: Col. and I breakfasted together this a.m. Hard at it today and got things into shape including this and my accounts. Father and Stanley at work. Hope they will make it all O.K. Future's rather pleasanter for me. Bidding friends adios. Wonder if forever. Mrs. Earle gave me a send off tonight. Mrs. Gage, Cheyneys and all friends on hand. A very pleasant evening. Finished packing finally this afternoon late. Packed a box with things to leave at Vickers. Left guitar and rifle at Berry's.

Friday, January 14, 1887: Well, goodbyes were said this a.m. and Maurice and I took the stage at 9:15. Met numbers of friends enroute. Dined at Tucson about 8:30, took sleeper, both of us, to Colton; passed comfortable night. Met Sam Drachman at Tucson who said he didn't have anything for me so arranged with M.

Saturday, January 15, 1887: Am again in California, old California. I feel better and also that a brighter future awaits me. Reached Colton about 10 and a Mr. Greenway met us, Supt. of King Mine. Maurice left me in his charge and went through to Santa Monica. Breakfasted here. Met Virgil Earp who looks well and seems to be going well. Can use his arm some.

George Parsons' friend John V. Vickers as a young man. A Pennsylvanian by birth, John arrived in Tombstone in early 1880 as a life insurance company representative, and stayed in southeastern Arizona for eighteen years engaging in ranching, mining, and real estate. In 1898 he moved to southern California and capitalized on the West Coast land boom and oil discoveries. In partnership with the Vail family, he ran cattle on Santa Rosa and Santa Cruz islands off the coast of Santa Barbara. Although John died in January 1913, and his brother Sumner passed away in March 1922, the Vail and Vickers Company is still active in southern California. *(Photo courtesy of the Santa Cruz Island Foundation)*

AFTERWORD

EARLY DAYS IN TOMBSTONE
Song of Drill and Sound of Six-shooter

By George W. Parsons

You asked me—an old Tombstoner—to give you a sketch of Tombstone in its early days, for the Arizona Number.* Yes, with pleasure, touching upon some of the incidents and a little of the life in those days—the time of the Schieffelins, Gird & Co.; when the song of the drill and sound of the six-shooter rang merrily together, and old Cochise, Juh and Victorio were in a class by themselves and gave solid instruction to Geronimo, Chatto and Nana in the art of hair-lifting and carving the poaching settler who dared to build his cabin within a hundred miles of the sacred precincts of San Carlos agency—the nursery of the downtrodden and helpless Apache, according to the Boston humanitarian idea.

I find in my journal an entry dated at Tucson, Tuesday, February 17, 1880, which reads as follows: "Early breakfast at Katie's before light." (Katie's last name escapes me at the present moment, but all Tombstoners will know who I mean when I refer to the stampede from Tombstone to Lower California, via Guaymas, when Katie headed the crowd in her buckskin trousers and other togs, and preserved her dignity at the same time.) [Parsons has mistaken Katie O'Hara for Nellie Cashman. They were partners, however, both in Tucson and for a while in Tombstone. But it was Nellie who went to Baja California.] "Stage on hand about 7 o'clock. Six of us on top, with driver; Bob Lewis, Ex-P.M. of Cleveland; W. P. Stanley, a fine old boy, my subsequent partner; Redfern, as true as steel; and one Stewart. My friend, Milton Clapp, and I faced to the rear and completed the top load. Pleasant day. Twenty-five miles out we changed horses at Cienega Wells and bowled along pleasantly another twenty-five miles to Ohnesorgan Station, on the mesa, where we met a relay of six-fresh horses, and found orders to drive fast to best the opposition stage. Fine drive, but driver was forced to be very cruel to the horses to obey orders, and the sixteen miles to Contention were made in an hour and a half—

*Published in the *Los Angeles Mining Review*, Vol. IX, No. 12, March 23, 1901, p. 13.

about eleven miles an hour. The horses were in a dead run and jump all of the time, up hill and down, passengers wildly clutching anything stationary, with a feeling of relief in one direction, however, that no Apaches or Rustlers could catch them. When at last we climbed down from our perch, one of the fine leaders was found to be nearly dead, and all the horses were badly winded. Four fresh horses carried us the remaining ten miles, and we reached our destination (Tombstone) at 6:30, only to find ourselves nearly an hour behind the opposition stage line, Kinnear's. A rough place, consisting of one street of shanties, some with canvas roofs. Hard crowd. Stopped at a restaurant (Brown's, as I now remember), and bundled in there bag and baggage. Good meal after a wash. Some street shooting in the morning, followed up later in the afternoon, about the time of our arrival, by two other parties, apparently not friends, from their marked hostility towards each other with rifles and six-shooters, which were finally captured before any gore was spilled. No law apparent other than miners' law, and that doesn't sit and deliberate very long, but acts promptly, we understand. The street looked oddly enough to me tonight, and reminded me of a frontier oil town. Good drainage. Mingled with the hardy miners tonight. Talk of killing some one in the air tonight. Everyone goes heeled. Jumping mining claims seems to be the chief cause of trouble. About 2,000 people here, with good big future ahead."

But, "tempora mutantur!" While Tombstone was in those days the liveliest mining town in the United States, it gradually settled down to the possession of a more or less peaceable community. Our reception was lively enough, especially so for "tenderfeet," but as we had come to stay, it didn't take us long to become identified with the town and its customs, although we got along very well at "breakfast" time, without the necessity of cutting a notch on our Colt's to whet the appetite.

Churches and schools multiplied; nevertheless, the early attempts to tame the unruly and bring all under proper restraint by the aid and help of the institutions provided for the moral betterment of all were at times attended with amusing results. I recall the attempts of the Rev. McIntyre, the first clergyman in the place, early in '80, to hold church services. Seated on old boxes and boards in a large tent, everything went all right, but when a hall was hired and a little luxury indulged in, church matters became confusion worse confounded. The hall faced on Allen and Fremont streets, had a common platform in the center, which was divided by a curtain, so that sounds were painfully perceptible from the Freemont-street side, and poor McIntyre's amens had to be well sounded in order to be distinguished from "All hands round" in the dance hall on the opposite side of the muslin curtain.

I remember a funny incident, too, which occurred in the little Episcopal Church, when one of my friends, wishing to be liberal at the evening service, desposited, as he supposed, a $5 gold piece on the plate, but which, sad to relate, proved to be a check resembling the coin, stating it to be "good for one drink at Charley H's." I will not remember who redeemed the check. Well, the boys were liberal in those days, and everything seemed to go, and that same spirit of liberality was prevalent everywhere.

Speaking of the press, though, reminds me that my old friend, Harry Brook, now of the *Los Angeles Times*, and I used to do a trick or two together in those days, and supply information "direct from the front," about the movements of the hostile Apaches, and what Harry doesn't know about newspapering isn't worth knowing. He was the "whole thing," a prodigious inventor of news, with my assistance at times, "from the front." He would set up the type, print the paper and later go out on a collecting tour with a six-shooter down his bootleg. Subscribers usually "coughed up" when Harry appeared.

A day that I recall, one that Tombstoners now living will not forget, was the one during which "Johnny behind the deuce" [Johnny O'Rourke] was brought into town from Charleston. That was the day they saw the Earps and Doc Holliday stand off the crowd bent on having the man who killed the engineer of the Charleston mill [W. P. Schneider]. That was a gallant preservation of law and order on the part of the intrepid Earp posse, and the nearest approach to a wholesale killing that Tombstone ever saw.

I remember one wild ride a party of us made on a hot summer day to the Three C's [Chiricahua Cattle Company] ranch in the Sulphur Spring Valley, forty-five miles distant, to rescue some ladies and a party at the ranch house. The party was picnicking in one of the pretty canyons of the Chiricahuas, when some cowboys dashed up and reported seventy hostiles approaching. In a few moments, flanked by the cowboys, the whole party was madly dashing over the plains in full view of the Indians. [Theodore] White, one of the party, held his baby and lashed the horses, his wife holding the lines, and all in the wagon hanging on for dear life. It was a mad run, but safely made. It was a hot ride for the courier who carried the news to Tombstone, but a hotter ride for those of us who went to the rescue and succeeded in chasing the Apaches toward the border.

The "hold-up" business was sadly interfered with when Big Dan Dowd, Red Sample, "Tex," and the others were finally run to earth, after their raid on Bisbee, where they killed poor Johnny Tappiner and several others, and rode out of town with their booty towards the line. It was a big haul, but not long enjoyed, as the $15,000 reward, "dead or alive," corraled them all, and I remember Ben Williams, of the Copper Queen Co., giving me $1000 in greenbacks on Toughnut street one day as receiver of reward funds. These healthy contributions retarded the road agent business very materially, and the bad man was so often turned down that Tombstone was soon rated a model mining camp.

INDEX

Guiager, Capt., 24, 25
Guiteau, Charles J., 4, 7

Hacker, Gus, 252, 257
Hackinson, 71, 73
Haines, Miss, 98
Hale, 75
Haley, John, 97, 100
Hall, Mrs, 79, 81
Hand, 126, 127
Handley, Jim, 111
Haney, Walter, 223
Hanna, 184
Hanson, Charles (Cap), 2, 3, 4, 5, 7, 14, 15, 17, 23, 24, 25, 26, 27, 29, 31
Harlow, Judge, 222
Hart, 81, 200
Hart, Miss, 152, 191
Hartman, 106
Harvey, Walter, 17, 19, 213
Harvey-Vail ranch (Empire ranch), 227
Haskins, Rev. Thomas W., 192, 194, 199, 200, 220, 222, 223, 230, 240, 244, 246, 247, 249, 250, 251, 261
Hatch, Dep. Sheriff Bob, 71, 146, 189, 194, 221, 242
Hatch, Frank, 154, 161
Havland, 144, 152
Hayes, 6, 7, 142
Hayne, Alston, 257
Hayne, Arthur, 88
Hawkins, 67, 123, 124, 151
Hawkins, Mrs., 69, 181, 185
Haynes, Judge John, 37, 195, 213
Heany, 197
Heith, John, 101
Helen's Dome, 215, 216, 218
Heliograph, 215, 216, 218, 232
Helm's ranch, 35
Hemming, 38
Hemset, 190
Hemset, Florence, 190
Henderson, Col. Jack, 28, , 126, 127
Hendley, Rev., 55, 56
Henney, 212
Hereford, AZ., 19, 61
Hermosillo, Sonora, 14, 16, 39, 84
Herring, Howard, 41, 64, 65, 70, 76
Herring, Judge William, 52, 60, 63, 64, 65, 66, 71, 72, 73, 74, 78, 89, 90, 96, 98, 101, 103, 106, 107, 111, 129, 131, 145, 149, 150, 164, 170, 174, 175, 181, 184, 187, 190, 191, 196, 198, 200, 203, 211, 214, 220, 222, 230, 234, 237, 238, 242, 244, 246, 248, 249, 252, 262
Herring, Mrs., 69, 100, 152, 189, 200, 239
Herring, Miss, 62, 76, 235
Herring, Miss Birdie, 82, 148, 186, 248

Herring, Henrietta (Etta), 247
Herring, Howard, 105, 111, 166, 176, 181, 184
Herring, Mamie, 105, 165, 245, 246
Herring, Miss Sarah, 82, 105, 108, 129, 243
Heyne, F. W., 33, 89, 91, 247
Hidden Treasure claim, 100
Hill, 34
Hines, Mrs., 186
Hirsch, F. M., 142
Hirsch, Morris, 123, 142, 144
Hoag, 100
Hoble, 39
Hoblitezall, Mr. 43
Hohstadt, John, 2, 3, 4, 6, 7, 14, 16, 17, 18, 19, 20, 22, 25, 26, 28, 30, 31, 44, 46, 61, 71, 72, 81, 97, 99, 121, 128, 131, 132, 172
Hohstadt, John, Jr., 1, 24, 29, 30, 45, 64, 126, 241
Hodstadt, Mrs. 3, 22, 26, 55
Hollenstein, 193
Holyoke, Miss, 51
Hooker, Henry C., 60, 166, 167, 168, 169, 252
Hooker, J. D., 60
Hoover, Judge, 170
Horn, Tom, 232
Hornbeck, E. O., 216
Howard, Billy, 106, 110, 118
Howard, Judge James G., 38
Howard, Tex, 93
Howe, E. R., 18, 34, 35, 39, 62, 91, 112, 162
Howe, H. G., 200, 224, 225, 226, 227, 228, 229
Howe, Miss Gerty, 164
Huachuca Mountains, 7, 53, 54, 81, 82
Huachuca reservoir, 105
Huachuca Water Co., 8, 70, 71, 172
Hubbard, Edward, 34
Hudson, Charles, 43
Hudson, Ed, 43, 71, 72, 88, 104, 180, 192
Hudson, T. F., 162, 163
Hudson, Miss, 43
Hudson & Co., 21, 107-10, 130
Hughes, L. C., 42
Huneke, A. J., 123, 124, 125, 126, 127, 150, 152, 182, 215, 219, 222, 223, 224, 230, 231, 233, 234, 238, 239, 242, 248, 249
Huians, Lon, 60
Hunter's Canyon, 82
Hunsaker, Miss Laura, 218
Hunsaker, James, 218
Hunsaker, W. J., 218
Hursch, M., 128
Hurlbert, Mr. & Mrs., 84
Hutchison, Dave, 170

Idaho claim, 254, 256, 257

80, 86, 96, 100, 114, 115, 116, 151, 225, 230

Parsons, George W., contributes to Billy Claiborne's death, 38; rejected by Nathalie, 57; interviewed by Chicago *Tribune*, 58-60; establishes mining agency with Maurice Clark, 91; inspects Spanish mine in California, 103; role during bank failure, 108-09; at Nacozari, Sonora, 111-29, 139-44; opinion of Crook's Indian policy, 202-11; participates in H. G. Howe's survey, 225-29; performs assessment work at Oro Blanco, 252-59; leaves Tombstone, 262-63

Parsons, Samuel M. (father), 51, 64, 89, 93, 95, 109, 116, 151, 170, 230

Parsons, Sam (brother), 57, 64, 85, 86, 88, 134, 185, 187, 200

Parsons, W. C., 192

Pascholy, Joseph, 76, 237

Pascholy, Mrs. (nee Hayes), 237

Pastuer, Sarah, 93

Patrick, 143

Paul, Sheriff Bob, 213

Payotte, Capt., 1

Peabody, Endicott, 8

Peabody Mine, 40, 70

Peacock Club, 65, 70, 72

Pearl claim, 62

Pearson, Rev. G. L., 183, 221, 251

Peck, Mrs., 162

Peel, Judge B. L., 33, 65, 71, 73, 81, 84, 87, 149

Peel, Miss, 34, 49, 50, 62, 69, 71, 74, 75, 77, 78, 82, 87, 89, 90, 91, 97, 98, 99, 101, 104, 108, 237

Peel, M. R., 86, 106

Pendleton, William, 158

Pennington, 74, 75, 76, 102

Pentagonal claim, 189

Pesqueira, Augustin, 136, 147, 212, 215, 220

Pesqueira, Ignacio, 14, 16, 21, 22, 27, 30, 44, 255, 258

Peterson, 66, 189, 190

Pima Indians, smuggling of, 1

Pine Canyon, 216

Pinney, Judge Daniel H., 38, 41, 42, 44, 49, 50, 51, 60, 61, 65, 83

Pito, Mac, 240, 250

Pito, Mrs., 262

Pluto claim, 55, 56

Poage, 33, 47, 50, 105

Point of Mountains, 167

Pomeroy, Miss, 43

Porter's Hotel, 42

Poston, Charles D., 252, 253, 256

Powell, Miss, 146

Powers, Patsy, 258

Prescott, Mr., 202, 240

Prescott, Mrs., 222, 240

Preston's sawmill, 81

Price, French, 77

Price, Mrs. L., 50

Price, Trenchard, 90, 212

Pridham, George, 35, 49, 50, 51, 61, 74, 103

Pridham, Mrs., 117

Prieto, Joaquin Diaz, Mexican Consul, 50, 52, 61, 64, 65, 75, 110, 149, 150, 151, 152, 153, 155, 182, 183, 197, 221, 230, 231, 233, 250

Prompter Mine, 62, 81, 97, 100, 105, 192, 193, 194, 197

Providencia, Sonora, 68, 70

Purcell, Hank, 67

Queener, Milt, 245

Quigley, Mrs., 156

Ramsey Canyon, 81, 160, 239

Randolph, 37

Randolph, Mr., 120

Rankin, Brayton Co., 121

Rankin, John, 25, 26, 29, 44, 53, 54, 55, 63, 64, 241

Ray, Jack, 69

Rayenard, Joe (French Joe), 81

Read, Charlie, 164

Redfern, J. L., 2, 3, 4, 5, 6, 7, 8, 14, 15, 16, 17, 18, 19, 20, 21, 22, 23, 23, 24, 25, 26, 27, 28, 30, 31, 32, 35, 36, 38, 39, 40, 41, 42, 46, 47, 50, 51, 65, 72, 83, 100, 104, 183

Redfern, Joseph, 257

Redfern, Mrs., 14, 21

Redfern, Miss M. E., 41, 43, 45, 47, 50, 61, 85, 104, 183

Reed, Charlie, 124

Reppy, Charles D., 56, 73, 80, 88, 97, 110, 130, 146, 190, 197, 233, 236, 243

Reppy, Mrs., 49, 72, 158, 231, 246

Reppy, Miss, 76

Revers, 118

Reynolds, Dick, 177

Rice, George, 33

Richards, Dr., 112, 116, 117, 120

Richards, Lon, 129, 130, 147

Richardson, Mrs., 8, 47, 49, 51, 65, 69, 73

Richardson, Miss, 64, 69

Riggs, Barney K., 250

Riggs, Brannick, 202

Roberts, Brad, 221

Roberts, Capt. C. S., 201, 205

Robertson, Dr., 18, 73

Robertson, Aleck, 180

Robertson, James S., 38, 39, 41, 107

Robertson, Joe, 256

Robertson, Mrs., 50, 76, 78, 79, 80

Robertson, Miss, 35

Robinson, Judge James S., 98, 195

Robles, 141, 143

Robley, 116, 120, 124

Design by   Lynn R. Bailey
Typography by   Western Lore Graphics, Inc.
Lithography by   Wholesale Lithographers, Inc.
Edition Binding by   Roswell Bookbinding, Phoenix